REFLECTIONS OF A PAR

A true tale, not of chosen heroes, but of
the loves, hates, fears, pride, courage
and endurance of ordinary men and women
embracing the defence of Dunkirk, Prison
Camps, Working Parties and the final march
from East Prussia to West Germany during
the winter of 1944-45

DEDICATED TO JOHN HUNTER
IN APPRECIATION
OF
VALUED FRIENDSHIP

Brothers In Arms
An evocative story of Territorial Army training, active combat and life as a prisoner of war in World War 2.
By C. Arthur Meads
Regimental Number 5383394

4th Battalion
Oxfordshire & Buckinghamshire
Light Infantry

Text copyright © 2013 Louise Beale
All Rights Reserved

Table of Contents

The Fledglings, 1939

Lavant, Near Chichester, 1939

Oxford, 1939

Mobilisation, 1939

Woolton Hill, Near Newbury, 1939-1940

The Crossing, 1940

Le Havre, France, 1940

St Romain, 1940

Attiches, 1940

Thumeries, 1940

Alsemberg, Belgium, 1940

Waterloo, 1940

Tournai, 1940

Bleharies, On the Banks of the River Scarpe, 1940

Nomain, France, 1940

Cassel, 1940

Watou, 1940

The March, 1940

Trier, Germany, 1940

Schubin, Poland, 1940

Arbbiets Kommando – Znin, Poland, 1940-1941

Gratz, Czechoslovakia, 1941

Marienburg, East Prussia, 1941

The Unknown Farm, East Prussia, 1941 – 1942

Marienburg, The Cheese Factory, 1942

Fisherbalki, East Prussia, 1942

Fisherbalki, East Prussia, The Farm, 1943

Marienburg, 1943-1944

Fort Fifteen, Poland, 1944

Thorn, Poland, 1944

Annaburg, Germany, 1944

Gothenburg, Sweden, 1944

England, 1944

Epilogue – An account of events after the separation of the brothers in December 1943 to June 1945 as narrated by Edgar

Fisharbalki, East Prussia, 1943-44, The Farm

The March 1944-45, East Prussia, Poland, Germany

The Release, Germany

The Last Lap and News of Revenge

The Fledglings, 1939

The warm October sun smiles down on us with misplaced generosity, dressed in our mid-winter and warlike attire, we stand in a line across the field waiting expectantly for the Sergeants word of command. In our 1918 vintage uniforms with drainpipe trousers, brass buttoned tunics, boots, greatcoats, webbing equipment draped on backs and chests, respirator on chests, anti-gas capes rolled at the back of our necks, rifle with a fixed bayonet held across our chests at 'High Port', respirator on our faces, steel helmets on our heads, we sweat like pigs as we wait, and we haven't moved yet!

A 'regular' this chap, supposed to know his onions! come along to toughen us up or bury us!

"When I tell you to advance, you will move off to your front at a walking pace holding your weapons across your body at 'High Port', which means you will at all times hold the rifle at the correct angle of forty five degrees across the body, you will proceed for one hundred yards".

"At the command 'Double time', you will jog the remaining fifty yards to your firing point at the range. On arrival, you will assume the correct 'prone' firing position and fire five rounds rapid into the target immediately to your front at two hundred yards range. UNDERSTOOD."

Christ, I'll never make it! Can't see a thing out of the glass eye pieces of the respirator, condensation has taken over again as usual despite the anti-mist ointment applied. A tiny clear patch remains down on the lower part of the right hand eye piece, if that fogs up might just as well lie down, got to be one lousy useless mask in the bloody army, I have it!

We're off. The line moves forward at the crisp bark of command. My enthusiasm is somewhat dulled by my inability to see clearly; move forward with apprehension in my heart. Pace reasonable at present, have to hold my chin up high, head tilted well back, right eye searching for the clear area on the eye piece. Stumble over large clumps of grass, stagger through them somehow, back of the helmet makes contact with the anti-gas cape rolled at the back of the neck moving the helmet forward, the front edge of the helmet rests on the top of the respirator, can't fall off anyway! Can just see the white marker at the firing point ahead, about fifty yards away, will have to break into a trot any minute now.

Galvanised by the Sergeants roar, we break into the dreaded trot, hear a rifle clatter to the ground almost immediately as some bloke hits the deck – expect to join him real soon. Helmet bobbing up and down on my head, it's as busy as a bloody Woodpecker – it's knocking me in to the ground with each blow. Vision mighty poor now, bump off of the man on my left, manage to stay on my feet, but only just – I leave a chain of muffled cussing. Right eye frantic now, fixed only on the dim white marker ahead, about ten feet to go, a frantic dive as the distance closes, crashing to the ground in a heap. Body shuddering, I lie there for several seconds fighting to channel each agonising breath into some degree of regularity. Got to complete the firing stage yet!

Body automatically arranges itself into the correct position for firing, angle of forty-five degrees to where I suppose the target should be, feet spread wide. Hand gropes beneath my body for the clip of the ammunition in the pouch. Am lying full on it, have to execute a half roll to reach the thing. Load rounds into the breach of the rifle smoothly and without thought, must get the shots off as soon as possible.

Can't see anything of the target! Can make out grass for about ten feet, nothing else, the bayonet looks long fixed on the end of the rifle, looks like a bleeding lance. Weights nothing, yet seems to drag the muzzle down. Two hundred yards he said, Ok, here goes! Adjust the sight to two hundred, offer a prayer to heaven that I am pointing the gun the right way, I let loose five rounds as rapidly as my shaking hands will permit. Lower rifle, apply safety catch, I listen for the call for 'stretcher bearer', but none comes, I have managed not to hit anyone, pure bloody luck!

Head droops forward onto the grass as I wait impatiently for the salvo of irregular shots to stop which will herald the shout of 'all clear' of gas. Brushing the helmet forward over the respirator, I eagerly rip the rubber bands of the respirator from my head in response to 'gas clear'. The repulsive object lies limply on the grass under my nose. It lies with the inside uppermost to the sky, the black rubber wet and glistening with moisture, two large eye pieces stare back at me like the eyes of an Octopus. I cannot believe that this thing could possibly save my life one day as I stare back at it with hate in my heart.

See, the sun is shining! There is no fog, pure fresh air rushes into my lungs. After a run like that you should be able to stick a bayonet into a man they say. Bloody impossible – for me anyway! Like a freshly landed trout on a river bank I lay gasping in the sun, cussing all Sergeants...this one in particular!

Lavant, Near Chichester, 1939

A busy period during the second half of 1938 and the first half of 1939 for the Territorial Army, young men and those not so young men can foresee the approaching of the many empty warnings uttered by our country to other offending nations. Men seek to learn something of the tools of the trade which they may be called upon to use in earnest in the not too distant future. By the summer of 1939 the 'Oxfords' can boast two Battalions, the 4th and the 5th where previously there had been one. My brother Edgar and I are in the 4th which is the parent Battalion.

Evenings are spent studying the effective use of the rifle at St Cross Road, Drill Hall, Oxford; Parades and 'square bashing' on the emerald green carpet of the adjacent University Sports field. Now and then we spend a Saturday crawling about in one of the local parks in what is loosely termed as a tactical exercise. All very light-hearted outwardly as we learn something of the secrets of weapons, women, and how to express oneself in colourful language.

The opportunity for training as a complete Battalion is presented only as the annual two week camp this year to be held at Lavant. The first lesson I learn at this camp is just how good Mum's cooking is! I view the pile of soggy cabbage and other daily gems with horror, but being starved one picks at bits and pieces.

Washing too is educational. No nice warm water, flannel, and scented soap. I eye the large cake of soap, the size of a brick, it looks just like the soap Mum uses to scrub the floor with at home! Note the old soldier over there – he cups his hands under the water, flinging the contents up into his face, rubs a bit of soap on to his hands and face. Make another bowl of water in his cupped hands he submerges his face into the pool accompanied by loud splutterings and blowing noises as he goes under; see how the deft hands cunning lift the water neatly round to the back of the neck as the hands meet. Even round the ears. In the twinkle of an eye he is finished, reaching for his towel he stands grinning at me with refreshed well-being. The crystal droplets of water fall from his face down to his khaki shirt, they form dark star-shaped patterns. The sleep of the night is well and truly driven from his eyes - he is ready to face a new day.

OK, if that's the way it's done, here goes! It's true; the shock of the cold water would stir a dead man! You can tell that I am the green one, my ears have to be content with a wipe form a wet finger and the droplets of water from my face do not form pretty star shaped patterns, but are lost in the rest of the water that soaks my chest and shoulders!

Other things are learned: backwards, forwards, round and round we march in the fields, arms drill, lectures on this, lectures on that, tactics by day, tactics by night, frightening ourselves to death with blank cartridges in the darkness of the night. Quite often we find ourselves dumped in a ditch, a clump of trees, or some other obscure and unpopulated location with orders to defend the thing to death from some enemy who we know darn well we won't recognise. Can lie there all day with a fistful of blank cartridges which we are expected to fire at someone or other. Apart from the odd shots going off around us the enemy never turns up. The fields remain completely empty of life. Only one thing to do: doze, smoke, and talk about sex!

Eventually an Officer will come strolling along. You look at him and wonder what you should do about him. He wears an armband which is an indication that he is the Umpire, but how do we know he isn't working for the other side? - might have pinched it. Should we shoot him? Capture him thereby showing a bit of initiative? Or just bloody well ignore him? Before our brains can decide his fate, he has decided ours! "You are all dead!"

We gaze at him in complete surprise! No idea what the hell has killed us. Haven't seen a bugger all day apart from him! But, he is an Officer, so we die as requested - we shall remain dead until some fatigue is thought up. He wanders off, sections of men are massacred all over the place as he wanders about. He thinks fighting men grow on trees! It looks as though we have made some dreadful tactical mistake somewhere, just by sitting on our arses all day where we were told to sit. Military tactics can be very confusing to the mind of a simple factory worker sometimes.

Spend a night out in the open for a change, bound to toughen us up! A field of long grass is chosen, looks inviting, bed down in that, lay down on the ground-sheet using the lumpy back pack as a pillow and greatcoat as a blanket; very romantic! Can see the stars directly above, count them if you can as you drift off through the strangely refreshing open air atmosphere of the night to a well-earned sleep.

The bugle blasts you awake, but all that meets the eyes is a low ground mist swirling over the bloke sleeping next to you. Everything is drenched in dew; our teeth are chattering from the cold; blisters have formed on our hands. Where the hell did they come from? The old soldiers tell us that we have chosen a bed of mustard grass; mustard grass! Never heard of it!

Once a week we have a long route march, long by our civilian standards, our feet groan in protest, but the Officers at our head stride out manfully regardless. Their very attitude clearly states: "We are civilians too, we can do it, you can, and will!"

Open day arrives. A great day for the parents, wives, girlfriends, and friends flocking to visit us; actually they have come to see how the army is treating their precious property. They eye the 'bell tents' that we live in with deep suspicion, must be cold in there, bet the rain gets in!

Cecil Arthur and Edgar Meads

The neatly folded blankets and other gear at the end of the bed shatters them. "Can't get you to put a darn thing away at home." One point to the army at least! They listen to our tales of suffering for our country, a cluck of sympathy; buy you a drink to cheer you up.

"Must have a photo of you with your rifle before I go", out comes the camera - you stand there like a fool fingering the rifle, would look daft standing to attention, so you stand 'at ease' instead wondering if you will come out looking like a soldier.

The joys and trepidations of venereal disease are vividly illustrated on film for the benefit of our young minds. Some of us are shattered! The subject becomes a talking point for some days, contemptuously dismissed as a load of old crap by the old soldiers, we younger ones however, become over cautious. Wouldn't be seen dead holding a girls hand for fear of infection! In twenty-four hours nature sweeps away our puny fears with gay abandon under the onslaught of so many pretty hands about!

Now that open day is over, parents gone, the highlight of our second week camp can be faced up to. A long distance run over open country, four miles, every man must start. Don't have to run the four miles but God help you if you don't cross that starting line - no excuse! Even a man on crutches needs a sick note.

Several hundred men mill about at the starting line, most are dressed in full 'going to town' uniform, peaked caps and ammunition boots far outnumber the puny half dozen P.T. kits walking about. They mean business, so do the rest of us for that matter!

Ok, everybody get set! On your markers! What marker? BANG!

A surge of massed boots create the thunder of a herd of buffalo as they cross the starting line.

I travel two, three yards over the starting line at the most, the ground is littered with panting bodies. We have qualified! Now we are free to spend the day as we wish. Men start running across the camp immediately to reach the bus that will take them into the town, if they have missed it they would think nothing of running the five miles if need be in order to catch the nearest pub open!

I watch the few real runners as they fade into the distance, tiny legs going like pistons, I salute them!

Army Training Camp, 1938, Edgar back row third from right, Arthur third from right centre row.

Oxford, 1939

A 'Royal' welcome awaits our return to the city. The place has gone mad! The station is packed with people waiting to greet us, they spill out of the station and into the street. Fighting our way gently through the mass, we elbow our way into the road in order to fall in to march. As far as the eye can see people line the street waiting for us to pass by. We can only gaze at them in complete and utter surprise.

Ok, let's make the best of it, this will never happen again I'll bet! Two Battalions, a lot of men, long time since the old city has seen so many on her streets. I pity the poor baggage party – they've got to unload the gear from the train, will miss the march and all this bloody glory.

A lot of room is needed to form up two Battalions, the citizens get gently shoved back to make more room. Soon, a long khaki snake stands ready for the order to move off, the band falls in at the head of the column - we are off! The mass of boots hit the hard surface of the road as one, left arms swing, rifles held down in the right hand at the 'Trail', we fall into the easy flow of the march with practised ease. Massed bugles open up. The stirring notes echo off the buildings, the crowds squeal in delight, who wouldn't be a young man at a time like this!

In response to those thousands of beaming faces we try to look the heroes they insist on making us. Over Carfax, down the High, only the mellow ageless buildings remain cool and unexcited with a dignity that says "We have seen it all before, century after century, but march on Sons of Oxford". Turning into Long Wall, we make our way up to the drill hall where we are dismissed until required again, perhaps another camp, perhaps something sooner, who knows these days.

Rifles back into the stores for safekeeping, other equipment we take home. Wait for the baggage party and collect our kit bags and then we are free to go home and pick up the threads of civilian life once again.

Mobilisation, 1939

A holiday in Bristol with relations, my girlfriend and I are just beginning to relax and enjoy ourselves when a nation-wide broadcast instruct all Territorial Units to report for mobilisation immediately. Bidding a hasty farewell to girlfriend and relations I catch the first train back to Oxford.

Returning first to my home to collect my uniform and equipment, I report to the Regimental Headquarters reflecting that in my hurry I had taken my girlfriend to Bristol with me but had now left her stranded to find her own way home.

Headquarters is a hive of activity. Men reporting in, drawing rifles from the stores. Falling in by platoon as their strength grows, mustering on the nearby sports field and waiting for the few missing men to report. We of the Mortar Platoon are told to report to an old cinema located in the Cowley Road; billets are being located in odd corners around the city.

Muster on the road outside H.Q. Fall in line to march, we await the word to move off. A few people stand about watching our activities, my wandering gaze falls on them, Hells Bells! Joan, my girlfriend stands over there, she is looking at me, she looks sad, no smile, wants to speak but we cannot, have just been called up to attention, we move off down the road at a brisk pace, away from Joan, again I have left her stranded!

A filthy and neglected structure the cinema, a flea-pit in every way, but it does boast a stage. Sweeping and scrubbing to make the floor fit to lay on is the order of the day we throw our kit down on the spot of our choice, some men choosing the stage, we settle in. Immediately I get detailed guard duty. Must stand out in the front of this dump, marching up and down and generally looking vicious. Won't be able to see Joan for another twenty-four hours, should think that this will be the end of my romance!

Standing in front of the place I try to look the part but find it very hard work to be dignified. Civilian workers from the factory where I work and who know me pass up and down the road on their cycles going to and from their work. The cheeky remarks thrown at me as they pass do nothing to boost my confidence. Bit of bloody military discipline is what they need is the worst thing I can think about them! Time drags! Can't think what the hell I am supposed to be guarding, not a thing inside worth pinching, had no instructions, don't think that there's an N.C.O. who knows how to give instructions on guard duty yet. But it passes, I get my evening pass and hasten to make my peace with Joan.

A small sports field on the Iffley Road is used as a temporary parade ground. Its size restricts too much movement, we mess about pulling rifles to pieces and putting them together again, marking time till something better comes along; somewhere to train in earnest.

Marching through the city on one of the numerous details we are used to the civilians who smile and wave but I am surprised and puzzled one day to see a group of three middle aged women watching us pass with neither a smile nor a wave. They are weeping. Silently they gaze, silently they weep. They disturb me, why do they weep? Have they more vision than the rest of us? Can they in their wisdom see beyond the flag waving and laughing faces to the reality of our possible future? I dismiss the women from my mind for the present. I think we shall soon have a job to do, probably a sticky job; tears won't do it, time for tears later!

At last Chamberlain has said it as we all knew he must, we are at war! I don't feel any different although I thought I would, perhaps later. Have to treat this bloody rifle better than a baby from now on!

A hell of a shriek from up on the stage followed by a crash, we have been at war for about thirty minutes and already we have our first casualty! A fellow sleeping on the trap door on the stage finds himself way down below as rotten timbers give way under his weight, a sore head but otherwise ok. He gets dusted off and promised a medal but we find him very hard to sooth for some reason.

Today we escort the Battalion Battle Flag into the safekeeping of the Chapel of Christchurch College, a colour party of fifty men. I consider the detail a great privilege.

Our first military church parade, march through St Clements, into the Marston Road where there's a large church. We fill it with khaki; the theme of the civilian priest's long sermon is to kill! Kill the enemy! In surprise I listen to the words uttered by the so-called 'man of God' in the so-called 'house of God'. No words of compassion or mercy, just kill! The memory of the hate in his words leave me with a cool attitude to the church and the symbols of the church.

Guard duty again! This time at Brigade H.Q. located at

University Parks. We march soon after dawn to relieve the existing detail. A large Victorian type property, probably pinched by the military as a H.Q. it looks comfortable, but then that sort of H.Q. would be!

No experience of mounting guard detail at all much less changing one! We have to feel our way slowly; our Guard Commander arms himself with a little Army Manual, slowly and surprisingly we find ourselves the active detail as we watch the relieved guards march away to a twenty-four hour rest period; we watch them go, green with envy. Have nothing to do for the first two hours, the instinctive soldier in me tells me to swill tea and sleep while I can. A dig in the ribs from a boot politely tells me that it is my turn to go on duty; two men go at once, one at the rear of the house and one at the front. I am chosen to take the front, pity, means I won't be able to relax at all.

Very important position this I am told, can expect to see one or two Brigadiers who pop in from time to time. Watch your step on salutes, Ok Sarge, you can rely on me! Full of confidence in his sentry the Guard Commander leaves me to get his head down. Standing 'at ease' I take stock of my surroundings. A narrow pavement with me stuck right in the middle of it; civilians will have to step off it and get on the road if they wish to pass, that will get their bloody backs up for a start! Can walk across the front of the house, a distance of about forty feet, turn around and come back again. This will require to be done every fifteen minutes or so.

A large five-barred-gate size entrance to the building, I stand close to it and decide to take the bull by the horns, try a turn! In my best version of the military text book manner that all men on guard duty should follow, I suddenly spring to attention with a crash of a boot on the pavement that almost knocked my hat off; shoulder arms, turn smartly to my right as noisily as I can. A woman on the other side of the street leaves the ground with shock at my sudden and unexpected move, I step out crisply and noisily, boots ring out a tattoo on the pavement as I eat up my forty feet of confiscated pavement, nice smooth 'about turn', march back, face front, order arms with a crash of rifle butt on the pavement, stand at ease. Not bad, should teach those snooty buggers outside Buckingham Palace a thing or two!

Getting bored with this lark, wish something would happen. Civilians pass by now and then, they gaze at the object standing outside the house probably wondering what the hell I am guarding – so do I! This looks interesting; a car has pulled up on the other side of the road, staff car. Two men in it, one at the front and one at the back, I examine them with the critical eye of a brand new and fairly enthusiastic sentry.

The bloke at the back is getting out, he slams the door shut and walks over the road in my direction, he's dead in line with me! A red cap, something big, better play safe and give him a 'Butt' salute. Snap to attention as he gets close sending the echo of my boot ringing down the street, rifle climbs nicely up on to my shoulder, a perfect forty-five degree slope, right arm snaps across the chest, fingers slap the butt. Drawing level with me he returns the salute pretty crisply for an Officer, his eyes search my face as he passes, he does not speak, probably too dazzled by my performance. I congratulate myself on the way I handled my first Brigadier.

Ten minutes later the guard commander comes out to see me; come to congratulate me I expect:

"Did you have a visitor just now?"

"Yes Sarge, a Red Cap"

"And what salute did you give him?"

"Butt salute of course Sarge"

"You bloody fool that was a General, in fact I think it was General Ironside! – you present arms to them just like you do the King!"

"Jesus bloody Christ Sarge – never seen a General before!"

Thirty minutes later a very deflated sentry is relieved. I slink back to the guardroom with visions of a blindfold and a firing squad at the crack of dawn. I have let the Platoon down, the Company down, the Battalion down, and worst of all, the Regiment down. I will live in disgrace for days! Arriving in the guardroom I try very hard to get drunk on tea!

Kicked awake for my second spell, no chances are taken this time by the Guard Commander; I get posted round the back out of harm's way. No bloody Generals will come round here anyway. Night is as black as pitch; I am dumped under a small apple tree and told to patrol the large garden, watch out for prowlers! The Sergeant with the nice friendly torch leaves me to find my own way about.

Can't see a thing, eyes take time to get used to it, know there is a high wall around the place somewhere but no sign of it yet. Clouds scurry across the sky creating constant changes in the degree of darkness. Shadows come and go; move about, they say there are narrow gravel paths twisting through the place edged with a one foot high ornamental hedge. Move forward gingerly feeling for the bushes with my boot, find a section, step over on to the gravel, does not matter which way I turn I've no idea where in the garden I am anyway! Bayonet thrust well forward I proceed to creep through the night. Bloody Hell! The gravel under my boots crunches with the noise of a tank approaching; could hear me a mile off, a steady slow planting of the boot down on the gravel, not too much weight. A strong wind is getting up, the cloudy scurry faster as though they are in a hell of a hurry to get somewhere; every shadow has designs on me!

A rapid series of thuds to the right, I freeze. Large black shadows over there one much bigger than the rest. Stare up into the dark sky which is a degree lighter than down here, can just make out a break line above the largest shadow. A tree! The thuds are coming from there! The wind is howling now, more thuds. Slowly forward, inch by inch, into the deeper blackness. A twig touches my hat, I freeze at the unexpected contact, deeper into the darkness my blood turns to water as the cascade of Horse Chestnuts bounce off my body. Half dead with shock I manage to locate the boundary wall; planting my back firmly against it I promise my heart we will stay there for the rest of the war if we can.

But the Guard Commander has other plans. I return to the guardroom to instant sleep, a tired and exhausted man.

Someone is shaking me like a dog shakes a rag doll. Urgent shouts of 'Turn out the guard' as the guard outside transmits his message. Snap up the webbing belt, hat on, grab rifle, tumble out into the darkness. I stand still, can't see a thing after the light of the guardroom, after a few seconds I move cautiously forward in the direction of the bellowing and near-frantic voice. Tracking the voice down I find that he has seen someone moving across the grounds. Certain of his facts? Yes! Having no other choice the Guard Commander orders an immediate search, spread out, a well spaced line to avoid sticking our bayonets into each other, we proceed with the man-hunt.

My patch of ground runs along the wall, full of small trees, thick shrubbery, and bushes. Probe with the bayonet but stand well back, very black here. There's the wall. A young tree. But what's that? My hovering bayonet has found something low down. In a very stern voice I tell 'IT' to come out; again I tell 'IT', no reply, ok, I take no chances, a forward and downward thrust of the bayonet, well directed to target, plenty of energy applied, but it is not as soft as expected – bloody hard in fact! The weapon won't come out – stuck fast. Hells Bells, a tree trunk, a sawn off tree trunk!

Great difficulty in getting the bayonet out at all, a decided curve will remain in it for the rest of its active life, but no intruder is found. Thank goodness.

Relieved at dawn we return to our billets at Cowley Road to the good news that we would be moving off the next day to a training area located round Newbury. Sounds good. Pretty easy place to get home from!

The 1st Battalion of the Oxfords have left for France; we wish them well.

Woolton Hill, Near Newbury, 1939-1940

A fleet of Oxford City buses take us to the Newbury area, speeding through Abingdon, Drayton, Steventon, past the Air Force Station at Harwell, through Newbury Town, taking the Andover Road we turn off for the sleepy little village of Woolton Hill.

Our new billet, a mansion! Run down, but still a mansion, rejoicing under the name of 'Burley House'. Sadly in need of repair, but a fine home for a bunch of infantry men. We look around our latest piece of property, almost with a sense of ownership. We of H.Q. Company have taken over the entire place; about three hundred strong, we fancy our chance a bit, feeling it's only fitting that we should have the mansion while the other Company's have less grandeur.

Allocated in the numerous rooms by platoon, we find ourselves with quite a good one, with a nice view of the long grass to the front of the house, which is probably all that is left of the lawn. Dumping our gear on the spot of our choice, we immediately search the place for six inch nails to bash into the wall, which does nothing to improve the market value of the house! Equipment draped from the walls to each mans satisfaction; we drape ourselves over the floor to survey our vandalism with satisfaction.

Lots of out-buildings and stables; these to be used as stores, workshops, cook-houses and dining rooms. Acres of grassland, these as vehicle transport parks, Bren-Gun carrier parks, room to train, room to move, ideal!

Released for the evening, time to explore the nearby village, get to know our hosts the people of the village. A nice cosy collection of cottages, couple of shops, a church, a village hall which has been turned into a recreation room and rest centre for us the troops. Tables and chairs fill the dance floor space, delicate table cloths grace each table to make it look just like home. Tea, buns, sandwiches, are served to us by volunteer girls and women of the village, they brighten our lives immediately.

A haven of peace, writing our letters, relax to think, a dance, sometimes an E.N.S.A. show, that big little man 'Arthur Askey' makes our hearts bleed with the struggle of his little fish and the Dam. A great welcome by the people of the village, they take this bunch of high spirited young men into their homes, keep them tame! Friendships and romances take root to blossom quickly.

Training is picked up by both hands, in deadly earnest now, we have no time to waste, as a Unit we are soft, need to toughen up! They do their best to oblige us, mortars come out of storage, remove the grease, get them ready for action. Now let's learn how to use them. From now on we live and breathe guns! Two fifteen hundredweight trucks, a despatch rider and a motorcycle are allocated to us, at least we of the Mortars are fully equipped. The Bren-Gun Carrier Platoon get their Armoured Caterpillar tracked vehicles. Bren-Guns and Anti-Tank weapons arrive, suddenly we are armed with more that rifles, we have a punch!

Virtually excused square bashing, except on special occasions, all H.Q. Platoons concentrate on their respective skills. Signals can operate on a more realistic scale. Cooks play about with strange heaps of mud, a mound of the stuff in a field, from it, a queer shaped door will enable some remarkably appetising dishes to be extracted, they actually look edible! The Sanitary Platoon use their imagination constructing weird and wonderful toilets. Some are more cunningly constructed than others, some so well concealed you don't stand a cat in hells chance of finding the bloody things before you need them!

Limited conscription having been introduced on a national scale, we receive a draft of about eighty men. Dressed in blue blazers and grey flannel trousers, we examine them with critical eyes, but soon they are dressed like soldiers. Sifted into various platoons, quickly they learn the ways of the Light Infantry, embracing it with surprising enthusiasm; a great bunch of lads!

Mortar drill going well, should be, they work us like dogs. Slow at first, working with nothing but an Army Manual, find out about all the bits and pieces first, study them as though they are your girlfriend's body, but get to know them better. Let's put them together. Right, we have a three inch mortar. Mount it. Dismount it. Mount it. Dismount it. Ok, let's do it faster, and faster, and faster. Room for improvement, by hell there is! Let's have a look at the sights; two air bubbles, just like on a spirit level, yes, but you don't build bloody walls with this.

Let's think in degrees shall we? A degree denotes a piece of ground covered by the barrel, it moves each time you wind off a degree, thus you point the barrel where the Gun Commander wants it pointed. Got it. Ok, let's practice with the sights on. Left degrees. Right degrees. Up degrees. Down degrees.

Where are the bombs? Let's have a look at them Yes, a ten pound bomb in weight, comes in a case of three, so one case gives a nice thirty pounds to hump about. Interesting. Can send this thing a distance of one thousand seven hundred yards, not bad, just like artillery, sort of! All bombs fired at a fixed target will fall in a cone shaped area one hundred yards in length, by fifty yards wide, each bomb will explode flinging shrapnel waist high for one hundred yards from point of impact, nasty little playmate, realise we have an effective weapon in our hands, we have got to become the best gun crew inside and outside Germany or bust!

Dig holes on the ground, six feet square by five feet deep, a nicely padded parapet of the loose soil, fit gun, me, and ammunition into it, make it snug and cosy, might be your home for days!

Trips to Salisbury Plain and Aldershot to fire live ammunition, high explosive and smoke bombs. Learn to lay smoke screen; learn the feel of the real stuff; lose the fear of handling it, soon, familiarity breeds almost contempt.

So the training goes. We are learning how to handle our weapons.

Unadorned the catering at this establishment. No fussing. If you are hungry, eat it. But, fussy home-bred eating habits die hard, resulting in every spare penny of pay being spent on food. On a wage of fourteen shillings a week, seven of which is allocated to my mother, a grand total of seven shillings a week is left; not often do I give way to the urge of painting Newbury Town red!

Sad as it may seem, week-end passes become an excuse to raid the larders of both my mother, and my girlfriends' mother. Both patient parents suffer the impertinent begging and scrounging with fortitude, never a complaint or reproof. Huge food parcels fill the luggage compartment of the buses as we wend our way back to camp, our departure, the signal for the harassed parents to fill up again before the next onslaught comes around. Not only do these women contribute their man, but half their larders as well!

Of the camp food I like the breakfast best; once you get used to that tray of fried eggs you're laughing. Small eggs, cooked by the cooks well before dawn I should think, warmed up for speed just before breakfast; they have a congealed look about them, a dead look, like a tray of big yellow fish eyes. Masses of curly bacon too would fill another tray, thick slices of bread and butter for the taking. Always gorged myself at this meal for fear I didn't like dinner!

Each day an officer comes around to our dining table just before we are due to eat. We must not touch a morsel until he has been. Our official food taster, he has got to do his drill first.

With the nervous and hesitant approach that Nero's food taster must have used every day of a probably short life, he tackles his task. A delicate sniff, a wise look around the staring faces, a tiny sip, or a tiny nibble, another wise look, he struggles to keep his face straight. Watching their antics every day with interest I breathlessly wait for one of them to make military history by rejecting something, or at least by dropping dead; but somehow, they never do either. The Sergeant cook stands close to the officers' elbow; he wears a pained expression on his face at the utter absurdity of inspecting his cooking. Trouble with his food – just ain't possible! His eyes bore into the Officers face, his respectful attitude daring him even to blink as he swallows the chosen morsel; silently he waits for the Officers head to nod which will indicate to all and sundry his approval; that the food used and the skill applied, is of the top quality. Having nodded after a lengthy pause, snappy salutes fly about, we can now eat the bloody stuff!

Currant cake for tea. Every day it's currant cake for tea, like a large wedding cake it stands in the place of honour in the centre of the table, a great slab of it dwarfing everything else on the table. Can't be any other kind of cake but this stuff in the whole wide world. Like dead flies the currants litter the table, at least, I think they are currants, pays to check for wings if you absently pick one up to pop in your mouth; it had to be known. Hunks of bread, hunks for butter, massive cans of jam, apricot jam, no other! The complicated shopping list of the cookhouse makes the mind boggle!

Introduced to the secrets of the emergency ration. A tin is waved about in the air, looks like a tin of tobacco. Full of good things they say, good when you are near to the point of dropping dead in your tracks from starvation; in fact, that's the only time you are allowed to use it and then only with permission. Filled with a chocolate-like substance carved up into little cubes; one of these cubes will be used each day, each cube constitutes a Christmas dinner to hear them talk! Very highly concentrated – they need to be – all sounds very unsavoury to me! Sooner put up with the bloody currant cake I think. Never did see the inside of the darn tin, bet a dollar, it was tobacco.

Show us a field dressing, a dirty brown square of cloth sewn into a little package. Rip one end, extract a folded brown bundle of cloth, unwind it; abut two yards of brown bandage, a patch of gauze fixed to one end, use this to stop the bleeding. If you can't do it yourself someone might come and do it for you. Comforting thought!

About time these lads lived in some holes thought some officer, so we move into some holes already dug for us, nice wet ones in a sea of mud. Permanent fixtures they are. You can see the boot prints of hundreds of other ammunition boots that have had the pleasure before us. A maze of slit trenches, each holds a section of men. Two days and one night we are in residence. The yellow mud clings to the clothes, rifle gets clogged, you sit on it, lean on it, bloody near eat it. Dressed in fighting order only, we shiver in misery, dead certain we shall all report sick as soon as we get out. Lugging containers of bully beef stew about we live like rats, just like our fathers did before us. We agree with them, living like this is hell, but it passes. None of us were physically sick, not even a cold! We are getting harder, tougher; we have left the softness of civvy Street a long way behind!

Winding up the days routine; trucks dash about the field, collecting the widely scattered equipment and men. Edwards of our platoon thinks he is Tarzan or something! As the fifteen cwt truck passes at speed, he takes a flying leap for the tailboard. Clever lad! He grips it with both hands, pulls himself up a bit trying to clear his feet off the ground; a deep hollow runs across the field directly in the path of the truck. The driver takes it at speed, as he has been trained to do, unaware of his passenger. Edwards' chin is about two inches above the top edge of the tail-board, he is in deep trouble as the rear of the truck dips down then snaps up. A shout of anguish as he flies through the air like a rocket. A sickening thud. He has settled. "Me teeth, I've lost me bloody teeth", he had too. Looks horrible, at least twenty years older, a sore jaw, nothing worse. Twenty years old he reckons he is, but in his gummy condition at present we wouldn't be seen out with him dead. Gummy old sod, bloody disgrace to the platoon, got to find his teeth quick before anybody sees him. Takes a good half hour to find the things, searching through the grass with great caution, not quite sure if the things will bite us on site. First one is found, then the other, both undamaged. Turn our back whilst he puts them in, can't stand the sight. When we turn round there stands our old mate, his pearly grin back in place, we can own him again – the platoon's honour is saved!

The Battalion is short on N.C.O.'s. Looking around the mortar platoon they decide that Edgar and I look like a couple of likely suckers and promote us to Lance Corporals; unpaid. Two pairs of single stripes are handed over with instructions to "Get 'em sewn on before Monday". Weekend leave, just the job for our girlfriends. Could not have brought more cooing from mother and the two girls if we had made Generals. My girl thinks I am top brass, don't see why I should let her think otherwise as I collect my just reward!

Dad sits quietly in a corner, he says nothing, just a soft knowledgeable smile plays about his lips. I know what is on his mind. He too was a hero once. When they brought him back from Mons in 1914, all shot to hell. In the last twenty-two years he has worked only two. Who the hell is going to employ a man who wastes his time having twenty-three major operations in hospital, the bloody 'Means test' people can look after the likes of him! He hasn't been a hero outside this family for twenty-two years. I know it saddens him to see us in uniform; he would rather do it all again himself just to protect us; but youth does not listen when he talks, only the hard way teaches youth. So, he smiles because we all want him to, it's too late to change anything now anyway.

Now we got a problem. All the men in the platoon eye us with suspicion. I have been among the foremost ranks when they say what a load of bastards the N.C.O.'s are! Now I have got to convince them that in actual fact N.C.O.'s are very nice people. Got to get around them somehow, otherwise they will be telling me to 'get stuffed' at the first order I give them; we got no mice in our platoon! I know every one of them is dead broke, I know too that the new Guard Room, starting tomorrow evening, is going to be the cookhouse. Get at them through their guts, that will win them over! I immediately volunteer for Guard Duty. Nobody volunteers for that. I get the job. Casually I tell the lads about all the grub myself and the guard detail can have, only want men. Have to get real tough with them, can't take them all; on such a low down trick was our satisfactory relationship based.

Beautiful guard details, twenty-four hours of top priority food for the poor men on guard. Warm cosy night, browsing the night away to the music of the sizzling frying pan, the tea-pot sings in harmony as it stews ready for instant action. Truly Paradise!

Time widens my experience, but to a brand-new Guard Commander like me an order is an order. Strict instructions that all personnel must report back into camp by a certain time; all men warned as they depart. One Sergeant returned very late, everyone else is tucked up in bed and asleep. Asking the Sergeant his reason he tells me to go to hell, big headed sod, thinks he walks on water. Ok Sarge, you are on a charge; can't believe his ears; speechless he walks off to bed. Company history I am making but I don't know it, Report and Charge duly submitted for action. An officer takes me into a nice quiet corner, talks to me just like my dad. "A junior doesn't place a senior on a charge, that sort of thing is not done you know". For some days I am an object of interest, fortunately we are short of sergeants in our platoon.

Training goes well on the guns, hard slogging work, but being willing surprisingly lightens the work. The use of live ammunition brings reality to our task.

Arrive at target site ready for action, dressed in fighting order, unload gun from truck, grab the forty-four pound weight of the mortar barrel, lift, sling it over the shoulder by its carrying sling, pick up two cases of bombs, each case holds three ten-pound bombs, sixty pound in weight, overall load, one hundred and forty pound; knees buckle; run to gun site and drop the load. Base plate, fling down to firing spot, slip barrel into socket of base plate, twist, it's locked into position. Lower muzzle of barrel, slip it through the collar of the tripod, fit sights. Other men have unpacked bombs, passed them down the line of kneeling men in position, ready to fire. A specially designed handling drill is used to pass the bombs, got to do that part right at speed. Got to do it automatically without thinking. Get a bomb in the barrel upside down you are dead certain to wet your pants. As smooth as butter, the weapon is ready for action within seconds; they wait for me now.

From my position in advance of the gun crew, I observe the target area. My shouted "Fire" instructions will determine the effectiveness of the mens' firing; under cover, they cannot see the target they must destroy. Study the ground to our front quickly; check the possibility of hidden folds of ground between us and the target; estimate the range with an eye and brain that remembers past errors; must establish the target within a 'bracket' first. If the first shot falls short, speedily raise the range; if it falls over, speedily decrease the range. Once we have fired our presence is known. They, the enemy, will hit back fast. Establish the range to centre of 'Bracket'. You're on target. OK, decision made – 800 yards. Shout back the range for the first shot; a slight pause as number 1 crew member adjusts the sights. A hollow muffled sounding 'bang' as the cartridge nesting within the cluster of tail fins on the tail of the bomb strikes the firing pin at the bottom of the barrel, followed by a loud whistle as the missile instantly disappears high into the air.

Eyes fixed on target, watching for the flash of flame and billow of smoke that will mark the point of impact. Have I read the ground right? There, just over target, fine. Raise the barrel, decrease range, shout back desired degrees. In seconds the second bomb is on it's way, landing short of target, good, 'bracket' established. Obtain a fixed range between the two shots. In seconds Number 1 shouts his readiness. Can order 'rapid fire'; see how many bombs we can get into the air before the first one strikes target, test our speed. 'Rapid fire' means rapid, the bombs pass along the line of kneeling men from one pair of hands to another. They pass with the smooth, well-oiled automatic ease of months of training to fall down in the open and hungry mouth of the waiting barrel in a perfect rhythm, each to be spewed out instantly. Ten, fifteen, twenty, twenty-five, six, seven, eight, the first bomb of the stick strikes target. Twenty-seven of its fellows eagerly chase it; they erupt rapidly one by one on and around the immediate vicinity of the target area in close packed formation of the one hundred yard 'cone'. In a sea of flame and smoke loud explosions echo back; nothing, but nothing can live in that area, especially men who lay on the ground.

Relax, the target is destroyed. Report back to the men, now to get the gun out quickly away from this position. Dismantle. Each man to his own task, can count the few seconds, the gun, ammunition, and men are on the truck waiting to move. The men look at me wondering what the hell I am hanging about for, I gaze at them because I am pleased; nothing part-time about this bunch any more, a smooth, co-ordinated, efficient, and deadly mortar crew I see. I love them!

Other drills, other exercises with live ammunition. Sometimes a dud bomb, we know the drill in theory. No need to panic! But, the first time it happens you hold your breath with slight shock, you pray to the God of War that he does not get rough, not yet! The thing went down the barrel smoothly but it has not come out; it's stuck down the bottom. Right, first thing to do; run back away from the gun, about one hundred yards; take cover; wait – see if it explodes, it should not, they tell us there is a safety valve built in to the bomb which prevents it exploding until it has travelled some distance through the air; at the same time they tell you not to trust their foolproof system! Wait about sixty seconds, if it has not blown the gun to pieces and parted your hair, run back to the gun and get the bloody thing out by hand!

Remove sights, twist the barrel to release from its lock in the base plate, lift the end of the barrel upwards gently to lower the muzzle. I stand, hands cupped together cunningly over the muzzle as the bomb slips down the length of the barrel slowly. In the centre of the pattern of fingers, a hole, through this long slender nose of the bomb will pass; allowing fingers to trap the fat shoulders; gently; into waiting hands; grasp firmly; quickly, screw the safety cap onto the nose; toss the thing aside; operation completed.

Try our hand at trench digging. A nice looking site at Snelmore Common on the outskirts of Newbury; looks fine until the couple of inches of top soil is removed to reveal a mass of knobbly granite stones. We cuss and swear over them, working like slaves we get down a couple of feet, the trench fills with water, a non-stop flow of water; got so bad the local water supply was being robbed. To our delight, the whole exercise was called off! What we learned about trench warfare one could write on a postage stamp!

Night operations as riflemen. Hold a piece of ground on a long extended front, stand to arms each morning at crack of dawn; attack can come from anywhere, things get played rough these days. Even though the attackers are our friends a clout from one of them is just as painful as any German one will be.

The ground to our front needs to be searched with keen eyes through the mist. There are some bloody maniacs round here. Watch out for the 'Mad Major' in particular; he will be creeping about somewhere. One of our own officers, a decent enough chap under normal conditions, but on this sort of game he is nuts on efficiency; springs out on drowsy sentries; frightens the bloody life out of them; grabs their weapons and runs like hell. See a figure staggering through the morning mist hugging a pile of rifles to his chest, it will be him. All guns retrievable only from him in his office.

Urgent appeal comes round the Battalion for R.A.F. Air Gunners. Edgar and I talk it over, decide to give it a try, like the thought of pretty blue uniforms; might even manage to get away from these holes in the ground – pay is bound to be better too. Our applications are turned down flat, spent too much time teaching us how to handle mortars, stay where you are.

Christmas is not far away, embarkation leave is to be included. At last we are considered fit to go overseas. That's fine, but to where? Speculation starts immediately. Plenty of experts in the ranks, rumours fly, every day brings fresh crops, tropical kit seen going into the stores, arctic kit seen going into the stores, I can see us doing a world tour if the gossip can be believed. Strange, not one of the experts actually saw what did go into the stores!

Battle dress is issued together with the newly designed webbing equipment; looks and feels quite comfortable. No brass to clean! That's a step in the right direction.

Edgar has just finished a twenty-four hour guard duty and is a very peeved man, one of his men had decided to give his rifle barrel a final clean just a few minutes before the Orderly Officer of the day was due to arrive to inspect the guard detail. An officer and the Company Sergeant Major arrived for the inspection. Edgar was horrified to see his man struggling to extract the cord of the jammed 'pull through' from the barrel of his rifle, no time to get it out; they had to turn out for inspection with the thing stuck in. Rifles presented for inspection, thumb nails of the right hand in correct position in the breach at the end of the rifle barrels, grunts of satisfaction from the Officer as he progressively peers down the muzzle of each mans rifle, not a bad turn out so far, but what's this? In total disbelief the officer gazes at the length of cord hanging out of the muzzle of the next mans rifle, for seconds he seems fascinated by the gently swinging weight at the end of the cord, Edgar has died a thousand deaths with shame as he waits for the blast of indignation that's got to come, it arrives in no uncertain terms, the Sergeant Major books Edgar on a charge.

Leave comes round quite quickly, we go home feeling like peacocks in our new uniforms, a cute little side hat on our heads. Our girls coo over us, we knock 'em cold.

Father is back in hospital with his leg wound, none of us are surprised least of all him having spent more than half of the last twenty years in the place, we know where to visit him, it's always the same place, they call it 'Queen Mary's Hospital'. Shattered ex-servicemen spend many years of their wrecked lives there still fighting the war most people reckoned finished in 1918. To reach this place you have to travel to Roehampton on the outskirts of

London.

We brothers know every inch of the place; it's as familiar to us as our home having spent so many of our childhood weekends and many Christmases visiting Father. We enter together on this our last physical contact with Father before we go overseas, the rhythm of our ammunition boots on the wooden floor of the army hut which serves as a ward is loud and disturbing, we break step to try to soften the noise of the heavy boots but it is impossible.

Every bed is filled with men in various stages of pain as they usually are, these ex-servicemen stare at the two battledress clad figures thudding into their silent world, they watch with interest as we converge onto the tent-like structure that protects Fathers leg from the weight of the bed clothes, we stare into his drawn, pain racked face and have to hide the ache in our hearts as always with a smile as he would wish us to. He smiles back at us with the light of pride beginning to brighten his eyes as he gazes at us standing one each side of him, tall, straight and strong in our youth, he looks around the ward to his other bed-ridden friends and shouts to them loudly 'My Sons'! This mass of men lying flat on their backs smile at us in genuine pleasure, a special breed of men, they look at us with approval, they award us a great honour by accepting us as of their mould. We say our farewell and leave Father in his all too familiar bed to fight his battle alone, to have yet another pin-point of shrapnel removed from his leg, but it never seems to improve or stop the flowing river of puss from the wound for long, he has had to live with the stench of the stuff for so long it's become a way of life to him.

Embarking leave is over all too soon. Shortly we leave for France. Parents, wives, girls and friends escort us to the waiting buses; sometimes us, sometimes they stagger under the weight of the largest food parcels that the hired Oxford Bus Company has seen yet. Surely mothers parcel is the largest of all, does she not contribute two sons to this Battalion. A forced Mum reckons she has packed enough food to keep her sons fit till the next time they come home on leave. A vastly different feeling in the air at this parting; a slightly forced gaiety fills the air. Emotions stir deep within, nobody admits to having such things of course, all you got to do is keep smiling; mostly it is simple but not always.

We are leaving for several months this time, promise we will come back of course. Promise a hundred times not to do anything silly; yes we will definitely stay out of trouble. Girls have given us many tokens of good-luck to safeguard us; bibles to bless us, and a crucifix to hang round our necks. Joan has given me a small bible and a crucifix to hang round my neck. I have little time for such outward symbols, such things are not necessary to walk with God, but, they are gifts of love and a blessing intended to protect a man going to war. They will be respected as such, the crucifix will adorn my neck as intended, the bible will nestle in my breast pocket together with my pay-book and photographs; they nestle over my heart deliberately with the romantic notion that one day they may help to soften a blow to that necessary and vital organ!

Last clinging farewell's as we climb on to the buses, tears from some of the women as the buses pull away; a two way traffic of kisses stopped only by the glass of the windows, they fall with the gentleness of thistle-down on those we aim at; but suddenly they are gone!

Bawdy songs pave our way back to Newbury; the air is 'blue' as the lads hide their emotions with versions of:

> Roll me over, In the clover
>
> Roll me over, lay me down and do it again

The strains of this military gem floats over the Berkshire Downs as we speed on our way.

France it is to be. Not rumour or gossip, but a fact. First we have got to have a few needles stuck in to us; some of them may flatten us; but we get twenty-four hours 'excused-duty' when we can lie in bed all day if we want. We love that sort!

Understand that the King wants to have a look at us before he sends us overseas as his representatives. Can't blame him if you think about it! Bags of unlimited 'spit and polish' on the great day, not that there is much to do with the new battledress. Give the old cap badge, boots, and teeth an extra polish to make up for it; but after this lot is over we want dull stuff, dead dull, no polish. A fine day to meet the King, clear and sunny, a good day for a march. Everyone is scrubbed clean, formed up into ranks and ready. A nice crisp word of command from the Officer in charge. Several hundred boots crash as one on the surface of the road in response to the second half of 'Oxfordshire'. As one man we fall into the rhythm of the march. Band and bugles at our head we go to keep our date with the King.

Typical! Too blasted early or something, so we march round and round the outskirts of the town, can't get on the racecourse yet; novelty wearing off; marched a good few miles so far. At last, they fit us in; troops all over the place, thousands of them! We stand in long lines, avenues quite wide between each unit; find myself in the front rank, should get a good view of him as he passes. Standing 'at ease', relaxed, chattering to each other to pass the time, we wait for him to come. Where the hell is he anyway? We have things to do!

Movement in the avenue directly in front of me! A bunch of officers, high rank some of them, sauntering along nice and casual, having a chat as they pass by; none of them look interesting; take no notice if us as far as I can see, they fade past, just a bunch of officers.

Troops moving off. Hell. Was he in that bunch that drifted past? Must have been...what a let down!

Obtain an evening pass into town; can't afford to let the chance slip; it will be my last visit. Missed the bus; a walk won't hurt. Reach the Newbury-Andover Road, a car pulls up by my side, an Army Captain the sole occupant; offers a lift in to town which I accept. Can't recognise his cap badge but he is very chatty. Too chatty for an Officer, asks a lot of questions about my unit, tells me nothing about his, don't like it one bit. Tell him to drop me off at the 'Gun' pub a couple of miles short of town which he does, feel I should report him to someone but the area is dead of life; he will be miles away by the time I reach town; the matter drops from my mind.

Have been busy over the last twenty-four hours! Stores and transports have gone ahead. Today we leave. For the last time we muster outside the village church to march away, not to return this time; most of the village population is here, among them many new found friends.

Moving off the easy swing of the marching 'at ease' is picked up. Our village friends move along with us as they escort us to the boundary of their little cluster of houses. Shouted "Farewell's" and "Good Luck's"' as children get under our feet; girls throw kisses; they fall behind. They are at our backs now. Nice people, a privilege to have shared their lives however brief. Thanks to their understanding and generosity our stay has been a pleasant one; we leave them; most of us forever.

Out into open country. A detail escorts a couple of men who had decided they have no wish to go overseas; domestic problems it is said, very little dignity about it for all concerned. We all feel embarrassed for them. Woodhay! A tiny country station out in the wilds, a waiting train, climb aboard, settle in for the trip to Southampton, soon we move off.

Several mysterious halts. Before long, outskirts of a City, sheds, warehouses, ships, Southampton. Unload, file into a large warehouse; nice girls stand behind even nice tea stalls, free buns and tea! Can undo our belts and sit down on the floor. Relax. We do so and await events.

The next event is in the shape of a bloke hawking little square objects. Probably dirty postcards. We do the man an injustice; they turn out to be French-English pocket books. On the ball this lad, most of us buy one, might be useful with the girls!

Cecil Arthur Meads

The Crossing, 1940

She waits for us patiently, a normal cross-channel boat christened 'St Helier'; regret having such insulting thoughts about her but I hope her bloody bottom is sound. Can go on board now; first on board must file directly down below, fill her up from the bottom upwards; I am among the first so I go way down, near the engine room in fact; can hear the engine throb on the steel bulkhead as I rest my head against it.

A large hold normally I would guess, but now it's rigged up with a sea of two tiered wooden bunks. I manage to get one but I'm not too happy with the distance I will have to travel if a torpedo comes sailing along. Unload our gear from our bodies, hang it on anything that protrudes, even if it's another blokes toe! Soon my gaze has to search for a way through the jungle of hanging rifles and equipment; they hang like bunches of grapes. My bunk is vibrating from the throb of the engine; the boat is not even moving yet! It's very hot and the packed bodies won't improve matters. Got to stay below until told otherwise which won't be until we are well out to sea. Engines next to my ear have increased their power, a deeper throb, vibration increasing. My bunk is responding with a will, the hanging gear is swaying gently to and fro, we are on the move.

Probably been going an hour I should think; she rolls a lot; don't like it much. Getting difficult to see across to the other side of the hold. Like an old London fog the area is thick with cigarette smoke; can hardly breathe in here. Can't got on deck yet, going to have some tea first, good, could do with some too.

I can see members of the cook-house staff on the way; they struggle between the bunks with huge containers digging their elbows into the packed men. They cuss and blind their fate, we relax while they work, won't hurt them, they get all the best grub anyway. Might have known there was no love in their hearts when they made that tea. Wish they had not bothered now. Thick like toffee the stuff could only have been made with jealousy weighing heavily on their hearts; the stuff is strong enough to kill an ox. Drowned in 'Carnation Milk', and, I suspect, a bleeding laxative. I get the stuff down in the absence of anything else. Shouldn't have done it, shouldn't have drunk the stuff, feel like a wet sack. Must get on deck quick! Stomach protesting violently, eyes desperately trying not to look at the swaying gear that just won't bloody well keep still,

I make my way towards the deck as fast as I can. Easier said than done, bodies lay about all over the place like so much litter, passageway and floors completely covered with chaps stretched out; no room to be sick down here anyway! Men playing cards, snores joining the chorus of chatter, some blokes even singing; how could they? Panic signals from my stomach now. I try to oblige as fast as I can, telling it to keep calm as I cautiously tip-toe through the khaki clad tulips in my number nine ammunition boots; by some miracle I did not hear one swear word directed at me.

At last! I have found daylight, fresh air, this will fix it. Hope fades fast, can't even see the rail around the ship's side which is solid with groaning bodies standing shoulder to shoulder as they deposit their tea overboard; pools of vomit splash over the deck, a few chaps keep it company. They look like dead men, faces a ghastly green shade; I get the feeling that this is not going to do me any good at all. Absolutely right. No sooner the thought than my stomach joins the happy throng, the intake of tea sails off into the wind, legs stagger blindly over the deck. With a will entirely of its' own, and with a promptness under these emergency conditions that would have brought comments of admiration to my lips under normal conditions, my arse finds a flat surface to sit on. Some sort of ledge I think. I don't even question it. It can go where the hell it likes as far as I'm concerned. Might be another fella I'm sitting on. Who cares! I sit wherever I am sitting for what seemed like a long time; think I feel a bit better; can risk opening my eyes; one quick peep, get the lay of the land, should say bloody sea I suppose! The section of rail to my front is clear; some of the men have gone; where they have gone is another matter; down below or flung themselves over the side? It's anybody's guess. Eyes fixed on the unadorned rail at the top, horizon about four feet above it; suddenly it's four feet below it. Jesus Christ! Quickly my eyes shut together tightly again. No improvement. Decide I may just as well die in my bunk as untidily on deck; I manfully stagger my way back through the mass of bodies without getting my head knocked off, see my bunk, Edgar is near it, he grins at me! My loving brother grins at my green complexion; I hate his guts because he is so cheerful; like a dying man I lay myself carefully down.

I manage a fitful doze, a radio blares somewhere, 'Lord Haw-Haw' the renegade Englishman is speaking; he welcomes our Division to France. My thoughts immediately fly to the unknown captain who has given me a lift to Newbury; could quite well have been one of the men gathering such information; regret I did not follow the matter through now.

Someone shouts "Land". I open my feeble eyes; most of the chaps have gone up on deck to see what there is to see; all I see is nasty swinging rifles and other gear; butterflies take over immediately in my stomach; I decide to stay just where I am, till the boat runs aground if need be!

Motion decidedly better now, almost nil in fact, better join the lads, see where the hell they are going to dump us.

Le Havre, France, 1940

A huge port; the boat is pulling in alongside an unloading dock; British and French liaison officers await us, among them I recognise our own second-in-command, he has had the job of organising our reception. In the next berth, the remains of a huge, burned out passenger liner; once the pride of the French Civil Line she now lies a depressing hulk; an act of sabotage it is said, a sad sight.

The air is good up here, the lack of violent movement is even better. Begin to take an interest in life once again. Look seawards where dozens of tiny French fishing boats are busy about their business, they toss like corks in the choppy inland waters; their crazy antics rekindle recently active chemicals in my body; frantic warning signals are sent immediately to my stomach warning me not to take liberties yet. I obey the delicate thing without hesitation and turn my eyes to something more solid and stable.

The port, that won't bloody move. Filled with massive sheds and warehouses with rolling open country beyond, covered in snow; can't see any signs of transport down there.

Off the ship at last. Falling in on the dockside I study the old tub that has brought us safely across; despite my unkind thoughts regarding her bottom. I have no hard feelings towards her; not her fault that Britain does, on occasions, breed some bloody lousy seamen!

Train it is to be, for a few miles anyway, then we will have to march for about eight miles. Very cold, more snow is in the air, we have no Greatcoats, dressed in Fighting Order, but the march will warm us up. Passenger coaches in small compartments, as in Britain minus a gangway, seats are wooden and uncomfortable. Piling our gear on the narrow parcel racks at the risk of dented heads, we wait for the next move. Not long in coming. The first jerk as the train moves forward brings down most of our gear on our heads. With curses we place it all back again, but the French driver seems to be one of those people who goes jerking his way through life, nothing will stay in those darn racks.

A wayside halt, "All out – Fall in on the road". Here we march, good job too, those racks were beginning to fray our nerves a bit. We leave the train at a place called 'Bolbec'. Shivering with cold as we 'Fall in' for the march, can't get on the move fast enough to suit us, band formed up at our head we move off into the open countryside. Big uneven cobbles, meant to last forever, probably will, but they were never meant to march on; especially when covered with snowy sludge. We slip and slide on them; curses get interwoven neatly with the words of our songs creating new versions.

Eating up the miles, village after village passes by; a few people come out of their houses to watch us pass by; they don't seem to be too impressed by what they see; perhaps our band and bugles, making enough noise to wake the dead, disturbs their peace; perhaps they have seen too many of us before in other years. Farming land by the look of it, difficult to tell with all this snow about. A few scattered cottages, farmhouses. All the women and female children seem to wear black clothing, a green sheen is clearly visible in the material of some of the garments, hard workers, people of the soil. Knotted scarves over some of the women's heads, some white, but mostly black; doesn't look as though there's much fun in their lives. They stare at us with sombre expressions.

Ahead, a fairly large town. The band strikes up on the outskirts just to let them know that the 'Oxfords' are coming. Entirely different reception, larger and more modern homes and buildings, people are dressed better and brighter; they have more time for fun I guess! The people flock to the sound of the music, greetings are shouted at us. The bugles open up right in the very centre of the place, tall buildings all around, the notes bounce back off the walls and re-echo down the street, the spectators scream in mad delight. Out through the town we go, these people have heard one of the very few British Bands in France, they have been privileged, whether they realise it or not!

Light getting bad, will have to stop for the night somewhere soon. Snow is falling pretty fast. Can just make out another large town ahead, understand that this is where we shall spend the night. Enter a large square, 'fall out', and wait billet allocation.

St Romain, 1940

Dusk; can't see much, shadowy figures of civilians loom up through the gloom and pass by with no apparent interest in our activities and disappear back into the gloom. Platoons peel off from the square as they are taken to billets for the night. Soon it is our turn, the French Liaison Officer accompanied by a seedy looking French civilian escorts us out of the square and down a lane. We have visions of a slap-up mansion, nice cosy rooms, home from home.

Through a five-barred gate into a field, a fairly large field full of fruit trees of some sort, probably the orchard adjacent to our mansion, we wind our way through the trees heading for the centre of the field; we reach it; our guides stop and point to a tiny two-storied brick built structure, here it is, hell, not much of a mansion! It's a storage place of some sort; a door in the wall on the ground floor held shut by a large padlock; can't see any notice but it says 'KEEP OUT' as plain as day.

The Frenchman points upwards to the second floor, yes, we see an opening; no door on it, no stairs either. How do we get up there? Bloody fly? We ask these questions of the Frenchmen, crowding round them in a bunch that does nothing to further international relations. The civilian dashes out into the gloom, presently to stagger back under the weight of a large ladder, props it against the wall under the opening; our escorts promptly head for home leaving us to it. Climbing up the ladder we discover that the loft is half full of hay. Taking up residence, we choose our spots and sling down our gear. Some blankets have arrived, one per man, could do with six per man actually to keep this cold out. No food from the cooks tonight but we can go into town for a couple of hours if we wish and get some grub if we can find any; we do wish!

Work out a sentry roster of one-hour stints, too cold for the usual two-hour sessions, sentry will have to keep moving as it is to avoid freezing! Each man to relieve each other, no fancy drill for this set-up. Posting the first man I go with the rest of the lads to find grub.

Complete blackout, can't see a darn thing, blankets hang over many doors of the dwellings. Behind one of them there's got to be somewhere to eat? Lift a doze, at last – a Cafe!

A blaze of light, instant warmth, people sitting round tiny tables drinking, some are eating. One man sits in a corner, my eyes fall and rivet on his jaws as they open wide to clamp together over the biggest crusty sandwich I have ever seen in my life. A bloody work of art the thing is, deserves to be enshrined. As the jaws close, the yellow yolk of the two eggs it contains runs in golden rivers down his chin. I can only point dumbly at the monster sandwich in response to the girl who is awaiting our requirements. Fit for a King! We love and simply adore this girl. Massive chunks of bread in which nestles two eggs, steaming hot bowls of coffee. Our bodies glow!

Must get back. Expect the sentry is like an icicle by now, he needs relieving and feeding. We give the lad a vivid description of the sandwiches; sounds like poetry to him; he leaves us with a glaze in his eyes to follow our directions. Hope he finds the place. Probably go mad if he doesn't. The remainder of us prepare to 'dig in' for the night, decide to take off our boots to give the old feet a rest, but keep them handy, burrow our way deep into the hay, feet well down, face the only part exposed; the hay smells nice anyway.

Hear No 1 sentry return from the Cafe, bet he feels better now! He beds down. The sentry below stamps his feet to get warm, will loosely keep changing the sentries during the night; won't be much sleep for anybody; too cold.

Dawn is slow in coming. Glad it won't be long now. Just want to get on the move again. Company bugler blowing his guts out telling us to get out of our cosy little beds; more than glad to oblige this time. His notes ring out loud and clear in the frosty air. He'll probably wake up half the bloody town at the same time!

Crawl out of our holes like men with acute attacks of lumbago, can hardly move, limbs as still as our rifles, bones feel brittle, going to snap like twigs at any second; groans fill the air as we try to limber up and get our circulation moving. Reach for my boots, better get them on, but hell...I can't, the things are frozen solid! The uppers are rock hard; no way can the feet be got into them until they have been thawed out. Other men are cussing too as they try to get their boots on. The things stand glaring back at us in defiance, might as well be carved from ebony for all the good they are to us. Got to get them softened up quick. Shouting down to the frozen sentry, we throw down a heap of hay begging him to get a fire going somehow, find wood, get some heat. This he does quickly, more for his own good than for ours we suspect!

Stranded in the loft, cussing the sentry because he is close to the fire than we are, we toss down our boots for him to arrange around the fire. There they stand, a long row of boots almost reaching right round the fire, they mock us; standing stiffly to attention, doing it better than we can on parade; some of them steam as the heat begins to work at them, like miniature steam engines, steaming with shame I should think! We dance about from foot to foot impatiently, trying to keep warm while we wait. A further heart rending howl splits the air. "My bloody Brylcream is solid". The anguish in the man's voice at the very through of not being able to smooth his curls down for the day is heart breaking. Other men get face flannels out hoping to lick their faces, but, they too are solid lumps in their dampness. Boots eventually yield enough to get into them, some have thawed too quickly, feel too tight, hope we don't march very far today; the Mortar Platoon is going to look a mighty sick bunch of cripples if we do!

Cookhouse has located us. A container of tea, fried bacon and bread is delivered; we wolf it down like starving dogs.

Bidding a rude farewell to the 'mansion' we hobble back to town. There we are delighted to see a fleet of waiting troop carriers, canvas covered backs. We are to get a lift, providing we don't freeze to death on the way, might even manage a doze.

Decide to take an interest in the passing scenery being as this 'tour' is at the government's expense. To my factory confined eyes everything is of interest that is different to our way of life, but, with the usual British criticism of anything alien, it, as usual gets condemned out of hand.

See two French soldiers come out of a Cafe, untidy looking objects, probably slept in beds but looking worse than us who have slept in hay. Tunics unbuttoned, crushed soft headgear perched on the backs of their heads, cigarettes drooping from their lips, they walk slowly across the pavement chattering as they go. Casually undoing the front of their trousers, two jets travel down the gutter to mingle and flow in a relieved stream! Dirty uncivilised bastards! Hope they get frostbite. Can't even be artistic about it; Christ, I have done better than that!

Standing on our piece of kerbstone outside where we lived, my brother and I, mere toddlers, our grubby fingers fumbled for equally grubby objects conveniently located between our legs. Two fine and delicate jets would arch high up into the air. Like magic, beautiful patterns would take shape on the surface of the road, even wriggly lines appeared sadly sometimes to be spoiled by the wind. But decent civilised behaviour was abruptly introduced in the shape of our Mothers' heavy and well directed hand leaving two small stinging ears ringing with "You dirty little devils". Jesus, what my Mother would do to those two blokes!

A few French military here and there, mostly infantry. We quite naturally measure them with our eyes as we pass. Some still wear the 'Blue Swallow' tail tunics of their 1914 fathers; others wear the more modern khaki coloured style. One man on sentry duty shakes us; his rifle leans against a wall, an easy chair stands on the pavement in case the poor dear gets tired, and he is busy chatting up a couple of girls! A battery of 75mm guns pass by, their best gun I understand, but I am surprised to see them still drawn by horses. Quite a few people are walking about in wooden clogs, Sabots I believe they call them.

A tricky drive for the lorry drivers in the snow covered roads but eventually they deliver us safely back to Bolbec where a train is awaiting our pleasure. Much activity in the vicinity as the Battalion is brought to the area. Cattle trucks stare down at us, we stare back at the words painted in white letters on the sides of the trucks; Chevaux 8, Hommes 40, quickly we grab our little translation books the canny customer had flogged us in Southampton to find out which of these two words we are. Find we are Hommes which makes us a bit sad, they might actually pack us in these trucks 40 men to each.

Plenty of straw, surprisingly no overcrowding, we settle in fairly comfortably, a lot of packing and loading, a long job; at dusk we move onwards to the next leg of our travels.

Travel all night, sleep well, tea and breakfast at Arras, our journey continues to Libercourt; here we detrain. Large packs are dumped at the station to be collected and delivered later. The Battalion will marsh on snow-bound roads to a village called Attiches not far from the Belgian frontier which is to become our training area.

We of the Mortar Platoon are caught for 'baggage party', missing the march we shall act as handlers of the baggage on and off of the trucks when they arrive, at least it's a warm job!

Attiches, 1940

An unadorned, plain working type of village. Terraced houses line each side of the main road which runs through it; not much greenery within the confines of the village. Here and there a cafe, one gents hair dressing establishment, a small factory that produces children's pushchairs, a church; side roads branch off from the main road containing clusters of workers houses, farm houses, and on the outskirts, a grand chateau.

Each platoon is allocated a billet; sometimes two platoons share one, depending on the space available. The Signals Platoon and we of the Mortars have to share a billet in a huge loft located over a large farmhouse; they have done us proud! Long and wide with plenty of room to move, biggest loft I have ever seen. Signals Platoon spread themselves over one end, we take the other. At each end there is a tall round iron stove; one for them and one for us; nice big four footers, round and fat, they glow a bright red. A dozen straight backed chairs stand in a ring around each stove ready for lounging on; soon as we settle in we promise the chairs we won't disappoint them. I see a beautiful vision as I look at the red hot stove, it's just like the ones you see in the cowboy films; get the chair back on two legs, nicely balanced, a well aimed spit on to the red cylinder, watch it bubble and fade into nothingness; we have got paradise here!

Sling down the gear on a chosen spot, troop across to the barn, fill a pilliasse with straw, hang photographs on the wall, we have settled in; at least the Signals Platoon have, we of the Mortars have got to provide guard duty. Hell, this is what we get for volunteering so much at Newbury! A bitter cold night, everyone takes short spells outside, even the Guard Commander. By morning we are shivering wrecks, our greatcoats are still on the road somewhere between us and Newbury; we don't expect to see the things again.

Twenty-four hour 'off duty' spell, decide to have a look round the village, try a couple of cafes, have a look in at the gents hair dressers – understand that a female cuts your hair. The cafe is interesting; every drink is the world must surely be ranged on the narrow shelves behind the counter, try a couple and leave the place very much in favour of having such a place set up in our billet! Have a hair cut – yes it's true! A lovely little female is slashing away with the scissors like a veteran. She stands close as she works her way seductively round you; her bosom, Christ, what a credit to France! They sail slowly across your front like a couple of trim destroyers; I can see the signal flags clearly, bloody sure they say 'England expects every man to do his duty'; but, being a bit weak on flags I don't take the chance, could get my throat cut if I have read them wrong!

Passing a row of detached houses, a door has opened suddenly as I draw level with it. An elderly female has stepped out on to the pavement and grabbed my arm. She is chattering and pulling me in through the door of her house directly into a living room, the door is slammed behind me; I have been abducted off of the public highway like a helpless maiden by a 'Tommy' collector! First impressions of the room - a step back in time, Victorian, lots of velvet drapes, lace, paper flowers, dainty china ornaments, old fashioned high backed chairs, a large round table in the centre of the room which all but fills it. Two people sitting at the table, an elderly man and a girl of about twenty, their faces split with wide grins as the view the captive; mum, dad and daughter I guess.

Mum is standing back beaming at me; I grin back like a halfwit, completely at a loss as to what is going to happen next! Mum takes charge and is speaking to me rapidly, not that the speed makes any difference I don't understand a word she says anyway. She is a fighter so she turns her battery on to dad instead; he is still beaming at me with delight, he nods his head in instant agreement with mum, gets up and crosses the room to a cupboard, gets out a bottle and four glasses. Looks good, perhaps we are all going to get drunk! The glasses are set out carefully on the table, daughter pours out red wine and hands me a glass; a glass all round; they all stand on their feet and move in close to me, dad is going to say something as he looks directly at me. He speaks one word and I know it! "Angleterre", solemnly we drink to England then we sit round the table, everyone beaming at each other with pleasure. Dad's filling up again; they stand, I stand, this time I am mighty quick, before they can open their mouths I make a brilliant statement: "France". Beams of pleasure, glasses kiss each other, are raised and drained, we all sit down again.

Formalities over I wonder what is coming next but mum is on the ball again, a rapid stream of chatter, I look at her blankly. She tries again, the others help her. I catch the words "Madame" and "Mademoiselle". Ah! Am I married? Mum has walked across the room and is pointing at a photograph of a bride and groom, she is pointing at me with her eyebrows raised in question. Taking the photograph of my girlfriend out of my pocket, I pass it over with my first impeccable French: "Mademoiselle". Three heads raise slightly, nod slowly, wisely, as though it's a bloody miracle and any girl will have me at all. Their faces light up with joy at the breakthrough they have achieved in the language barrier. Mum grabs the photo first; dad and daughter look over her shoulder, immediate coos of pleasure, chatter among themselves, beaming glances at me as three fingers stab at the picture. I gaze at them mesmerized.

Dad has picked up an important point, mum and daughter agree with him; they all fix their eyes on me at once. I get ready for the blow as mum gets cracking. Showing me the picture, her finger is pointing at my girlfriends breasts! To make certain that I understand her she places the picture down on the table and stands squarely in front of me and decides to illustrate. Fingers closed together, hand flat, she places the edges of her hands on her chest just above her own breasts; a forward and outward movement, down, back, upwards, to the lower parts of her breasts. She has illustrated two large balloons in the air! They all stand beaming at my good luck, cooing like pigeons. I not my head in agreement, indeed they are a fine pair.

Mum has spotted something outside the window. With her face very serious, the others look out too; they are all very serious as mum grabs me by the arm and drags me to the window. Pointing out at a nice looking girl who is walking down the street on the other side of the road, the three of them shake their heads from side to side, their mouths droop in disapproval. I take another look at the girl, she looks bloody good to me! Mum can see that I haven't quite got the point, a determined sort she is going to make her point if it kills her. Placing her hand briefly between her daughters' legs and pointing again out of the window she vigorously shakes her head, we've now got three shaking heads and three sad mouths drooping at the corners. OK, I've got the point. The girl outside is a prostitute. I must not have anything to do with her. I nod my head to convey that I have got the message, they beam in relief.

Panic signals are sounding in my brain; got to get out of this lot quick. For a fella who has virtually never left his mothers apron strings apart from when the Territorial Army took him away, the standard of this drawing room conversation is frightening. Having parents who never bothered to explain about the birds and the bees, it was a bit of a shock to me to discover entirely by accident at the tender age of sixteen, that a buck needed a bleeding doe to get another rabbit. Already in this dainty room we have discussed tits and fannies, that only leaves one more object, somebody's penis, could be mine too!

A frantic act as I look at my watch, get up, grab their hands each in turn, thank goodness my limited French can fade me out politely. "Merci Madame, Mademoiselle, Monsieur". I flee from those well-meaning and hospitable people like a whipped cur, my tail between my legs, back to the safety of the Platoon where such topics of conversation are expected and can be dealt with easily.

Leather jerkins are issued, intended to keep out the bitter cold weather. Sleeveless, they help keep out the wind. Still no sign of the greatcoats, some bugger must have flogged them I would think. Training is picked up where we left off in England. Crawling about in snow like a load of seal; without white clothing it was very difficult to blend in with the stuff, we could be seen a mile away. Now for map reading; getting really educated now! For the first time it is brought home to me that a map is not just a flat piece of paper with just roads, rivers, and railway lines; other things spring to the knowledgeable eye, hills, mountains, forests, slopes, depressions, tracks, the flat paper as you look at it becomes a birds eye view of the real country.

Compass reading, connect it with map references. "Think you know how?" "Sure." "Ok, take a patrol out tonight". "Hell"! A mantle of blue snow with bright stars above it; it is freezing cold but I sweat in apprehension. A tiny speck on the map, in this featureless landscape which looks like a wedding cake without ornamentation, I have got to find this tiny speck first time out, no wonder I sweat, the men will have my guts for garters if I don't. Got to look confident, work it out slowly but surely. It comes as a great surprise to me when I actually find the thing, the magic of the exercise enthrals me for days. A 'Red Letter' day, Edgar and I actually get paid for our stripes at last! Big deal, considering we are now doing the work of Sergeants, but at least we can buy a few more eggs and chips.

The washing of our grimy bodies is taken care of at the miner's pit-head at 'Abbeville'. File into a large washroom, white tiled shower cubicles in a row, opposite the showers on the facing wall a row of small metal hooks with men's names on little metal plates.

Long ropes are attached fastened by slip knots, the ropes snake up to the ceiling. I look up, there above our heads hanging from the other end of the ropes are the miners working clothes, dirty filthy garments stored well out of the way, an ingenious wardrobe.

Little time for leisure generally other than at local level, trips are arranged to visit E.N.S.A. shows at 'Lille' and 'Douai', together with some other fluctuations.

Relations with the men are good with one exception, Cooper has a nasty chip on his shoulder, seems to hate my guts for some reason, is insolent in front of the other men. Will have to watch him closely, don't want to put him on a 'charge', it's not the way to handle his type, a miserable fella, I expect his mother loves him though!

Working parties are frequent, heavy work on concrete pill-boxes, large strong-points, anti-tank traps, unloading steel rods, bags of cement from goods wagons, all of it unattractive labour. Each unit takes its turn at the work, usually in the 'Seclin Canal' area. Sometimes we are knee deep in water throwing out the wet clammy soil from a ten foot deep hole, soil that refuses to leave the spade; you throw yourself to death without achieving anything. Take a wheel-barrow full of wet cement up a winding track of narrow planks; the track winds up thirty, forty, fifty feet. Can't actually see the wheel on the plank, got to judge it, keep it central; if it runs off the plank you don't stand a cat in hells chance of holding the weight of the thing, men are working below, if you plaster them, you're a dead man! Can't rest once you start, can't set down the metal rests of the barrow as the planks are not wide enough, just got to keep going, a slow cautious trip up but an even slower one back. I pray that the bloody cement mixer will blow up, but it never does. The best thing about the work party is the hunk of bread, cheese, and a massive raw onion, served with lashings of tea. We eat and drink with relish.

Wedding plans are discussed by letter with Joan, date settled, wedding fixed for the early part of May on my first leave.

Take a trip to 'Vimy Ridge', a memorial to Canadian troops of the First World War. Travel by truck, passing through the town of 'Lens', this road is the best cobbled road that I have ever seen, a work of art, tiny square cobbles laid in neat fan shaped patter, flat as a billiard table. Leave 'Lens', out into the open country, immediately you see a high ridge crowned by a finger which stabs into the sky; the monument. I stand at the base of the beautiful white soaring column, look upwards slowly at the many names, don't try to count them, it tells you the number, thirty thousand; yes, thirty thousand men! See the trenches, still there in places, forty, fifty feet apart. The fields around are wildly pitted with deep holes, a crazy endless churned up wilderness, green now, green with the growth of some twenty years of peace. Can't laugh or even smile in this place, not where thirty thousand men have died. Instead you feel a deep sadness, sadness for their deaths, sadness that once again the young men are here today dressed in the same colour to do the job again. Surely thirty thousand deaths should have earned more than twenty years of peace; but no, they didn't; the god of war wants more. We leave the place to its temporary peace, silent and depressed.

Some replacements among our senior officers, a new Battalion C.O., a new H.Q.C.O., both regular service men, we now expect the final polish to our training to come fast.

It does. Within a few days the training intensifies. Representative N.C.O.'s are chosen from each platoon to attend a crash course on 'small arms' training. Normally a three week course, it is to be completed in one week. Chosen to represent the Mortars, I go along to the small school chosen as the training centre. Tough unsmiling instructors take us through our paces, fresh approaches to handling weapons we think we know quite well, but we are going to know them a bloody sight better before this lot is finished with us. Let's have another look at the rifle, bren-gun, grenade, bayonet, two inch mortar. Yes, let's have another look.

Let's start with the rifle. What's the name of that bit? And that bit? This bit? What does it do? O.k. Strip it, assemble it. Good. Do it again, and again, and again. Fine. But you had your bloody eyes open, could see what you were doing. Let's do it blindfold. See how good you are by touch. Jesus, what are we going to form, a blind Battalion? None of your lip my lad. DO IT!

Grenades get primed, un-primed, and primed. Learn how to throw them to hit the target first time.

Bren-guns: strip, assemble, strip, assemble. The barrel gets hot, bloody hot, will expand with the heat, needs changing, take it out thus, insert the spare barrel you should have with you. Haven't got a spare barrel handy – tough luck! The barrel is still too hot, got to cool it down, dip it in water, that's what you got to do. What, no water about? Only one thing to do, piss on it; don't want a piss? Hunt around, always someone pissing themselves under fire!

Let's try the bayonet next. Guarantee to make you good in twenty-four hours. Bloody good. Don't get over excited using this thing. Don't give them the whole length of it, two inches will do the trick. Just stick it in two inches, that's all you need. I can see myself marking off two inches from the point with a bit of chalk or something, trying not to stick it into a man more than two inches. Will probably get myself killed for being too pre-occupied; wish he hadn't mentioned the bloody two inches.

A ring of men face outwards, we stand 'at ease', rifles with bayonets fixed held in the hand ready. In the circle stands the instructor armed with a wooden broom handle type of pole. One end is padded with cloth; attached to the other end is a hoop of wire. We wait for a tap on the shoulder. He taps at random, could be anyone next. The tap will request and expect instant action ending with a thrust of the bayonet into the centre of the ring which will be somewhere in the region of his knees. A tap on my shoulder; instant turn straight from the 'at ease' position. Rifle up into both hands ready to thrust as I turn; eyes eagerly seeking the whereabouts of the ring. Thrust on sight, do it again and again, and again. Get it right, get it on target, get the reflexes to move faster, come on now, MOVE!

Now we will try the 'butt stroke'. The instructor reverses his pole, the padded fist is down by his hip, the wire ring points forward as would a bayonet. This time we thrust for his left shoulder. Another tap on my shoulder; a well co-ordinated fast turn; thrust straight at his shoulder. He has moved. Like greased-lightening his pole goes to the left of my rifle pushing it sideways. The bayonet is deflected passed his left shoulder, the padded butt is swinging round in a clipped arch; it is stopped in flight only by my jaw! He demonstrates again and again. That's it. "Now you try" he says, "but gently, your butt is not padded". I kiss his jaw with the butt until he is satisfied I've got it right. Now thrust to his right shoulder, another dirty butt stroke, lands on a different part of his face.

Remember too that instead of butt strokes, drop on one knee, get under the other blokes weapon, under his thrust, grab a hand full of soil, sand, stones or anything that comes to hand, throw it in the other blokes face, eyes and then stick him. Chest to chest? Ok then bring your knee up into his groin, do it quick before he does it to you, then stick him.

Soon the weight of the rifle is nothing. Reflexes work faster than thinking, we move smoothly as fast as the bat of an eyelid, and with confidence. Dirty business bayonet fighting; have no intention of getting that bloody close. Read a lot about the British love for cold steel; load of crap; I don't love it! Don't know anyone else that loves it either; so bloody scared of it that I practice and practice. Not until the instructors have given their approval do I relax a bit.

Two inch mortar, map reading, range finding, use of cover, camouflage, and physical training winds up the course. I return to the platoon a mental and physical wreck my brain seething with new methods of instruction.

Edgar and I are told that the men will have to stand to attention when they wish to speak to us on parade. The regulars do it so we have to do it as well. We have reached a compromise with the men that they only have to do this when officers are around. We believe we can do our jobs as efficiently without that. Ordered to start the new instruction the very next morning. Get the men out on parade nice and early, dressed in vest, trousers and boots, the nearest that we can get to P.T. gear, our first lesson is physical training; never had to do this before. Standing in front of me the men look at me with expectant eyes. They shiver in the fresh morning air; can hear the poor things teeth chattering. Better get them warmed up before they drop dead. The shock of having to do these exercises is bad enough! Got them running on the spot now. Just about fit to drop by the looks of them. Go through a few gentle exercises to lower their blood pressure. Release them for breakfast. A couple of them stagger in, must most of them have enjoyed it much to their surprise, and mine!

Breakfast over; we parade in the farmer's field at the back of his barn for small arms instruction. Like me when I first went on the course, they think they know it all. I wonder how they will take the new approach. In order to judge the deliverance of the instruction, Edgar and I will give pre-arranged signals. Thumbs up if Ok, thumbs down if it is lousy. The lousy signal will require a change of tactics. Thumbs up! Warming to my subject I give them the treatment, bayonet fighting they love, gives them a chance to frighten me to death once or twice. There is only one man who grumbles and it has to be Cooper as usual, got to deal with him very soon. I feel that the whole platoon is waiting for my reaction to his acid tongue. Only one way to deal with his kind, get the gloves out, let him get it off his chest, whatever it is.

A few days later things come to a head. I tell him that I will get the gloves from the stores, that he can have it out in the barn if he wishes, he agrees. To my horror the stores are packed up and ready for a move, I cannot have the gloves. I return to the billet and tell Cooper, an immediate torrent of abuse, he doesn't believe that I tried to get them. Later, sitting around the stove in the billet, a half dozen of us, Cooper sits opposite me. Other men, about twenty in all lounge about the billet. Cooper goes to town with his mouth, loudly sending a stream of obscenities at me, I ride it for quite a while but I am getting very angry, all the men are looking at me wondering what I am going to do.

Another stream of abuse is encouraged by my inaction, suddenly I see red, in two strides I reach him with my right fist swinging upwards from the hip with all my weight behind it, he is half out of his chair as my punch lands full in his mouth. Cooper and his chair are in a heap over on the other side of the room as I stand there waiting for his return onslaught. It's the first time that I have ever hit a man in the explosive heat of anger. It feels bloody marvellous! A wild exhilaration fills my whole being as I wait.

He is getting to his feet slowly; I note that there is blood on his lip with deep satisfaction. He is walking slowly over to me, not yet attempting to retaliate, he can hardly speak for the hate that has flooded his mind, he stands close to me and tells me that he is going to shoot me as soon as we get into action, it's the worst threat he can think of. Another voice speaks quietly from behind me; it is Edgar my brother, he is speaking to Cooper. "If the Corporal is shot under circumstances that do not clearly establish a German bullet I will shoot you without question in retaliation. It is clearly to your benefit to see that the Corporal is not shot at all". Cooper knows Edgar, and I know Edgar, and we know that he will carry out his threat if need be. An effective counter threat from Edgar; I am more than glad of his support at the time.

Having committed just about the worst crime in the military book, that of striking a man in my charge, there can only be one possible result, the loss of the single stripe, but hell, it was worth it. I decide not to report the matter - wagging tongues will do that for me, think I'll just wait and see what happens. To my amazement nothing happens! Cooper gives no further trouble, the men are even more friendly, everyone seems pleased that the matter has been settled, but I still watch Cooper very closely for although this kind of threat is not uncommon it is not to be taken lightly.

Spring is in the air, I can smell it as the air gets sweeter to the nostrils, softer with the promise of natures miracles just around the corner. See those tiny close packed buds; I await their bursting into green glory with impatience. It's been a long hard winter, the coldest for many years, but apart from and attack of flu which swept through the ranks to some degree everyone is fit and hard as nails.

Thoughts dwell on leave quite often, could do with a spell at home, wedding plans are tidied up and everyone is ready to go, all they need is me. Edgar has permission to take his leave with me; he is to be the best man at the 'Do'. I'm told that I should have a little talk with the medical officer and the padre being as I am getting married, I'll think about it.

A directive offers the older men in the Battalion the chance to go back to England, these men have served with the unit for many years, some since the last war! Many of them are in the H.Q. Company Band and would serve as stretcher bearers if things got sticky, perhaps some of their reflexes have slowed a bit. Some take the opportunity and go; others are more stubborn and stay. Leave the first love of their lives, how stupid can some people get? Leave the Battalion – they take the offer as an unexpected insult. Sergeant Williams is such a man, he bristles with indignation. A tough wiry little man, he looks as though he is in his fifties I guess, leave his friends just when trouble might break? His friends advise him to go, go while he has the strength to move, but he says his wife would nag him to death, she would kill him, he reckons he is safer with us, he stays.

Made the mistake of getting frivolous while in charge of the detail today; marching the men down the main village street, a gorgeous looking girl is walking along the pavement towards us, I'll give the lads a treat and at the same time salute such a beauty. All eyes are on her as she approaches, she will pass on our right, I call the men up to attention as we draw level, a snappy "Eyes right", as one the heads snap to the right, their eyes subject the poor thing to a barrage of admiration, wide grins split all faces. The girl has gone a deep crimson colour with embarrassment, her face turns away, she wants the ground to open up and swallow her; she has passed. With the order "Eyes front, march at ease" we are back to our normal comfortable rolling gait, the men appreciated the gesture.

Back in billets a messenger is waiting to see me: "Corporal?"

"Yes?"

"Message for you from the Company Commander, he is watching your antics from the window of Company Offices and says 'DO SUCH A THING AGAIN AND YOU'RE BUSTED'".

There's talk flying about regarding a stint on the Maginot Line. Not in the nice cosy underground system of defences but in the trenches in advance of them. Just to ease our minds on the matter we get stories from men in other units who have been up there, these tell of the lousy filthy conditions in the trenches, the nasty and dangerous patrols into no-man's land, and of a particular box barrage speciality of artillery used by Gerry when he wants prisoners. All sounds most unfriendly and rough, don't want any part of it, fortunately though it does not materialise.

Don't want to see another pilchard as long as I live. Sick to death of them. Every day each man gets a tin of pilchards in tomato sauce. The picture of the darn fish leaping over the waves on the label is enough to send my stomach churning without even opening the tin; I guess another cheap offer from somewhere has been made to the Catering Officer.

Just can't eat the things, not while there is a cafe down the road with chips! Consider throwing them away, the billet is getting stacked up with unopened tine, at this rate the whole country will soon be littered with them. Decide to ask the farmers' wife if she can make use of them. Yes, she can, only too delighted to relieve us of them; we hand over a stock large enough to feed the whole village.

Better think about the recommended visit to the Medical Officer I suppose. Won't bother to visit the Padre on this occasion though, can't quite see what advice he can give me about getting married that I don't already know. A fine man the Padre, a man's man, listened to many of his sermons with great interest. A very sincere man in everything he does, never hear him telling you to kill anyone, not like that bastard priest back in England at St Clement Church. Our priest is a gentle man, a man to respect, but I won't bother him on this matter.

Listen to the expected lecture from the Medical Officer on the correct tactics for sex warfare. Agree with his diplomatic and delicately worded suggestion that it would be wise not to saddle the girl with children at this time due to the possibility of me getting my bloody head blown off in the not too distant future, can help myself to rubber goods from the box in the waiting room, take as many as I like, I do, I take three packets just to make sure. I am going into business. Never owned such things in my life before. Men talk about the things as though not a day goes by but you get through a packet. The old soldiers especially, to hear them, each and every one uses more of these than they do cigarettes, load of empty talk of course, like most of us.

Retire to my sleeping space, take one out, study it. Never seen one in 'mint condition' before: seen one or two littered about our English landscape from time to time, ugly obscene things, an insult to the beauty of nature. My critical eye studies the flat round object lying in the palm of my hand, a cold calculating piece of rubber eager to get cracking probably. Difficult to associate it with the tender and beautiful lovemaking visions that fill my mind. Christ, at what stage would you climb into the bloody thing anyway? Good point, that surely will need working out with great delicacy, but time and love will I expect solve the problem. I tuck them safely away inside my Battle-Dress pocket ready for instant action when the time comes.

Half a dozen of us have been invited to supper by the farmer's wife downstairs. We look forward to a change in our diet with keen anticipation. The whole family is present, looks to be a grand affair. Mum staggers in with a huge dish in her hands, places it in the centre of the table; Dad sits at the head of the table in his lord and master position, oozing confidence in his wife's cooking abilities. Mum takes the lid off the dish, a cloud of hot steam rolls up in the warm atmosphere of the cosy room, you duck back from it, soon it clears. Eager eyes look into the monster dish to see what masterpiece it contains. Potatoes! Whipped to the consistency of whipped cream, snow white, tiny flecks of green in the mixture in abundance, a study in white and green.

Mum is back with another dish, a large flat one this time, it contains dozens of fish, fish that lie in well ordered rows, each a rich golden yellow colour, tiny breadcrumb s cling thickly to each fish, they look like gems from the East. Strange, they are the same size as the bloody pilchards. Can't be, can it? Yes says mum, they are. Well I'm blowed! A bottle in mums hand full of yellow liquid, olive oil, gentle delicate droplets go into the potatoes, a quick stir mixing it well in. She serves half a dozen fish per man and a mountain of potatoes. God, there can't possibly be better food that this anywhere in the world, our pilchards too!

What is this green stuff we ask, takes fifteen minutes to work out the answer: dandelion shoots! What! Those bloody weeds that grow at the side of the road? Yes! We look at her with fresh eyes henceforth, she is a goddess. We are overawed by her culinary skills; no wonder Dad sticks his chest out.

Home leave starts, on the first batch goes Private Cooper.

Spring is well and truly here, life is sweet, tactical exercises out in the open country are a pleasure. Acting as a rifle section we have been ordered to take up position in a small wood, later to be reinforced by a bren-gun carrier. Reaching the wood in full advance of the section to establish a position, I am aware of a beautiful scent in the air, the scent of flowers somewhere. Can catch glimpses of white through the young growth of leaves on the trees. Looks like snow but there is none about these days. Closer, the scent is like wine to the senses, smells just like I imagine paradise to be. Part the low hanging branches, stop dead in my tracks; I am in paradise, a carpet of staggering beauty. Breathlessly I stare in disbelief at the billions of Lily of the Valley spread out before me. A carpet of snow, vivid green of the spiky leaves stab the air, the tiny fragile white bells boastfully peal their message of joy to my heart without the slightest trouble. Every nook, every fold of the ground, filled as far as the eye can see, sheer heaven. But God, I must walk into them, crush them with these bloody number nine boots, got to find a suitable position for the lads. I place my boots on them with horror, not daring to look down at the slaughter I inflict.

The men too are spellbound by this magic place, we choose our position; lay ourselves down full length on the most dreamlike couch we will ever have. Our ugly guns protrude through the trees, pointing outwards, our very presence is sacrilege.

The throb of a heavy engine, the carrier; it approaches rapidly across the open meadow. We make our presence known; it turns roughly in our direction, a road of power, noisy squealing caterpillar tracks, like a bat out of hell it crashes into and over bushes creating a hell of destruction in the carpet of snow. Deep ugly ruts filled with the tiny crushed and mangled bells, thousands of bells together with clods of soil fill the air. These things mark its passing as the monster manoeuvres into position. The dog of war has arrived. Mere flowers mean nothing, indeed human lives don't mean much, it has priority over these plentiful things. Has not man decreed it to be so?

My friends tell me that I should take a trip to Lille, have a look at the houses of pleasure that abounds in a quarter known as A.B.C. Street, widen your outlook I am told, but somehow I feel that my outlook in that field is plenty wide enough. I don't bother to take the trip.

Thumeries, 1940

Arrived at the small industrial town of Thumeries which is located between Lille and Douai. Our billet this time is opposite a factory full of female labour. They erupt out of the gates in a flood as the demented siren shatters the peace of the town. A laughing, cheeky, chattering bunch, they match our whistles and calls across the street with ease.

Less than two weeks to go for leave and wedding bells but me and my best man to be, Edgar, feel a bit apprehensive about our chances. A certain something in the air, something electric, not a wise time to choose to get married, not spring, not the time for loving, not for a soldier at war. It's the time when armies flex their muscles, wake from their long winter sleep, begin to oil their guns. Read any history book and you will see that this is so. No, I have definitely not timed it right!

There it is. All leave cancelled until further notice. Bang goes the wedding. Joan has as near as hell been left standing at the altar, a rough love-life the poor girl is having, very rough.

Someone has found a loose N.C.O. stripe lying about somewhere; they have given it to me, fools! They have given it to the wrong man; Edgar is a better soldier than I can ever be. Got to sew the thing on now, one thing I love is sewing, Jesus!

Placed on two hour stand by notice; things have exploded at the Frontiers, Belgium and Holland have been attacked.

A noisy dawn, heavy guns are greeting the day, they sound quite close from all directions around us. Run out into the street, people cover the pavements in groups, others scattered in the road, all heads are turned up towards the sky. Tiny black specs twist and turn in a crazy diving tangle; fighter aircraft. Machine guns chatter up there, black balls stab the pale blue of the sky, black balls fringed with white, as shells explode they turn all white to hang in large cotton-wool lumps, soon to be gathered and stretched into long drifting wisps by the winds above. A ball of fire hangs for a few seconds then begins a tight spiralling fall to earth, it spins like a boy's top. There, another, this one falls more slowly, in wider circles, with the gentleness and grace of a falling Autumn leaf. In two seconds we behold the death of two men. Some cheers from the crowds as the two flaming coffins come down to meet the earth; they have convinced themselves that the two coffins are German. Impossible to tell, they are too high to identify, the people do but indulge in wishful thinking and forget they cheer the terror and death throes of two men.

Orders to hit the road in two hours; we go in to Belgium. Ammunition is issued, weapons are made ready with a fussiness as never before, full fighting order, the time for games is over, let's find out what we are made of! A short march, embus on to lorries by Company, we peel off from the lines of lorries and hit the road spaced out for safety from aircraft. Glad in a way that things are moving, fed up with the continual training. If we've got to have a war let's get it over with. The date is the 14th of May.

Over the frontier now; the people wave and scream at us from the doorways in greeting. The Belgian people, like the people of Oxford, once again treat us like heroes, we have done nothing yet, wish they would wait a bit, let's see what happens first.

Note immediately the lack of any defensive positions. No trenches, no tank traps or strong points of any description. So much for neutrality, now the things are needed! Many halts along the route, great caution is shown before we enter large villages and towns. Anti-aircraft guns here and there along the wayside, some go into action at high flying aircraft.

Here and there a house that has been hit by a bomb, smoke spirals rising into the blue sky.

Each halt the signal for a mad rush of civilians to the rear of each lorry, gifts are thrust into our hands, cigarettes, glasses of wine, sweets, chocolate, cake, other tit-bits and flowers. Flowers, yes by Christ, flowers! I pass these down to the front of the lorry quickly; the lorry is filling up fast with the men of Oxford decorated with a bunch of flowers each. Don't know what to do with them, can't insult these people by refusing them so they get rammed into the front of the Battle-Dress blouse. I finish up with a large bunch of lilac as big as half a tree. The darn blooms are jammed under my chin, up past my ears, to spread out on each side of my face in large sprays. My face peeps out at the passing world a little blank. I feel a bloody sissy. The lads insist on telling me I look bleeding beautiful. I hate their guts!

Stop after stop the same story. Gifts, more gifts, kisses, shouted messages of good luck.

A woman is shouting at me in English: "Where did you get that lilac from?"

Sounds a silly question to me, but I tell her "I don't know, a hand just thrust them into mine".

"Throw them away quickly; lilac is an omen of bad luck in this country".

I gaze at her a bit confused, she pleads with me to throw them away, I promise to do just that, she smiles, pleased. Fine thing, here I am dashing in like the U.S. Cavalry to their aid, been in the country less than an hour and some bugger wants the break my neck already, strange feeling. An unknown hand among a sea of hands has offered poison, I wonder how many others.

Our ride is peaceful, not bothered by hostile aircraft, but panic is in the air, you can smell it.

Daylight is fading as we enter a town. Having passed through Orchies, Ath, Enghein, and Hal we have arrived at Alsemberg; here we debus.

Alsemburg, Belgium, 1940

Dumped in the centre of the place, not too large what bit of it we can see. Standing at the side of the road waiting billet allocation, passing Belgian troops prove to be of interest, they fill the road, Infantry mounted on push-bikes. Rifles slung over their back, they grip the handlebars of their steeds with their hands rigidly, moving quite slowly calls for all their concentration to avoid bumping into each other. In loose massed formation, their eyes stare directly ahead, tired men intent only on placing distance between them and that which they wish to leave behind. Pretty little silk tassels hang from the front of each mans forage cap, dancing across the caps from side to side as the heads tilt with the physical effort of pedalling. A lot of men have passed, they travel the opposite way to that which we face, a point worth bearing in mind.

The road is clear, our billet is across the road, it looks like the front of a small cinema. Enter, it's a place to hold a dance, or meeting, or like us, to wait for a punch up. Large empty floor, can undo our equipment but not take it off, must standby for anything that may arise, meanwhile we can rest, get some sleep. No argument with that order, we try hard. We do get some sleep but it is fitful. The mind is too tense waiting for something to happen. A noisy morning, every bren-gun in town lets rip at some enemy bombers flying over the roof tops. Telephone and electronic cables of the town suffered severely I understand from our own guns!

A lazy day of waiting; dusk rushes at us all too soon. A heavy rumbling outside on the road, we poke our noses out. Yes, tanks, big ones! Too dark to identify them as they pass, sparks fly from the road surface as the tracks meet the cobbles, six in all, a single tiny blue tail-light marks the passing of each monster. They too travel in a different direction than us, another point well worth bearing in mind. Looks as though everyone is leaving us to it!

A red glow in the night sky, blood red, it lies in the direction from whence came the tanks. Heavy gun fire is growing but is still distant, it rumbles ominously from the depths of the red sky.

"O.K. on your feet. Fall in outside."

Not far off midnight, black as hell outside except for that red glow which casts a pink light on whatever faces it. Oxford voices calling to each other in the dark as platoons fall into place reporting their readiness to march. Nobody mentions the distant guns; you would think they heard them every day of their lives. Move off, keep close together, will soon be moving off the road out into open country, that will be fun!

Off the road now, turn directly into the red sky, but the only comments are curses as the feet stumble over unseen tufts of grass, otherwise silence, each mans thoughts are his own at this time. Been stumbling through the darkness for some time now, the red glow never seems to get any closer, the darkness doesn't seem so intense, dawn can't be too far away.

Jackson, one of the gun crew, suddenly asks me if it will be alright when we get up there; surprised at his question I realise that he is searching for a straw of comfort to grasp. I tell him without hesitation that it will be a piece of cake, no need to worry. To my surprise he appears to relax, that was what he wanted to hear. I have lied through my teeth to the lad, I know nothing more about it than he does, he knows that but still he is comforted.

Dawn is beginning to peep out shyly as we half scared warriors. Glad to see its promise, about bloody time, will be able to see where we tread at last. The red glowing sky is fading to pink, it still eludes us; as the light gets stronger it grows weaker. Soon, the shadowy shapes of trees begin to form, an isolated house or bungalow looms, shutters at the windows, dwellings with an abandoned air about them. The guns are beginning to fade away as though the approaching new day forbids such things.

Just about daylight, guns are silent, the whole world is silent, dead. A large open plain to our front, across the other side a forest can be seen, we are heading for its' cover. We tread hallowed ground, ground soaked with British blood before. They tell us this place is called Waterloo - fine spot to choose for our first fight I must say, got an optimistic general around here if he expects us to repeat that performance!

Almost three-quarters of the way over the open plain, not far to go to the shelter of the trees. A beautiful morning; clear; the air is soft with the magic of the month of May. The sun is just beginning to smile upon us, all is peaceful as we swing easily over the short springy grass. A casual sweep of the sky with the eyes for enemy aircraft; no, nothing in sight. A few more people steps; a sudden shock wave of sound - the deafening roar of aircraft engines and machine guns from above. Without thought we are flat on our faces. Get down first; locate the disturbance afterwards; our training is coming to the fore.

Almost above our heads, seemingly coming from nowhere, eight aircraft fly in a twisting diving tangle. No more than seven hundred feet high, not interested in us in the least, they are busy with their own little war. Seven carry the white cross of Germany, the eighth is British, a Westland Lysander. No fighter aircraft this, obviously been jumped by the seven Messerschmitts; they can only consider him easy meat; they are giving our lad a rough time. A crazy flying fool as he struggles to escape, he keeps low, twisting and turning in less than five hundred feet of air space. They can't get below him, they can only climb upwards a short way, peel desperately into a dive with guns blazing in a follow the leader circle downwards; a sharp pull out of the dive to climb upwards and repeat the performance again.

Daylight can be seen through our plane in a dozen places, but still he flies. He flies mostly on his side, first right, then left in tight impossible variations. I swear his wing tips cuts furrows into the soil; he has the cunning of a trapped fox. We have stopped breathing long ago, our hearts are in our mouths for him; his fight for survival is superb, his handling of his craft masterly, he teaches those Germans how to fly!

A sudden sharp and impossible turn, virtually on his wing tip as he hugs the ground, he has gone from view behind a row of poplar trees that line the road. Above the tree tops the tip of his flat wing can be seen as he travels at high speed along the gully of trees flying on his side. There, at the end of the trees, he climbs upwards steeply into the sky and is away. We are on our feet, rifles thrust upwards high above our heads as we scream in triumph for him; he is away, like a bat out of hell!

The Messerschmitts are still above us, they circle around stunned by the escape of their easy victim. We hit the deck again watching them. Suddenly, they dive in runs over us, spraying their bullets at random over the area where we lay, probably emptying their guns I guess. After a few runs they turn and leave, a couple of men have slight wounds, but nothing to worry about.

Eyes are fixed on the cover of the trees now, we need to get there quick, no more hanging about in the open; let's move!

Waterloo, 1940

A fine big forest this, bags of cover. Wide avenues of majestic trees tower upwards, topped by wide spreading branches that touch their neighbours. A subdued light in here, each tree the width of a good road from its neighbour, could drive four trucks in line abreast between them. I think I have read about this place! Close my eyes, can easily see Wellingtons' brightly uniformed troopers skirmish with the French way back! A peaceful march under the green umbrella, the carpet of leaf mould deadens our boots, we move almost with the silence of gliding ghosts.

The edge of the forest is marked by a line of bushes; part these and you see a flat expanse of grassland about four hundred yards in width, it drops off sheet into a valley. A village nestles on the far edge of the valley maybe three-quarters of a mile away. Here we halt and wait for orders. The order comes fast and is to the point.

"Dig in, we hold this position to the last man. There will be no retreat!"

It doesn't matter how good your hearing is, even if you can hear a pin drop a mile away, when an order like that is tossed at you for the first time, despite yourself, you will reply, "Eh?". The order will get repeated, politely if you are lucky, and you will be told where to start digging. I feel sad about it; not worried or even frightened, just sad. All sounds a bit drastic, sort of thing you read about or see at the pictures. I then start looking at the other blokes, wondering who in fact the last one will be? If it's me I'm going to run like hell!

The sadness gradually turns to anger, anger at the thought that this will be my first fight and probably my last, just a tiny bit too brief really. My angry gaze wanders over to the other side of the valley beyond the village, Jerry is over there they reckon, his bloody fault!

Spent the last six months making ourselves specialists on a certain weapon, what do we do? Finish up in a trench as riflemen! Can't use the Mortar in these trees, the tree tops are too thick. The army manual on mortar training specifically states that guns should be behind the troops they support, on occasions they can fall in line, but never, never in front of your own troops. So what happens!

"Take one gun; site it in the middle of the meadow three hundred yards in front of our line of troops".

Typical! Might have bloody guessed!

Edgar, Myself, and three men make up the crew. Nothing to

worry about we are told. We will dig our gun-pit one hundred yards back from the lip of the valley. In front of us is a Vickers machine gun crew, two men, they perch on the lip of the valley and their fire will cover the floor of the valley when Jerry starts to cross it; our task is to lay a carpet of bombs over the floor of the valley as soon as the Vickers gun fires.

Dead easy, the only trouble will be if Jerry actually comes over the edge of the valley, we are going to get a bullet in the teeth from them and a bullet up the arse form some trigger happy man of Oxford from behind. Jesus! Choose our spot and start digging, soil harder than the softness of the woodland loam, we soon begin to sweat; a couple of feet down; I must get forward and view the target area to establish the range.

Easy target - get a fixed range, a narrow valley floor, range three hundred yards. The shots will fill the floor area, just a bit of traverse from side to side will do it; all we want is the signal shots from the machine gun, we open fire when they do, a piece of cake!

A deep throbbing sound has filled my brain as I work on the target; aircraft! The sound comes from behind us, a hell of a lot of them! Can't see them though, the trees are too tall but the noise is getting deafening, must be ours coming from behind. The air vibrates with the massed engines; they break cover over the tops of the trees. Germans - bloody great bombers, they fill the sky! The lads have disappeared, they are down the hole, I gallop back to join them. As I do a stupefying shriek of hundreds of bombs being released is heard, the nerves tear apart, the heart freezes as I dive into the hole. They're coming directly at us, the exposed back crawls as the body grovels itself deep into the earth. This is it, we have had it!

A shattering explosion that leaves the mind dulled, we heard it, feel Ok. So, they missed us, can't believe it, the explosion came from across the valley, the village isn't there any more - instead a great mass of flame and smoke marks the spot where it was. It has completely disappeared. Dazed with shock we can only stand and stare at the sight, but not for too long!

We finish digging our gun pit in record time! It is a work of art, loose soil heaped round the edge; we can stand up in safety inside it. Gun, men, and ammunition neatly installed, eyes search the far side of the valley for movement; the mind keeps checking that everything is in fact ready, sights set correctly, bomb safety caps removed, bombs laid down correctly so that we can pick them up at speed. Yes, all is ready if they come; nothing else to do now but wait and think.

If things get rough around here some of us are going to get hurt, but I'll bet that I am the only bloke in the platoon that has a 'war wound' already, got it in the last war too! As a child I recall being persistently puzzled by a scar which I viewed every time I went for a pee. Got quite worried about it, had grown out of the 'winkle' stage and had qualified for the 'dicky' stage I remember. Edgar and I had talked the problem over, compared our possessions. No, he had no scar on his 'dicky'. Get quite worried about it, shop around in the school lavatories looking at other lads possessions. No, they had no scar! Had to turn to my mother in the end, "Hey Mum, what's this scar on my 'dicky'?"

A truthful woman my mother, she was forced to confess her shame. A German Zeppelin was bombing London; mum was alone with two babies and had to go to the air shelter immediately, but how? She couldn't carry two babies at once. I was sleeping peacefully but she had a hell of a job getting me off to sleep in the first place, pity to wake me, she decided to let me sleep in peace and off she went taking Edgar, the brand new baby, with her. On her return I was screaming my head off, telling me that the nasty Zeppelin won't get me did nothing to stop my mouth. She decided that I had probably messed my nappy again and proceeded to check only to reveal the awful truth! My cries had nothing to do with the nasty Zeppelin, but they had a lot to do with the safety pin that had pierced my tiny little penis! I forgave my mother many years ago for leaving me to get blown to pieces by a bomb, but could never find it in my heart to forgive her for being so careless with that safety pin!

Getting quite dark now, all is silent in the immediate vicinity, so sign of our defence line behind us, as silent as the grave back there. Gunfire over the other side of the valley, sounds like machine guns, flares are beginning to go up, they soar up into the sky falling in a gentle arch down in our direction, they are German flares, they fall some distance from the further edge of the valley, at least they will more or less indicate the progress and whereabouts of Jerry. The deathly silence on our side of the valley is un-canny, a seed takes shape in the mind that we are on our own, but that's silly, plenty of other men around us in the darkness, getting jumpy, that's all.

About forty eight hours since I have had a real good sleep, strange, I don't feel tired at present, just bloody hungry, had nothing to eat since the tit-bits on the way up into this country. A bright moon has burst upon us lighting our world into clear cut patterns of black and silver. The trees behind us cast deep shadows; we speak in whispers, normal pitched voiced sound like trumpet blares in this strange unreal place. Can just make out the machine gun post ahead, all is quiet there, hope they haven't gone to sleep.

Firing getting heavier across the valley, flares seem a bit closer, beginning to get a bit worried about the atmosphere somehow. All of us are on edge, this waiting is getting us down, things are beginning to feel just too unnatural somehow, too quiet to our rear, getting too noisy to our front, still no sign of the machine gunners, we feel there is something wrong.

Fed up! Look for something to do, decide to have a smoke, get down on to the floor of the pit and light up with hands shielding the flame. A deep drag, the smoke rises up into the air, in horror we watch as the smoke rises upwards with the clarity of smoke signals into the clear moonlit night. Hell, a Jerry could see that a mile away. Frantically we stamp it out, the strong smell of the smoke drifts up and fills our nostrils, even this would be a dead give-away to any lurking Jerry. Got to do something about it, got to find out how things are up front, too quiet up there, something is very wrong, I can feel it in my bones.

Brief the lads - I will go forward on a certain line and return on the same line, if anything approaches on another route they shoot and ask questions afterwards. Out of the pit, a silent crouching run forward towards the machine gun post, got to be bloody careful that I don't frighten them, could easily get myself shot here! Creep up to the entrance, a soft call to identify myself, silence greets me, another call, a bit closer, closer, another call, still no reply! A low entrance, not galloping into there until I check further, something is definitely wrong. Fix my bayonet, ease the safety catch of the rifle forward ready for a shot if necessary, stick the bayoneted rifle into the black cavern probing the interior, a sweep from side to side, I feel nothing but what I think are walls; nothing for it I shall have to go in and check fully. Take off the bayonet, it will impede the speed of my entrance. A wild forward fling of the body inwards, a roll, up on one knee, rifle up, but the place is empty of men!

A soft moonlight within, a cosy well prepared position roofed with branches, part sandbag walls, a ledge cut from the earth bank on which stands the Vickers machine gun, its muzzle peeping through a long loophole which covers the valley floor. The moonlight enters the loophole to fall directly on the gun, it looks new. Beautiful and deadly as its blue black gleams, brass cartridges sparkle like jewels in the light as they cascade downwards in the belt to the ammunition box standing at its side, it looks eager to spring into action but the men who can make it sing have gone. Not retired, just run away, the bastards have run; well might we wait for their warning shots! Nothing stands between us and Jerry now - I turn cold at the possibilities of what might have happened if we had not checked! These bastards have insulted a well know Northern Regiment, panic has seized them. How long have they been gone? Is the valley full of Germans at this very moment? Christ, better check! A scrutiny through the loophole, flares are falling on the furthest slopes of the valley, they help my vision, no, no sign of men. All is clear on the floor as far as I can see, better report back to the lads.

Edgar and the lads are happy to see me, beginning to think that I had got lost. The language directed at the two missing machine gunners should strike both of them dead with any luck. We have now got to decide what to do. Our fears have been confirmed. Something is wrong; everything is too dead for comfort. Decide to send a man back to the forest to check how things are, tell him to take a fixed route and return the same way, if he deviates, we shoot, we don't trust our rear now. We don't even trust God at this moment.

The rest of us face outwards to cover all directions, if bombers can come from behind us we don't see why German infantry can't. The trees look menacing, shadows seem to move, we are in a highly nervous state and bloody certain that we are on our own now. The man has been gone an hour now and there's no sign of his return, got himself lost we suspect. Edgar volunteers to go and see what he can find out; he crawls out of the pit and is away to our rear.

Three of us left here now, I cover the front while the others cover the rear and sides, eyes strain out of their sockets watching the valley, flares getting too close for comfort now, I expect to see figures rising above the edge of the valley at any moment. Christ, why doesn't someone come from the rear? What the hell are they playing at?

The two lads are fine, outwardly quite calm, no sign of panic, good lads. Time drags, hope Edgar gets back soon with some news, movement to our rear! A large black shape is creeping along the edge of the wood - can't identify it, could be anything! We line up across the back of the pit, line our rifles up on the mysterious shape, fingers on the triggers. We ignore the valley for the immediate visible danger. Closer now it's turning roughly towards us, two hundred yards away. Yes, it looks like a truck, moving so slowly, closer, we can just hear the engine, a mere whisper, a voice calling my name in a subdued shout - Edgars voice! A flood of relief sweeps though my body.

The front wheels of the truck are almost in the gun pit as it comes to a halt. Two figures jump down, frantic whispers, "For Christ sake load up quick, get out fast, tell you later". Dismantle the gun in record time; sling it silently on to the truck, ammunition, men climb on board as we watch the edge of the valley. Instantly the truck creeps round in a tight turn back towards the trees away from the valley, we leave only the hole in the ground behind to mark our presence.

Edgar relates his activities as we travel. On reaching the forest he had found it deserted. The unit had pulled out! Unperturbed he had set about the task of finding them again. Along the forward edge of the trees he had found a rifle section of D Company, but they too had known nothing. An officer and half a dozen men, they had been waiting patiently for the attack or someone to come along with fresh orders. Whichever happened to come first they will deal with it. They, like us, had sat tight while Edgar had wandered about the country looking for our lost Battalion. Creeping along deserted moonlit roads for several miles he had spotted three trucks approaching him at dead slow speed. From his cover he had identified them as 15cwt Bedfords. Stepping out as they drew level he was greeted with: "Bloody fool, jumping out like that". Our Company Commander had his revolver lined up on Edgar's stomach.

"What are you doing here?"

"Looking for a truck to get the Mortar crew out" replied Edgar.

"No time to go back for them, they are considered lost, get up on the rear truck at once".

A most disrespectful Edgar to his Commanding Officer: "Leave them be buggered", climbing on the last truck he had plans. The front truck moved off silently followed by a second, then a third, coming to a crossroads the leading truck turned right, away from the front line area, the second truck followed, as they approached the point of turn Edgar had told the driver to turn left back towards us, the driver had obeyed Edgar without question even though he had already told Edgar that the supporting flanks of the line had collapsed under German pressure. Our Unit was in danger of being cut off, hence the mad retirement. A race to beat Jerry to the next line of defence is the order of the day.

With only a vague idea of where we might be these two men had cruised about until they had found us. We proceed to pick up the rifle section, the old Bedford looks like an overcrowded bus. Only Edgar has any idea which direction the Unit might lay, but first he has got to find, and recognise, the crossroads. Up one road, down another, the engine a faint whisper, the tyres on the gravel is the loudest noise of all. A long straight road, the undergrowth comes up close to the road; our eyes stare at it as we glide slowly past. We wait for the blast of gunfire from every bush that we pass, could even be from our own men in this unreal world; our fingers nervously play with our rifle trigger in anticipation.

Have travelled about a mile along this road, don't like it! Convinced we are going the wrong way, deeper into territory abandoned to Jerry! The back of the neck crawls, your heart tells you it is so. Your brain is screaming "Turn back"! With one accord almost everyone whispers to the driver to turn around quickly, we all have the same feeling. Silently, expertly, he does so. We glide back the way we have come from. Can't keep my bloody eyes open, to hell with it, despite myself I fall asleep.

Somebody is pushing me, a voice is telling me to get down. A hand on my arm, a brief hazy glimpse of trucks parked under some tree, a babble of subdued Oxford voices: my legs are moving, following my guiding hand, a few steps, the voice tells me to sleep; I drop where I stand, instantly asleep!

Violent shaking! "Get up" a voice of urgency, I tell the voice to bugger off. It is insistent "Got to move, Jerry is on the other side of the forest". At the mention of Jerry my mind climbs from the drugged depths, my eyes open to greet another dawn with a sour look of disapproval. My arm is through my rifle sling where it should be; don't remember putting it there, instinct I suppose. Get to my feet, men are falling in for the march, most of the Mortar platoon is there, see the man I had sent off last night but who did not come back. Will find out about him later; four other men are missing, got mixed up with some other unit I understand, they might turn up later.

My mind is clearing a bit, can take stock of things. But for Edgar and the unknown driver there wouldn't be a Mortar platoon left this morning; events are beginning to weed out the men from the boys already. Leave the shelter of the forest. Out into open country, march in open order, extended single files, eyes continually searching the sky, we know now how suddenly they can strike. A steady pace that will eat up the miles at the rate of about five an hour. We have still got to reach the next line of defence.

Feel a lot better now that the fears of the night are past. Begin to take an interest in my surroundings. A fine warm sunny morning, aircraft pass to and fro, German but at present they ignore us, intent on other business. On to a road, a wide road, usually very busy I would guess but now it is silent and empty. The only sound is our boots, marching as one, one line of men each side of the road, close to hand, wide ditches; they are our friends, nothing bad to say about them at all even if they are full of mud. If a hostile aircraft takes an interest in us we will embrace those ditches with a speed and tenderness unbelievable in Civvy Street.

Village after village, silent, empty of people. Most dwellings fastened tight with shutters at the windows. Here and there signs of looting, doors, shutters and windows smashed, goods scattered about, some spill out of the doorways out into the road. Domestic animals wander the streets unattended, cats and dogs with a wild look in their eyes as they search for food, but mostly we hear the frantic howl of dogs fastened by their owners, they howl as they slowly starve at their bonds. Cattle gaze mournfully at us as we pass, their udders swollen to gigantic proportions, milking time has long since passed, their soft eyes plead with us to stop a while to relieve them of their precious yield, but we dare not.

Depressing signs of panic by the military, weapons and equipment litters each side of the road, I can but wonder what kind of man can throw away a tiny revolver; it lies with all the other debris of the fear of men.

The day advances, the miles mount up beneath our boots, a couple of enemy aircraft empty their guns at us but we have no casualties, men are getting footsore, their rifles toss from shoulder to shoulder seeking relief, nobody talks much, nothing much to say, no breath to spare, shoot some dogs, their troubles are ended.

A commotion ahead on the road. Some sort of factory, looks pretty large, it's a brewery. A mountain of wooden beer crates piled high at the side of the road, half a dozen British lads are busy emptying them, they work with the dedication of salesmen giving away free samples of a produce the strongly believe in, entirely absorbed in their task of giving each passing man two bottles, they have no intention of leaving this vital lubrication for Jerry.

Some of the men stand comfortably leaning on the crates, reaching into them lazily with one hand, holding out two bottles to me as the pass by at arm's length away, they work with the bored efficiency of men on a conveyor belt. They are obviously men who cut their teeth on bottles, others have a harder task, their customers pass by on the other side of the road, they have distance to travel. They gallop backwards and forwards wearing themselves to shadows in their determined efforts not to miss a man; they run into trouble now and then when they collide in the middle of the road, they lose momentum, lose the smooth rhythm. The passing file of men slow up, almost mark time briefly, fitting themselves to the rhythm of the delivery boys, shouts of abuse at them for being slow, shouts of "Hurry up! You're buggering up the column!" Uncomplaining the delivery boys increase their efforts to a mad frenzy. They are angels in khaki! Who can panic with men like them around? You would never guess that Jerry is just one jump behind to look at them.

Pass over some rail tracks, a nearby sign points the way to Mons, the name strikes a chord in the mind. Dad was wounded near Mons in 1914. He lay on a rail track unattended for three days, almost bled to death. My mind asks "Is this the very track?" Strange, we travel quite close to the route of his retreat, now we are retreating too, our family seems to be cursed with military retreats.

Shortly afterwards a halt at the side of the road for ten minutes. Everyone can sit down except the N.C.O.'s. Jesus, we have got to stand! Propping our rifles under our guts we flop over them for some relief. Darkness falls fast. Leaving the road we head for cover and position for the night. There is a canal in the area somewhere, the Charleroi Canal they call it. Among small grass-covered hills, they rise up slightly in a range of large bumps like a miniature range of mountains, lots of hollows between the slopes for use as cover.

We of the Mortars are not required to do anything at present, the rifle companies will form the protective screen, we can get our heads down. A bit of ground mist lies in the hollows, a bit fresh, stretch out, head up the slope, can't lie on my back, pack is in the way, arm through the rifle sling, immediate sleep.

Shouting! Brain registers the word 'Gas'. Helmet off with one hand while the other rips open the respirator case flap, fit mask, replace helmet. Daylight is just breaking, mist thicker, it swirls upwards over the top of the low hills, a bit chilly. Is that gas? looks like plain common mist to me, certain it is. Somebody says there is tear gas about, claim they can feel the stuff stinging their hands and faces. Got to be a load of crap, I think it's just pure fresh air, but I can't chance testing it! "Gas clear". I take the mask off with relief, had the thing on for about twenty minutes. Plenty of activity, chaps galloping about, I sit still, rest while I can, clothes quite wet.

Ok, "Fall in", retrace our steps to the road, resume the march. Dead cattle scattered about in the fields, almost all of them lie on their backs, strangely bloated, their legs point directly up into the sky like sticks. A strange smell about this morning, an unpleasant smell, different to other days, the air is suddenly not clean any more, tainted with dead things, some seen, some not. More dogs shot on our route, desperate now they will eat anything, even humans, may well be some lying about here. The smell in the air is DEATH.

The front window of a small shop has been smashed by looters, its goods scattered over the road, cigarettes and sweets among them, grab a handful of cigarettes as I pass, yes, we too will have to help ourselves now, we've got to, nobody has the time to give us rations. Search nearby houses when we halt, if they are locked we smash our way in. Search for food, most houses have cellars, some contain large earthenware jars filled with eggs, eggs hard boiled and pickled in white vinegar, we fill our pockets. Sometimes we find a hard bread-like biscuit, a bottle of champagne, or a fat cigar.

Some men feeling the pace a bit as they hobble along with blisters, their mates carry their rifles to ease their load; some of the tough nuts carry three rifles.

A two-pounder anti-tank gun under cover at the side of the road, its muzzle and its crew face the other way to that which we travel. A stack of ammunition ready to hand, a lonely job these men have, they stay behind as we pass, they cover our rear, only Jerry will pass this way after us, we shout our greetings to them as we pass.

Another silent and deserted village, rows of terraced houses. A door burst open in one of them as we pass, almost at my elbow! A young girl of about sixteen stands on the pavement for a few seconds, a wild look in her eyes as she runs at me a plucks at my arm, a rush of words in English: "Help me! My mother is in labour!" She is staring up into my face as she walks several paces by my side but my mind has not registered what she has just said quickly enough for her, she dances back to the next man frantically repeating her appeal. What the hell did she say? Christ, a baby, what a time to pick! Looking round for her, she is well back down the line, still pleading with the columns of marching men who dare not stop, but God, we pray that someone can do something somehow.

The column moves on without a pause which it must, on out of the village with its two lonely inhabitants. A heavy machine gun with its two men dug into the side of the road, they too face the other way, they too we leave to their lonely task. Getting used to the abandoned litter that lines each side of the road, the sign of other men's panic. What other men do is their business, it is not our way though.

The men are moaning like hell, sick of this weary marching backwards. They have endless questions: "Why do we run? When the hell do we fight?".

Daylight is fading, need to take up defensive positions for the night, off the road, out into open country for a short way, rolling hilly country. I am told to dig into a hillside, target a bridge, drop bombs on it at a given signal. Edgar's gun crew have the same target, but they will fire from a different site, in an orchard somewhere on our flank. By the light of a bright moon we dig a shallow pit below the crest of the hill. A flat topped hill, a meadow stretching away into the moonlit distance, a steep slope falls away to our left for about one hundred yards, a track runs around the base of the slope following a wide stream. Men, gun, and ammunition installed, we set up a night aid for fixed line firing in front of the gun by sticking in the ground a small lamp attached to a short spiked rod, line the rod on to the target, pull a length of cord attached to the lamp from your position in the gun pit and the light will come on, line your sights up on to the light if the first shot has moved the gun, you are back on target, a second pull of the cord will shut the light off. All set, we settle and wait for the possible signal.

Moon high, a dead world immediately around us. To our front some distance away flares begin to light up the sky, like shooting stars they burst on the scene to fall slowly back to earth, some small arms fire here and there but it's not close. Eyes continually search for movement across the meadow. There, to the right, something is moving, several of them! They are drifting slowly towards us, large objects, they come closer. Hell, they are bloody cows! They have seen something over this way that interests them and straight as an arrow they drift along in a long line towards us. And we are supposed to be well concealed! I retreat to the gun pit hoping that they will pass us by, but they don't. They stand instead in a half circle around the marker lamp. They glance down at us in our pit, we are standing motionless, hoping that they can't see us or that they will ignore us and go away, but they won't. I am sweating blood; I imagine that every German within miles can see these cows staring at us.

Ok, so there is bound to be a bold one among them, a nosey one, a show off. She has moved forward a bit, stretching her neck towards the lamp, sniffs at this strange thing, decides that she likes the small of it and decides to give it a lick. Blast, she will push it out of line with the target. She licks it twice, decides to move round a bit, she now faces the glass face of the lamp, her nose goes forward for another sniff, as it reaches the lamp I switch on the light, flick it on and off, that should frighten her, does it hell. She likes the colour, thinks it's a different flavour I suppose! Must not frighten them too much, must avoid stampeding them at all costs, make their antics look as natural as possible to any eyes that might be watching.

They're fed up with the lamp, the pit looks interesting, so they come down and have a look at it and a closer look at us. We are surrounded by them, they stand and gaze at us, some of them stretch their necks to take a delicate sniff, they ignore our frantic whispers of "Shoo, shoo" and waving arms. If we can get one to lead off, the others will follow, dig them with our rifle butts, they shy away but some come straight back. In desperation we prick one or two with the bayonet, one of them finally gets fed up with the unfriendly treatment and walks away, presently the others follow in a long string. We can get on with the war now!

We resume our observation to our front, I watch the cows retrace their steps back to the other side of the field and disappear as they presumably go down a slope, they have gone out of our lives forever; I hope! Flares still soar upwards lighting up the night sky, scattered shots, bursts of machine gun fire, but in our immediate vicinity, all is quiet. Most of the lads doze as the hours pass slowly without any action, no signal to fire has been given.

Something moving, over to the left; a running figure, it runs along the track at the base of the slope, following the stream, he will pass us on our left, I shall have to intercept him, check him out, could be a Jerry! Tell the lads what I aim to do; the man is coming along fast. Fix my bayonet, safety catch of my rifle forward, I run down the slope on the silent grass, reach the track in front of him by about forty yards, he has his head down; he has not seen me. Twenty feet away, I stand, tell him to halt! He skids to a shaky halt, he is still shaking with shock as the point of my bayonet rests on his chest, he is in battle-dress, no weapons, no helmet, he could be anything; I question him. Says he is from a rifle company, on his way to Battalion H.Q. with a message, could be, but I don't like the look of him. Question him further, his English sounds Ok, I've got no facilities to hold him, apart from shooting him, can only let him go, pretty sure he is British but I suspect he is making a run for it, with reluctance I tell him to go on his way.

Dawn at last. Leave the positions, move off down the slope to the stream, follow the track. A truck has tipped off the bank into the stream, a khaki clad figure lies pinned beneath the truck, face down in the mud. About two feet of water flows over him, the water plays gently with the hair on his head. Rejoin the remainder of the platoon; they too seem to have had animal trouble during the night.

A cosy enough spot among the fruit trees, no pit needed, plenty of shelter, set up gun, lay on target, watch for the signal, and relax! Out of the deep shadows of the tree an express train hits them in the shape of an infuriated ram. They scatter for their lives and limbs, trembling with shock as the beast charges through their ranks. He applies his brakes, turns straight back into the charge at the humans who dare to invade his domain. Again they scatter, again he charges, again they scatter. They're getting fed up with him, he's got to be stopped, can't shoot him it would make too much noise and give their position away, only one thing to do, bayonet him! Nobody wants to do it, they all look at each other waiting for some cold-blooded sod to volunteer, they scatter again whilst they hesitate. Edgar fixes his bayonet, the animal must be killed, and quickly! No need to chase the ram, he will come, just stand firm and let him run onto the weapon. He makes a wild rush on to the bayonet, his body eagerly takes the full length of the blade, a terrible scream from the animal fills the stillness of the night, the blood of the watching men turns to ice at the anguished and almost human sound, God! It would have been quieter to shoot him! For the Mortar Platoon it had been the night of the animals!

This marching is getting us down, more than half asleep, our legs move automatically, stomachs scream for food, we are all sick to death of pickled eggs, fat cigars and champagne. I piss pure champagne, oh, how the idle rich would envy me, I'd give the lot for a woodbine and a cup of tea!

A very old man sits at the side of the road entirely on his own, his feet rest on the floor of the ditch, he sits upright on the gentle slope, only his head rests forward on his chest as though he takes a doze. Something about his stillness and silence is strange an ominous, Edgar walks over to him to see if he is ok, he is dead, machine gun bullets from an aircraft fill his back, we leave him in peace sitting in his piece of ditch.

Pass groups of British troops resting at the side of the road; they look worn out even by our standards, a mixed bunch, look like the remnants of different units.

Shells begin to fall on the town as the column is entering it, some of the platoon are past the point of no return and have already entered, the rest of us skirt round the place in safety, we never see the men of our platoon who entered the town again, they are lost in the milling sea of khaki.

Dozens of vehicles of all shapes and sizes lie abandoned, either broken down or run out of petrol, in useless heaps they taunt our aching feet with what might have been. In three short days I have forgotten how the world used to be, things around here have gone to pot. We live, feel and smell like animals.

The man is dressed is the uniform of a British officer, he stands in the road telling the passing troops to throw away their weapons, it's their only chance of getting away he says, he tells Edgar to throw away the anti-tank gun he has picked up and carries, Edgar tells him to get stuffed. He accepts the rebuff without a word. Must keep our eyes open for Fifth Column activities now, people with a grudge against their own nation are helping the Germans, they even take a hand in fighting how and when they can, they snipe at you when you pass, or signal targets to German aircraft, they create traffic jams and any other little trick which comes into their minds. Nice people!

Lonely 'do or die' Germans drop by parachute behind our lines, they wear any sort of clothing, some even disguise themselves as priests, some wear battle-dress. Need to be very careful when rounding them up, some have a nasty habit of concealing a grenade in their upraised hand as they appear to surrender. We take orders from nobody unless we know them.

A town ahead, begin to enter the outskirts, a row of small workers cottages, one second we march upright as men, the next, we grovel in the ditches as the air is torn asunder with the nerve racking screams of diving aircraft and falling bombs. The bombs fall in the centre of the town, they are not aimed at us. Huge billows of smoke follow the sounds of the explosions. The Stukas dive with the speed of lightening, each time, the town shudders in agony.

I am under the front window of a cottage, a plank crosses the ditch from the front door to the road, my head is close to the plank as I crouch in the ditch, wonder that I didn't brain myself on it. The door has opened, a woman walks into the middle of the plank, stops, she is looking down at me, she wears a long dress, I practically touch the hem, she does not speak, just looks at me. Looking into her face I can see that she is in a state of shock, she looks mesmerised, her eyes move off me, they follow the line of men sheltering in her ditch, her eyes move slowly across the road, follow the line of steel helmets, in the other ditch, her head turns towards the diving Stukas, her body jumps violently as each of the bombs strike home, her eyes come back to me at her feet. She is staring in a puzzled, perplexed manner, her face crumples, tears run down, for seconds she stands, body shuddering, still she stares at me. I want the ground to open up and swallow me, I can do nothing to comfort her, all I can feel is the guilt as I crouch in her ditch. She acts as though only at this very moment does she accept that a war is being fought on her doorstep. She turns back and goes into her house without haste, closing the door gently but firmly.

The bombers leave, we scramble out of the ditches, fall in, resume the march. Skirting the town we find transport waiting for us, an assortment of trucks, we locate our 15cwt Bedfords by some miracle, they carry our guns, we are glad to meet up with them again.

The road is choked with men and vehicles, men beg lifts, men from all units, some march with order, others walk in isolated groups, others rest at the wayside. The trucks move along slowly, men cling to every possible foothold, but most of them have to walk, they watch us pass with desperate faces.

A woman with two tiny children approaches Edgar's truck as it crawls along, she begs a lift for herself and her children, but he cannot help, strict orders say he can't, sadly he has to refuse her. A man in civvies, big, fat and prosperous looking, pushes the woman and children out of the way as he offers Edgar a large box of fat cigars in return for a lift. In anger Edgar tells him to piss off with his bribe, we gaze at the misery of the refugees sick at heart, but we have strict orders not to become involved, they are something apart, something that's in the way of our war machine, they are a bother, you look at them, but you must not stop to help them, we are here to be manoeuvred, sooner or later we shall fight, so clear the mind of refugees, just build up the anger for the fight.

A bren-gun carrier at the side of the road, half a dozen men lounge around it looking relaxed and comfortable as though waiting for a bus, bright red kilts that hits the eyes like stabbing rays of sunlight in the drab sea of khaki, they wave as we pass, men of the Camerons.

Bad news, the band instruments have been captured; Jerry has slapped us in the face!

Tournai, 1940

Entering a rather large town, a slow entry, transport jammed nose to tail, we move forward in fits and starts. Small terraced houses line both sides of the street, an unending chain of them with no break between. Well into the town and still the same terraced houses, another halt, sit waiting it out.

A sudden scream. "All out. Enemy aircraft. ALL OUT!" Like greased lightening we spring over the tailboard, boots beat an irregular tattoo out onto the cobbles as they land in a mad scramble, across the pavement, stand with back against the nearest house wall, nowhere else to go anyway. Eyes turned upwards by the sudden deafening roar of low flying engines immediately above our heads. Bloody hell, waves of gigantic bombers are flying directly down the street just above the house tops. The engines in the narrow gully of houses erupts into a crescendo of nerve shattering sound. The whole world is vibrating madly.

For a split second we stare at the sky in disbelief at the slowness with which they fly, anything as big as them must fall out of the sky. Heinkels. Back firm against the wall, rifle already at the shoulder, hand working the bolt in a frenzy. Can't miss, aim at the fuselage, the engine, hundreds of other rifles and some bren-guns have added their chatter to the noise. See the clusters of bombs leave the wide open bomb bays, which stare at you like wide open barn doors as they spew out their loads. Coming straight at you. Can't run anywhere. No time for fear, just keep firing!

A loud screech as the falling bombs add their music, they fall inside the house that I lean against, tearing through its heart, I feel the wall shudder on my shoulder blades from the shock. Glass, dust, and other fragments spurt from the window at my elbow to shoot across the street, glass pieces and tiles cascade about my ears dancing on the road and pavement as they strike. The wall heaves outwards as the guts of the house drops then recovers, it stands firm, settles, the house has died but there is no time to think, nothing to do but Fire! Fire! Fire!

The aircraft has passed; you are still standing, feeling alright, your body is filled with wild exhilaration that you have been able to hit back. Your throat is dry, you realise that you have been screaming at them at the top of your voice in a flurry of obscenities as you fired. Look around, everyone still on their feet in the immediate vicinity, no casualties, but the sky over the centre of the town is black with smoke and dust. The bombers fly on, seemingly unperturbed by the hundreds of bullets that have been pumped into them

Urgent orders: "Get out quick, before they return". Silent lorry engines break into life, men run to the lorries, clamber aboard, slowly we move forward picking up speed faster than before, the road has been cleared, head for the open country, let's find some ditches! Clear the town, halt, rifle companies deploy, Jerry is close somewhere so they say. Refugees fill the roads from the battered town, if we have to start shooting, they are in the way!

Fifty men lost on the raid, some trucks destroyed, petrol and ammunition also been lost, but FIFTY MEN! All at one blow! The traffic hold up and air raid was engineered by Fifth-Column it is said, a man has been caught and shot.

See no sign of Jerry ground troops, later perhaps, load up, move on.

Bleharies, On the Banks of the River Scarpe, 1940

How nice, at long last they have promised us a fight! Having debussed we stand at the side of the road awaiting orders. A small village, deserted like most of them, on the left hand side of the road a stretch of grassland approximately forty feet wide, it runs from the roadside to the bank of a river which runs parallel with the road. About a fifty feet width of water, flat open country extends beyond for about two miles to reach distant woods which drift upwards as the ground rises. Jerry is just over there by those slopes they reckon.

A row of terraced cottages on the right hand side of the road, they have a perfect view across the road, the river and the sweep of open country. Behind these cottages the ground rises steeply for about two hundred feet, houses dot the slope, a narrow road leads up to the top of the hill.

We are to stay as long as is necessary. We fit into a defensive line that must keep Jerry on the other side of the river; we have permission to argue with them about it. You can tell it's different. When they detail the section they don't say "There's your billet", but "Get in there and bloody well get dug in".

We of the Mortars are told to take over some of the cottages opposite, we decide on four men to a house, two up and two down at the front windows. People don't seem to leave their keys dangling on a bit of string in their front doors round here. Kick the door open with the boot, Edgar and I take the upstairs window, climb the narrow stairs into the front bedroom. A large iron bead stead fills most of the floor area; there is also a wardrobe, a dressing table, small bedside table, a linen chest, good. Drag the linen chest over, it fits perfectly under the window ledge, a good arm-rest to fire from. Rifle butts smash out the glass, it falls outwards on to the street to join the tinkle of other falling glass, kneel down, try the position out, perfect! A wide sweep of the ground on the other side of the river, lay the guns down on the chest, a heap of spare ammunition on each side of the weapons, we are ready!

A good view, front row you might say. Look over the water that will stop their tanks, the scene is beautiful and peaceful, just as peaceful as any other country view, can't imagine it spewing danger of any sort, but I know it is deceptive, not a true picture. Nothing moves over there, stare as much as you like, it's as dead as a door nail.

An anti-tank gun digs in on the edge of the river, rifle sections move along the street taking up their positions. Follow the river to the left you see nothing but clear unobstructed banks. Follow it to the right, the eye meets a house built directly on to the edge of the river bank, from behind this house a long straight road leads directly into German held territory, trees line each side of the road. There's a bridge behind the house but we cannot see it from our position at the window.

Still no movement. No bloody Germans within miles we feel. Edgar tries the bed, not bad, spreading his number ten boots wide, a stack of pillows under his head, he has a perfect view of the target area and comfort as well. Search the house for food, but no luck, the cupboards are bare. See the arrival of some trucks near the house along by the bridge, perhaps our Mortars have arrived? Decide to investigate. I leave Edgar to the slogging labour of resting on the bed. Yes, our Mortars are here, can see the two trucks. On reaching them an unknown fellow hands me a letter, a letter from home. In total disbelief I stare at it, it's completely unreal, has no part in this mad world. I am not pleased, it reminds me of soft civilised things I have no time to think about, I can't get a cup of tea but a letter, yes!

A sudden terrific explosion from nowhere, the mind is drenched in a shock wave of sound. The letter flies out of my hand as I am flung across the road, pieces of debris rain down around, dancing before settling as though fitted with springs. A column of smoke and dust billows up in to the sky from behind the house by the bridge. Other men are picking themselves up off the ground as well, ears ringing; we look at each other in shocked surprise. The silly bastards have blown the bridge. Indeed they have, never thought to tell anyone they were going to do it. Enough explosives there to blow up the houses of parliament! Collecting my wits and my letter I return to the cottage to share the comforts of Edgar's bed. But not for long, kicked off the bed just as I am getting comfortable. We are detailed to take up positions with our Mortars.

Out of the house, Edgar's gun crew turn one way, we turn the other. Up the narrow road that leads to the top of the hill and the back of the village, we walk as the truck slowly follows us. Pass riflemen busy digging slit trenches in gardens, fortifying houses, see Joe a friend I work with in civvy street, we wave greetings as I pass.

Pass under an iron railway bridge that crosses the road at the top of the hill, enter another road that runs across our front from left to right, pause and study the advantages that each direction offers with regards to cover for setting up the Mortar. To the right a few low bungalow type dwellings, not too good. To the left, one large bungalow type dwelling and a clump of trees, that's better, turn left and investigate further. The railway embankment runs along on our left, the road we tread takes a sharp right turn away from the dwelling and trees just before we reach them, but the railway embankment continues straight on to skirt the trees, beside the trees and in front of the dwelling a patch of grassland. On to the grass, clamber up the embankment, cross rail tracks to study the potential target area. Fantastic, from this position, our bombs will sail over the village, our men, the river with ease, everything is within easy range, a good spot for a Mortar.

Unload the gun and ammunition; dig a gun pit deep into the side of the embankment. Gun, crew and ammunition soon snugly installed, range on to the far bank of the river, will lay a carpet of high explosives one hundred yards back from the river's edge if they come, we are ready. Before dark the whole defensive position is ready. There is a determined feeling in the air, been a lot of grins in evidence during the day. Nobody expects it to be funny, the grins haven't been that sort, just grins of satisfaction because the running is over. Darkness falls slowly but surely, we take sentry duty in turn, each man waking the other for spells.

Odd bursts of gunfire start up to our front, gradually the volume increases, suddenly the whole front erupts, shells begin to come over, German ones, they burst to our rear, listening to them, I decide Dad was right, they do sound like bloody trains, the loud screeches sound like London subway! Climb up on to the railway line to observe our front, gun flashes can be seen; obviously we are under attack, time to lay our carpet of bombs, the lads down there fire at something pretty close.

Open fire, our bombs whistle up into the blackness of the night followed by the crump as they explode. Traverse - first right, then left, spread out a nice curtain of hell, feed the hungry barrel as fast as our arms can move. A dud, Christ, get it out quick! No time for fancy safety drills, nobody even suggests it, they are for training, not for when muck is flying about.

Shells pass over travelling the other way. A silent cheer at the comforting thought that they are ours, a two way traffic of the things fill the night sky. Jerry's shells are falling shorter very fast now, to the right of the gun site a bit. They are on us, stop firing, dive deep down into the gun pit. The shells fall into the grove of trees forty yards to our right, a salvo falls in tattoo, shattering our senses. The air is filled with the sound of trees splitting, branches, chunks of tree trunk, and turf fly past our hole, half choking in the smoke as we sweat blood! Soon they drop short, falling on the village gradually to die away and stop. The small arms fire slackens just after midnight, our artillery ceases fire, but we stay in our lovely hole until dawn, shivering in the morning mist.

Full daylight, cross the railway lines, scan the target area, see nothing, no sign of life on the ground but in the air a tiny aircraft is approaching our lines from the German side. Flying low, bloody low, it reaches us and flies along our front a couple of times, comes up, looks around the top of the hill, unhurried, not a care in the world. He can feel that we can't he? They own the bloody sky don't they? We don't seem to have anything! Thousands of bullets are thrown up at him, everyone has a go, but still he flies. He goes when he is good and ready not before, he disappears from whence he came.

Snipers are active to our front, they were left behind during the night. Our lads are trying to locate them, bren-guns rake the trees that line the road on the other side, several hits are claimed and figures are seen to fall out from the green tops, but we are getting casualties too, some very nasty and some dead.

Decide to dig ourselves a shell-proof shelter, our gun pit leaves our backs exposed to shells dropping immediately behind us. Choose a measured spot just one jump from our gun pit and start digging. Approximately nine feet long by four feet wide, about four feet deep, build up the soil around the edges, drag thick branches over the top, pile up with thick timber and top it with chunks of turf leaving a small opening at one end. We are home and dry, a lovely hole, will stop anything except a direct hit!

Message of goodwill received from the rifle company to our front. Our supporting fire last night was welcomed. Moving figures were seen in the flash-light of the bombs, if this is so, they won't have any more. The message concludes with "You will draw enemy fire, please piss off!" Delighted that our fire was effective but we decide to ignore the rude initiation to leave.

Isolated bursts of firing as men spot targets. Our heavy guns open up sending salvos to the rear of Jerry positions, a nice comforting sound, our guns.

A lonely isolated bungalow located to our rear, we investigate it for food. Shutters hang open, windows shattered, climb in through one, no other damage visible, a nicely kept place, had been left spotless. No panic departure this, obviously a calm, temporary sort of exit as thought the people had just popped down to the corner shop. The house is a bit dusty now though, we mentally apologise to the lady of the house for our presence.

Find the larder, a large one, a walk in type, room for lots of grub. The offering this day consists of a piece of cooked meat, a bowl of uncooked rice, and two tiny pigeons eggs on a small dish. I stare at the two tiny eggs in surprise, the fragile delicacy and the soft roundness of the things fascinate me, can't leave them here, they might get broken! They are not worth eating, wouldn't know that you had had them, better take them with me, might meet up with a pigeon. Lying in my filthy hand they look what they are, beautifully shaped works of art. Wrapping them carefully in a soft cloth I place them carefully aside to take with me. A solitary cow has been located at the rear of the dwelling; she is undamaged and bursting to give milk to the first one to come along. With the sickening superiority of a country lad scoring over a bunch of townies one of the lads who reckons he can milk her goes off with a saucepan to do just that.

The meat, a bit of thought required; at least a week old, don't know what kind it is, best not to think of that part of it, its looks good, bloody delicious in fact. Poisoned grub would also look good, fifth column and all that, possible, better find out. Corporals come cheap, I tear a small piece off, chew it, can't hang about too long, give myself thirty seconds to drop dead, I don't, we carve it up between us. The milk has arrived, we add the rice and place both on a small fire we have lit to cook it, it boils over, the milk has boiled anyway, that makes it cooked, we eat the stuff just as a shell lands outside the house.

Like streaks of lightening we gallop for our new shelter, in its darkness the ground shakes, soil crumbles from the wall, Jesus, is it going to cave in? Branches and turf rain down on our roof. Soon the shells pass, they sound heavier than last night, probably bigger guns, but our guns are hitting back, we hear the music of their passing.

Slip off singly back to the bungalow, clean off the grime of five days dirt from our faces, our bodies will have to make do for a bit longer. Retrieve the pigeon's eggs; tuck them in a corner of the gun pit, in their wrappings that should be a safe spot.

Decide to check out front, climb the embankment to get a good view of the target area, must cross two sets of railway lines, opposite on the other side of the tracks there is a small allotment sized hut, presumably used for tools by the rail staff. If I can get there I shall have some sort of cover. The four rails run as straight as an arrow in both directions merging into sharp points of distance. Step over the first rail, boot planted on the timber sleeper, walking upright, I concentrate on placing my boot just right, over the second rail, over the third. Eyes register that my boot is on the timber as it should be, they also see the bright white scar of wood that has just appeared like magic about an inch from the side of my boot, splinters fly into the air, my brain screams, SNIPER. Fortunately my reflexes are one step ahead of my brain, they have already flattened me between the rails. A sniper, he had me in his sights, Jesus!

One more track to get over, looks a bit steep from down here. With caution my body melts over it with the professionalism of a dirty black slug. I swear I go up one side and down the other without a fraction of daylight between me and the rail. The shed is just one jump away, a roll, a jump, I make it. Standing directly behind the shed now, the shot came from the right, move round to the left of the shed putting it between me and the sniper, I hope! Scan the open country, no movement, hard to believe that they are out here at all, but that grass is long, could hide any number of men.

I jump about six inches with shock, a voice is speaking at my elbow, a cultured voice talking about ranges. An English voice, it comes from inside the shed. Completely unaware that anyone was as close as this to our position, I speak to make my presence known, hope I make him jump six inches too! I dart round to the front to go in. An Artillery Officer sits inside, a field telephone in his lap, perfectly comfortable and relaxed, he grins at me like a Cheshire cat. Every inch of the target area is under his eye, we chat as our eyes search.

We both spot them at the same time, both shout, both point. A dozen men have risen from the grass just over a thousand yards away. They walk across our front from right to left, well spaced out, a section moving into position, they're either stupid or impertinent. The officer is moving fast. Ok I'll take them. Already he gives the range into the phone, a few rapid words, the phone again rests in his lap, he watches the target. In seconds I hear the shells on their way, so too do the distant section of Germans. They melt into the grass instantly out of sight, but the shells have landed; the ground they occupy has erupted into violent flame and smoke, the area of explosions widens around the, a seething mass of churning earth. The officer grunts with satisfaction, reports into his phone that the target has been destroyed. I wait a while but no further movement is seen from the enemy, he is right, they have been destroyed, it took less than five minutes. I am deeply impressed by the efficiency of the operation but the smoothness of the killings leave a shudder up my spine.

A mad dash back across the railway lines, giving the sniper no time to line up his sights, land in a head among the lads as I leap off the embankment. They eye me with disapproval; I frightened the life out of them. One man posted during the night, each taking it in turn as the others snatch some sleep. The odd shell comes over, doesn't fall near us, bursts of small arms fire goes on and on which disturbs our sleep.

Dawn creeps up, another fine day; the sun breaks out to smile impartially on all men on both sides of the river it refuses to take sides. The Jerry spotter plane comes over on his morning visit, again very low and completely relaxed. The whole front shoots at him at will as though trying their hand at a low flying duck, but he flies on, his feathers unruffled. He infuriates us! He must be full of lead. His inspection over he returns to his own lines. Check the eggs, they look fine, feel responsible for them now that I have moved them!

Sniping increased today; fresh marksmen have taken up position during the night. Ordered to saturate the grassland on the far bank, snipers suspected of sheltering in its lush growth. We cover a fair size area when shelling interrupts our firing. The shells fall in the tree to our right forcing us to take shelter, certain they are searching for us now, they have got the right area, if they alter their sights a couple of degrees, we are dead men.

Resume firing as soon as the shelling stops only to be interrupted by the arrival of two French officers, they walk calmly into our position and start speaking rapidly in a mixture of French and English. Would we stop firing? Our bombs are landing among

French troops situated to our right! They couldn't have insulted our marksmanship more if they tried! They are both armed only with revolvers, I tell them to buzz off or get shot. They buzz off, deeply offended.

Hear one of the rifle company lads decided to sneak a couple of hours sleep in a real bed last night, breaking into one of the houses he stumbled upstairs in the darkness, hands searching for the bed, found it, he laid down with a sigh of relief but, instant alertness, he feels someone else already in the bed. Someone very still, cold, and stiff, frightened to death he strikes a match, the light revealed the body of an old man laid out reverently by his grieving relatives before they left the house, he had been dead for many days. The soldier fled his unexpected bedfellow, the thought of his surprise and probable speed of exit tickles us to death.

A nice relaxed rest in the sun, getting paid for it too, but rest is abruptly interrupted by an officer from one of our rifle company's. A very excited young man, a mere kid; he waves his revolver about in the air, dancing from one leg to another in his agitation: "Come with me Corporal. Quickly".

He darts off in the direction of the road a few yards away from our position. Grabbing my rifle I follow him. He stands in the centre of the road jumping about with excited jerky movements of a badly operated string puppet, arm raised, he us pointing down the centre of the road. "Shoot that man".

'That man' is walking along the centre of the road towards us with the casual air of someone out on an early morning stroll, he is about one hundred yards away, seen him before, he's one of the Frenchmen who tried to get us to stop firing, he is looking to his left as he walks, turns his head towards us, immediately he stops in his tracks, a quick about face, he is running away as fast as he can. Now why would a Frenchman run away from us? What is he doing here anyway? The officer is doing his nut because I have not sighted on him yet, I'm forced to agree with him, the Frenchman has acted guiltily. Rifle at my shoulder, I sight half way down his back just below the shoulder blades, take first pressure, ease into second pressure, hold my breath as the last hairs touch of pressure arrives.

"Stop. Don't shoot". A sharp blow from my rifle butt to my jaw as the Officer knocks down the muzzle. He is away, chasing after the Frenchman as fast as his legs can carry him, the Officers revolver is still waving wildly in the air. Bloody barmy, got cold feet about shooting him. Doesn't realise that if he catches him he will probably have to shoot him himself now! They disappear down the road, both running hard, neither gaining on the other. Mentally washing my hands of all officers I return to resume my interrupted rest in the sun.

Reflecting on the two Frenchmen and our officer walking up to our position and taking us by surprise, I realise how easily people can creep up on us. Scare myself to death at the thought of the nasty types hanging about here, they could easily do the same; know darn well that I will have to scout around the rear of our position to ease my mind. On to the road, follow it round to the rear of our position, a sunken road has developed, gravel banks approximately thirty feet high, they run for about two hundred yards, no sign of life back here.

Hear shells travelling my way. The first one to explode is on top of the bank to my right, I dive into the bank on my left simply because it is closer, crouch down, face and body flattened into the gravel as the remainder of the salvo bursts on top of the bank on both sides of the road. A high pitched twanging noise fills the air, it sounds like a thousand released bow strings must surely sound, comes from behind, there. Up on top of the bank, a telegraph pole, it whips from side to side with the frenzied rhythm of a released steel spring, bends with the ease of a willow twig, broken wires crank though the air like giant whips. For seconds my fascination overrides the fear of the shells. Another salvo on the way, they all explode on the bank behind, shock waves flatten me into the gravel, terrific blow in the back, on the belt over the right kidney, I stiffen with shock, my breath virtually stops.

It is said that when you get a bad one you don't feel the pain at first. For several seconds I lie still afraid what movement of the body might tell. Got to feel round there, see if there is any blood, my right hand goes round my back with reluctance, fingers feeling the area nervously. Belt feels alright, not pierced, doesn't feel wet but i have to drag the cowardly hand back round to my front. My equally cowardly eyes have a yellow streak a yard wide, they fear to look at my hand, might see red, my blood! All is well, my hand is white, a dirty white to be true but white none the less, no red, no blood, I let loose a sigh of relief. I flex my back, punch it, seems alright, feels fine. Got to get out of here, my arse is sticking out into the road like a target, as the third salvo comes over I make a mad dash back to the gun position, lungs bursting as I join the lads back in the safety of the shelter.

Very impressed with our hole in the ground, it takes a surprising amount of hammering, without it, I fear we would have been goners long ago. A reasonably quiet night, no major panics; in the morning we have our usual visit from our friend in the spotter plane, give him his breakfast of lead which he seems to digest with relish as he flies back to his own lines in infuriating safety.

A second attack develops covered by extensive artillery fire. Small arms fire from our front as targets are spotted and engaged. Most of our time is spent keeping our heads down. Concentrated shell fire round our position, I think they know where our mortars are, I fear for the two eggs! Check them, they look fine and healthy, they have a beautiful soft creamy white bloom that contrasts vividly with the colour of my dirty paw. Things are getting torn apart round here but these delicate things still survive, I will see that they do.

Have heard no British shells go over in reply today, decide to check over the railway lines, visit the artillery officer, slither over the tracks in my best snake act yet. The shed is empty, they must have pulled out, a pity, we will miss them.

Some Jerries actually made it across the water got into a wood, but men of C Company chased them back again at the point of the bayonet, good lads!

Got to move from our position, shells too hot, gun barrel knocked off line once from blast, just got to move. Whistle the truck, load up, place the eggs carefully in a safe corner of the truck, we move back into the sunken road, set up the gun and wait for orders. Jumped from the frying pan into the fire! Shelling becomes heavier, splinters fly from the hard surface of the road, an even warmer spot, again we must move, move back about three hundred yards to a farmhouse, out of the shellfire here it is quieter. Quite dark now, can't set up the gun here, the only observation point is the roof of the farmhouse. Being no steeplejack I shudder at the thought of trying to climb up onto the roof in the darkness. Relax, see what happens.

Orders to get out! Got to slink away without letting Jerry know that we part company for a while, we to it to the sound of heavy gunfire along the banks of the river as the rifle companies disengage. Rifle companies moving back through the darkness, shadowy figures marching in disciplined order, no panic here, only regret leaving such a good position, but our flanks have collapsed so rumour has it, we have to move to survive.

Had a fair try at them though, held them for three and a half days, they know we are around anyway, we have let off steam! Our turn to move off, lads all loaded up, they wait only for me. Swinging up on to the truck as it moves off my first number nine boot swings over and is in swiftly to be followed by the other. The eggs didn't stand a bloody chance, I lift my boot from the flat pathetic bundle appalled at my carelessness! I do the only decent thing left to do for them, I cast the soggy cloth and its shattered contents overboard into the depths of the passing night.

Going back to a good defensive line this time they say, a well prepared line, calling it the Gort line, it had better be good! Move back something like ten miles, H.Q. Company takes over some farm buildings, hang about all day watching waves of enemy bombers passing overhead and dodging sporadic shelling, see nothing of Edgar and his gun crew, it is the best part of four days since we last met. After dark a march, a long march of about eighteen miles. As dawn breaks we enter a straggling village called 'Nomain'. We are back in France.

Nomain, France, 1940

Delighted to meet up with Edgar and his reduced Mortar crew of two men at last, they are dreadfully exhausted buy reasonably cheerful having suffered no wounds so far, like us they suffer only from shortage of men. A chance for sleep and a bit of food in this place they tell us, we will be on the move later in the day. Told the location of the cook-house, we head for it with the haste of starving dogs, a mess tin full of tea, good, a slice of fried meat loaf, not enough to feed a goldfish, that's all there is, take it or leave it, we take it! As we eat Edgar tells me of the fortunes of his gun crew back on the river at Bleharies.

From the cottage where we had left them to take up our position, he had received instructions to support B Company who were located outside the village on the extreme right flank of the Battalions front and were dug into positions on the river bank. Thus the two Mortars were to be sited approximately half a mile apart. Arriving on the bank of the river they were surprised to find it almost empty of water, it obviously being a tributary of some kind. Twenty-five yards back from the river bank and running parallel was a belt of trees, guessing that the trees would become a target area for shells when they arrived, Edgar decided to dig the mortar a pit directly into the bank of the river. Tall reeds growing there provided some shelter, quite close to them was a tall tree. Soon the job was completed, safely installed and covered with netting and reeds they took stock of the target area, responsible to cover a four-hundred yards front, about three platoons of rifle company men were spread out in holes in the ground on the opposite side of the river to their front, something like thirty or forty men, not many to cover four hundred yards, with worried Edgar quite a bit.

Small meadows located directly to their front criss-crossed by hedgerows, a group of small houses about eight hundred yards distant, beyond them the stick-like mast of a barge could be seen on a canal about sixteen hundred yards distant. A barn on the left flank, behind it long straight tree lined road coming from German territory to halt at the blown-up bridge in the village. Sweeping open country on their right flank but this area was covered by a Regiment of French-Moroccan troops, laying the mortar on chosen targets within the sector they were soon ready and waiting, their eyes searching for enemy movement.

Movement on the road, a large civilian van was travelling from deep within German territory. As it reached the bridge it screeched to a halt in a half turned position as though ready for a fast getaway, three men descended from the vehicle, young active men dressed in civilian clothes, they walked to the bridge, surveyed the water and our side of the river, many eyes watched them closely from cover but they did not know what to do about it, should they shoot them? Could well be Germans in civvy clothes checking our positions, but they had no orders to fire as yet, they watched the men climb back into the vehicle and drive back from whence they came with some apprehension. Doubts are settled on the matter shortly afterwards, orders issued to shoot anything that comes to the further edge of the river and attempts to turn back, nothing must return to German territory after gazing on our positions, now they knew.

Nightfall presents them with a brilliant moonlit landscape but a strong breeze rustles the reeds around the gun pit, their nerves scream with the strain of listening, they feel certain that every German in France is creeping up on them. Edgar tried closing his eyes in an effort to improve his hearing but he kept falling asleep and falling over, dare not lie down, must stand to keep awake. Fixed his bayonet on his rifle in the end in desperation, rested his hand on the point, placed his chin gently on his hand, as he fell asleep the weight of his head on his hand dries it down on the point and pricks him.

Suddenly his blood turned to water, something crawling through the reeds towards him, he died a thousand deaths as he lined up his rifle on to the spot, taking first pressure and almost pulling the trigger as the dark shadow emerged and quickly identified himself as the Company Sergeant Major, he is closely followed by a French Liaison Officer. They apologise for startling him, tell him that they have been checking the lines of responsibility with the French – Moroccans net door, all he could muster in reply was a very weak "Have you?". A close thing, they almost died then if they did but know it!

Heavy gunfire in the next sector on their left flank during the night but they are troubled only by badly frayed nerves and are startled by a light German spotter plane that swooped along the length of the river with its engine shut off, it shot past them like a large silent bat. Sweeping the target area through his glasses Edgar was interested to see a German step out from behind the cover of a house at eight hundred yards distance and examine our lines though his glasses, he reported the man's presence to Company H.Q.

Two specs spotted walking along the road towards the bridge from German territory, it took a long time for the old man and woman to materialise and reach the bridge, they stood gazing into the water in a helpless fashion. Large bundles on their backs, they look like genuine refugees, but you could not be certain, many pairs of eyes examine their every move, every fibre of Edgar's body is willing them to travel along the bank of the river, not to travel back along that road. The man stood waving his arms a lot, he wanted to go along the edge of the river in the direction of Tournai, but the woman argues about it. They stand arguing for several minutes, she looked as though she wanted to turn back and go along the road, back in to German territory, he gave in to her, and in doing so sealed their fate. They turned, slowly retraced their steps back the way they had come still arguing, but they didn't have to walk far, maybe fifty yards, then God knows how many Vickers and Bren-guns opened up from our side of the river, they fell onto the cobbled road in two shattered heaps, Edgar was sad that the old man had not been stronger, had not won the argument.

As if it was the signal they had been waiting for, the German artillery immediately erupted, laying down a terrific barrage of high explosive shells on their positions, all hell had broken loose! In the distance Edgar could see a small observation balloon hanging in the sky which was directing the German fire, they were spot on to the line of trees twenty-five yards to their rear and he and his men could do nothing but grovel into the earth, their backs felt naked. After a while Jerry changed from high explosive shells to air bursting shrapnel, it simply rained shrapnel, the rifle sections to the front couldn't stand it, they doubled back quickly across the river to take what shelter they could among the trees. The Mortar crew hugged the gun pit for several minutes until a shell hit the tree standing close to them, the complete top was severed and fell on to the gun pit, by the skin of their teeth no-one was hurt but it was time to move. Quickly they moved the mortar back into the shelter of the trees digging a fresh gun pit in record time. Machine gun fire was striking the ground about ten feet in front of their new site, but having to shout back ranges from forward of the gun for observation, Edgar made sure that he darted from tree to tree quickly and observed fire from behind the thickest tree available!

Machine gun fire was buzzing around them in streams but they could not see the German gunners, it was not until they noticed that the German troops were firing red flares up into the sky when their own artillery shells were falling too close to them that they knew where they were. The flares left a tell-tale mark in the sky as they soared upwards from the long grass, the Mortar then drenched the spots with high explosive bombs in rapid fire. Noticing ditches along the side of the road the Mortar crew also saturated the road to stop Jerry crawling along the ditches, and thus gaining the bridge.

Spotted a German machine gunner in the barn on their left flank, he was giving our lads a bad time near the bridge, the Mortar found the target with the first two bombs at 550 yards, a stick of five bombs to follow plunged into the barn, a second stick of five arrived on target as the structure collapsed, the machine gunner within had had it.

As the Jerry's got closer their shelling slackened for a while, but soon a heavy barrage descended again, the reason became clear when they noticed that the Jerry infantry were pulling back, they had managed to stop them! Branches and bundles of wood were quickly laid across the river bed on to the mud and slime, and with a struggle some Bren-gun carriers managed to cross to the other side of the river, they dashed across the fields chasing the German infantry back beyond the distant canal.

The rifle company left the shelter of the trees and re-crossed the river bed to give support to the carriers, they advanced in a thin extended line, suddenly there was machine gun fire from just in front of the line of advancing men. Six men on the left flank fell, the officer leading them ran across to the left flank firing his revolver into something lying on the ground in the long grass, a lone German had been left behind, not knowing that his mates had pulled back, death was his reward. Two of our men dead, four wounded, they brought them back across the river bed on a Bren-gun carrier.

Told to fire at the distant barge, all they could see was the thin stick of the mast, firing at almost maximum range they eventually see debris sailing into the air followed by the disappearance of the mast.

The rifle company and the remaining Bren-gun carriers return to their positions among the trees after chasing Jerry back. The carriers have great difficulty in re-crossing, one got stuck fast in the mud, as they struggled to free it a shell struck the side of the vehicle; they got the men out, one was wounded in the shoulder, another sat silently in his seat white and staring, he was badly shocked, they could not see his tunic for the number of bandoliers of ammunition draped around him, he wore a jacket of bullets!

Shelling continued as night fell, they got the impression that they must have upset Jerry quite a bit, millions of stars were out twinkling down on them. Edgar stood forward of the mortar pit, watching their front as he leaned against a tree, suddenly he was sailing through the air as a shell landed near the gun pit behind him. Picking himself up he ran back to the pit fearing the worst, but weak trembling voices from the pit assured him that they were alright. In the early morning light he can see that the shell had ploughed into the soft ground just three feet from the edge of the gun pit, it had missed the stack of bombs by a mere one foot, a huge jagged, nine inch long chunk of shining metal glittered in the tree trunk he had been standing against, just a few inches above where his head had been, it was so sharp he cut his finger as he touched it, the metal gleamed with the multi-colours of intense heat.

Morning brings steady shelling but no machine gun fire, Edgar decides to search for food, wandering down into the cellar of the first house he saw, hoping to find a jar of pickled eggs or something. Feeling about in the dark his hands encountered something cold and clammy to the touch, hanging from the ceiling is a plucked chicken, taking his find to the company cook-house he asks them to cook it for him, will collect it later.

German infantry kept their distance as their artillery softened up our lines. He watched some German bomber overhead returning from a raid behind our lines, anti-aircraft shells mushroom around them thick and fast, suddenly one of the aircraft is hit, flames and smoke pour down from it as it begins falling in the slow death throes of descent in wide circles. One man has jumped out, Edgar watched the parachute open safely, the Jerry was well clear of the aircraft which travelled away from him, but in fascinated and disbelieving horror Edgar saw the plane complete another circle and in passing catch the parachute on to the tail plane. Suddenly the plane dives straight down to earth, the tiny speck of a man trailing after it, they crashed on to the road just behind Edgar's position. Later Edgar found the tail unit of the plane not far from Battalion H.Q. and near it only bits of parachute material and a luger pistol, of the man there was no sign!

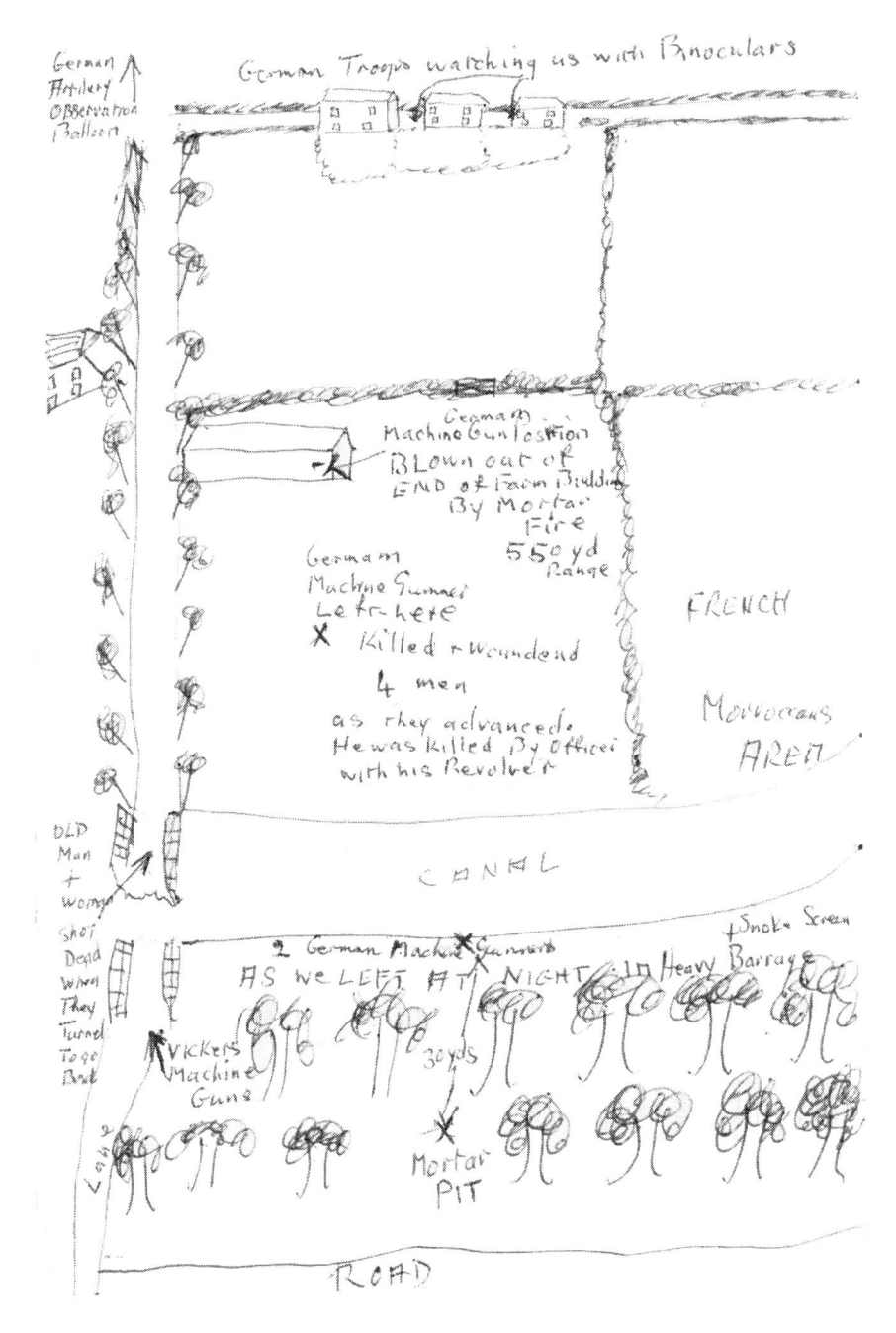

[Hand-drawn map with the following annotations:]

- German Artillery Observation Balloon
- German Troops watching us with Binoculars
- German Machine Gun Position BLOWN out of END of Farm Building By Mortar Fire 550 yd Range
- German Machine Gunner Left here X Killed + Wounded 4 men as they advanced. He was killed By Officer with his Revolver
- FRENCH Moroccans AREA
- CANAL
- OLD Man + Woman SHOT Dead when They Turned To go Back
- 2 German Machine Gunners AS WE LEFT AT NIGHT IN Heavy Barrage
- Smoke Screen
- Vickers Machine Guns
- 30 yds
- Mortar PIT
- ROAD

Late in the afternoon German infantry begin to close in and as dusk fell our lines were deluged with thick smoke screens from German artillery. Thick choking stuff that forced them to put on their respirators to breathe, visibility was almost nil in the smoke and darkness. Machine gun fire started cutting into our lines, the men crouched on the edge of the trees, staring into the darkness and drifting smoke with their bayonets fixed. Suddenly about thirty feet in front of them Edgar could see flashes from the muzzles of two machine guns, one was firing along the river bank towards the bridge, the other fired towards the Moroccan sector. Jesus, there were Jerry guns on our side of the river. As Edgar and his men watched the flashes a voice called Edgar's name from somewhere behind, he kept answering the voice to guide it to him, it was their truck driver come to take them out. Hurriedly they moved the mortar back through the trees back on to the road to Battalion H.Q. Loading up on to the truck almost in their sleep, for three and a half days they'd had neither sleep nor food, they never did get that bloody chicken!

As they pulled away from the machine guns and smoke the last thing Edgar saw as his eyes closed was the dead body of an Oxford lad we knew lying at the side of the road. Edgar felt a great sorrow because he wouldn't be coming with us.

Opening his eyes to daylight he was greeted by a beautiful sunny morning, trees surrounding him, trees heavy with the beauty and magic of delicate pink blossom, he stared at the wonderland of colour not understanding where he was, he shivered as he tried to move on his bed of comb cases, it was so quiet he could hear birds singing, the spell of the peaceful moment filled his heart with the great wonder of things forgotten.

Edgar and I finished our meal, we can get our heads down in a kids school they tell us. Stretching ourselves down among the children's benches we manage a few hours sleep ignoring the signs of interrupted lessons from other days.

On the way to load on to lorries we walk in the ditch at the side of the road, German shells fall on the hard surface of the road itself, we hit the bottom of the ditch each time they explode. A French battery of seventy-five artillery guns are busy firing from a field close by in reply, the crash of the guns as they fire is comforting to hear. A hedge beside us as we walk, from behind it a sudden unexpected thundering crash of shots as a British artillery battery opens fire, we almost die of shock not knowing that the buggers were there! Eventually load on to lorries late at night, move off into the darkness. Almost immediately heads nod forward down to the chest swinging from side to side with the motion of the truck. Weariness takes over, the mind is a complete blank, live from minute to minute, time to wonder where we are going and what will happen when and if we get there.

A violent lurch as the lorry wheel strikes a deep hole in the road, the eyes snap open with a start to behold a flame lit street, we are passing between houses that burn like torches in the night. The bomb crater in the road that our lorry has struck recedes from us as do the figures of the French priest and the other three civilians that are loading dead civilian bodies on to the wagon that stands near them. The bodies lie on the wagon with the neatness of stacked rail sleepers. The eyes and mind briefly absorb the scene as the chin settles back on the chest, as the mind drifts back in to sleep is registered a muttered: "We are passing through Armentieres."

Dawn, still travelling, had some delays in the night, don't worry about them though, someone always sorts these things out. The early vivid greens of spring growth recedes from the back of the lorry spoilt only by the ugly abandoned flotsam of war on the road.

Full daylight, going up a steep hill, as we climb, the countryside begins to drop away sharply on each side of the road; soon a sheer drop, more than four hundred feet high. Now running on a level stretch of road, we have reached the top, the country below us is like viewing a map, we are about six hundred feet high now.

The lorries halt, we unload at the entrance of a town called Cassel.

Cassell, 1940

A town perched on top of a sharp edged ridge astride the Lille-Dunkirk road, it commands a panoramic view of the surrounding countryside below. Our new defensive position, ours to hold at all cost. Can see for about twenty to twenty-five miles from up here. Will see Jerry coming anyway!

Far up at the side of the road, the first few houses of the town can be seen just along the road. Move off, usual single file on each side of the road, the men ahead on my side skirt some obstruction in the road. A French army gun limber of some sort, or it was once, now it lies smashed at the side of the road. In front of it is a mountain of raw flesh recognisable as two horses only by the hooves and a bit of harness. Near them, a figure of a man lies covered with a blood soaked blanket. A pair of French army boots protrude from under the edge of the blanket. Blood has run down the slope of the hill finding several routes between the large cobbles only to merge into a pool that has congealed, we skirt him in silence.

About one hundred yards to go to reach the first house of the town. On our left a grove of trees and shrubs, opposite, the town cemetery, a large one, surrounded by a six foot high privet hedge. The cemetery lies at a lower level than the road, a wide cobbled path leads down into the cemetery from the road. Reach the first houses as the road bends sharply to the left. Terraced houses very tall, at least four floors high, follow the road for a hundred yards between the tall buildings. A sharp right turn, on the corner a cycle shop, its windows full of new machines. Smaller dwellings in this stretch, still terraced, pass an ornamental archway, through it a view of open countryside lying below the town can be seen. Next to it a shop which sells pots and pans, they gleam with newness in the window, next a drapers shop, gay coloured pieced of cloth. Houses a further two hundred yards, out into a square, fall out at the side of the road, wait for further instructions.

Military traffic passing through, they go directly across the square to disappear out of the other side. Dunkirk lies down the road, they will be there well before nightfall, it's only about thirteen miles away. Two badly damaged British troop carrying lorries in the centre of the square, flowing traffic all going one way wend their way round them. The figure of a solitary man in Battle-dress sits more or less upright at the back of one of the lorries, sitting on a wooden plank that runs along the side of the uncovered back, he rests against the side of the lorry as though patiently waiting for the vehicle to move off again. He has been decapitated! Over there, by the wall of the houses lies another dead man, he too has been decapitated, his arms have been placed across the front of his body, they meet low down and are covered with bright yellow gauntlet gloves which gleam with the startling bright yellow of daffodils. You can tell they are brand-new, their brightness forms the only colour in the square.

A French civilian lorry turns into the square from the other side, it catches the eye immediately, it's so old, must have got it out of a museum. 1914 vintage I should think but it seems to move well enough. The only vehicle moving this way, he has a job picking his way against the traffic flowing against him. We watch his progress, he reaches us, has to stop, has to wait for somebody to let him into the narrow road that leads out of the town. Very low side walls fitted to the lorry, he stops virtually under my nose, he carries a cargo of death. Shattered civilian bodies fill the back of his lorry, men, women, and children, all in a ghastly heap, a mantle of white dust covers them, dust from their shattered homes, victims of an air-raid, the town buries its dead today. Soon the lorry can move into the narrow street, the street that leads to the cemetery which we passed as we entered the town.

A decision is reached regarding our fate, we are taken across the square, turn into the coast road, two large buildings to our right, turn into one of them, a large yard full of hustling, busting men, see lots of familiar faces which we have not seen for many days, Edgar and I are greeted with: "Hello, you two buggers still together?" Cooks are working frantically to get the cooking gear going; they know that if they don't feed us soon now that the Company is more or less gathered to together we will skin them alive!

The building is the local Police Station, now to be used as our Battalion H.Q., the nerve centre of our lives. We are told that in all probability we can expect a German armoured column to come this way, our job is to stop them, keep the road to Dunkirk open for as long as possible, if we can get a rest first we don't mind the job, somebody has to do it I suppose.

Away in the distance a huge black column of smoke rises up into the blue sky, spreading out into an ugly cloud, oil tanks at Dunkirk, Jerry aircraft fly past, many of them at eye level with our elevation, expect them to come thicker later, our heads will soon be moving as tennis spectators do I don't doubt. Where the hell is our Air Force anyway? Come to that, where the hell are our tanks anyway? Hear the Guards Battalions have been busy with their bayonets at Arras in a counter attack.

The food, whatever it is, is hot, which makes it fantastic! Splash some water on our faces, even have a shave, nice to see my chin again. Explore the large building next door, a Post Office, full of letters and parcels stopped in flight to their intended receivers; someone, somewhere, was waiting for an urgent package which has since lost its urgency, they lie collecting only dust. Some may complete their journey some day, perhaps none of them will, they wait patiently while men fight it out, they have all the time in the world. The country below us looks quiet and peaceful enough, but it is not to be trusted. Companies are digging in, temporary protective screens must be thrown into position, patrols must explore the perimeter of the town.

Edgar is given a group of men to form a protective screen around the H.Q. building, out on the forward slopes, dig in, an all night watch, I am detailed to join part of a patrol outside the town under the command of a Sergeant. A 15cwt truck, open back, planks each side propped up by petrol cans, five men sit in two rows, our rifles upright between our knees, move out of the town taking the coast road. A road block ahead, slow down to negotiate huge tree trunks that lie in a staggered pattern across the road, checked through, we remind the fellows that we expect to be coming back, we hope, probably after dark.

Never felt so stupid as I do now. Been creeping up and down miles of roads for far too long looking for trouble, sitting wedged together, couldn't move fast if we wanted to. Like sitting ducks all in a row, a kid could blast us from any hedge, darker it gets the less I like it. All good things come to an end, we turn for the town not having seen a thing thank goodness. Approach the road block with great caution, they let us through safely.

Good news! We have the Gloucesters; four anti-aircraft guns and some anti-tank guns are now with us. We have a good position here, only one road leads through the town, tanks can only use each end of the road, the fall of ground to the country below will, I hope, be too steep for tanks to climb up most parts. Below us the village of Hazelbrook; in position there, our sister Battalion of the Bucks, below us too facing the south west approaches, D Company of the Oxfords are taking up positions in the south of Bavinchove.

A quiet, uninterrupted, but watchful night, morning calls for a close scrutiny of the country below. Aircraft fly about, fires burn in the distance, each sending up its signal of distress. Convoys start rolling through the town heading for the coast. Have a look through some bombed houses, find the usual eggs, champagne, and a bottle of brandy. Instructed to report to A Company located approximately facing the south-east approaches to the town, their backs are towards Dunkirk.

Company headquarters based in a cellar of one of the small terraced houses, the Ironmongers, Drapers, and Cycle shops are in their territory, together with the cemetery. Told to retire to the cycle shop until required, we move the gun and ammunition into a garage nearby to await events. Commandeered to direct traffic through the town, our dispatch rider becomes a casualty, allowing a bloody great lorry to run over his foot! Always a show off, he stands with legs astride his machine in the middle of the road, a sharp turn is necessary at that point, one lorry trying to turn on a sixpence catches his foot, crushing it, load him into an ambulance with other casualties, send them off to the coast with our blessing, will miss him, not because he is a tough fighting man, but he is about the best scrounger in the Battalion. Always on a roving commission he feeds the members of his own platoon with many a tit-bit be has probably pinches!

Have expected trouble all day but it has not arrived yet. Edgars crew, together with a Bren-gun carrier, went out of town looking for a reported German machine gun nest, they could not find it. Getting dark now, though traffic is drying up, we settle down to a watchful night. No problems though the night, make tea, drinking it from real china cups, eat our collective bits and pieces of food off real plates, feeling too civilised for words. We even have a shave; as we congratulate ourselves on our turn out shelling bursts upon us, they have arrived.

Report to A Company H.Q. for orders, they tell me to sit tight but to hold ourselves in readiness. Return to the lads, decide to get our heads down while we have the chance. Listening to the weight of shells coming over we decide to retire to the cellar. A faint light seeps into the cellar from a grating, almost the whole of the floor space is taken up by a rigged-up bed. Mattresses and bedding in abundance, the fella must have had a big family. The ceiling is arched and low with about two foot clearance over the bed. To get on the bed you sort of roll on to it but you can't sit up on it once you're there, to get back off you just roll.

Decide to have a look out on the street before I retire; all hell is breaking loose up there, feel uneasy. Up into the doorway of the shop, peer down the street, three figures have just turned the corner from the cemetery. Walking very slowly, they are coming towards me, two stretcher bearers supporting a third man who hangs limply between them, they hold one each of his arms around their necks virtually carrying him; a badly wounded man, bet he could do with a drink. Race back upstairs for my bottle of brandy, get back to the street before they get level, walk out to meet them. He looks bad, bloody bad, a bullet through the centre of his stomach, he is conscious, deathly pale, his eyes are fixed on the bottle in my hand. Not supposed to give men with gut wounds drinks so they say, but how the hell can I say no to this man, I hand him the bottle, he gulps his fill, he says nothing but his eyes thank me. Men of D Company have been overrun by armoured vehicles and infantry. They are fighting desperately say the stretcher bearers, things are looking bad down there, they go on their way slowly towards the dressing station with their burden. I wait for twenty minutes or more to see if any more come up, but none do, I return to the cellar with my bottle.

Fit only for a contortionist this bed; can't just sit down on the edge and roll back into place, knock your brains out on the low ceiling if you tried. Must slide head first, face down in a low crouching position almost as though you intend to get on your knees as when a child to say your end of the day prayers; crawl into position flat on your belly, turn on your back, ignoring the bloody pack on your back if you can. Our rifles are tucked at our sides as we lie in the gloom, arms through rifle slings, a round ready up the spout, only the quick movement of the safety catch is required if we need to shoot fast. Tin hats shoved forward over our faces in case the roof falls in, drift away into sleep with the ease of babies as the crash of exploding shells and falling walls above gradually recedes into the background of our mind to disappear completely into the blesses nothingness of sleep.

The world has exploded! Jerked upright by the shock of the blow, a million stars shoot through my brain as my tin hat meets the ceiling just above my face, a split second of dazed nothingness. My body is already moving through the thick cloud of choking dust towards the crack of daylight in the darkness where there was none before. Climb through, run out and away, out into the open space of the road, the other lads are with me. Looking back at the house which was our haven we see that the room upstairs where we ate and rested has gone, it rests on the roof of the cellar with the rest of the heart of the house. The cellar has held the weight, has decided not to become our tomb; lost my bloody bottle of brandy though! The shell has ploughed through the roof, down into the centre of the house before exploding, its harvest rests on the stock of new cycles, they protrude from the rubble, bits of twisted metal. Return to the garage, check the gun and ammunition, all is well, we are still in business.

Strong enemy attack developing on A Company front; concentrated tanks and infantry coming our way fast. Orders received to open fire on Jerry as he moves into a range of six hundred yards. Outside the cycle shop an alley runs at right angles to the main road, from our gun site the last cottage that flanks this end of town stands about forty feet away, the alley runs straight for approximately eighty yards, at the end, a large grove of trees. Open fire at six hundred yards, the bombs sail over the wood like rain as we fall into the rhythm of feeding the gun; we fire in a frenzy of speed. My mind shuts out almost everything else other than the job at hand, almost, but not quite. My eyes see the explosion as a shell lands at the end of the alley, my ears tell of yet another one coming over and I know that it will fall in a measured distance which will bring it somewhere near us, we all know this but we cannot stop now, no time, our men down front need our fire. The shell lands on a cottage to our right ploughing its way deep inside. The cottage erupts outwards, our rhythm has not been broken.

A tug on the left side of my jaw; Jackson is standing facing me on the other side of the gun barrel, he is staring at me with a look of shocked horror. Something wet is running down my chin, his face as I watch is beginning to crumble, he is going to cry. I feel my chin, my hand comes away wet and red, work my jaw up and down, feels fine, I scream at him that I am alright, carry on firing. We pick up the lost rhythm, Jackson is alright now, he was expecting me to topple over, the spurt of blood looked worse to him than it really is. Other shells coming over but we know that they will fall behind us, they usually fire in creeping steps of about fifty feet between each shot, these won't bother us. We don't have to worry, at least not until they start their pattern again, we will have to play the guessing game again, make sure they have not changed the pattern just to fool us. Cease fire, return to the damaged cottages, rest until next time. The scratch on my jaw causes no trouble but it bleeds like a stuck pig, blood soaks the front of my blouse.

Hear that Edgars gun crew have been busy, they were told to give a hard-pressed D Company supporting fire, they attempted to reach them taking the road out of town, they were fascinated watching armour piercing shells bouncing off the road surface just in front of their truck as the German tank which was firing at them traversed its gun. Their fascination was rudely interrupted by a lone German machine gunner popping up out of a ditch at the side of the road just thirty feet in front of them, he stood with legs braced apart as he emptied his machine gun at his target, although he had point blank target and the element of surprise on his side he missed them completely. The lads stared at him in surprise as he ducked back out of sight. Stopping their truck they disembarked and fanned out in defensive positions. A Bren-gun carriers chance arrival on the scene saved them the job of hunting the German gunner, the carrier crew were happy to take on the job.

Unable to reach D Company due to tank shelling, their mortar now aids us on the Company A front, already they have hit one German tank, striking it with a bomb just forwards of its turret, the thing lies stationary and smoking, its companions are giving the spot a wide berth as they accelerate quickly round it. A Lance-Corporal wanders into our group as we relax, he understands we can do with some help. He is from the Transport Platoon but he has no transport left. Could we use him? Too true we can. I know the lad, good man to have around.

The air vibrates with the song of shells and mortar bombs travelling and exploding, bullets fly about in streams of white fire, houses are burning, smoke hangs over the town, you have to shout when you speak, telephone wires and other cables hang in low curves at different levels. We are told not to stand up on moving trucks as the unseen cable wires will slice our heads from our shoulders like a knife.

Urgent call from A Company, concentration of enemy tanks and armoured fighting vehicles immediately to their front. We mount the gun in the same position as before but the enemy is closer this time, the fall of our bombs must be observed to avoid hitting our own men. The Transport Corporal immediately volunteers to go forward through the trees to do this, another one of the lads wants to join him as a half-way-stage observer. Off they both go leaving two of us to work the gun, testing range five hundred yards, over goes the first shot, eyes fixed on the bottom of the lane waiting for someone to emerge and shout back the effect. Hell of a lot of shooting in the trees, small arms fire, dare not fire another round until I know where the first one went. Already I sweat for our men in the forwards positions wondering if I have hit any of them! Wait several minutes, the figure of an officer has stepped out from the cover of the trees, his arms urgently signal me not to fire any more, it's as I feared, too close I guess, wait a bit before we move. The amount of shooting in the trees worries me, I half expect to see a bloody German step out into the lane the shots are that close. Dismount the gun, move it under cover back towards A Company H.Q.

As I feared, Jerry had got within forty feet of our forward positions. Lots of crawling about in the grass by men on both sides, rifle shooting at close range, the Transport Corporal has been shot in the back, the mortar man has shrapnel in his arm, the Corporal is in a bad way. Only a counter charge led by the Company Sergeant Major has dislodged Jerry, our gun has lost yet another two good men.

Walk back to A Company H.Q. to see what's going on, have got to negotiate the ornamental archway on the way, it lies between us and H.Q. A German sniper has taken charge of it, he fires from the wide-open country below us somewhere, haven't been able to locate the bugger yet. Reach the arch, no good poking your nose round to see if the coast is clear, he will shoot the bloody thing off; he is a good shot. Sometimes you double up and fling yourself across the space, sometimes get back a bit to build up speed and streak across like a flash of light. You can go across any way you darn well fancy, but however fast you move you can be sure of one thing, he will get a shot in, usually he manages to spray you with brick dust. Yes, that's one bleeder we want to get!

Reach H.Q.; two men on the road outside, one man lies on the ground the upper muscles of his left arm have been blown away, Edgar kneels over him, frantically trying to stop the gushing blood with an inadequate field dressing. There had been a direct hit on the mortar, more wounded men are at the back of the house. Enter the house, another man lies in the passage, deathly white but conscious, his stomach is pitted with shrapnel. Out in the garden men lie about all over the place; one man walks about in a circle, a dazed look on his face, shrapnel pieces in his chest. An Artillery Officer doing observation duty is the worst casualty, he lies fully conscious, peppered from head to foot with shrapnel, only his eyes can move as they try to fight down the panic within. The black entrance hole of the German mortar bomb stares at you from the soft earth between the base plate and the tripod of the mortar, the barrel lies over at a crazy angle. Jesus Christ, they should all be dead - but for the softness of the earth they would be. One foot from the side of the gun runs a wide concrete path, their escape is unbelievable. A personal duel had developed between Edgar's mortar and a Jerry mortar, a shot in a million landing where it did, sending men flying feet through the air, two mortar men and two artillery men taken away wounded, we are now down to one effective Mortar Crew of four men.

Edgars face is a mess, got himself mixed up between a jar of petrol and an exploding shell, his face got covered in burning petrol, he looks an ugly bugger now. Huge bags of water blister hang from his face, his eyebrows and curly eyelashes have gone, his face is the colour of a lobster, he walks round with the upper buttons of his blouse undone. The collar and upper part of his blouse is turned inwards to keep them away from his skin, he can hardly even bear the air to touch it, but the stubborn so and so won't report to the medical, claims he can't, got to look after me he reckons!

A busy day, a rough day; shelling and mortar fire is diminishing as it gets darker, had a lot of casualties, managed to get the wounded off to Dunkirk. Good work done by the anti-tank and anti-aircraft guns, firing over open sights they have knocked out thirty tanks; gunners and guns however have been lost to the uncanny accuracy of the Jerry guns. A few fires still burn but most have died away to leave drifting smoke. Some traffic has passed through town today but not as much as usual, suspect the roads are being cut somewhere.

Understand that some of our kilted friends passed through town, called into our Drapers shop looking for a change of underpants, they had to make do with pretty laced female stock which can only add to their plumage!

No grub. Having trouble with the cooking fires we understand, haven't been able to keep them alight due to shell concussion, a fine thing; got to feed ourselves again I suppose. A quiet night, sleep comes in fits and starts; eyes pierce the darkness wondering what they are up to out there. Rifle companies send out patrols every few hours but little contact is made; we can only wait and see what tomorrow brings.

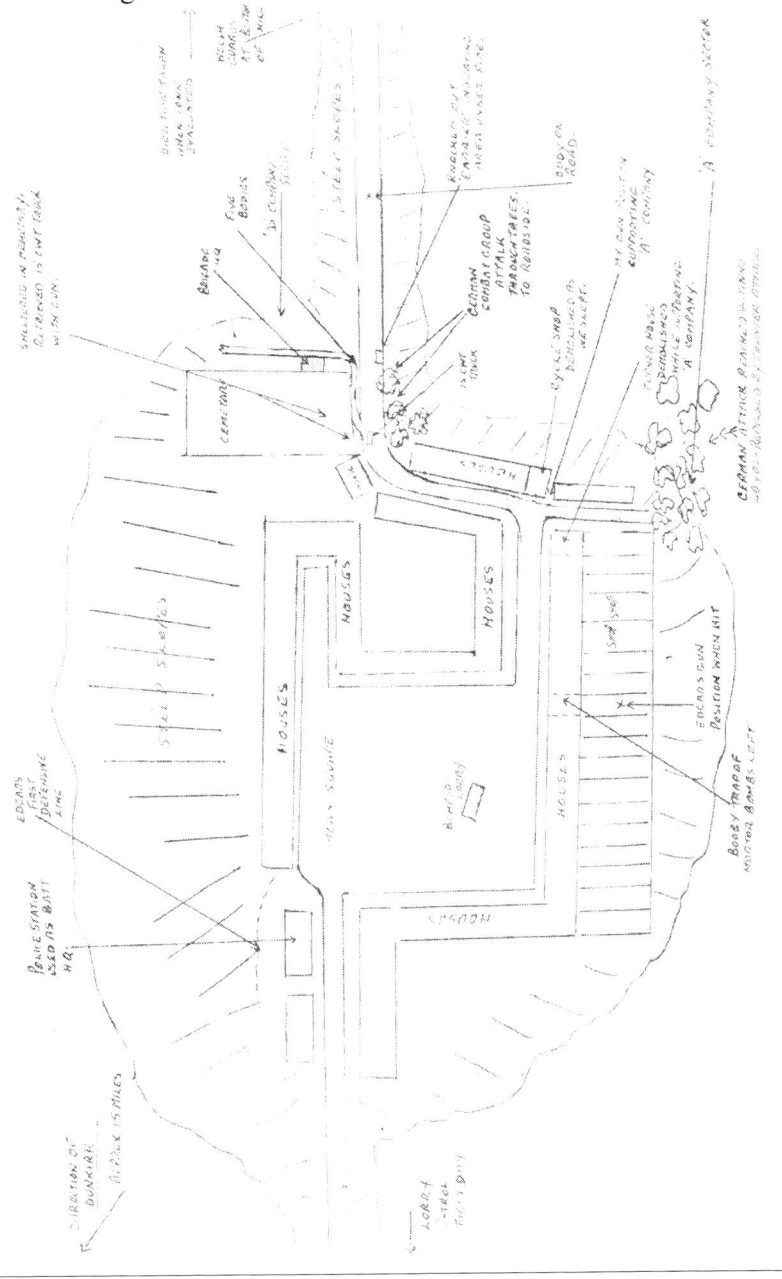

The ironmongers stock is taking a bashing on the quiet; anyone this end of town who requires a pot for some reason just leaps across the snipers little bit of territory, enters the shop, makes his choice and leaps back across the sniper sights again. Must be driving the bloody bloke crazy with frustration, plenty of near misses but he has not hit anyone yet, not at this spot anyway!

Dawn is announced with enemy gunfire; shells fall on to the town adding to the rubble that already lies in heaps. Ammunition is getting short, got to get some from somewhere if we are to stay in business. Told that a stock of ammunition has been located but I will have to fetch it, it lies out of town; a transport of Welsh Guards have it, they wait for me to collect some from them at the bottom of the long hill on the south side of town. Sounds reasonable, if the Guards are down there it must be safe. My instructions are clear and simple: drive out of the town, past the cemetery, as you pass the cemetery you will see a knocked out carrier on the right hand side of the road, head past it, go like hell for the bottom of the hill because once you pass the carrier you are under fire the whole way! I like the nice conversational style they use when they tell you these things after you have already said that you are prepared to go. Need a couple of men to help load up the bombs and a driver for the truck. Two of the lads volunteer, all we want now is the driver.

A fifteen hundredweight truck arrives, a canvas hood on the back. The driver, a little man, usually drives the C.O.'s staff car about, he has no work at the moment, he also has no choice in the matter, the poor little man has been detailed into it. Not sure if he is happy about it or not, he says nothing; tell him what we've got to do, the way I tell it, it sounds simple, a straight forward sort of run, just down the hill and up again, it's only the last bit about being under fire that makes him blink and makes me stutter.

Load the lads into the back, they lie flat on the floor, I sit in the front with the driver, hope he can drive. Speed is what we need on this trip, speed; no intention of hanging about. A short distance to get out of town, turn into the straight stretch, past the cemetery, the carrier is just ahead. The driver's foot is standing on the accelerator; we roar past the carrier, out into the open. The blokes with guns that might shoot at us are on the right hand side of the road I am told, that puts the driver between them and me. A half safe sort of feeling creeps over me until I remember that he is the only bugger that can driver between the lot of us - he is the last one that we need to be hit.

Looking afresh at the sheer drops on each side of the road, Jesus, we would sail out into space like a bloody rocket!

The old Bedford truck is giving us all she has as we hurtle down the steep grade, taking a dead straight course across the bends, almost half way, something ahead in the centre of the road. In the seconds warning he was given somehow the driver has somehow managed to miss the object by inches, it flashes past under my gaze. God, a body, headless and legless; British! Not aware of any shots at us so far, don't know if anything has happened at the back of the truck though. We reach the bottom, large lorries stand at the side of the road, chaps in battledress mill around them. We pull up with a screech of brakes, turn the truck round ready for the return trip; our arrival is expected, men stand ready to pass over as many bombs as we can carry. The springs groan under the weight, stacked up in walls on each side of the truck, they might offer some sort of cover for the lads on the return trip. Ok, fine, we have the stuff, all we've got to do is get back with it. We came down like a bat out of hell but we were empty then.

Get well back on the flat surface of the road for a good run up, the driver builds up speed with a determination that leaves nothing to be desired by any of us. A good start as we hit the upgrade hard, quite well up before the old dear reminds us that after all she is only a 15 cwt, not a bloody ammunition carrier. She is losing speed but pulling her heart out, what more could you ask? I study the deceptively empty country below us as we climb higher, I now sit on the right hand side, I shield the driver. Past the body, half way up, still no shots; three quarters of the way up, beginning to thank our lucky stars when a string of beads cuts across the front of the windshield, a stream of white fire, looks pretty. Bloody tracers, about two inches in front of the two tiny square bits of glass that act as windscreens the stream of fire travels with us keeping the same distance in front as the gunner traverses. Yes, he is doing the correct thing on a moving target, let's hope he keeps moving, if he stops traversing for the time it takes to blink an eye I am dead! Nowhere to duck, nothing to do, just sit and look at them spellbound. The driver has made no comment as they pass in front of his eyes, he stares grimly ahead, every nerve stretched to get speed out of the truck, his reaction is as though the string of tracers are not there. Eyes strain for sight of the carrier, I cannot believe that the gunner has not realised that he travels a shade too fast on his traverse, that we will not run into his fire as he hopes, but, he hasn't realised it yet and the carrier is in sight. The driver is willing us along, his mouth open as he shouts, we have passed the carrier in a rush of speed, we have made it!

Slow down as we reach the cemetery, turn into town, reach A Company H.Q., get down, my legs feel like water. Shouts and bellows coming from the back of the truck; Christ, they have been hit. Rush around to the back and peer in; gone are the nicely stacked piles of bomb cases, instead, a tangled mass of bomb cases, arms, legs, and heads meet our gaze. The twisting and turning on our trip up the hill had tipped over the load beneath which are the men almost flattened by the weight but otherwise unhurt.

The little driver leaves us, drives away in his truck, a great little man, cool as a cucumber, we wish him luck.

Relax a bit, catch up with the gossip. Bren-gun carriers have been having fun, one of them caught about fifty Jerrys resting up in a field, charged through the hedgerow and shot them down, took them completely by surprise. I see the Padre running down the street, a cheery wave and a smile from him as he passes; there goes my idea of a true man of God. He's busier than most of us I would guess, burying the dead of this town. A few more tanks have been knocked out today but most of the anti-tank and anti-aircraft guns have been destroyed or are almost out of ammunition. Food is getting scarce, difficult to find anything to eat but there is enough drink about to get every man in town under the table with ease.

Enter a badly bombed house, on the scrounge; I stand in the lounge, I can look straight up to the blue sky through three floors, a whole family wiped out in this room. Two other lads are having a look round, searching the debris for anything of use. A sideboard is up against the wall, I pull open the drawer, it's empty except for a miniature gun which lies in the centre of a dark green felt lining. An automatic, gleaming nickel plate, pearl handle, made to slip into a female handbag; I lay it in the palm of my hand, close my hand, it all but disappears from sight it's so small. A scream of anguish from behind me; I turn, startled. The figure of a woman stands in the centre of the room, a very old woman dressed completely in black, a heavy veil covers her head, face and shoulders, snow white hair gleams through the net, her face is a masked shadow. Her arms are stretched upwards to the sky, fingers claw at the heavens, her face too is tilted upwards as she moans her suffering and anguish to God.

These alien beings desecrate the tomb of her dead family they disturb her pilgrimage to the shrine of her grief. My blood has turned to ice; the pretty little gun drops from my fingers back into the drawer, myself and the others run from her sight, out of the ruins, I feel sick with shame.

The shells are easing off, soon to stop, they bombard us with softer weapons for a change. Now they are trying persuasion, leaflets are floating down from the sky like autumn leaves. A nicely executed map is illustrated showing us completely surrounded. They tell us not to waste our time, resistance is pointless, might as well lay down our arms. Must have heard that we are out of toilet paper. We thank them from the bottom of our hearts, but whom the hell do they think they are dealing with?

As darkness falls there is a phone call for me, it's the major, second in command of the Battalion. Would I send over one shot from the mortar every fifteen minutes through the night just to let the bastards know that we are still awake and waiting? To be sure I will. A long night, shots at random out into the blackness of the night, they fall with a flash of brilliant flame here, there and everywhere. Apart from our monotonous cough small arms fire stabs the darkness in bursts from all directions. Sure thing, we are surrounded, but in general a peaceful night.

A new day is heralded with heavy shelling and bombing, heavier shells, shells that penetrate deeper, do a lot more damage, make a lot more noise. The Major is one of the days early casualties, killed as a shell ploughed through Battalion H.Q., a bad start to the day with many casualties. A grandstand seat of enemy tanks moving about, infantry moving into position, fresh gun positions being prepared, we haven't an effective heavy gun left that can reach the enemy.

Orders to report to Brigade H.Q. Brigade H.Q.? Didn't know we had one! Where the hell is it? "Go to the cemetery, follow the sunken track, it will take you there." Nothing else to do, will see if we can find it but first we need a truck and a driver to carry us. Another 15 cwt truck but this time without a canvas hood on the back; at the wheel our old friend of yesterday, the little driver. He smiles nervously at seeing us again so soon but says nothing. Load up the gun and ammunition, Edgar and the crew on the back, we set sail. Turn at the cycle shop, pass between the tall terraced houses, turn at Dead Horse corner as we call it for obvious reason, fifty yards along the road is the cemetery. Halt the vehicle opposite the entrance to the cemetery, no need for the crew to dismount until I have found the H.Q. and found out what they want of us, it's can't be nice, whatever it is.

Stand on the road and survey the cemetery and its layout. Immediately at my feet is a cobbled driveway which leads straight into the cemetery, it goes down at an angle of about forty-five degrees and is about fifteen feet long. To the side of the slope on the right hand side is a dirt track which leads downwards then bears right along the face of a six foot high hedgerow into a gully which is formed by the hedge and an earth embankment which runs up the road. Ok, all I've got to do it seems is follow the dirt track alongside the hedge, somewhere along its length should be Brigade H.Q. The knocked out carrier which marks the stretch of road under fire is further along the road about eighty yards but here it is safe. I leave the lads laid out in the back of the truck relaxing in the sun.

Follow the track across the front of the hedge, the leaves brush my left shoulder as I move along, the embankment is on my immediate right; look right, my eyes meet the back of the heads of a section of riflemen, eight in number, they face across the road, their eyes level with its surface. I too as I walk can just manage to see across the roads surface, approximately forty feet across and on the other side are trees and bushes, all is peaceful as I pass them, the riflemen look relaxed and comfortable. The hedge turns at left angles to the road, the track follows it, I follow the track. The hedge now runs the depth of the cemetery, probably a hundred and fifty yards. I can see a low roof top ahead peeping over the top of the hedge, no other dwelling in sight, that must be it.

The leaves still brush my left shoulder as I walk, on my right low wide open country sweeps away, my eyes scan it for trouble, nothing in sight, I could be alone in the world. Halfway along the hedgerow is a scruffy looking bungalow with a doorway round the side. A wide open door, I stand by the door and peer in. Place is full of top brass! Some sit at tables studying maps as big as tablecloths which are spread out over the rough tables, some walk around, others talk in groups. Staff Sergeants flash about the place like busy little bees, some of them glance at me standing by the door as they pass to and fro. Puzzled frowns crease their brows but they have no time to ask why the hell I hang about. Others look at me without seeing me at all, they are so busy, immersed in their own thoughts. My thoughts are busy too, I wonder why the hell I should hang about here for about fifteen minutes after having been sent for, could be getting my head down instead of wasting time here! At last, a Staff Sergeant can't stand the sight of me propped up against the door frame any longer; he changes direction as he walks across the room, heading for me he asks, "What the hell do you want". I tell him that I want nothing, what the hell do they want? Off he goes into the back of the room out of sight, a few minutes later he returns, "You're not wanted now, return to your unit." With pleasure! Was probably a suicide job anyway!

Back on the track, retracing my steps back to the lads, they will be pleased to hear that there is nothing special to do. My right shoulder now brushes the hedgerow and the wide open country now on my left still looks empty of trouble. It looks beautiful and peaceful as such country scenes should. I walk along completely at peace with the world, warm sun on my face, rifle swung over my shoulder, perfectly relaxed, prepared to love everybody.

Bullets passing overhead, a couple of feet I guess; they come straight down the track from my front, to high to do me any harm, probably spent ones, not aimed aim me. Nothing to worry about, plenty of shots going off around, but nothing to do with me; I proceed, perfectly relaxed, still at peace with the world. Approach the corner of the hedge where the track turns, a couple of feet to go, rifle still slung over my shoulder. Turn the corner, stop dead in my track; at my feet lie five dead men. Spend a second staring at them in surprise, loosely thrown into a heap they lie so still; my eyes sweep the bank where the rifle section had been, nobody there. Up on to the road where the truck stands in the open, streams of machine gun tracer bullets fill the air around it, seven, eight, nine streams of tracer, but no sign of the lads.

Tracers pass my nose by six inches, leaves and twigs sting my face; the hedge is a good three feet thick, slow work for a man in full equipment to break his way through, I go through it as though it is butter. A tangled heap of arms and legs down on the lower level of the cemetery, on my feet, leaping for the cover of the nearest tombstone as I un-sling my rifle, gain shelter behind the tombstone but it's too close to the hedge. I must double back from the stone a bit to get room to fire if they come through the hedge; I move back from stone to stone, twenty, thirty, forty feet, that's better, can nail them if they come through now. Look around the cemetery, Edgar and the other lads are safe behind their individual tomb stones, they wave their presence to me, I breathe a sigh of relief at the sight of them, especially at Edgars' silly grin.

About eight Germans, a combat troop that have penetrated the trees, each man with a light machine gun, tracers flood through the hedge to ricochet off the stones to hum away like angry bees. The hedge is too thick to see through, they fire blindly into the cemetery hoping to hit us.

Getting browned off sitting here; doesn't look as though they are coming through the hedge, but I am worried about the truck stuck up there on the road, got to get it out somehow, can't afford to lose the gun. Study the situation: to get the truck out we have to have a driver, only one driver here, our little friend, he will have to come. If we line up behind the metal wheel we might be able to reach the truck that way, a quick reverse for fifty yards, and we will be safe. I shout my proposal to Edgar and the other lads, they will give what covering fire is required while my little friend and I tackle the job, afterwards they will retire through the rear of the cemetery, through back gardens, through the houses, back to the safety of town.

I join the little man behind his tombstone, explain how we can probably do it, he merely nods his understanding, superb little chap! He says that the ignition key is in the dash, just needs a turn. I will go first and he will follow. We leap from stone to stone, gain the foot of the cobbled slope, it looks a bloody long way up to the truck. Line myself up with the rear wheel, tracers fly over and under the vehicle, the driver tells me that he is ready to start. Doesn't talk much this lad, but when he does he is to the point, bloody rushing me now!

We move off up the slope, inching our bodies, the driver is almost up my arse he is so close, but I don't blame him, it's the only cover he has. We are more than half way up but that was the easy part, well below the surface of the road; ahead the fun bit, gradually inch up to road level. From here on they may spot us, the last six feet to the wheel, can see the tracers leaving the bushes at the other side of the road, know they have not seen us yet, the tracers still pass over our heads by a good foot. The wheel looks smaller as we reach it, smaller than it did from back in the cemetery, but the steel feels good to the touch. Inch upwards on to my feet, keep the body arched forward to take advantage of the cover of the trucks side wall, keep the bloody head down. The driver is on his knees at my feet, slowly he is moving to his feet, balancing on his toes, crouched, he is ready for his vital spring forward. I must now leap forward from my standing position to the door-less cab, reach in, turn the ignition key, if it starts the driver must leap into his seat and reverse; fine. If she doesn't start, we have a hell of a leap back down to the cemetery!

I look down at the driver, we dare only speak with the eyes, his face is calm enough, his eyes tell me that he is ready to go when I am; wait a second, wait for a lull in the stream of tracer that passes under the truck, we have to cross that space, once I move we are both committed openly, they will be able to see us, rifle slung on my shoulder out of the way of my hands, ready to leap, the driver does not carry a rifle, he is free of that burden, eyes rivet on the tracers. Now. A frantic leap forward, the mind is filled only with the picture of the key, eyes search the dashboard, there my fingers turn the thing the way the driver has instructed, instantly the beautiful, magnificent Bedford coughs into life. I turn looking for the driver but he is on his feet and moving forward, I grab him, helping his leap as I lift him into his seat like a sack of potatoes, fear has given me the strength of Sampson. His practiced hand smashes the gear in to reverse, his boot stands on the accelerator; we shoot backwards at a terrific speed, I hang on by the skin of my teeth, backwards into the shelter of the first house, we are safe.

We halt and catch our breath, we grin stupidly at each other in sheer relief and surprise that we have done it, that we still have the gun; wait a few minutes, Edgar and the rest of the lads burst through the front door of a nearby house, all are safe, climb aboard the truck, head back to A Company H.Q.

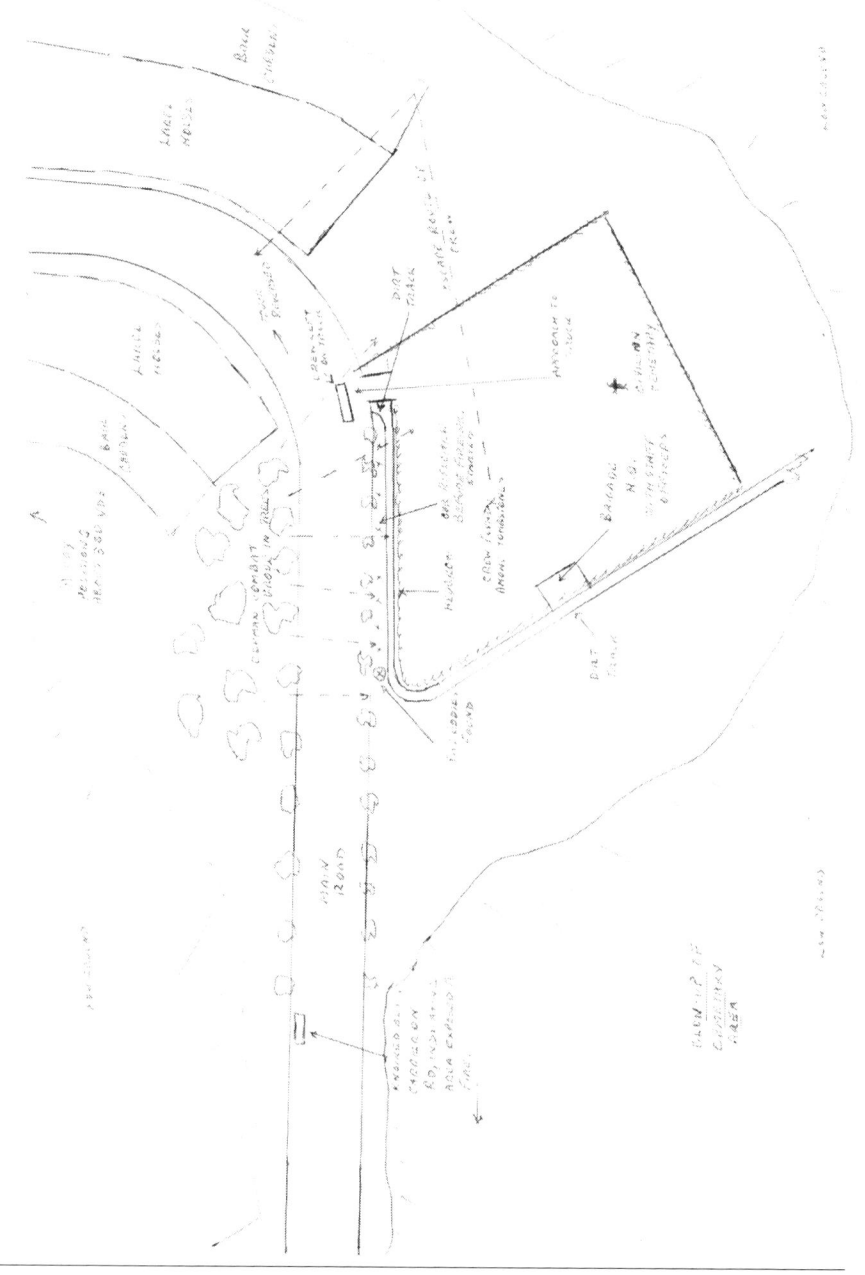

Shots still stream across the road in to the now empty cemetery as we leave, report the intrusion to A Company who will clear them out. Unload the ammunition and gun into our storage room of H.Q., we say farewell to our wonderful little driver, he leaves us once again to return to the peace of normal shelling.

Talk of fifth columnist activities going on in town, have noticed nothing myself, they reckon one has been caught and shot at the rear of Battalion H.Q. Report reached town of something like seventy of our lads being killed after being captured by Jerry, report brought in by a witness, the men were shut in a barn and killed by hand grenades, our resolve not to give in to them if possible is strengthened by a deep burning anger.

Orders to fire on an area, part woodland, part meadows, Jerries seen moving there. Set the mortar up in the back garden of H.Q., open fire at twelve hundred yards range, soon a rain of bursting bombs carpet the area as the ever hungry gun barrel is fed as fast as we can go. A lorry has broken from the cover of the woodland out into the open, he is trying to make a run for it, but it disappears in to a massive sheet of flame as it explodes; it has moved into the path of one of our bombs, black objects fly out of the cloud of smoke as its load of ammunition disintegrates. Cease fire, relax, but watch our front.

Spot the German armoured car beak from cover about six hundred yards away, he travels too fast across the open stretch of our mortar to bear; it travels swiftly, suddenly an invisible hand strikes it a violent blow, see how it tosses upwards in to the air to roll several times before coming to rest like a kids smashed toy. Our remaining anti-tank guns are busy.

Empty bottles to be collected, fill them with petrol, use them against the tanks that will surely get into the town next time they attack. If we throw these bottles and follow up with a grenade that will do the trick, a piece of cake. Darkness falls, everybody is watchful, staring into the darkness, bags of weight built up during the day against us, when are they going to use it? probably with the coming of the dawn. The town is bright with the flames of burning buildings resulting from the days shelling; must watch where you stand, a backcloth of flame gives a perfect silhouette to the ambitious sniper.

New orders come through; we are to move from this place, held it long enough, now we can cut our way to the coast if we can, leave in two hours, march with light weapons. A riot of destruction, trucks, lorries, heavy guns, all the stores and ammunition that cannot be taken with us has to be destroyed, we are to leave them nothing. Mortar sights are smashed to a pulp under the butts of our rifles, remove the firing pins from the barrels of the guns, bury them deep in the vegetable garden in separate place. Start removing the cartridges from the tail units of the bombs, using our jack-knives is a slow job, not the correct tool for this job. Christ, we will never be able to get them all out in time; have to set up some sort of booby trap instead, can't leave them intact without trying something. The Company stores truck is outside the window, they prepare its destruction in the quickest possible way, two or three cans of petrol under the truck, a trail of petrol leads to a safe distance, ignite it, the tiny flame races over the ground to meet the cans, a terrific explosion as the truck erupts skywards in a sheet of flame to join the many other fires. Help ourselves to ammunition, we load ourselves up with three hundred rounds apiece, I have a fear of running out of ammunition.

Men are beginning to muster out in the street, shall have to do something about the mortar bombs now that there is no danger of our lads wondering in on the stuff. Bombs are stacked up in the neat pile of cases, remove the top layer of cases, pull the pin from the grenade, lie the grenade tenderly in the groove between two bombs, finger holds down the spring lever, lay a case of three bombs on to the lever, thirty pound weight now holds it down, remove finger, replace the top layer, it all looks very innocent to the first German that tries to move them, I am now ready to go.

Out into the street, join the long line of men that is forming up to move through the night in single file, each man to keep in contact with the man in front of him, lose contact, no one will stop to search for you, the line must not be broken if we are to survive. First we go to a place called Watou, other British troops are there, join up with them, then head for the coast. As we wait in the street bullets start flying about our heads wildly, every-body ducks; a store of rifle ammunition has gone up in a nearby house and as the bullets are caught in the flames they explode like fire crackers.

Morale is high, we have had a good go at them, done our best, can't do more. If we get over this lot we shall see the boat they say, but let's see what tomorrow brings, meanwhile I feel as if I could eat a horse and sleep for a bloody week.

We are moving; the men snake in a long line ahead, past the snipers archway, he can stick it up his arse, it's his! We go past the remains of the cycle shop, between the tall terraced houses, follow the road as it turns right at dead horse corner, pass between the cemetery and the grove of trees. I peer down to the sunken track as I pass thinking of the five dead men that must still be lying down there, but it's too dark to see, the night is as black as pitch. It is now 2230 hours, a time when all decent people should be thinking of going to bed. Past the broken down Bren-gun carrier marking the road under fire, our backs are now to the burning town, down the slope of the hill into the blackness below.

We walk off the cobble on to the dirt at the side, it's silent for the boots; stop that rattle of equipment, drift through the night, touch the man in front every few minutes to make sure that he is there, no talking, if you must swear do it in a whisper. Moving out of town on the Lille road, Dunkirk lies at our backs. I wonder about this fact for a while, would rather have headed straight for the coast, but I expect the officers know what they are doing. I hope so! A few bursts of shots stab the darkness from Jerry lines but this is not surprising. Nearing the bottom of the hill we are now in utter and total darkness. I look back up at the town, a farewell glance, it stands high, a flaming torch, a beacon that men can see for many miles, some men of the Gloucesters are still up there firing guns into the night to cover our stealthy withdrawal. They will stay to the end in an attempt to fool Jerry, make him think that the place is still held, the rest of us are trying our luck.

All kinds on this trip, men of the Gloucesters, Artillery, East Riding Yeomanry, Oxfords and a few other miscellaneous units. My mind is quite relaxed, not worried, the possibility of a boat is a fantastic dream that might come off, but it's only a dream as yet; place it at the back of my mind nice and handy to digest now and then, but don't let it fill my mind completely. A lot of Jerries stand in the way, get over them first, then dream, just keep my eyes on the bloody man in front, that's all I've got to do for now, that's all I've got time for!

Rough ground under foot, we are still moving out into open country, a light touch on my back as Edgar checks that I am still there, I check the man in front, he is there, ok. Many long silent halts, unexplainable, standing so still and quiet in the darkness. I get impatient at these halts, want to press on through the night, not waste the precious mantle of blackness, but someone is leading us through this black world by compass, his is a terrible responsibility, he has got to get it right, my job is but to follow. A whispered word is passed back from man to man "Forward", we have to make bloody sure the man behind us has got it clear before we move off, but we must hang on to the man in front for a second, don't let him out of touch, don't break the line.

A blazing farmhouse, a torch of flame, all on its own out here in the blackness, lit deliberately of course, lit by the bastards to watch our progress, they know we are out, I feel it in my bones. Trees stand out in stark silhouette against the flames as I feel we must do to watching eyes; walking in single file as we do they probably count us as we pass. Seeing the flames I feel that we are in for trouble. Back into the utter blackness, stumble through unseen hedges, branches sweep my face, a frantic endless touching of the man in front, though a fence, get caught on wire, rip myself free, no delay tolerated.

Another fire, part of a dead village; we skirt the fire and move on. A sudden unexpected and frightening noise as our boots strike the hard surface of a road, I am appalled at the noise made by so many boots in the stillness of the night. A shot from up front; we hit the surface of the road with our bellies as tracer bullets stream over our heads. Several bursts, then silence returns; we lie still and wait. A whispered "Ok, on your feet, MOVE." The machine gun has been silenced by someone's bayonet but an Officer has died to free the way for us. Somewhere out in the darkness our carriers are trying to spearhead the way for us, they are trying to do the work of tanks on our behalf.

A whispered word passes back down the line rapidly, the line has been broken by the shooting back on the road, nothing can be done about it now, we can only press on. Our strength has been about halved; two parties now stumble through the night, contact has been lost. Not quite so dark now, a greyness in the sky, solid but blurred shapes of trees begin to emerge.

My legs are sodden from the knees down with morning dew. Not much feeling left in my body, no emotions of any kind in my mind, my thoughts dwell only on the anticipated bursts of fire that will come from somewhere sooner or later. Not particularly worried about it, just want to get to grips with it, get it over one way or the other. First daylight, can see where the hell we tread now, trouble is, so can Jerry. Walking alongside a wide deep ditch, a long ribbon of men in front, a few behind, the line was broken not far behind us in the night.

The sudden roar of a low flying aircraft from out of nowhere; it swoops low along the line of men from the rear to the front, just above our heads. Some silly bugger shouts "Don't look up, he will see the whites of your faces". The bloody thing almost took our tin hats off. He looks familiar, looks like our friend from the canal in Belgium; he swoops upwards from his run over us to climb high into the air heading directly to our front to disappear from view. The ditch ends, an expanse of flat wide open country ahead of us, we head straight across it, there is no cover. The front of the file moves to the left into the open, men fall into place to walk shoulder to shoulder. We at the end of the file finish up on the extreme right flank of the long line that now marches forward to its front. It reminds me of a line of Grenadiers going into battle. I've got a nasty feeling that this approach is not quite right, not these days.

Edgar is the last man on the right flank, I am the second, Jackson of the Mortars is third, then there is an Officer. The rest of the men are unknown to me, something like four hundred men stretch away on our left across the plain, the Colonel has the centre position. A farmhouse on our extreme left front, a small grove of trees on the extreme right front, we shall pass between them, about two hundred yards to go to reach them. Order passed along the line to extend the ranks, open out, we stretch out to the right flank as the men do so.

About a mile away to our front is a belt of trees running from left to right ending where low, grass covered hills take over on the right. Peeping over the tops of the trees is a church spire which marks our destination, or at least our first stop, Watou, British troops there, join up with them and then make tracks for the coast. Nobody has much to say; mostly it's a walk of silence, most of us know that it's been too bloody easy so far. Our eyes search the country for flashes of field-grey uniforms, they won't let go of us this easy.

Drawing level with the farmhouse and the grove of trees; the trees are about eighty feet to Edgars right, he says that he thinks he should pop over and see if there are any Jerries in the grove, Jesus, he is looking for trouble! He is fighting mad this morning, I think he has been taking a nip out of his water bottle during the night and I know it carries something stronger than water. However, I persuade him to stay with the main body, I believe that there is strength in number on this sort of lark, at least that's what I tell him, but in actual fact I know that if he was to go wandering over there I would have to go along to look out for him and I don't feel a bloody bit brave this morning. Rifles held loosely across the front of our bodies at 'High-Port', just past the farmhouse and trees, shots ring out on the left. The whole line stops dead in its tracks. Many rifles went off then. Who fired? Wait; don't move. Nobody has hit the deck; they must have been our shots.

Can move forward, not too fast, keep well spaced out. Word comes down the line that a couple of German motor-cyclists have been shot, they came round a corner in the road straight into our lads, shot to pieces before they could turn their machines, bloody shock should have killed them anyway I would have thought, it certainly would have killed me.

Figures of men running across our front in the middle distance, they run with their backs to us, running up the nearest of the low hills, look like Germans. Somebody from the centre of the line shouts "See, they are running away from us". I'm not so sure, they could be running to their bloody guns couldn't they; these bastards don't run, not with the stuff they have got!

A steady pace forward, more than half way to the belt of trees, some movement can be seen in the area. An order comes along the line for the flanks to slow up, going too fast, fall back, get the line straight. Looking along the line I can see it's true. The line is very much bow shaped; we shorten step to let the centre catch up but still keep moving. We cross a narrow road, back on to a dead flat field of young seedlings, a ditch ahead, the line is still bent. We reach the ditch, Edgar is the first man to reach it, a high wide jump, he has landed on the other side. I take off as he lands, in mid air I see Edgars right leg move forward into his first stride, as his legs part, tracers cut between them passing under his crutch. I have changed direction in mid air, am now down in the ditch, Edgar lands with a thud beside me, he is unhurt. The shots came from the left front, other guns have joined in, all hell has broken loose.

Six of us are in the ditch, everyone else is pinned down in open field; behind us screams fill the air as men are hit. I raise my head to see where the Jerry guns are, the banks of the ditch dances as the tracers tear in about our heads. Try again, more shots fill the air. Can see nothing but a stretch of soil that rises upwards from the ditch for about four feet to meet and early morning blue sky, eyes rivet on the limited skyline expecting to see it filling with German Infantry at any second. There's six of us in front of all the others; Bloody Hell! Take stock of what we have, one officer with a revolver, Edgar, Jackson, one stranger and me all have rifles, there's another man without any weapons at all, don't know who he is, looks like a Company Officer type.

Moans from behind us, three men lie four feet away from the edge of the ditch, they have been hit but are still alive. One cries for water, another for his mother, we try to get them in by reaching backwards extending the arm to pull, fingers cannot reach, tracers immediately sing about our heads flinging chunks of soil into our faces. The bullets hit the three men, they grow silent, the moans are heard no more.

The ditch to our left runs straight for about fifty feet to take a sharp bend to our front; to our right the ditch runs for about eighty yards, at the end, a low hill overlooks it, rolling open country can be seen beyond and a clump of trees probably two miles away. Have seen nothing of Jerry yet, cannot raise my head to look; screams and moans from the men laid out on the billiard table behind us fill our senses. We can do nothing to help them, can see nothing to fire at yet. The Officer has said nothing, he sits silently on the floor of the ditch.

Mortar bombs coming over, they land behind us among the men. We mortar men know quite well what they will do to the men lying on the open ground. Jesus Christ, the Officer is standing up, tracers wrap themselves around his neck, we wait for him to drop; after a few seconds he gets down again, muttering, "My God, they have surrendered". He takes no notice of us but speaks to himself.

Tank engines starting up to our front, shouts of "Tanks!" from behind us.

A shot from inside the ditch, the Officer is slumped on the ground, his revolver lies near.

Must take a look to the rear, see what the situation is. A quick half stand, the immediate response of tracers miss me to churn up the soil at my elbow to race back across the bodies of the three men lying behind. Yes, it is true; the plain is dotted with white handkerchiefs tied to bayonets; they are getting shot to pieces, they have had to give in.

Listen to the tank engines to the front as they approach, my heart turns to ice. Where will they cross this ditch, for cross it they must to reach the lads behind. My eyes search left although I already know that it is not the way to go. Eyes search right, that's the only way, but wait, up there on the top of the grassy hill, a bloody German! He comes over the brow of the hill walking upright, looking down to the ground at his feet, in his right hand there is a light machine gun which he carries by the tiny handle above the barrel, looks as though he hasn't a care in the world, he's about two hundred yards away. He is selecting a spot to fire from, walking around like a fussy dog before it settles. Quickly; he is heading back towards the skyline of the hill. I take aim, as I do so he drops to the ground and nestles himself comfortably behind the skyline, his head and shoulders can clearly be seen together with his gun as he settles it into his shoulder, he directly overlooks the length of the ditch.

Take careful aim, the barrel of my rifle rests on Edgars shoulder, pull the trigger. A shout of anguish from Edgar, the muzzle was too close to his ear, he is deafened. The German has gone, don't believe for one moment that I have hit him, not that good a shot, probably a near miss, but he has gone, the danger has been removed for the present.

Tanks sound dreadfully close now, the squeal of their tracks fill my brain, the roar of the engines sound just about on top of us. My eyes strain at the limited skyline searching for the first glimpse of the thing towering above. Which way do we jump? Will there be time before their guns open up? My ears strain at the guessing game, we are going to die, we know it, I say to myself "God help me" and I am immediately disgusted with myself for saying, now I choose to ask favours.

Going a bit to the left, my breath has stopped as the last moment arrives; it's to the left, there across the ditch, thirty feet to the left, a big bloody tank stands stationary across the ditch; a large white cross painted on its side. A man stands half way out of the turret, dressed in black, headphones over a soft hat, a revolver in his hand which he is waving about wildly in the air as he shouts in English "Stand up". He has his back to us, he shouts to the men behind us, he has not seen us; we freeze into the side of the ditch. We could blow his bloody head off easy, tempted to do so, but if we do his gunner will probably fire on to the white handkerchiefs thinking it has come from them, best let him go. The tank moves back among the men to our rear, firing has stopped not that the tanks have reached us, we lie quietly for a few minutes our eyes fixed to our left where the tank had been. Men are jumping the ditch, our men, they run towards Jerry lines, the tanks are rounding them up like sheepdogs.

The man without a weapon is moving, he is going to stand up, I pull him back down and ask him what the hell he is doing; he says that he is going to give in. I point out that if he stands up he will give us all away, he says that if they catch him trying to escape they will shoot him - I tell him that if he stands up *I* will shoot him! With my rifle pointed at his guts he considers my proposition, he looks into my eyes and can see that I will if I have to. He decides that he will not stand up, he will come with us for a break to our right, try and get into the grove of trees that we can see across country about two miles away. I remove the map and binoculars from the body of the Officer, pick up his revolver, tuck the map into the front of my blouse, binoculars round my neck, give the revolver to the unarmed man, we are ready to try our luck.

Head to the right, crawl like slugs for about one hundred yards, across our front another ditch. This ditch is deeper, full of black muddy water, the banks have tall reeds growing in each side, step into the muck, it comes up to my knees, can stand with a slight stoop. Decide that we had better travel as light as possible, tell the lads to dump all equipment except their belts, bayonets, and cotton bandoliers of ammunition. Pouches, packs, respirators and straps are pushed deep into the mud out of sight. Bend low, proceed slowly, silently, don't disturb the reeds. Sixty, eighty yards, the ditch ends up slap against the road; no tunnel or drainpipe only a shallow dry ditch which runs alongside the road.

Got to cross this road but not here, too close to the Jerries; can't turn back, must take the shallow ditch, at least it runs in the right direction. I lead the way into it, followed by Edgar, Jackson and the other two men; slow, cautious moves, feel much more exposed here. Forty, fifty yards, Christ, the ditch is getting shallower, another twenty yards and it starts to disappear into the flatness of the meadow. We're stuck, can't go any further, can't got back. Can't go across the road yet, it is too open, one man might make it, but not five.

Nothing to do but lie still, hope we are not seen, wait for darkness, what's the time, five thirty am, bloody hell, some wait! Tired, starved, and completely buggered, I tell the men to sleep, I will keep watch, but I don't I fall asleep as well despite my best resolve.

A noise, a lorry approaching the road; I turn my head slightly to get the maximum vision up the bank of the ditch. About two feet of soil then a sea of blue sky broken only by bayonets of short grass. I peer back at the lads, Edgar and two others are awake their tense eyes stare at me, nothing to say, just flatten into the dirt, hope the lorry passes. It's almost level now, there, it is past in a flash. My ears strain for the sound of brakes being applied or a slowing up of its speed but it speeds on its way. I had seen nothing of it as it passed, worried about the difference in elevation for a while but too tired to work anything out, just lie dead still, nothing else to do.

Glance backwards and find myself looking directly at a German soldier up on the brow of the grassy hill. He too is roaming about with a light machine gun in his hand, if he turns this way he will look directly down on us. Edgar is awake and has spotted him too, the others sleep. Faces down against the soil, we watch him; dare not shoot, if we miss his gun will make short work of all of us, only shoot if he spots us. He makes no sign that he has seen us and wanders over the skyline to disappear. We breathe again.

I sleep, come to, drift off, sleep again; my eyes won't stay open, the lids are far too heavy. Hear boots on the road. Several pairs of boots walking along the road, not marching but walking in an irregular tattoo; coming bloody close. Edgars eyes are on me, the others are stirring, two of them are lying on their rifles, Jesus Christ. I bury down further into the soil, my face stretched up from the flatness, my eyes strain from their sockets watching the blue skyline, praying that the boots go past. They stop, about seven men I guess. A few seconds of utter stillness then the blue skyline is filled with a revolver, a German revolver, it points into my face; a hand, the top of a helmet, a face peering down, the face splits, it speaks in English "The war is over for you Tommy. Stand up".

The face, helmet and gun disappears as he steps back out of sight, giving himself shooting room I guess! Edgar has a grenade in his hand, but we can't see them, don't know how many or where they stand on the road. If I stand up shooting, Edgar will let it go, he and Jackson will follow me, don't know about the others, no idea what they will do. Expect they all have light machine guns anyway, they know where we are, we don't know where they are, hopeless, and we are buggered anyway. I stand up, arms clawing the sky; there are six of them, one Corporal, five Privates. The Corporal stands at the other side of the road, well back; his men stand in a semi-circle round our position, but again well back. Each man is armed with a machine pistol, all guns at the moment seem to point at my belly button. Climb up on to the bank, tell the lads to stand up, leave their weapons. They do so, climbing out of the ditch to stand alongside me.

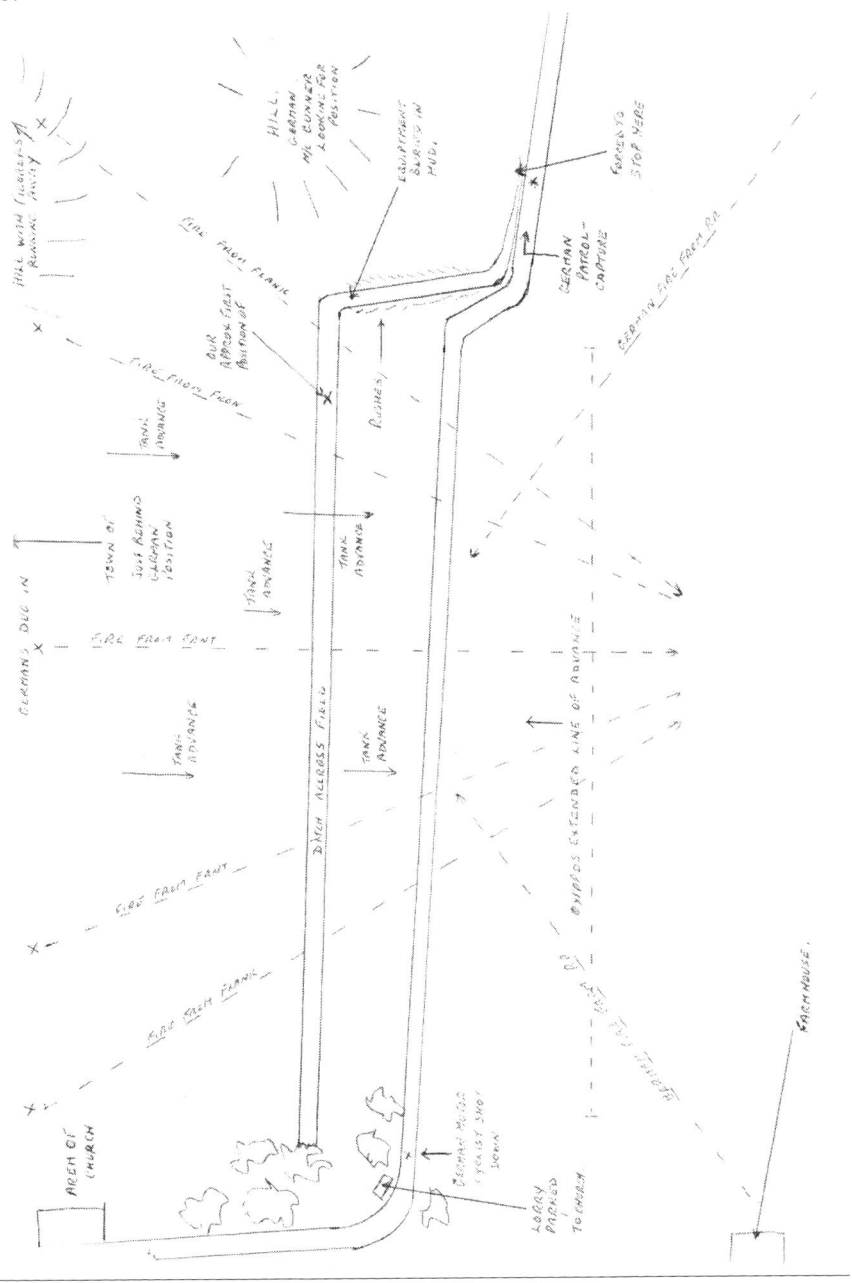

Watou, 1940

Jackson stands on my left, his face is crumbling again, he is bloody crying; tears roll down his cheeks. A good man, but Christ, he cries with the ease of a woman. I am filled with a deep anger at him for crying in front of these Germans; Ok, he expects to get shot, don't we all, nobody has told us that we will, but we expect it anyway. I think about it without any sense of fear, my mind and body is mostly dead anyway. A thought fleetingly races through my mind, I haven't seen much of life, I feel a mild regret about it but nothing else. No other thoughts, no other emotions, if it comes we can only show the bastards how to meet it, that's all there is to do, nothing else matters, nothing!

Edgar stands to my right hand side, his left shoulder behind my right, he is still the only one of us who does not have his hands up in the air, he can't, he still has the grenade cupped in his hands. I can read his mind like a book, if they shoot, he will drop the grenade on the road, some of them will travel with us. The Corporal has read our thoughts, he is speaking, "You have been told that we will shoot you, that is not true, you will work in Germany." I let out a mild sigh of relief at his words, he has said it, maybe they won't shoot, perhaps he is speaking the truth, perhaps there is a chance to live, if we don't do something stupid, perhaps!

The Corporals pistol is stuck in my guts as he moves in close to me, he lifts the binoculars from my chest, hooks the strap over my head, places it round his own neck, pulls out the map from the front of my blouse, tucks it into his pocket, moves back to the other side of the road. He is looking at Jackson with a frown on his face, indicating him he asks "What is the matter with that man?" I mutter something about shell shock, he accepts the explanation; how can I explain away a man that is crying!

He tells me to throw away my bayonet, I reach across my body with my right hand to oblige the fellow, to withdraw the weapon. The five machine gunners have jerked down into low crouches, all guns swing as one back on to my bloody belly button again, I freeze the movement of my right hand, remain dead still. The Corporal shouts "No! Don't draw it. Undo the belt, let it drop to the ground!" Jesus Christ, I must look wild, scared the bloody life out of them. Gently I undo the buckle of the belt, together with the bayonet it drops to the ground at my feet, the gunners relax, stand upright, turn their guns back to the other wild men.

The Corporal has spotted that Edgar has something in his hand, he asks me what it is. Edgar answers by opening his hand, holds it up in front of him, the grenade nestles like a large egg in his bloody great ham fisted hand; the pin has been straightened, pulled through, the ends of the pin is flush with the neck. A split second of time is the measured distance it needs to travel to death. The Corporal looks at the thing calmly, no panic, he knows and we all know that if Edgar chooses to give a gentle pull and drop it we shall all travel the same route. Seconds of dead silence, the gunners are still, Edgar is thinking; everything will have to wait until he is ready, he is a stubborn bugger!

A sudden toss of his hand, the thing is sailing through the air towards the Corporal who deftly catches it in his hand as would any good cricket player. He holds it under his nose looking at it for a second as though it was a second rate article compared to theirs, tosses it over his shoulder nonchalantly. It falls in the ditch behind him, I instinctively turn sideways a bit, presenting a smaller target but the pin stays in. The Corporal didn't even turn round to see where the thing fell, either he is a cool customer or he has no imagination.

"You will run along the road in front of us, we will run behind you, do not try any tricks." He is indicating the direction in which we are to run, back the way we came. My back crawls as I turn, now they can do it so easy. "Run now!" We are running, eleven pairs of boots tattoo the roads surface, equipment rattles as they follow us closely. Past the grassy hill, past the ditch with the dirty black water, draw level with the field of battle, khaki figures lie on the ground, the plain is covered with them, some are sitting upright, others rest on an arm, but most of them lie still and quiet.

There, one of our mortar men; he lies close to the road, sees us, shouts a greeting, his eyes light up with joy at seeing friendly and known faces, he screams with delight, we cannot stop, a we run past we ask him how he is, bullets in his thigh, shout to him that he will be ok, will soon get attention. The sadness in his eyes as his friends have to leave him hurts the most!

Run for several hundred yards, shots still ring out in isolated bursts, some of our stubborn types still having a go I suppose. A tall hedge, a large hole dug into its roots, it houses a heavy machine gun, its position sweeps the plain which we have crossed, its bullets have killed our men, the crew rests beside it, they had an easy target today. A large open backed lorry behind the hedge, it is full of Battle-dress clad figures, two folding steps lead up to the lorry, the Corporal says we must climb aboard; he leads the way up into the lorry, turns, offers his hand to help each man up. I am last, a hefty kick in the rump helps me on my way, I turn, one of the machine gunners is giving vent to his feelings for the British; he glares at me with hatred in his eyes, if he had been in charge we would still be lying in the ditch but not breathing! The Corporal has seen him do it, he screams at the man who stiffens into a frozen ramrod, the man scarcely breathes as the Corporal relieves his feelings on the matter. A sudden forward jerk that all but tosses us out again, recover our footing, the vehicle settles into a steady pace.

The Corporal stands wedged close to me as we sway with the movement; fingers clutching at the stripes on my arm, I look down at them, the Corporals fingers. A question, "Are you a Corporal?" "Yes." His fingers go to the silver braid around the collar of his jacket, "I too am a Corporal." Good for him, pretty too. "Would you like a drink?" He is offering his water bottle, "Not water, cognac!" In that case "Yes!", I take the bottle, have a swig, offer it back to him, "No, No, pass it round the comrades!" I pass it round the comrades, it comes back empty.

"What happened to your face?" he asks, I tell him shell burst. "What happened to that mans face?" Following his pointed finger I find Edgar is on the end of it, so I tell him that too was shell burst. "Where have you come from?" Here come the questions; I tell him I forget. "What Regiment are you?" Don't know. "Where were you going? No idea. He is grinning! "Alright Tommy I will tell you!" "You are the Oxford Bucks infantry, you come from Cassel, you come here because you think other Tommies are here, we have been waiting for you to come this way for three days." To make his day he tells me the name of my Commanding Officer, he beams as he finishes his little joke, leaving me speechless with surprise.

A church, a tall spire pierces the heavens, the spire that I saw peeping over the top of the trees a life-time ago, how many deaths ago? Down from the lorry, German troops mill about the place, infantry, tank men, transport, as numerous as autumn leaves on the ground, two lines of heavily armed infantry men form an avenue up to the church entrance, we file between them like a large wedding party, enter the church. Truly a house of God, large and imposing, room for a very large congregation, it has one today; the numbers would swell any vicars heart. Shoulder to shoulder we stand between rows of seats, can't sit down yet, we might snatch a rest, that's bad for people in our situation. The walls of the church are lined with armed guards, they hold their weapons ready, other guards stroll up and down the aisle trying to look tough, their eyes don't leave us.

The air is filled with the hum of British voices, shouts echo across the church as faces are recognised, questions about missing friends, the tally of dead and wounded climbs rapidly, becomes frightening, counted among the dead our old friend Sergeant Williams who reckoned he dare not leave us when he had the chance for fear of his wife. He died swiftly with a bullet between the eyes, you wonder why you are alive, examine the fact that you are a prisoner with surprise, considered death or wounds, never a prisoner!

Ignore the Jerries that bustle about as if they are not there, unless of course you get a push which sends you reeling into your mates. Feel something being snatched from my hip pocket, a walking arsenal of a guard with his machine pistol in his hand, bandoliers of ammunition round his chest, stick grenades festoon his belt and top boots. In his hand he has a Bren-gun magazine, waving it under my nose he looks very cross. Of course, I picked it up last night somewhere, rammed it in my pocket, thought it might be useful, forgot all about it! He still rants away, chastising me as though I am a naughty boy; about time I said something to him just to relieve my feelings. Holding the bastards eyes I stare him out and tell him to get stuffed. My comment stops him, he looks at me hard, guesses I have said something not very polite, but he can't do anything further, not here, not yet!

Discordant music fills the air, a playful Jerry tries his hand at the organ, our voices rise in competition with the thing. The noise becomes deafening, a guard walks over, stands with his lips pursed into a circle finger to lips, indicating that we must be quiet, we tell him to get stuffed as well. He walks away shaking his head. Guards study us as though we are rare animals, can't quite make us out. We should look miserable, defeated, shouldn't laugh, smile, ignore them, even wink at them. Already they think that we are mad. They can't see the shock within us, the hearts that have sunk with sadness at our losses, those faces that we won't see again, they can't hear the prayers we say in this place, all they see is a dirty lot of Battle-dresses; Battle-dresses are British and being British the language of defiance in the absence of weapons is to tell them to get stuffed!

Out of the church, fall in, hundreds of Jerry troops surround us, feel quite flattered. March into town, enter the square, a solid mass of men in khaki sit on the ground in the centre of it, we fit around the edges, face outwards across the road, twenty feet away heavy machine guns in position facing us, one every few yards around the whole square, each gun has its crew of two men, one behind, his hands on the handles, thumbs hover over the firing button, his number two lies flat on his side, hands reaching up holding the belt with its golden cartridge case in line ready to feed, the black hole of its muzzle looks like the bloody Mersey tunnel from here. Is this it? Are they going to fire? They won't miss anyway, lot of men to shoot down!

Ok, nowhere to go, nothing to do but turn your back to the bastards. Don't look scared, light a fag, turn to your neighbour, say something, anything! Don't look frightened, not in front of these things that watch you so intently, for Christ sake don't look scared! Several hours spent sitting in the square then orders to get up on our feet to march, fall in to ranks five deep, the heart has lifted that w still breathe. The column heads out of town.

The March, 1940

Signs of heavy fighting outside of town; battered vehicles, masses of equipment, mostly British. German troops marching, others on transporters drawing massive guns, tanks, rolling stock of all kinds flood the road going the other way. Most of the men carry cameras slung about their bodies, they look like tourists, many shout with excitement at the sight of us, fingers point as they scream "Tommy"; they realise that they are looking at something special! Out come the cameras, others are not too impressed, they spit in our faces instead; they too take pictures but for different reasons, we spoil all their pictures by raised hands with two fingers stabbing upwards to heaven, or by sticking out our tongues, or looking at them with leering faces – children's games revived especially for the occasion!

Graves dot the roadside, the British ones marked with an upturned rifle, helmet hanging from the rifle butt, if it's near a house we sometimes see a few flowers secretly placed on them but mostly they are unadorned. The German graves have neat uniform factory made crosses, each have a border of whitewashed stones and a bunch of flowers.

British motorcycle over there, burned out, covered with a black bubbly substance which is in a mass on the saddle and tank area, runs down over the engine, I realise that I am looking at the remains of a man. Burned out lorries are also close by, they too are covered in heaps of the stuff where once the floor used to be.

Men are darting out of the column picking up discarded pieces of equipment that may be of use, the guards shout in anger; a respirator case, it lies by the side of the road, by the ditch; I make a dart for it, bend to pick it up, my eyes stare straight into a face in the ditch. A young face, about eighteen years old, he lies three quarters covered by soil, his head and right shoulder protrude from the heap of soil hastily flung over him and others which it covers more fully; he sits upright, head resting on his right shoulder, he looks at peace, a look spoiled only by the gaping wound in his forehead. No rifle marks the nasty grave of him and others. Quickly, back to the column, the guard is getting excited; take out the mask, throw it away, I have a bag!

The dust from the endless passing column of troops chokes us, yellow dust, it clings to our lungs, thirst is driving us mad, the sun beats down driving us into the ground.

French women start to enter our lives, timidly they stand in front of their little cottages with buckets, containers of all sizes and shapes filled with crystal clear water, pools of paradise. They place their gifts as near to the roadside as they can, standing behind their offering like little mice, children stand with them, their faces are full of sorrow as they gaze at us.

Men rush at the water in droves, dipping their hands in deep, they rush back to the column sucking at the contents of their cupped hands, a trail of splash marks on the dry road marks their passage. The guards get angry at the women who disorganise the march, they shout, rave and threaten them, but the women stand their ground weathering the wrath. One or two guards are nasty, they kick the containers over, the water runs away rapidly to soak into the dry earth. Rifles are un-slung, a few shots into the air above our heads, we fall back into order until the next time.

My neighbour is arguing with the guard who marches next to

him, neither can speak the others language, but by Christ, don't they argue! Our lad has opened his mouth and said that British helmets are better than German ones, British ones are stronger, German ones are pure rubbish. In exasperation the guard tells him to let him have his helmet, taking it in one hand the guard removes his own; holding one helmet firmly in each hand with arms flung back wide he brings the helmets together with a crash of steel on steel. Silently he hands the lad back his helmet, a horrible dent has appeared in it, the German helmet is unmarked; never heard another word from my neighbour, he sulks for the rest of the day.

Day is drawing to a close, enter a town, no idea where it is, couldn't care less anyway, all I want to do is sleep. A civilian prison, makes a change, always suspected I would finish up in one! High walls surround the place, a large compound, can't get a bed in the cells, French prisoners already installed there, we will sleep under the stars. Tiny fires burn feeble lights here and there, stoked up by Frenchmen who blow at the tiny bits of paper and wood to get the maximum heat to warm up mysterious portions of meat and evil looking liquids. Faces present an amazing variety of purple shades resulting from the desperate efforts. Thin lazy spirals of smoke drift upwards into the soft evening air like weak distress signals, we stare at the preparations sick with envy, our stomachs screaming for food.

Many French coloured troops; large men from Morocco, faces glisten as a facet on wet coal, their faces split into wide grins at the slightest excuse presenting rows of brilliant white teeth. Friendly people, more so than the white troops, but Jesus, don't they stink – even more than we do! A group beam with pleasure as they tell us that they don't feel too bad having recently eaten a misguided dog that made the mistake of expecting a pat on the head, bloody savages! Sleep like a log, dawn presents us with another beautiful day, just as well.

Out on the road, no food, pull our belts in another notch instead. The French are placed on front of us in the column of march, many, many thousands of them. A fresh batch of guards for the day, not like yesterdays crowd, they were fighting men, most of them understood our problem to a large degree. Todays bunch are second rate soldiers, a load of vindictive rubbish; they drive us hard, taunt us with invading England, going to take Buckingham Palace. Privately, they can have the bloody thing as far as I am concerned, but they will have to buy it, not pinch it. Laugh in their faces, tell them there's plenty more where we came from who are going to knock hell out of them. God, how big we talk. But pride is all we have left, it feeds us like a drug, our hearts burst with the pride of being British among the hostile sea of field grey, we have no weapons but we still got to fight, every way we can.

The women have started work early today, there they stand with their little buckets passively defying the wrath of the guards, daring them to do their worst. Some guards accept the challenge kicking over the buckets, pushing the women violently. A roar of anger from the British section of the column, men surge towards the guards. Shots fired over our heads, other guards run up to the spot, an ugly few seconds, the column finds its line again. The women have refilled their buckets, they stand again in exactly the same spots as the side of the road as before, it's a long column, plenty more men coming along yet, plenty of thirsty throats to come, they settle firmly on their site looking straight through the Germans as though they were invisible. They have a self imposed task to perform, to hell with the Germans!

Edgar spots a pack on the ground, picks it up, now we have two bags. Watch an item being struck by passing boots, it gets trodden on, I watch it travel its perilous way through the forest of boots as it comes closer, a mess tin; bend, pick it up, it's mine. It is a French mess tin, consists really of two, one within the other, tucked inside is a queer looking piece of meat which defies identity and a safety razor, fine, we've got some grub. Tuck the things into my bag, Edgar and I are elated at the thought of our forthcoming meal at the end of the day, things are looking up, two bags, two mess tins, a razor and a chunk of meat!

Getting mad at the Frenchmen in front of us, we try to march in step, makes life easier if you pick up a swing, but they shuffle along forcing us to lose our stride, not too much love between us I'm afraid!

A large hospital which looks to be full of Jerry wounded, a lovely sight! The walking wounded stand at the side of the road to see us pass, they stand quite close, almost rub shoulders with one bloke who stands too close to allow a clear passage, his right arm is heavily bandaged and in a sling, our eyes meet as we pass, I wink at him! If I had touched him with a hot cigarette he couldn't have jumped any more with shock. His face immediately darkens with hatred, I guess he must have had some British lead in him at some time, needs another bit!

March for several hours on end without a break, always in the endless dust of passing military might. The amount of it worries me, they'll have to get their fingers out at home if they are to beat this lot! Passing a row of cottages, a door opens, framed in the door we witness a tender scene of farewell between a man and a woman. A French soldier, he places a large suitcase down on the doorstep, turns to kiss her tenderly, swings the suitcase up on to his shoulder, he is running to catch up with the column, the loaded case bounces on his shoulder, in danger of losing it he clutches wildly with both hands to hold it fast. This man's country is still at war, yet he waits in his house for the column to pass, going to face prison life with all the comforts of home, packed and ready. He and his kind sicken me, the women and their buckets are the true people of France, not bastards like him!

Some of the lads with the strength slip away from the march, a clump of trees on the roadside, a quick check to the spaced guards, a sudden dive, they are gone. Sometimes they make it and are away to fresh adventures; sometimes they are brought back somewhat battered.

Thirty, thirty-five miles a day, keep them moving, wear them out, keep them out of mischief, the policy is plain. Into a large field, enter one half, got to be searched before we get into the other half. The French have disappeared, dumped into another field. Several German Corporals do the searching, each one is flanked by a couple of men with guns that point at us as the Corporals hands run over our bodies, full of enthusiasm for their task these blokes. Pity you if you are the proud possessor of a belt full of Regimental Cap Badges, because you are going to lose it mate. Never fails, they pinch it, now hold your pants up, that's all you got to do!

My turn. Arms claw the air in respect to the guns, the Corporals hands get busy, odd bits of French money, last few cigarettes, matches, army pay book, Joan's tiny bible, photos, jack knife, examines my wrist watch, not good enough to pinch, he lets me keep it. Certain he has not missed anything, he has; something at the front of my blouse, his hand eagerly dives into my inside pocket, he looks closely at me with a 'can't catch me' expression, I've no idea what the hell he has found. I wait as eagerly as he does to see what the daylight will show us. In triumph his hand has emerged, it grasps whatever it is in his fist; he opens his hand, its secrets are there for all to see and admire. Flat on the big palm there are three packets of rubber goods for the use of a male; blast, I'd forgotten all about them.

They are killing themselves with laughter, they think they have the randiest bastard in the British Army in front of them; they giggle at my poker face, cracking jokes which I don't understand at my expense. Little do they know that the nearest I have been to the inside of a female pair of pants was on the washing line. I stare back at them, not sharing the humour. Wonder what he will do about them? He speaks to me, grinning, very deliberately he replaces the things back into my pocket and pushes me away as cleared.

Soup is being dished up, we are lucky, we have mess tins, most men have nothing but their steel helmets, they use those! A long line of men moving up to the German Army cooks who are all dressed like the head chef at the Ritz, all in white with tall hats. On reaching them a ladle of murky washing up water from a large iron container, no solids, is dished out, at least it's hot! Machine guns circle the field, armed sentries circulate freely among us. As I pass one of them he sinks his boot into my rump, I stop, turn to look at him, he is un-slinging his rifle, wants me to lose my temper, hit him, he can shoot me then, I swallow my anger and walk away.

Settle on the soft grass for the night, sleep is interrupted several times during the night by quite a lot of gunfire, a crazy surge of hope that our troops are about somewhere near, that they might rescue us, but not, the gunfire ceases, quietness returns, go back to sleep. Morning brings the usual muster ; on the road, French in front, but there are no black faces this morning. Where are they? The shots last night! Surely not. But, voices say that they have been shot, I don't know, but nothing would surprise me about these people.

There must be some sort of secret signal among these French women flying through the air from one to another. Wish to Christ that they would stop it, I fear for their safety as they come rushing out of their houses laden with buckets full of water, they rush to the roadside quickly before the men get opposite, every bloody container in the house stands in neat rows, the owners eyes are filled with sadness as she waits for the men to draw level with her water. What wonderful brave people they are, I can almost weep for them.

Some of the passing German Army transport drivers have found a new sport. Quite fun really, all you've got to do is swerve your lorry into the passing column of prisoners, bound to knock down half a dozen of them, on a good sized column, can do it two or three times, dead easy. Good fun!

A black coffin nicely arranged on a cart at the side of the road so that all the passing British can see it ; painted on the side in nice white letters the world Chamberlain. A large party of Jerries stand by it grinning broadly, it's a joke it seems but it's lost on me, are they saying that he is dead or what? Don't care a bugger about Chamberlain one way or the other, got enough troubles to get on with without his!

Some of the guards today are ancient, the march is killing them, almost as bad as we are; they are supposed to be fit, won't be when this day is out. One fatherly type gives his days ration of food to one of the lads, he does it in the most furtive way possible, terrified that his mates will see him!

Another field. A ladle of soup and then sleep, blessed sleep, it takes everything away for a while.

Each day is hot, and dusty. March the thirty or more miles each day, feet are holding up well, no blisters yet, many men fall by the wayside each day, sometimes they pass us in lorries, other times they seem to disappear off the face of the earth. My thumb is hooked in the respirator strap that crosses my chest, my fingers grip round it hanging on, seems to help me along somehow, keeps me moving. Signposts keep repeating the same information but with different mileage, ask the guards why we march in circles, they tell us that exchange talks are going on. A load of crap; we are marching round collecting men. See how the column gets longer every day, but there is nothing we can do about it, nothing, they have the guns. An endless grind now, the rhythm of the early days marching has been lost. The French in front have completely defeated it, we walk as they do, each man to the best of his ability. As we grow weaker it becomes obvious that every man must look to his own survival, the mind is a virtual blank, the important thing in life is to get one foot in front of the other, get over the march, reach a field, maybe some food, maybe better than last time, if not, there is always sleep to escape it all.

From the high ground the column winds down the road as far as the eye can see, away round the distant bend to disappear into the far distance, my heart sinks at the sight of so many French and British captives. I wonder what the hell is going on in this bloody war! A commotion about half a mile ahead; men run like ants to the side of the road, dart back to the column again, looks as though they have found something to eat. Soon as it is close, a sadly reduced heap of mangolds from last years crop, a heap of soil, buried in its black richness are gems. Quickly! On to the mound, join the other ants, my hands dig into the soil feeling for a round object, grip it hard, for Gods sake don't let go. Grasp it to the chest as I run back to the column, get out of the way quickly, other desperate men swarm round me. As big as a coconut, solid, fit for a King; I rub it clean on my jacket, sink my teeth into the roundness of it, chew happily, feel the juices in my mouth, feel the solidity hit my empty stomach. Taste is of no account – I'm eating!

Another field for the night, another search, a mountain of British steel helmets greet us at the camp entrance, a large notice board, on it in English in big bold letters: THROW YOUR HELMET ON THIS HEAP – REFUSE AND YOU WILL BE SHOT. Fed up with carrying the bloody thing anyway, I send mine to the top of the heap, not worth getting shot for, not when a German helmet can dent it!

Gave us a treat today, coffee, ersatz coffee, made from acorns, bitter stuff, difficult to tell which one is to be drunk, the coffee or the soup, both being liquids, both being wet. Settle down for the night, darkness falling rapidly, every man is flat on his back, a solid carpet of bodies. One figure has caught my eye, it's upright, threading its way slowly between the men, stops now and then, men sit up and talk to it, something strange about it, watch as it comes closer towards me. Can't be. It is; a man in the uniform of the Salvation Army. He has a book in his hand, he writes as he talks to the men, soon he stands over us, ask if he can take our names and addresses, write home for us, let our folks know that we are alive. Instant suspicion. Beyond surprises, my mind races, what is Jerry up to now? Is this a trick? He stands waiting, can't place his accent, can't tell if he is French or German, genuine or fake, but hell, there's a remote chance to get news to mother, she will be worried sick with the two of us, take a chance, give him what he asks, pray it works!

This morning heralds the seventh day on the march - a special day, my bloody birthday! A fine place to be on your birthday I must say, a beautiful clear and sunny day as it should be on such a great event, today is the fifth of June. Don't expect any pleasant surprises though, to get through the day peacefully will suffice, finish it in one piece, well and truly soaked with the dew but marching soon dries it out, who cares. Young guards this morning, youngest we have seen for many days, they proudly announce that they are Bavarians. Fair enough, so they are Bavarians - some of them have push bikes with them an unusual feature for guards.

Muster us on to the road ready to march, waiting to start, the French are slow in coming. Some guards busy themselves cutting long pliable sticks from the hedgerow as they wait, they test them by swishing them through the air, we watch their activities closely. French to the front as usual, move off, get rid of the stiffness in my legs, sometimes they are painful at this stage, but then they know little else these days, just watch the feet, they are the chief worry, if they go all is lost.

A long grind but a halt at last, not so the French, they are still marching. We sit at the side of the road, going to let us catch them up with our normal march pace I expect, the French are three maybe four hundred yards away, still we sit. The guards have been active while we rest, some have moved along the road on their cycles, spaced themselves out between us and the French, some have sticks, others fix bayonets to their rifles. The French are probably about five hundred yards away now, we rise to our feet, fall in ready to march, we'll soon catch them up.

Sticks fall about our shoulders, shots are fired over our heads, they prod us with bayonets that draw blood. Run, run you bastards, run; they have us on the run, they have gone stark staring mad. We run to dodge the blows, draw level with the next guard, he swings his rifle full into the column, me fall, men ease up to help them, they have to leave them under a rain of blows, each guards as we reach him is a frenzied madman lashing out wildly with bayonet, rifle or stick. Shots from the rear, they are shooting them. Men who fall out are dying! Lorries pass from the rear to the front carrying men in khaki, but they are Frenchmen, no British from the rear are seen at all. Catch up with the French, lungs bursting, body trembling with exhaustion, fall into a walk, regulate my breathing, stop the pain in my chest.

Let the French fall away to our front as we halt once again, see the guards pedal off on their cycles to take up their stations in this game with our lives, see them test their sticks in readiness for our passing, grip their rifles nice and firmly, ready for that short stab or swing of the butt, up rifles on our feet, running like sheep, arms ready to ward off the blow if we can. They scream with pleasure as they strike, each guard a gauntlet of violence to dodge if we can.

Men fall out, are lost to the rear, shots ring out from the rear, the lorry passes but still it is only filled with Frenchmen. Catch up with the French, fall back into a walk, legs jump with nerves, heart pounds, lungs burst, chest will explode!

They are satisfied for the moment with their game, they need a rest, need to relax for a bit, let us march for a couple of hours without a break, then a halt, watch them fall into the dreaded pattern. Up on your feet, run you bastards, run. My mind and body is dead, my legs respond to the hundreds of other running boots around me, only my eyes are active, my arm is ready to ward off the savage mad blow.

A British lad lies at the side of the road, he was not quick enough to dodge a blow, he lies there with his arms held out beseechingly to the column as we run past, tears stream down his face as he screams to be picked up, to be carried, not to be left. For God's sake don't catch his eye with yours, don't read the dreadful appeal you know is there, don't look at the hopeless undreamed of fear that you know is in their depths, don't let him read the agonising pain and helpless misery in your eyes that will tell him there is no hope. For Christ's sake don't let it be my eyes that tell him, he is behind us, we run on leaving him to the madmen with the guns.

A rifle butt swings at Edgars head, he ducks wildly as he runs, it parts his hair it's so close, literally parts his hair. Thank God, he is past, safe for the moment; if he hadn't ducked, what then? Couldn't possibly have left him, not my brother, not to die alone, not with these dogs, we would both have died on this road, this day, simple as that; couldn't leave him with these dogs!

In front of me a rifle butt strikes a man hard, he slithers to a halt from the run, in a blind rage he strikes out at the guard with his fist, but he is off balance; the blow misses the guards face by inches, the momentum of the blow carries the man's body round in a complete circle, his back to the guard. The guard's rifle juts up into the man's back, the trigger is pulled, the man falls to the ground, his chest blown out! A frantic leap over his body to avoid being brought down, the air is full of shots, screams of frenzy from the guards, swinging rifle butts and jabbing bayonets as we catch up with the French, fall into a walk; we are entering a town, march through it to the other side and enter a field.

The men are in uproar at the days treatment. Senior N.C.O.'s demand from the camp guards that an Officer is made available at once, a high ranking Officer at that. One promptly arrives, a complaint is made, he promises to investigate, can expect an answer in the morning; we will not march until we get a reply next morning. The Officer returns, he reports that a man responsible for the shootings has been executed, taken into a field and shot, gives his word as an Officer that it is true. We have to take his word, I suspect it's probably true, Germans don't play at these things.

Eighth day of muster for the march, eye the fresh batch of guards for the day; a middle aged lot, they look a fairly peaceful bunch. The French have disappeared, glad to see the back of them, the rift between us definitely aggravated by the Germans for their own ends, but it was easy to do, the seeds have been there all along. A steady pace all day, we keep going but only just, can't stand much more of it, a bit easier on our own than it would have been with the French about, we march in step as military men should, try to look like soldiers, British soldiers, not a bloody rabble. Life today is good after yesterdays hell.

No field to rest in tonight, instead we march into a large railway siding, a long line of rolling stock stands waiting. Large flat topped wagons, in between every three wagons a cattle truck, perched on top at each end of these machine guns have been fixed, their field of fire the flat surface wagons and the tracks at the side of the lines. Men squat behind the guns ready, they eye their possible targets with interest as we arrive, we eye them with equal interest but for different reasons.

Ok, up on the wagons; Edgar and I are quite close to the things so we are among the first to board, get to the centre, sit back to back, lean against each other, feet stretched out. Soon the surface of the wagon is covered, filled up, but several hundred men still mill about on the ground, got to get on board somehow, squeeze up, make room, draw up our knees, tuck them under our chins, make bloody room! The guards are getting excited and threaten to shoot anyone who does not get on the wagons, there is no room, but for Christ sake pull them up, get them on. Last men up are in a hell of a spot, perched round the edge, arms linked to keep their seats, Christ, what's going to happen when the train moves, when it starts swaying, when the pressure of bodies sway in response, when the mass of bodies to the centre fall asleep?

Dusk falls as the train moves off, slowly at first, but gathering speed as darkness becomes total, soon to be racing through the night.

The shadowy figures of the guards up on the tops of the wagons seem to be firmly fixed against the wild swaying that has developed more's the pity, the bastards won't fall off. Shots break out, bursts from machine guns, someone has fallen off, they don't intend to leave anyone behind, not breathing. Hair dances crazily in the rushing wind, soon I doze - subconscious mind registers shots, screams, wild swaying of my body from side to side, rhythm of the wheels, rushing wind. Terrible cramp in legs which can't be moved, my feet are anchored by someone's arse, will never be able to straighten them again, drift back to sleep. Dawn is breaking at last, a grey light, shots from time to time, many gaps round the edges of the wagon, men are missing, some from the ends of the wagon, they would have met a swift death on the track under the wheels, they stood no chance, others have gone over the sides, they were the targets for the guns, the track must be littered with victims.

Full daylight, the train is slowing, soon to pull into another siding, unload. God, the agony of moving; stiffened limbs drop to the ground, hit it hard, legs fold a bit, but come on, get moving legs, don't give in now! Another train awaits our pleasure, passenger coaches, doing us proud. File aboard in a nice civilised manner, no rushing, no overcrowding, a seat for every man just like in civvy street. It's soft and luxurious, my rump accepts the luxury with suspicion, but it's alright, I can relax, lean back, feel the softness of another lost world. A long open coach, seats ranged the length of it on both sides. A guard sits at one end, a casual type, wants tor relax, we let him do so with pleasure.

We are moving; look out of the large window. A beautiful, magnificent scene, no sign of damage or the flotsam of war, pine clad hills rise steeply from the sides of the rail tracks to disappear into a haze of green distance. Study the soft green of the regimented ranks of trees, would like to lose myself deep within their cool shaded loveliness, deep within the darkest shadow, but impossible. Relax instead in the soft sunlight that comes through the window, count my blessings, am I not alive, Edgar too. Yes, just relax.

Guard is quite friendly for one of them, tell us that we are travelling through Luxembourg, but won't say where to, doesn't matter, will find out soon. Another railway siding, move out of the coach, fall in at the side of the track for marching, move off, soon the outskirts of a town comes in to view.

Trier, Germany, 1940

Flags fly, red flags, swastikas form the centre pattern, everywhere I look red flags, we are in Germany. Civilians stand watching us file past, blank, not much expression, German civilians. We stare back at them as we go through the town, up a winding hill, a barbed wire camp ahead, brick built structures inside, through the gates, counted in, break away, flop on the ground, rest. A frontier town, in the Zeigfried line they say, we are on the threshold of Germany, but not as we expected we would be, the words of that stupid song mock us, we have no washing to hang up on the line.

Soup, ertatz coffee, a loaf of bread. Soup is thicker than anything we have known so far, cabbage, sour tasting stuff called sauerkraut, dislike it intensely but it is solid, get it down! Dark brown bread, one loaf between five men, great worry to get it cut, no knife, chase around the camp to find someone with a precious knife, someone somewhere is bound to have one even though we have been searched about eight times, someone will have one. How to cut the thing into five equal parts, this way, no that way. Who is going to have the soft centre part? Less crust on it, won't last long, the four end pieces are best, each piece carries four surfaces of hard crust that you can chew on, you can suck it till if gets soft. We'll take it in turns to have the centre, take it in turns to cut the loaf up, nobody wants the job, the responsibility of counting the crumbs is too great. Feel the other four pairs of eyes on you as you cut, each starving pair has measured the bread to the very millimetre, for God's sake cut it right and equal otherwise your name is mud.

Can expect this ration daily whilst we are here, but don't expect to be here long, this being a transit camp. Nothing to do but look around for faces that we may know, sit around talking, endless search for war news, trying to build up a picture of our personal calamity. There's water in the camp but no soap, rinse my face, let it dry in the sun. Smokes ran out days ago, our stomachs rumble with hunger, but somehow we live with it, can get used to anything if we try. Sleeping on the compound ground is no hardship, getting quite fond of counting the stars that glitter above in all their glory, see how many I can count before sleep snatches me off into its thankful oblivion.

Today we move on. Had a couple of days rest, our spirits have revived somewhat having no marching, moving by train they say, the trip will take a couple of days. One loaf per man is issued, got to last the trip so don't eat it all at once we are warned. Fall in ready to march, counted out the gate as we leave. They flop a small spoonful of jam on the side of the loaf which we hold up ready, make it last they say. How can I carry a bloody loaf with a dollop of jam stuck to the side; lick it off, safest place to put it is in my gut.

Down the hill, past the silent, staring civilians, into the railway siding. A long line of cattle trucks, French rolling stock, march straight down the length of the train, count off men in casual bunches of fifty minimum per truck, climb aboard, door crashes shut, bolts applied, as usual the last men aboard are the unlucky ones. The walls are filled with reclining men so the last ones in have to sit in the centre, sit back to get some relief. A subdued light enters the interior from the opening at one end, I am sitting directly opposite, the square of blue sky is a vivid jewel; it's the only normal looking thing around here.

A large open-topped tin stands in one corner, our latrine! Legs are a problem, can't dispose of them anywhere, either they are over or under another man. Can't lie down, get interwoven with other legs, they disappear into a layer of them, can see some bugger picking up the wrong pair out of this mess! For hours we don't go anywhere at all, remain stationery stewing in the overheated interior as the sun smiles down on the world outside.

The loaves of bread lie in our laps, mockingly inviting us to eat. Start picking bits of crust off, chew on it, soon you can't stand messing about, pull off a piece and start chewing. Men perform intricate juggling acts with their feet as they thread their way between bodies to the tin in the corner, the balance of a tight-rope walker is necessary to reach it. With the skill of men just beginning to learn the art of wagon shunting, the train moves forward in a series of violent jerks, eventually to gather speed, we race along in a wild swaying movement as though trying to make up for lost time.

No, it will not be possible to use the tin; first because of the swaying of the train, second because the men sitting by the thing are already getting well and truly splashed with its prime contents. In full sympathy with the men who are getting the unwelcome and stinking ducking we look to the floor boards, worry the cracks, open them up a bit, that will do, other functions of nature will have to be dealt with if and when it becomes necessary.

To be sitting opposite the patch of light is a great privilege, most of the men can't see it at all, but the jewel is spoiled by the barbed wire that is criss-crossed across the outside, the ugly points on the wire stand out in sharp silhouette.

Wish the bread could be shoved somewhere out of sight but the bloody stuff lies about everywhere you look. Can't see it lasting too long, already some of the loaves have been well eaten into, hard to look at it when our stomachs keep shouting. No room to move, can't move from the spot we sit on, bloody hard.

Sometimes we sing, sometimes we don't, mostly we don't, nothing to sing about. Mostly is a doze or sleep, sometimes the train is moving, sometimes not, the patch changes colour, clouds, or a grey softness, night descends to be followed by utter blackness within our world. Sleep, just sleep, lie like a wet rag, limp, only the cramp pains that sometimes shoot along the leg reminds me that my legs are fixed to me, simply no idea where the bloody things are though, somewhere in that tangle.

The patch is white, summer clouds scurry past, patches of blue, place stinks to high heaven, so what. My mind is mostly blank, loaf well eaten into, won't last much longer, just as well, hate eating in front of men who have already finished theirs, let's all draw level. A couple of days they said, shouldn't be much longer. Soft dark blue patch, black inside, complete silence, utter stillness about everyone, nothing to say, we lie like dead things. The patch has changed colour to a light blue, another day. Hot within, strange, haven't needed to relieve myself, haven't seen anyone else either, just as well, can't be bothered to get the bloody thing out anyway, as for the other, no need yet.

A shuddering halt followed by the usual silence just like so many others. Voices outside – shouted commands in German. Boots crunching on gravel, the clatter of many, many rifle bolts being cleared as men insert bullets as we say 'up the spout'. The world is suddenly full of interest, other people on this planet, someone fumbling with the bolts on the door, a crash as the door slides open, noisy bastards. Daylight floods in, we blink out of the opening to the sun-lit world outside.

Faces peer in at us, they are attached to bodies that stand on a rail track; we gaze down at them, not moving, don't know if we can anyway! A solid line of infantry stand across the far side of a second set of tracks, shoulder to shoulder, guns bristle in our direction, like a row of bloody hedgehogs. Busy looking N.C.O.'s walk up and down the track; we lie still waiting for something to happen, probably to get out of our rest camp.

Jesus Christ, tripping down the line between the tracks in their daintiest manner come nurses! Females, of a sort; the fat matronly sort! Faces like carved wood, dark blue dresses, white aprons slung over their ample chests, delicate little white hats perched on top of their heads decorated with a red cross. Two soldiers struggle manfully with a large container which they carry between them, the nurses each carry a delicate soup lade in their ham fists. Stopping at the door of each truck they offer coffee with an expression that dares you to take it. Somehow they fall short of the angel of mercy image.

Doors slam shut with a crash fit to wake the dead, back into the gloom, we are not getting off, the mind sinks back in to nothingness, the tensed body muscles slip back to their fixed positions. Lost track of the colours up on the wall, just a variety of the same colours, blue, white, grey, black, they get mixed up, run into one another, the colours have gone crazy, there is no pattern. Bloody cheek, two strange heads obstruct my precious view of the square of light; two men have managed to drag themselves to their feet and now hang on fast to the edge of the opening, they are looking along the track as best they can for railway stations.

Patiently they wait, in their hands are hard lumps of excreta; draw level with the station, out go the missiles among the waiting passengers with shouts of triumph "Take that you bastards". Every throw is applauded by a warm glow within me at the thought of the outraged indignation with which every gift must have been received by the surprised Germans. Hope to Christ they hit someone in the teeth within it; to my mind, both these lads deserve the bloody V.C.!

A twilight world, endless stops or the rhythm of the wheels. Utter silence within, the aggressive ones have run out of both ammunition and strength. Think it's the fifth day, bread went days ago, drift back into blackness, makes time pass quickly, makes it fly.

Another stop, silence; utter stillness for several minutes. The soft light of dusk outside; boots, voices, hands at the bolts. Door crashed back, outlines of men's heads peering in, rifles slung on their shoulders, bayonets stab upwards into the soft evening air. Fine thing, now we can get out I can't bloody well move. My legs are dead, don't even know where they are; roll over on my side, bit of space now, some of the lads have disappeared, get up on hands and knees, my legs follow me to the edge of the truck, peer over the edge, Jesus, a good five foot drop, men lie about down there trying to get on their feet, having a bloody job too!

Only one way to get down, roll out, hit the deck with a thump that helps to wake me up; roll out of the way before some other body flattens me. Legs won't work, just won't work; can't lift them, how bloody stupid, can't stand up! One or two of the lads have made it, they stand on two feet like we used to, swaying like trees in a high wind but they stand upright like men. They stagger over to the men still struggling to literally find their feet, come on, climb up me, pull yourself up man! Guards stand watching the circus with disbelieving eyes, never had such a soft lot as us in their lives before, we couldn't swat a fly! Up on my feet at last, the world spins, join up with others, two, three of us cling together, slowly, one foot forward, weight on it, that's it, that's the way to walk, now the other one forward, weight on it, gently, slowly, Christ, we are moving. Hang on now, don't let go, don't let go!

The guards walk slowly in front of us, a few steps, wait for us to catch them up, another few steps, turn, wait for us to catch them up, we progress through the darkness. The world is full of nothing but the effort of learning to walk again, heads down, watch the boots, will them to move forward, but don't for Christ sake let go of each other! Some men tell of other men they have left behind in some of the wagons, men who couldn't crawl out, men brushed by the hand of death for a variety of reasons, but the mind leaves little room to dwell on their fate being filled only with the business of walking.

A light pierces the darkness, it illuminated a wide-open barbed wire gate. Guards posted at each side, staring at us, pass them, soft underfoot, feels like sand? Outline of a large marquee, into one end, dim light burns, bodies all over the place, space over there, reach it, drop like a stone, instantly the world blacks out.

Schubin, Poland, 1940

Daybreak: the sand is like a feather bed, don't want to leave it, body drained of energy but my legs have enjoyed their stretch, men are painfully stirring, better move, see what's about, look outside, see if there's any grub about. A huge marquee, the type used at home for garden parties, flower shows. About two hundred bloody ugly flowers fill the place at the moment, stretched out like dead men, just asleep I hope. My legs are not too bad, they actually work, they get me outside.

Not too large a compound, something like a couple of hundred yards in diameter, no buildings inside, ten foot posts round the perimeter, barbed wire in a single strand woven into a pattern of small squares, British working parties listlessly mess about with roll of fresh barbed wire, it's to be fixed to another line of ten foot poles which stand already erected inside the fence. Building our own bloody prison camp! Adjacent to the compound there is a much smaller enclosure; within, a large brick built structure, a few men in Polish military uniforms wander about, they take no notice of our overtures, look very nervous, we think perhaps they have a very good reason for ignoring us, we do not press the point.

A large square hole has been dug in the ground to one side of the parade ground, approximately thirty foot dimension, along one side a raised pole which forms the seat of the latrine, a haze of big fat flies fill the air above it, nothing else of interest in the bloody place!

Called on to parade. Stand in nice easy lines of five men but the stupid bastards can't count over twenty five, can't get it right. We mock them with cheers each time they have to start again, something like two thousand men in the camp, Jesus, it will take them all day – but we are not going anywhere!

Search the area for men of the Oxfords, find three. Joe who works with us in civvy street, David my civvy street barber, and Edward a Militia lad who joined us at Newbury. We team up to share rations and other comforts that such a union can bring to each other.

Bread and soup is dished up, soup is back to the taste and consistency of dish water, bread is eaten at once, no question of saving any, three days hunger has shattered all will power. Food fills our minds, everything else is blacked out; we dream of it, talk of it all day, sit and discuss the merits of every edible thing known to man and beast, recall with horror the number of occasions we have refused food in the past, swear to God that it will never happen again as long as we live.

Polish civilian workers come into the camp on various jobs, contacts are made, scraps of food and tobacco are exchanged for personal belongings. As things get more desperate valuables have to be bartered, a gold ring for a slice of bread, watches, necklaces, slowly the pretty ornaments of normality leave us to serve our immediate needs. Guards join in the rich pickings, we work through our goods for the good of the team, no room for sentimentality, everything has to go. No Pole or German is interested in my pocket bible but with a pinch of tobacco and a page of St Mark or St Matthew I have got a gold mine! Page by page the practical work of the gospel really is getting blessed.

One tap only in camp, it sends out a pathetic trickle of water as thin as a pencil, impossible for the thing to cater for the basic needs of so many men, most of us cannot get near it, we view from a distance the endless queue that winds round the compound, we rely on the ersatz coffee for drinking.

Don't walk about much, have no energy for it, when we do, it is a dreadful physical effort. Men are going down fast with dysentery, they sit or lie on the ground in pools of their own foulness, tears of mortification fill their eyes, sooner or later though strength may return perhaps to drag themselves towards the solitary tap to attempt to clean themselves, perhaps they will reach it, perhaps they won't, few other men have the strength to help them, there are too many of them, men are dying, sixteen have died this week.

Joe, David, Edwards and myself have escaped the purge of dysentery so far, but Edgar is in a bad state, repulsive slime runs down his legs from his body, we have nothing to clean him with. Joe and I lift him to his feet daily, his arms around our necks, we take his weight as best we can to walk him round a bit to keep his legs functioning, we can do nothing more. A Polish doctor comes on the scene from God knows where, he gives the suffering lads a spoonful of powdered charcoal which the dried condition of their mouths find impossible to swallow, also some sulphur tablets, he solemnly advises against eating anything for the next twenty-four hours.

Several of the lads are taken outside the camp on various jobs of work for the day, one of them is brought back to camp in a coffin, we ask the guards how he had died, they replied that he just up and died. They place the coffin in a small stone storage hut for the night; during the night one of the lads breaks in to the hut to examine the body, as suspected, the man had been shot, shot in the back.

Most men have had their hair cut off completely, our barber friend is kept very busy for many days shearing me with his tiny nail scissors, most of us now look like inmates of a penal colony.

The sanitary pit is filled to overflowing, the muck laps over the edges of the pit and flows over the flat surface surround, billions of maggots provide a heaving surface around the pole we sit on, we stand in the revolting mess daily. Men fall in the stuff from weakness, squatting on the pole they lose their sense of balance and fall backwards in on it, someone gets them out before they drown, then cleans them off somehow, God knows how!

The small horse-drawn cart enters the camp every day laden with a heap of fresh cut grass. The cart is at once surrounded by prisoners pinching its load. The old Polish driver goes blue in the face trying to keep us off, cracking his whip over our heads, the air is blue with Polish swearwords, but we've got to have a smoke, dry his grass out, it smokes, he wends his way through the camp fighting his losing battle.

His horse suffers too, someone in the camp is making some very nice rings for the fingers from horse tail hair, which we are busy pinching the old man's grass, some nasty bastard is pinching the very tail off his horse. Find a few raspberry canes in an old garden, a few leaves cling to them, nicely dried too, a change of blend. Roll them in a piece of paper from the good book, happily we choke our way through it, passing the weed from man to man. Explore other desperate blends; the crushed bark of a tree; a leather bootlace patiently shaved into thin sliced with a blunt razor blade; each blend doing its best to choke us to death.

The soup today looks like whitewash; it turns out to be milk, milk with tiny bits of fish in it, we stare at the offering in disbelief, not believing our luck, ask the guards why the honour us so, they tell us that an American delegation is due today to visit the camp to check the condition of the place and to check that we are being treated correctly. Never did see a sign of a Yank in the camp, but at least the threat of their visit got us some milk, next day things return smoothly to the disgusting swill.

Edgar has recovered somewhat from his dysentery, he can stand upright on his own two feet again, he gets caught for a work detail on the barbed wire within the camp, the guard tells them that he requires a roll of wire without the barbs, the lads ask the guards for gloves to do the job, the request strikes the guard as very amusing. The lads struggle all day twisting off the vicious barbs with their bare fingers, they finish the days with badly torn hands.

I am delighted to collect potatoes from the camp store. Enter the Polish compound, have seen no sign of the Polish inmates for some days, we wonder what has happened to them, they have just faded away. Enter the brick built structure, down into a cellar, a faint light enters from a skylight, against the wall a heap of black rotting potatoes, the air is filled with an acid smell that offends the nostrils. A large fork is thrust into my hands, I have got to load the potatoes into baskets; can just about lift the fork itself, but cannot lift it with any sort of load on it. Drop the fork on the ground, down on my knees, pick up the potatoes instead in double handfuls; the stench becomes unbearable as my hands disturb the soft stinking pulp, my head reels with the fumes, fling the revolting mess into the basket, other men take them away.

Ration parade; there, beside the soup container, boxes filled with the stinking potatoes, placed there as extras to the soup ration today. Men still fight to be first in the queue, take the stuff and eat it without hesitation.

My wandering gaze falls on a lad sitting on the ground clad only in his birthday suit, he is busily searching his clothing, he picks out objects from time to time, squeezing the objects between his thumb nails, picks out several more, pops them - the bloody man's lousy! Tentatively take a look at our own clothes, lice calmly stroll about by the dozen, fat healthy beasts, hundreds of tiny white eggs infest the seams, we gaze at the things in shocked horror, we too are well and truly lousy. Once discovered, they fill our lives next to the hunt for food; the more you kill the more they multiply, they torment day and night, scratching my body at night I find that I am covered with scratch marks, it's a losing battle, we have to live with them. Our bodies have seen daylight for the first time in more than six weeks but only to hunt for the fat white creatures whose transparent bodies carry our stolen blood in them. To anoint our bodies with water is a dream for the future, someday, somewhere, perhaps.

Jerry searches the camp for men of Irish birth to form an Irish Brigade to fight the British, offering bags of food and other comforts of life to all volunteers, don't hear of them getting anyone though, difficult to judge. Officers come round asking how many regular Army men in camp, they go away shattered when they realise that most of us are only part-time soldiers. Silly buggers though that they had the hard core of our Army in their hands.

Couple of lads from the Camerons in camp with their colourful red kilts which are greatly admired by Jerry; almost every day groups of them come into the camp and ask if they can tank a photo of these lads, the two of them realising they are on a god thing to allow them to do so at a price, with an eyes to the length of material per kilt involved Jerry offers to buy them. Only when the kilts are infested with lice in every fold do the lads agree to sell, but they don't look the same men without them; just look like two convicts like the rest of us.

Bread ration runs out, give us biscuits instead, large square objects with the dimensions of a large dog biscuit, which they could quite well be! Hard as rocks, can't break them, but we can suck them all day and all night until they disappear, we go to sleep hoping we get another one next morning.

Are to be registered for Geneva at last. Will feel a little safer when it is done, until then we are as nothing on Gods earth, easy to claim they have never set eyes on us. In our filthy starved condition, a board is hung round our necks, on it is chalked the Stalag Number and the Prison Number, a photograph is taken, they assume we look like this normally I suppose. Finger prints are taken, Army identity discs taken away, a metal plate and a piece of string to hand the thing round our necks, we are now official Kried Gefangenen. People again of sorts, in time our folks will know of our fate.

Men who have retained items of value for strong sentimental reasons are forced to hand the over, for safe keeping it is said, they now regret not having traded them in for food. Solemnly the items are sealed into large envelopes with name, number, and Stalag written on them. The performance does nothing to instil the men with confidence that they will ever see the goods again.

Scabious is among our ranks it is said; Jesus, is that all. Got to be examined to find the infected ones, going to have some treatment. On parade, a smart looking German Medical Officer, shirts off, file past him. Stop, let him have a look at our filthy hides; disdainfully he looks closely at the skin, some of us have to go to the right, some have to go to the left. Those that go to the right can leave the parade, they are termed clean, those of us on the left are the infected ones, the untouchables! About thirty of us wait in the centre of the parade ground wondering what it is all about and how they propose to cure us. With a bullet? No, not quite as dramatic as that, yet! A soldier stagger on to the parade ground with a large oil drum on his shoulder, drops it on the ground, opens the lid, stand respectfully by awaiting the Officers wishes. We are told to strip everything off. Reluctantly we take off all our clothes, my skin shudders at the unaccustomed attack of daylight on the whole body at once. File past the drum, it contains a liquid that looks like olive oil, cup my hands into it, rub it over every part of my body until it glistens, put my clothes back on, I can go. Cure finished, we now have a load of sticky oil to contend with as well as dirt and bloody lice!

Arbeits Kommando's (working parties) are being made up and sent out. Edgar, Joe and me are on the same party, the rest of our friends we lose. Stagger out of the place with no regrets, happy to be on the move, great difficulty in walking, pace very slow, feel dreadfully week. Reach the railway siding, clamber up into the cattle trucks with great difficulty; no overcrowding this time, room to lie down, room to stretch. Time to sleep, leave the hunger behind, leave the whole bloody world behind for a while.

Crashing door as it is flung open, out of the wagon, fall in to march, about three hundred of us listlessly fall in line, rough cobbles underfoot, move off. Pass a few houses, a church, groves of trees. March for a couple of miles, more houses, near them a barbed wire enclosure, double gates wide open to welcome us, guards stroll about. We go through the gate, counted in slowly, gates shut, break away into the compound. What next?

Arbbiets Kommando – Znin, Poland, 1940-1941

A long brick building within the compound, a small open space to the front of the building approximately one hundred yards in diameter, a single posted barbed wire fence surround, single strand wire interwoven in squares, sentries patrol immediately outside the wire in a continuous circle. Four long rooms in the building, one washroom and three living quarters, flat timbered platforms run the length of each room on both sides, one side is double tiered. Our beds, lie shoulder to shoulder in long rows, window overlooks the compound, can look straight down on the guards as they patrol their beats. Opposite the building another small square building with a large boiling receptacle inside, a cookhouse! On each flank of the main building two other small rooms, one is to be our hospital, the other will be a small shop, yes by Christ, a shop!

Nothing in the shop at present but by next week it will have loaves of bread, bottles of beer, cigarettes, and pencils. To purchase these treasures we will have to work, do a weeks work, they will give us bits of paper that will actually get us a loaf of bread in return. Start work tomorrow.

A large factory near the camp, between it and the camp a huge pit in the ground, three quarters filled with waste material from the factory, down in its depths can be seen a line of push wagons on a small gauge rail track, beyond, some trees, above them peeps a church spire, a strange shaped spire, a mass of ornate knobs and in intricate curves, unlike any I have ever seen before, a strange design.

Soup, coffee and a fifth of a loaf of bread is issued. Go to sleep wondering how anybody is going to get any work out of us. Tomorrow will tell!

Up bright and early next morning, roll-call in the compound, move slowly out of camp, down into the pit just outside the wire, straight to the line of trucks. A line of wooden planks on the ground alongside the trucks, stand on them, the place is muddy. Each man is given a long handled shovel; immediately to our front and within reach is a cliff of jelly-like substance, the waste of sugar beet we are told, must dig the shovel into the stuff. It's quite firm, should cut into blocks with ease, get a block on the shovel, supposed to lift it and swing it backwards into the small steel wagon that stands behind me, no need to move the feet at all, sounds like a piece of cake!

Left the empty shovel and dig into the jelly, can just about make it, get a small block on, can't bloody lift it. Get a much smaller piece, ok, now try a swing back into the wagon. The shovel falls to the ground, can't lift upwards. For seconds I stand still, gather strength, try again. Lift man! Lift up into the wagon, it's there! Shovel back into the jelly, dig it in man; a small piece, right, get a swing into the sodding truck. Lift; swing backwards; in! Utter joy flows through my body, my heart sings with relief, now another one, gently now, build up slowly, get the muscles to work again, stand up straight like a bloody man. That one went back smoothly and in one move, my whole body screams with the joy of being able to function, life is about to return! A pitiful load this first day, but we are happy and amazed that anything has been moved at all. Sleep is that of utterly exhausted but happy men.

Each day we stagger through the work, praying for the week to pass quickly, get paid, get some extra bread, maybe even a smoke. Patient guards seem to understand the agony of this first week, they do not hustle us. It arrives, the great day. Tiny bits of pink paper are handed to us - goods are in the shop, can buy some of them ; an instant queue. It's in my hand; Edgar too has one. Other men have them - loaves of bread, all to ourselves; cigarettes too. Gaze at the rich golden glossy brown colour of the fantastic crust that covers the whole loaf, bring it to the nose, sniff in the rich smell of it, run the hands over its holiness. This dreamed of object, feel the smoothness, the rich roundness of it; quick, for Christ's sake find a knife, sink the teeth into it. God, life is good! Have a cigarette, thin objects, thinner than pencils, half its length is a hollow tube, the tobacco is jet black. Light up, a deep drag, deep into the lungs, instantly the senses reel, an acute dizziness, going to pass out, sit down, quick. God, a kick like a horse, tastes dreadful, but it's better than nothing, it's heaven.

The Camp Commandant, a perky little Corporal, prisoner in England in the last war, likes the English he says, they treated him well, wants to do his best for us, we shall see. A cake of soap per man is issued, about the size of a matchbox, hard stuff that provides little lather, greenish in colour, same colour as their uniforms, bloody field grey! Use the stuff to help hack off our chin growth as well, at last we can wash in a fashion. The body has to stand the shock of water treatment for the first time for roughly two and a half months, it doesn't take kindly to the disturbance, but it is too late for the fleas and lice, they are here to stay, they are the masters!

A few weeks, work is changed, break up into smaller working parties, move off into the town, we are happy about this, can see a bit of life, see what is going on in the outside world, we work at a variety of jobs. Enter the town, not a bad little place to look at, probably a lot better before the bombs had ripped half of it apart, signs of pretty heavy fighting here and there, signs of Polish resistance. Many people walk the streets, the Polish people are easy to pick out, they wear a special cloth badge of identity on their chests, diamond shaped, backing colour mauve, a yellow border round the outer edge, a yellow letter 'P' in the centre, branded! They step off of their own pavements to make way for the Germans, yes, it's easy to pick them out.

Strength is returning fast with the extra bread and better soup, so too is our self respect, confidence and pride in who we are; our march into town is as military as we can make it, a nice smooth, free and easy swing of the body, a lot of German eyes are on us in this town, some people ask the guards who we are. Englanders, they reply. There is magic in the bloody word as it falls on our ears, wouldn't be anything else in the world at this time, in this place. Poles gaze at us as we pass, we smile at them; Hey, you with the badge that you so proudly wear on your chest, we smile at you in greeting, we are your friends, we are here with you; temporarily disabled, but not defeated, look at us and take heart. They look at us, some openly wave back, some content themselves with a weak smile, some are too frightened of the Germans that surround them and just look furtively.

Find ourselves on a party who have to move heaps of soil from one spot to another, load the soil into a little steel push wagon on a small gauge track, other lads have to push them about two hundred yards, tip them out, other men level the soil, we seem to be laying out a park of some sort. Long handled shovels are dished out to us; funny thing, now that we have proved to ourselves that we can work, that our bodies are recovering, we have no intention of doing so, not for these square headed bastards. Got to work it just right, move just enough to be seen to work when the guard is watching, but stop when he turns his back; just work enough to qualify for the grub, that's all we have to do, nothing else except break every bloody thing we can lay our hands on. Lovely shovels; must have been designed especially with us in mind, handles just the right length for leaning on. Cup the hands over the end of the handle, adjust the angle; fits under the chin just right, easy fast movement to slide the hand down the handle into the working position as the guard turns to face you.

The chaps on the wagons seem to be having trouble, track runs down a slope fortunately for them when they are loaded, but for some reason the wagons never seem to reach the end of the line smoothly, keeps tipping over, a slow refilling of the wagons, try again. Been working half a day, only got two wagon loads down so far, Polish workers act out at being appalled by the chain of accidents for the benefit of the guard, but we know they are delighted with our bits of resistance.

Poles start slipping us titbits of food, pinches of tobacco, cigarettes, now and then an egg, as the days pass they get bolder at it, start taking risks. Sometimes they ask the guard if they can give us something, sometimes they can, sometimes they can't. When they can't we know we have got a bastard guard on our hands, in any case, by asking, the Pole has declared himself for us, a bad thing for any Pole to do openly in this town, they are treated like dogs.

Plenty of German troops in town, Hitler Youth groups as well, they all sing at the tops of their voices as they march, set pieces, special tunes. Voices seem to be spread out along the ranks in the same way that a choir master would place them, nothing like our free and easy choice of songs, they sound like a choir too, bursting into song on the shouted command: Eins, Zwei, Drei, Fier. On four they're off like bloody thrushes. The Hitler Youth groups carry spades instead of rifles, handle the things the same way as rifles, beautiful bright sparking spades, hard to believe they ever touch the soil, easy to swap them for rifles as soon as the kids come of age, they are almost fully trained fighting men already, but I can't believe they are as joyful as their songs make out, some of them look a bloody sight more miserable than we feel.

An Officer stands under a tree, he shoots at a cat with his revolver. The cat has taken shelter in the branches of the tree, the Officer is having great fun but it takes many shots before he can bring it down, a Pole tells me that they shoot all cats and dogs on sight in Poland, they need the fat for soap making.

Sit on my bum on a couple of bricks on the ground, a hammer in my hand, it taps at the other bricks that must be reduced to little pieces of hardcore for a road, a stubborn brick, been tapping at it on and off all morning. The guard looks on as fed up with the proceedings as I am, but, I am moving, he can't complain. A Polish worker sits at my side, has a bit of English; in a mixture of English, Polish, French, German and wildly waving arms we converse very well. He holds his hands under my nose as he tells me that he is a professional pianist, has played at the Royal Albert Hall in London, but he will never be able to do so again, his hands are ruined by hard labour since the Germans came, a very sad man. He tells of the charge of the Polish Cavalry against the German tanks in the recent fighting, only to be mown down as wheat before the scythe.

Pull out the piece of bread that I have brought along for lunch, bite and chew as we talk, no need to look at the bread as it travels to my mouth, it knows where my mouth is, another bite, a loud buzzing in my mouth.

A stab of pain! Open my mouth as I yelp, out flies a wasp, he wings his way upwards into the blue sky buzzing angrily in outraged indignation, I have been stung. Bet it's a bloody German wasp. Gradually my tongue swells to fill my whole mouth, my Polish friend is very distressed for me at my misfortune.

A rough night, no good going to the hospital, all they have is paper bandages and white Aspro type tablets which are intended to cure gunshot wounds, broken limbs, and all other kinds of ill including toothache and mental disorders but they are not guaranteed to cure stings. All is well next morning, tongue back to normal dimensions, another lesson learned, look before you bite.

Marching back to camp at the end of the days work, pass the railway sidings, a long line of cattle trucks stand there, doors wide open, a thin layer of straw on the floor of each truck, men, women, and children sit inside gazing listlessly out at the passing world. Sometimes small bundles of clothing are seen here and there, but most have nothing with them at all, a few of the smaller children play in front of the wagons as children will. Slave Labour; snatched from their homes in what they stand up in for transportation to Germany, there they will work. Guards patrol the length of the train, each man armed to the teeth.

The camp life has settled into a routine, up in the morning, roll call, out to work, return, roll call, soup and bread issue. Hunt lice most of the evening as we talk, or indulge in a sing song, sleep to get rid of another day. The little Commandant is proud of his Englanders, thinks we are his toys, shows us off to everyone at every opportunity. Likes to give the word of command himself when on parade or on the march, but gets worried at our response to him, too ragged, not snappy enough, he knows we can do better. Silly little bugger doesn't realise how we resent taking orders from a German throat. Tell him we want our own Company Sergeant Major to give us orders instead, he goes half way, agreeing to give orders only on the march, he still wants to show off in town. He watches our response to the Company Sergeant Majors commands in camp with deep resentment, walks about with a hurt expression is his eyes for days. On the march we are fine until the Commandant gives the halt, always given on the wrong foot, we slide to a terribly disorganised stop, we curl up with shame under the critical eyes of watching German soldiers.

News of Italy in the war does not depress us at all; just another hurdle to climb. Jerry soldiers don't seem to be too impressed either.

The Commandant is pleased to be able to announce on evening parade that he has obtained a concession for us, he has good news, can have more beer or more bread in the shop for purchase. The choice is up to us, can't have both, can discuss it on parade, vote by a show of hands. I turn to Edgar and say "To hell with the beer, let's have the bread". A tornado hits me; rolling on the ground in a wild frenzy as I strike at the body that is on top of me raining blows to my body, we roll among a forest of boots in the middle of the parade, somebody in Battle-dress clings to me. I lash out, trying to get rid of him; hands grab us, pull us apart, hold us fast, a big brute stands facing me breathing fire and brimstone, he wants beer he says. So, I happened to voice a different opinion to his, that's all it is about! The Commandant stands between us wagging his finger under each of our noses in turn as though we are naughty boys.

"Should be ashamed of yourselves, Englanders fighting together, should be helping each other, not fighting. Come on now, shake hands, be friends!" He looks shattered at our behaviour, we don't want to shake hands at all, we want to murder each other, but he insists that we do; grabbing our hands he brings them together, makes us shake, parade reforms, vote is taken, bread wins! God knows where the Commandant's prison camp was in England during the last war, but must have been on the playing fields of Eton, he really thinks we are gentlemen and sporty. For many days afterwards my antagonist and I circle round each other in the space of the confined compound, each never daring to turn his back to the other.

A cleared bomb site in the centre of town, two main roads flank it, a good site for wandering Polish people to drop gifts, have to keep the eyes peeled for them, they look so innocent. Once they drop it you got to move like greased lightening to pick it up, get it out of sight of the guard to protect the Pole. We tap away at bits of rubble with our hammers, but that is only secondary, these Poles take such risks for our sake, we sweat for them sometimes. One girl in particular, about twenty, beautiful, lovely figure, sometimes she drops things, disappears; other times she alters her tactics, asks the guards permission, sometimes lucky, she will hand her gift to us openly with a lovely smile. If she is refused permission she keeps passing backwards and forwards across the site waiting for the guard to turn his back and judging the passing Germans. She worries us sick for her safety, shoo her away as much as you like, a waste of bloody breath, the little devil has devoted herself to easing our creature comforts and that's that; sooner or later she is going to get caught. Many German soldiers think she is beautiful too, they chat her up, she is gay and laughing when with them but we know she is only using them to get established in the area just to get closer to us, we know that a gift lies in her handbag as she talks to them. For weeks she has us on tenterhooks as she makes her daily appearance but one day she does not arrive, nor the next, nor the next. Something has happened to her, we never see the vision again, we fear the worst for her, we didn't even know her name.

The man has got to be a sex maniac. Every time he is our guard for the day he will produce his dirty photographs, will call a few of us over to where he stands among the ruined walls of the cottages, secretively he flashes pictures of men and women starkers in some pretty fanciful sexual contortions. He is leaving himself wide open with this lot of prisoners if he did but know it, among his listeners are men who have served their sexual apprenticeship in the Indian Army, their tales on the subject make my hair curl; some have served on remote frontier hill stations, Jesus, even the bloody goats weren't safe when they were about. They give the poor fool technical advice, new positions to try, special Indian and English versions. His eyes gleam in anticipation as he listens, God; if he tries any one of them he will never get out. Germany is about to lose another good fighting man we reckon.

Legs getting in a bad state, scratching in the night has caused ulcers to break out, lower part of the legs smothered in deep holes in the flesh which leaves the shin bone exposed in places. Paper bandages the only treatment available to try and keep them clean but the lice like the wounds, they move in under the bandage, enter the wounds, drives me mad, playing leapfrog within. But I am lucky, some men's legs are in a terrible state, they can't walk, no good going sick if you can't walk, so, work proceeds as usual.

Some of the men have taken over the cookhouse, cook our food which improves as a result, no increase in rations, they handle it better, that's all.

A tooth has been bothering me for some weeks, have to have it out, no refinements here to try and save it, a tooth is either in or it's out. Commandant arranges for a German Regimental dentist to extract it. Go to the guards quarters, he doesn't mess about, identifies the offending molar, immediately grips and pulls it out leaving the rest of me to go through the roof. A reassuring pat on the shoulder as I leave, tells me that I will live which is a nice thing to hear from the lips of a German.

A right mixed bag in this camp. Men from many infantry units mostly, some captured in France, others in Norway. Amazed at the number of men here who have seen fighting in the late Spanish Civil War, some fought for Franco, others for the Government forces. One naval man in the camp, he complains bitterly at having to put up with a load of army types but nothing can be done about it; captured in Norway, he is a bitter man. His ship was off the coast of Norway when they spotted some troops on the shore signalling for help, looked like Norwegian troops, had to pick them up. Lowered a boat, a long row to shore, lots of sweat, check to ensure they were Norwegian troops, uniforms very similar to Jerry, looked ok, pulled in to shore. The Germans helped them to pull in their boat and then told them they were prisoners. He swears blind that he wouldn't even help his bloody grandmother to cross the road after that little effort.

Another lad was captured on the job in a brothel. He complains bitterly because Jerry didn't have the decency to let him finish, we think he hates Jerry more than any of us. Yet another lad was stationed thirty miles behind the fighting lines, at least he thought he was, his job to service transport. He found no trouble at all in answering the smart military looking type who had stepped out from behind the hedge and said "Good Morning" so politely. After all it was a beautiful May morning, a fine morning for his usual stroll to his workshop, but when the man said "Tommy, the war for you is over" and on glancing at the man again, he saw a nasty little revolver pointing at him did he believe his ears, but he is still a very dazed man.

Pay day is quite a circus, every week the Commandant likes to have his pay day parade in the English fashion. A tiny table in the centre of the parade ground, the Commandant and his right hand man sit behind it, call out your number, march up to the table reasonably smartly, stand loosely to attention, take the paper, about turn, march back. The men from our Brigade of Guards always make his day, he curls up with pleasure when one of them goes out to him. Perfectly trained they can do nothing by half measures, they do it in the only way they know how, backs like ramrods, reach the table, halt, crash of boot on soil as it is driven downwards almost from the knee; only very rigid control stops them carrying the drill through to the salute, the about turn with its exaggerated and clear cut movements leaves the Commandant glowing with pride at his Tommy charges.

Some men swear that when they lay their shirts on the ground they move with lice, I believe them, there's enough of them in camp to pull a bloody cart!

A few letters from home have reached the camp, the rest of us are sick with envy of the men who have received them but we are refreshed by the possibility of others arriving soon. The lucky men pass the letters round for others to read, see, here is proof of a delicate invisible thread that reaches out to England, to our home!

Eleventh of November today, we are going to honour our dead at eleven am, don't care a damn what Jerry says or does about it. On the mid-town site chipping at the rubble, have told the guard of our intention, don't think he is quite clear what we intend to do but he will find out. Drop tools, fall into a single rank, dress by right marker, one of our number calls us to attention, we stand stiff and straight for two minutes while the German world goes to hell. The guard stands in front of us staring, not quite certain how to take it, looks round at the passing military and civilians who also stare, decide to wait a while and see. Soon the command to dismiss, a smart breakaway, resettle our behinds on the bricks of our choice, resume tapping at the rubble, we are content, have paid our respects to our dead mates and reminded the passing Germans that we are a disciplined military body. The guard looks quite pleased too at our display, he looks at the passersby as though to say "What are you going to do about it?" Jesus, how they love any tiny thing military!

The ever helpful Commandant has collected about a hundred books printed in English from somewhere, releases them into the camp, the lucky men with them are immediately bombarded with requests to have them next. A complicated system, being tossed a name of the next man in line to have a book, you have to find him, establish who he has promised it to, find him, get another name, find him, and so forth. What with chasing lice and chasing the last name on a verbal list, you can spend several days detective work before getting your name attached to the list, enough to drive you bloody mad, the next thing is to pray that someone along the line doesn't forget. Captured three books during the course of several months, became deeply submerged in the trials and tribulations of Mr Dickens 'Little Dorrit', envied the long sleep of a Rip Van Winkle type of character in a book printed in 1840, read the bible from end to end but don't feel any better for it.

We move with the speed of exhausted slugs, leaning on the long handled shovels in the sun is so comfortable, if the guard would keep his back turned long enough a fella could snatch a doze standing upright with the ease of a horse.

Some noisy troops down on the road are firing live ammunition on a range, can recognise the cough of a mortar among the weapons. Hit the deck fast, that was shrapnel which passed overhead then, bit close, look around, all the other lads are on the deck as well, only the guard is standing upright on his feet looking down at his charges in startled amazement. Ok, can get up, nobody is shooting at us, just a piece of mortar bomb come too close by accident, the guard tells us that he did not think prisoners could move so fast, we tell him his turn will come, of that we are dead certain.

The column will pass the heap of coal at the side of the road very shortly, it's on the other side of the road but that's a small problem; we have no fuel, it's getting chilly. A nice straight column until it gets level with the black gold, a sudden decided bend formulates in the line that touches the coal for an instant, still the column moves forward, pace unaltered, just the mysterious bend in it that ripples past the heap. Many, many hands shoot out of the column with the speed of light, the attitude of the owners of the hands is pure innocence, no idea what the thieving hands are doing; each hand grabs a piece of coal, into a pocket, the pronounced curve straightens out only when the heap is past, the guards gaze at the scene quite mesmerised, they don't believe they have really seen it happen, they say nothing.

A change of working party, a small cinema nearing completion, Polish workers lay blocks of wood in a Herring pattern on the floor, they tell me they are good for carving. Pinch a dozen, get them back into the camp over a period of several days; pinch two six inch nails, flatten one at the pointed end, a Pole grinds it to a cutting edge, cut off the point of the other , a Pole gives it a cross cut across the blunt end. I have a chisel and a punch, a piece of wood as a mallet, I have tools to carve. Draw flowers on the surface of a block, cut down into the pencilled lines, remove the surplus wood surround; shape the flower petals, leaves, stems, punch a pattern on the flat surround, colour the flowers with crayons from the camp shop. A nail driven into the top of the block of wood, bend, we have a picture to hang on the wall; soon, the walls carry many pictures of flowers, they hang with the few precious photos.

A few yards from the cinema stands the church spire that can been seen for the camp, as side door stands open, nobody about, the guard has drifted off somewhere, deice to have a look inside. Cautiously poke my head in through the door, the place is empty, a fairy land of bright and vivid colour, brilliant read, blues, white, and masses of gold, an Alladins cave of gold. Angels, Virgin Marys, ornate when compared with the soft mellowed stone churches at home, here, it's a riot of colour. A few flowers here and there, someone trying to show some degree of normality but the peace in here is a lie; it's not the truth of the world outside. I step outside into the world of men who have no time for the peace within, their conscious moments are devoted to the battle for survival.

The guard uses his rifle butt on the men whenever he can, easily the most disliked guard in the camp at the moment. Marching across the square of the town, he hits a man hard, a howl of anger from the men in the immediate vicinity; the guard has disappeared into a mass of men about thirty strong who crowd round him. The column has halted, all is confusion, the Commandant pushes his way through the crowd looking for his man; they open out to let him through, one of our lads holds the guards rifle in his hands whilst others hold the guard who looks the worse for wear. Hand the rifle to the

Commandant telling him to stop the guard using his rifle butt or he will be having a nasty accident, after a few days the guard is seen no more.

Carl comes out of a different mould, if you are detailed to his working party he will keep disappearing , going round the local Polish houses begging titbits for his prisoners, at the end of the day he takes the greatest pleasure in sharing the stuff out between the men, a gentle young man, difficult to believe he is a German.

Hitler Youth lads cannot resist the temptation of trying out their English on us, full of confidence when they first approach, it does not take long to disillusion them; they are so bad, have to tell most of them that their English is rubbish, they leave us quite upset, but, one or two speak it well. Fancy little revolvers they carry, they tell how they go to the Jewish Ghetto in Warsaw, shoot at any living thing that they see move within for target practice regardless of sex, we do our nuts at the casual way they tell it. Tell them they are sons of bitches, they don't understand, never learned that one at school, spell it out for them letter by letter, it comes out Bastards. They register shocked surprise at our words, walk away from them, tell the guard they are annoying us, they don't bother us any more.

A strange happening even by our standard, a German soldier is noticed trying to attract our attention as he rides past on a push bike; up one road, down the other, round again, clearly he wants to communicate without the guard seeing him. He is in a different unit to the guard, red piping round his tunic collar, Coastal Artillery. Watch him closely, what's he up to? Watch his hands as he passes this time, there he has done it, thrown a packet of tobacco, quickly, pick it up before the guard spots it, he has peddled off like a maniac once the deed has been done. Back again the next day, same circular ride round the site, he has us on tenterhooks, when will he throw his gift? Again, like a hand grenade the packet falls among us, recover it quickly, he is off, wobbling furiously down the road soon to be out of sight, we never see the unknown soldier again.

The Polish girl is lovely, you just have to smile at her as she passes on the pavement, a radiant smile in return, but the guard doesn't like her taking the liberty of smiling at us. He walks across to her, sinks his knee into her groin, beats her bowed head and shoulders. A roar of anger from our ranks, his rifle is in his hands as he returns to face us. Take great care to analyze the guard before we smile at the Poles from now on!

Hope of a beautiful and practical form has reached out her hand and blessed us in the shape of a small bulk issue of Red Cross food. Not much, but sufficient to send us crazy with joy. A tin of Nestles condensed milk between two men, a tin of beef between two, half a dozen cubes of chocolate, three cigarettes each. All of us are in a hysterical state, scream with joy at the English printed on the labels, read the words time after time, these things have actually come all the way from England to nestle in our hands. Eyes gaze at the tins with reverence, open the tin of milk, stick a finger into it, suck the finger, God, what ecstasy! Spread a little on a piece of bread, not too much for Christ's sake, got to make it last. Taste the milk, close the eyes, keep the taste in, don't let it go ever. Close the tin, stand it somewhere safe and firm, the thought of upsetting it upsets us, almost nail them down in our anxiety. Beef from the Argentine, like bully beef, the good smell of it is like wine to our heads, the taste makes us purr like cats. Golden Dollar cigarettes, fat English type, see the golden tobacco inside the milk white cylinder of paper, break them in half; two or three puffs of pure heaven, out with it, two or three more puffs remain in it before I dare start on the other half. Three cigarettes, half per day, six days they will last, six days of heaven. We sleep content, Britain's hand has reached out and touched us very gently - she hasn't forgotten us after all.

A letter from home for Edgar, the first between us, all are well at home, relieved to hear that we are alive; Edgar has been reported missing for three months, me for four months, must have been hell at home, wondering all that time. My girlfriend has decided not to wait for me, getting herself married off, the news leaves me cold; more interested in survival than females but many men are losing their wives, let alone mere girlfriends. Many letters deliver this shattering blow, women back home are earning themselves a bad name round here.

The cinema job is about finished, the opening day not far away, have to go along to fill in a trench with soil, pipes have been laid in the trench, we have got to cover them over. Suspect they are drainage pipes from the toilet, pity to leave them intact, wait till the guard wonders off, a nice looking lot of shattered pipes got covered over reverently, going to have trouble the first bugger that pulls the chain. Grand opening next day, a few lads go along to do a few last bits of work around the place, they worry about it a bit; feel they should do something to help make it a grand opening for the important local party members who are bound to be there. Get a nice big jar, fill it with lice and fleas from the abundant stock in camp; very important task the man in charge of the livestock has, got to keep the poor little mites warm all day until the last minute, keep them inside his shirt next to his body, at the last minute before leaving he must tip them over the seats, spread them out a bit, there are plenty to go round! A nice restful nights sleep thanks to the thought of the many discreet scratching and stretched bladders there must be at the 'pictures' tonight.

Clothing getting worse for wear, boots have holes in them, winters are rough round here we understand, wonder how we will ride it.

The friendly Camp Commandant is in disgrace, has been taken away, two of the lads cut through the single strand wire and are away over the hills, their mates have managed to cover for them for a couple of days. The replacement Commandant is also a Corporal, be breathes fire and brimstone all the time; has closed the camp shop for a couple of weeks, shall miss the extra bread, but to hell with him. He gets his guards to chase us out of bed in the morning in no uncertain terms, thinks he is frightening us, bloody fool.

The two lads are back in camp in a couple of days, looking as though they have been bashed about a bit, have us on parade to gaze at them, they threaten us with all sorts of terrible things if anyone else tries it, we listen and stare back at them bored to death. A good spontaneous try by the two lads but too many odds stacked against them from the start; spell of solitary confinement on bread and water for a couple of weeks is their lot, sentence to be served out at the main Stalag.

Mail drifting through from time to time, they tell of our parents being able to send clothing of sorts, which they are hastening to do. Red Cross food parcels are slow, intended to be available one parcel a week per man, they arrive one between two only occasionally; still a Godsend with their tins of green peas, carrots, stew, jam, butter or margarine, biscuits, fruit, salad spread, and toilet paper which is so valuable to us as cigarette paper and writing paper, many a diary is started and maintained.

Getting mad with the new Commandant though, he thinks the tins look suspicious, might contain weapons or something stupid like that, his men sometimes pierce the tins, probe inside, sometimes open the lot, tip them together, we do our nut! Opened tins forces us to eat the contents at once, the housekeeping gets upset, protest strongly and noisily, gradually he drops the practice.

A questionnaire from the Red Cross asking for information on missing men, deaths reported only if directly witnessed, a depressingly long list is sent back to Stalag.

A boot repair service is introduced by the Commandant, quite a simple direct method really, stick a sharp knife into the boot upper where it joins the sole, cut all the way round the upper, the sole will fall away. Place an inch thick piece of flat wood which has been cut to your foot size, insert the wood up into the upper, it fits with room to spare, a piece of wire to fit round the outside of the upper, staples fasten over the wire, drive them through the upper and into the wood, there your boots are repaired, re-soled. Get your foot into the reduced toe space if you can, be a cripple in a week, soon half the camp strength is a load of hobbling workers, the Commandant has boobed.

Need not have worried about winter clothes, our hosts are going to cater for us, have got to hand in our rags for new rig outs. Empty the pockets of the old faithful Battle-dress, search inside the pockets, bloody hell, the rubber goods, still look as good as new, still ready for action, they haunt me, chuck them away. No, better than that, give them out to the lads, they will think I am Father Christmas!

Men lie sprawled abut on their platforms below me, climb down casually with the rubber goods clutched in my hand, walk over to them, hand one to the first man, don't say anything just give it to him and walk on to the next man, give him one; get rid of them, some mighty dazed men stare at the objects in their hands, they are speechless. I wait through the silence grinning at them, sudden screams of delight, we roll about helpless with mirth; have to relate how I got them, but the age of the things doesn't worry them, each man I note, carefully tucks his treasure safely into his pocket, an optimistic bunch, Jesus!

A mountain of clothes out in the compound, our new uniforms have arrived, a pile of tunics, another of trousers, cotton vests, long cotton underpants, hats, greatcoats, a pile of small square dish cloths, a mountain of wooden clogs. All shades of khaki, garments of all shapes, French, Polish, and others very mysterious and of unknown origin. Line up for issue, one item of each tossed to each man, one pair of clogs, one pair of dish cloths. Back to billet, see what the hell we have got: tunic not a bad fit; Polish trousers? thin riding breeches of some sort, a slight bulge at the sides of the legs suggests cavalry, lower half of the pants finish in a cylinder of linen intended to be covered by top boots or puttee. Made to fit a man half my length, the linen cylinders finish half way down the calf of the leg, the rest is bare flesh, then they too are Polish.

Greatcoat too tight across the chest - when buttoned difficult to breathe, two blue patches on the side of the collar, pretty red sea anchors are embroidered on each, a bullet hole in the chest suggests that the former owner is probably no longer with us, French marine I think. Wooden clogs like large boats, gleaming new untreated white wood, slip in the bare foot, large enough anyway but I need socks. Ah, the dish cloths, square, a little larger than gents handkerchiefs, lie one down flat on the floor; place the foot into the centre, pick up the four corners, slip the foot into the clog, let go of the four corners of the cloth, they will flap in the breeze as I walk.

Early Prisoner of War days, note clogs footwear and old Polish uniform bits and pieces.

Pale view vest and underpants, pieces of tape at wrists and ankles, you can tie them into pretty bows, we look like nothing on Gods earth! Recognise Edgar only by his face, otherwise he looks like a clown, we all look like clowns, our British image has been lost which saddens us. Got to do something about the bare leg though, cut two three inch wide strips off the side of my blanket, wind them round the exposed areas of the legs as puttees, the circus attire is complete.

Christmas of 1940 come and goes, we are not in the mood for such things, to remember is too painful.

The Scots among us are made of sterner stuff, not going to give up their New Year come hell or high water. Many of them have been saving their camp money for beer, denying themselves vital bread in order to give their friends a drink. My Scottish friend cries on my shoulder because his bloody beer has run out, real tears, he is mortified because he can't give me another, I tell him I don't want another bloody drink; makes no difference, he wants to weep, that's that, reckons he has insulted me!

Mac who sleeps beneath us is better off, he has quite a lot of beer, has difficulty getting his friends to drink from his mess tin; not surprising really, we all know he pisses in it at night. Persuade him instead to give us a dance, mark a cross on the floor, hum, sing, and whistle his Highland tunes, he dances the beautiful graceful steps to our hearts delight, see how the tempo works up, a few genuine Highland shrieks echo through the night soon to be joined by a lot of synthetic English versions. The guards patrolling the wire outside must surely feel their bloody hair stand on end! Mac sits for hours playing his chanter, it's his most treasured possession, poor Mac, his mental state is deteriorating fast.

Snow is the big problem in our lives now that we have wooden clogs, marching on the stuff is almost impossible, the snow clings to the untreated wood, builds up into huge balls of ice after twenty or thirty yards. Try to kick the stuff off, the clog goes sailing through the air, no way of getting rid of it until you reach the end of the march at which time each man is six inches taller than when he started. Ankles are at serious risk of breaking as we balance on the balls, you might get one ball to fall off under its own weight of which will leave you with one foot six inches higher than the other, you're in worse trouble then. Sledges pass us on the road as we struggle along, fairy-like bells tinkle and fill the air with their music, the steel runners swish through the snow, passengers are wrapped up nice and warm in their layers of blankets. Snowflakes float gently down to kiss our faces, but the Christmas card scene can go to hell as far as we are concerned, it's all lost on us.

The river - very wide, boats frozen in solid, they will stay there until the return o spring, until then they won't be going anywhere.

Across the road a sentry stands outside the German Military Headquarters, he can hardly be seen under the weight of the clothes he wears, his top boots stand inside a massive pair of felt over-boots, a long sheepskin coat hangs down to his feet, face covered by a balaclava, sheepskin gloves on his hands, the poor thing should be warm.

The guard leads us out into the centre of the river, a Polish worker stands waiting for us, a long wide toothed saw in his hand, a lead weight on one end of it, a handle at the other end, a hammer, chisel, a large pair of tongs at his feet. Chip a hole down through the ice, a good twelve inches thick, reach the water, drop in the saw. He starts cutting, soon large square blocks float in the water, pull them out with the tongs, push them over the ice surface to the bank, load up into waiting horse-drawn carts. Polish drivers will take the loads back to the camp where they are to be stored outside the compound. Another working party waits to unload the ice, stack the blocks into a long pyramid approximately one hundred feet in length, cover the ice with a foot thick layer of saw-dust, top it with a six inch covering of soil, this it is said, will keep the ice in perfect condition until the following August, not if I know our lads will this lot last that long!

A bucket shaped iron grill is raised off of the ice surface on three legs, it holds a fire to warm the guard, in between loads we surround the fire, elbowing the guard to the outside, he can have it only when we are working. Lunch break, too cold to sit about, have to do something to keep warm, two pieces of wood make a snow plough, clear a large circular space of snow from the ice, we skate around on our clogs singing the Skaters Waltz at the top of our voices. Intricate figure eights are executed with ease, the guard and towns people stare at us with their mouths open, they think we are mad, no sense of humour these bastards, that's their trouble.

Cold enough to freeze the vital statistics off a brass monkey, good idea to hang our blankets out, might kill the lice. Killed all those who hatched out, they lie curled up, legs pointed to heaven, but the eggs are strong and healthy, doesn't get rid of them. Well worth the exercise though, managed to make the guards mad, not enough fences to hang all the blankets on so we hang them on the barbed wire instead which blocked out the guards view of us; instant panic stations, lots of running around shouting, we took them down after one or two guards looked at though they were going to have a fit.

Men going down with all kinds of illnesses, bad cases have a rough time on the tablets and paper bandages, some just disappear back to the main Stalag, we don't know how they make out, ulcerated legs slow in healing, some ghastly wounds about.

A camp newspaper is introduced, the call it the 'Camp', gives us all the war news, German version of course. Pleased that they are going to so much trouble to convince us that they are winning, proves to us that they are not. Tell us every time they bomb London and other cities, never lose any aircraft, keep sinking the same capital ships of ours time after time, it does nothing to us except provide us with toilet paper.

A beautiful vision walked into our room last night, right in the middle of a delousing session, flanked by four tough looking body guards she glided into the room, her sexy swaying hips caught the eye immediately as she walked the length of the room, turned daintily, walked back and out. Hair beautifully arranged, makeup applied with practised skill, smart dress, shoes, well padded and provocative breasts. Only the body guards saved her from a fate worse than death. The vision disappeared through the door back from whence she came leaving a room full of drooling mouths hanging open like barn doors, no idea who the chap was, but he looked good enough to eat!

The potatoes are stored outside the wire, out of normal reach, daily details go out to dig out our requirements. About time we caused Jerry some bother, leave a few holes in the soil, the frost will do the rest, it does, they go rotten, they will have to get some more from somewhere if they want us to work, we go short for a few days but that's the luck of the draw.

Have an extra man in camp tonight, guards found him on their first count which in itself is and achievement for them, didn't believe it of course, have another count just to make sure but he is still there, Jesus. Count again, still he is there, the whole guard detail is running around like blue arsed flies, expect to lose a man, not find one! I must agree with them, sounds impossible but it is a fact, the lad got fed up, walked away from his working party, wandered about Poland for a couple of days, got tired, cold and hungry, spotted one of our working parties, decided to join it to get some grub. The guard in charge of the party had no idea he had an extra man, all they got to do now is find out which party he came with. Takes them a couple of days to establish this fact and identify him, send him back to the Stalag to get rid of him, they are too shattered to do him any harm, the Commandant has a few extra grey hairs over the matter.

The guards walk their lonely beat round and round the outside of the wire, not fit for a dog to be outside tonight, one keeps passing backwards and forwards beneath our windows, he looks cold and browned off. A couple of the lads decide to brighten things up for him, streaks of red substance on the face of one of them, straw from a palliasse hangs over his face from underneath his hat, two pieces of white comb hang from his mouth to form two horrible fangs. They have acquired a torch, hold it under the chin, he frightens the life out of you as the soft light illuminates his face in the darkness after 'lights out'.

Loud urgent tapping on the window as the guard passes below, the light floods the diabolical grimacing face, guard stops dead in his tracks as he looks up at the window. Thinking it over, decides to ignore it, passes back and forth without looking up at the persistent taps, but he can't win, his patience runs out at last, looks up again in response to the taps. He has exploded into action, rifle up at his shoulder as he lets loose a volley of shots at the window, the sound of the shots crashes into the silence of the night with a hell of a racket. Pandemonium has broken out around the camp, lights flood the rooms, shouting around the wire and in the guards quarters, we sit up on our bed spaces waiting to see what is going to happen next. The diabolical face and his mate have disappeared like magic, you could not pick them out from any other of the sleepy faces that surround you, nobody has been hurt, all the shots missed the window anyway!

A mad rush of heavy boots tattooing up the wooden stairs, half a dozen guards armed to the teeth rush in to the room, they fan out covering as many of us as possible with their weapons. The Commandant is hot on their heels, in his hand is his revolver which he waves wildly in the air, never seen a man in such a passion, Jesus, is he mad? He is a raving lunatic, screaming at the top of his voice, his revolver moves slowly along each one of us perched on the upper platform as he swears to God he is going to shoot the lot of us. We stay dead silent gazing down at him with the surprised look in our eyes of men who have been rudely woken up from a well earned sleep. His face has gone a deep purple now, the veins stand out in his neck in thick cords, his revolver is beginning to shake a bit from nervous tension as it comes back along the line, he knows the only one he wants is among them, but he can't shoot the lot, he would have no bloody working party left. He runs out of steam in the end, no more breath left, deflates like a balloon, leaving the room closely followed by his men, lights go out, we settle down to sleep in between giggles.

The young lad that sleeps near us is taken ill quite suddenly, he lay for three days before he died of pneumonia, we feel so sad for him.

The blizzard struck suddenly as we worked in town, visibility drops to only a few feet, the guards decide to return to us to camp due to the worsening conditions. On the way back, jock of the Camerons decides he is fed up and will go 'over the hill'. We tell him he is nuts, will never make it in these conditions. We know her has only decided on the spur of the moment. But he is a stubborn lad, he casually peels off from the line of march as soon as the guards back is turned, a few steps and his figure is lost in the swirling snow. Arriving back at the camp minus Jock, the Camp Commandant decides to have his roll call by bed count instead of outside. We make up Jocks bed with greatcoats to make it look as though he sleeps blissfully beneath the blanket. The hump of greatcoats duly gets counted in by the unsuspecting guard who reports all men present and correct to his Commandant, the camp settles down for the night.

    A hell of a racket wakes us up well past midnight, lots of shouting down by the main gate, looking through the window, we can make out the figures of a group of guards and can it be? Yes, it looks like Jock. Lights come on in the rooms, we sit up waiting to see what is going to happen. Boots on the stairs, the Commandant, a couple of guards and Jock enters the room. Jock leads them to his bed, they all stand looking at his bed, Jock is as mad as hell, he thumps his bed with the made up figure still sleeping blissfully with his hand as he shouts: "This is my bed you stupid bastards". The Commandant grasps the blanket and pulls it off to reveal the greatcoats, he explodes into a white heat of rage, his revolver is out, says he is going to shoot the bloody lot of us again. We gaze back at him with bored and innocent faces. He leaves in the end deflated as usual without shooting anybody, his sleep for the night completely ruined. Jock relates his story to us in the dark amidst our hysterical giggles.

    He has spent several hours in the blizzard beating his brains out on one Polish house after another, but none of the doors would open to his frantic banging, he realised in the end that people do not open their doors to bangs in the night in this country for very good reasons. With nowhere to go, and frozen stiff, he had to admit defeat and headed back to camp. The guard on the gate did not seem to be too surprised to see Jock roaming about, he asked him what the hell he wanted. Jock tells him that it is his camp and that he wants to get in to get to bed, but the guard is no fool, he knows that they have nobody missing, that their headcount was correct. He tells Jock to go away – must have the wrong camp! Jock and the guard argue about it for many minutes, the guard calls the Commandant out of his bed in the end to settle the matter, but he too tells Jock to go away; he has no one missing from his camp. Things are looking desperate for Jock – the bastards won't let him into his own prison camp, Jesus Christ! He tells them in the end that he can actually show them his own bed if they will let him, they take him up on this point quite confident that he can't. But of course he did.

We have a fellow in our room we call Yorky, he has formulated a five years plan for Britain winning the war for German consumption. He slides over the recent French balls-up as part of the plan as he tells the guards that by the fifth year we shall smash them to pulp. The guards listen to his lectures on the subject daily, wide eyed with wonder.

One of the guards is a very sad man, his Scottish wife waits for him in Scotland, his son is in the British Army, he returned to Germany to bury his mother, they would not let him go back, truly a prisoner among prisoners. Another guard is an opera singer; when we get fed up on the job, we will request him to give us a song, instantly he will burst in to a rich selection of opera gems at the top of his voice regardless of passing townsfolk, you can see the joy light up his face as he sings he beloved songs. Yet another guard is a very old man, a very tired old soldier, he has fought many battles in his time and is tired of war. Says he was a prisoner in the Great War, was kept in Scotland and was treated very well indeed. He loves to come into our room whenever he is off duty and will sit talking to the lad Yorky for many hours. When out on a working party if he wants to go to the toilet, he will take off all his equipment and lay it neatly on the ground with his rifle and ask the lads to keep their eye on it while her drops his pants. A nice old chap, we are all very sorry when he suddenly became very ill and died.

The snow has gone at last, spring is rushing in at us. The town is full of German troops, they are all over the place, a German Padre with the troops offers to give us a service in the local church, welcoming anything for a change, the camp accepts his offer. Right, now is the major chance to show these Jerries that we can march, our Sergeant Major from the Welsh Guards is going to give the orders; some of the lads even get hold of boot black and give their wooden clogs a birthday. Ok, get fell in; crisp clear cut orders, every clog hits the cobbles as one. Right lads, getting near the church; doesn't matter about the church, but what does matter is that bloody load of

Jerry troops opposite. Get ready now lads, wait for it, HALT. With an unbelievable loud crash of wood on cobbles the massed clogs hit as one with a clean cut precision that would have done credit to any British guards battalion, our hearts burst with pride as the German troops stare at us in complete surprise.

People hang out of the windows of their houses to see what body of men made such a noise, my eyes sweep upwards to the windows above my head. A girl leans out of a window directly above me looking down, she leans well out for a better look. Looking directly at me, I admire her bare shoulders and breasts to the full for a few moments until she realises why I am grinning at her. Quickly she withdraws back into the room like a startled bird, a tantalising glimpse of another world, rationed just like every other bloody thing!

A four storied and badly bombed hotel stands in the main square of the tow; they tell us that they want us to pull it down, demolish it brick by brick. No idea how to tackle such a job, but like ants we swarm over it, just bash away at any odd bit you fancy. As long as we all work on the same level at once, nobody will get hurt, only a guard maybe if they don't move out of the way fast enough. Hammers, picks, shovels and crowbars do their work of destruction well, the whole town gets covered in a blanket of dust as we send walls crashing down to hell. Men perch on outcrops of brickwork chipping away at the very bricks they stand on, bricks hurtle past the ears of the guards we don't like bringing many a suspicious look and angry remark. As though we would.

Spend several months on the job, have it down as clean as a whistle, strangely the only casualty happens to be a guard nobody cares about. He fell through a hole in the floor three stories up, he hung there for several seconds shouting blue murder, his rifle slung across his shoulders caught across the hole and held him for a while. Funny thing, the lads working near him suddenly got very busy and very deaf. He fell through, hit the floor very hard indeed, they carted him out of our way, another good man lost!

Huge granite boulders form the foundations of the hotel, each a good six feet in diameter; they give us sledge hammers with instructions to break them up into tiny pieces, four men to each boulder. Even we know that to break these things one needs to locate which way the grain runs. Spend a week walking round them and looking wise and giving an experimental tap with our hammers, each time we tap, the hammer bounces right off again as though the things are made of rubber. Guard gets fed up with our puny efforts in the end, takes a good look at the stones himself, with the cocky know-all wisdom of all Germans. He tells us just where the grain is, but we see to it that our love taps don't prove him right, we tell him he has guessed wrong. Guard gets wise at last, knows we have no intention of breaking the stones, he sends for a Polish civilian worker to do the job.

The expert duly arrives, raising his hat to the member of the master race as all Polish males have to do, a very old gaunt individual, a white snuff stained moustache. He doesn't look like he has the strength to roll a cigarette let alone break granite rocks, he has a twinkle in his eye as he listens to the guards instructions. He walks around the stone examining it with a practiced eye, makes his decision, produces a light hammer and chisel from the secret folds of his clothes, cuts a shallow line near the top of the stone; details one of us to hold a wedge while another of us gives it a hefty swipe with a sledge hammer, the massive stone lies split in two like an apple. In no time at all the stones are reduced to tiny pieces easily lifted. The old man grins at us in satisfaction at a job well done, we are pleased for him, he has shown the guard that Germans don't know everything.

Fall in to march back to camp on a side road, the head of the column enters the town square just as a German infantry battalion marches across our front. The Camp Commandant is screaming orders fit to bust, he screams in German which we choose not to understand. Too late, our column has already carved straight into the infantry column and is going straight through them like a tank. Utter confusion in the German ranks, they scream in shocked indignation, but the column of deaf mutes does not stop. The German Infantry Commander has our Commandant standing in front of him like a frozen ramrod as he screams in to his face. We march on without orders followed by the guards, intent only on getting back to camp to see what titbits we have managed to collect during the day.

Half way back to camp, the Commandant catches us up, he keeps running the length of the column in a most excited condition, looks as though he is going to have a fit. In through the camp gate, halt, about face; there he is, his anger is tying him in knots, the revolver is out again, it is waving dangerously in the air.

Edgar and I stand in the second rank, Joe stands in the front rank just in front of us. Something about Joes face catches the Commandants eye, he moves in close to Joe, they stand almost chest to chest, Joe is a head taller than the Commandant. As he waves the revolver upwards in to Joes face the muzzle is just under Joes nose, the Commandant is screaming in to Joes face as he threatens him with the gun. Joe hasn't even flinched, he looks down at the raving lunatic under his nose, he stands as steady as a bloody rock. His right hand reaches into his trouser pocket, out comes a bit of rag. Moving his hand round the revolver stuck in his face, he blows his nose hard in to the piece of rag and cooly polishes the organ, slowly the rag is replaced into his pocket. My breath has stopped. The finger on the trigger is in such a frenzied state it must be a whisper from death. The cooly delivered insult has stopped the Commandant screaming, instead he is visibly swelling before our eyes with indignation; his whole body shivers, he stares wildly in to Joes face, several seconds of deathly silence. Suddenly the Commandant deflates, his whole body visibly collapses, he dismisses the parade, walks out of the compound. Christ, thought we were going to bury a mate then!

Edgar and I get clothing parcels from home, shirts, socks, wool jersey and gloves, balaclava, pyjamas and chocolate. Pyjamas immediately pressed into service as vests and pants, some chocolate we barter for eggs, bread and tobacco. We flash our bits of chocolate and large cakes of scented soap to the guards and German civilians which makes them mad. Can't understand how we who are losing the war can get it and they can't. Tea now, that's a good item to flog, we use it first, then dry the stuff out again, seal it back into the packet nice and carefully, can get a couple of loaves for a packet of tea!

The old Pole has worked with our lads for many months, he is over seventy years old, loves to try and teach us Polish words, but he is in despair most of the time because our English tongues can't twist around his beloved and beautiful sounds correctly. The fact that he is almost stone deaf adds spice to the lessons. Riding his cycle against the flow of traffic one day, not knowing the rules; some German speaking Poles who strut about with an armband and a rifle shout at him to halt, he doesn't hear them, so they fire some shots at him causing him to fall off his bike. As one man the lads immediately pelt the so called Folkdeutch Police with full size bricks forcing them to beat a hasty retreat from the scene.

Busy demolishing a thick tough old wall, it's monotonous work until we start digging up human skulls and two rusty old bayonets, very impressed with the perfect condition of the teeth. We stand the skulls on the heap of soil. The grinning teeth face the passing German civilians earning many a tut-tut and wagging head at our disrespectful handling of the unknown dead.

We are leaving this place, pack up the junk we have, searched as we leave. I lose my diary, more than a years comments wiped away in a second. They close the gates behind us for the last time, physical wrecks when we entered this place, we leave with strength in our arms and hearts, wiser men in the gentle art of survival. March to the railway yard, load on to cattle trucks, room to move. We leave the Polish town of misery called Znin behind us.

Gratz, Czechoslovakia, 1941

Confined to the truck for three days, many long silent hours when the train remains stationary, other times when it rushes about like a mad thing. Move about within the confines of the truck as much as possible, keep the legs in order, cut holes in the floor to relieve ourselves, here and there a hole in the side of the truck just big enough to piss through, never know, might be lucky, might drown some German on a passing station. Live on our Red Cross food, bits and pieced that we may have, but the guts scream for food all the same.

Eventually another camp, a large one. Pass through the gate, a double and very high barbed wire fence, masses of loose wire in a crazy tangle between the fences, cross a moat, another double barbed wire fence, through a second gate, get counted in.

The guards of the camp welcome us with broad grins, one of them shouts out "Up the Territorial Army". Hell, how does he know? His accent is very broad American, they all chatter away in English of some sort, delighted to have us they say, they are Czechs, we have entered a Red Cross parcel depot, entered heaven in other words. The luck of some people is unbelievable, us for instance. The guards tell us that we are just over the border and in Czechoslovakia.

Nice to ease up on the hate a bit in this camp, we actually like all the guards, it's only their uniforms that spoils them. Three Red Cross food parcels issued per man, blimey, truly heaven. A letter card to write home, delousing of greatcoats, toss away the lice ridden clown uniforms, underclothes and wooden clogs, a mighty washing of the body, new Battle-dress uniforms, new army boots, underclothes, hats, heaven be praised. We truly look British again!

Here and there well hidden Regimental cap badges spring out into the light of day as they gleam on the new British hats, look closely at the lucky owner of the badge. I swear the man's chest has swollen another inch from stinking pride.

Large barn like wooden sheds, bunks built three tiers high, fall out of a top bunk, you could break your neck. Men mill about, gossip and fanciful war news fills the air. Washing so much these days with our scented soap, beginning to smell like cissies.

Stay in the camp four days, move out, back to the cattle trucks, cut new holes for toilets, settle down to relax, sing a few dirty songs, sleep, get rid of time.

Marienburg, East Prussia, 1941

Largest town so far, beautiful medieval houses scattered about, a large castle, lots of people on the street who hurry about their business, most of them carry briefcases as women at home carry shopping bags, they take little or no notice of us as we pass on our way. A big camp ahead, the real thing, high double fences, masses of tangled wire within, watch towers round the perimeter. Inside, six feet from the main fence a single strand of barbed wire, about four feet off the ground, place a foot inside that wire without permission, you're dead instantly from the guns of the watch towers above.

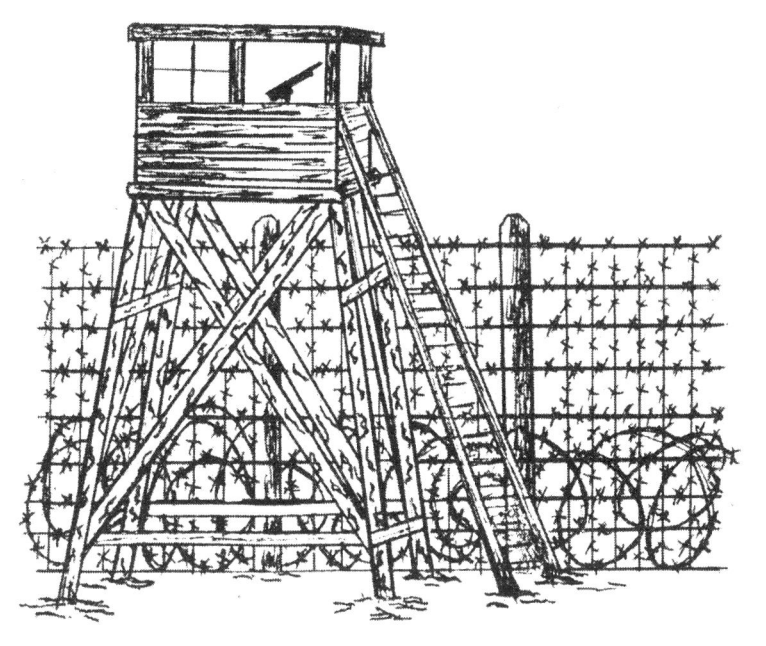

A transit camp, nobody stays here long unless they are working on administration, in the hospital, are the permanently sick, or buried in the cemetery just outside the wire. Nice gesture sticking them outside the wire, free in a way I suppose, but the thought of being buried in this alien land forever fills me with horror.

Daily working parties have to go out to do odd jobs around the town, this work earns nothing extra in the way of food unless something is picked up or pinched. Camp soup is pigs swill; to earn better food one must go on to a permanent working party, these come up from time to time.

A long line of wooden huts, they contain double tiered sleeping platforms, a large wash-house, numerous taps for cold water, wash basins. Behind the wash-house are the toilets, poles of timber perched over a large ditch, a trickle of water flows past at the bottom of it, a hospital hut with several beds and no stocks of preventative goods. Within the compound a further small area fenced off with high posts and barbed wire, the 'Glass-House' the place to serve sentences of solitary confinement on bread and water, a collection of huts for cook-house and storage, a lousy depressing dump!

Roll calls twice a day, it's nothing to spend two hours on one check, these guards are no better at counting than the ones at Znin; only wants one of our lads to feel playful, move about in the ranks, they have had it, the changing totals make them tear their hair out.

Edgar, Joe and I are detailed for a working party next day. Load up on to open backed lorries, standing room only, to the outskirts of the town. Debus at a large military aerodrome which appears to be nearing completion, large open spaces between large buildings, mounds of soil lie about, men break up into small working parties doing all sorts of mysterious jobs. I find myself leaning on a long handled shovel at automatic rest gazing at a large heap of soil which I am supposed to level into a flower bed, don't feel like it but better move my arms a little now and then. In between the occasional movement I study the surroundings. Luftwaffe men stroll about looking very busy, they ignore the very presence of we common prisoners as though we are not there, they just about ignore the very presence of the infantry guards as well, they walk with the usual snooty superior attitude that all Air Force personnel seem to manage when in the presence of common infantry types, seems to be an international complaint.

Hangers and administrative blocks, living quarters, can't see any sign of aircraft. Going to be a big place one day, hope our folks know about it! Should be worth a bomb or two, they can come right this minute, love to see them at any bloody time!

Move at least a couple of barrow loads all day, don't see much of the guard, he doesn't seem to care a damn. Some nice looking girls seem to congregate in a building across from me, nice to see their bodies flow along, nice smiles as they pass, can't be German, got to be Polish.

Third day at this task, have covered a few square yards with a nice flat surface, room for a couple of yards of cabbage plants. Lost in admiration as I examine my skilful contribution to the German war effort, didn't hear the first gentle call from the doorway of the building near me, heard the second one though. She stands framed in the doorway beckoning me over, her long finger is curling downwards in a 'come hither' signal, coast clear, drop the shovel, gallop across to her, softly chattering in Polish she draws me inside the doorway. Acres of polished floor space, bright gleaming cooking boilers, dozens of lovely smiling girls standing about looking at me, all dressed in white, every pair of gorgeous eyes sparkly with friendliness. One pair, attached to a nice body, is walking slowly over to me with a plate in her hand; full of soup, a spoon in it, hands it to me, tells me to eat it quickly. Cheeky grinning faces watch me eat, I grin back, choking myself to get it down; there, it has gone. Hand back the plate, check outside for the guard, all clear, a quick wave of thanks to the girls, out on to the site, my mind is in a trance. I have just seen a bunch of lovely angels.

Hug the building the next day, watch out for them this time, sure enough, the long slender finger is doing its come hither act, wait my chance, across and in. Bit more organised today, a girl stands just inside the door, plate of thick soup and a spoon held out ready, quickly acknowledge the waving hands, get the stuff down. They seem so cool about what they are doing, don't look in the least worried. Must say, Luftwaffe grub is better than ours, a wave of thanks, back out to the waiting heap of soil.

A different shovel on a different site, a few smashed cottages, clear away the rubble, guard keeps popping off somewhere for a quick drink or a quick woman. A German military hospital just down the road, some wounded walking about heavily bandaged, does the old heart good to see them, somebody somewhere is knocking them about.

A young woman comes out of one of the undamaged cottages, walks slowly and unnecessarily close to me without stopping, talking to me as she passes in perfect English, she has asked me if I am alright. She is English, from Manchester, she turns, comes back towards her house, married to a German technician who works in a factory, the war is going well for us, don't worry, look after yourself, can't stop now, dangerous. A fast hurried blur of words, she is gone, back into the safety of her little cottage, I see her no more, but nothing surprises me in this mad and dangerous country.

Other days, other working parties. First important job is always to sound out the guard you're saddled with for the day, test his mood, see how many liberties you can take with him, see how little work you can get away with; most of them want the quiet life as we do, but others will shoot you at the drop of a hat.

A large forest of pine trees, some have been cut down, trimmed and cut to the length of pit props, our job is to collect them and stack them into neat piles ready for loading on to lorries. A beautiful world of whispering bright green as the gentle breeze sways the branches, the green tops, long endless straight lines of chocolate coloured trunks, pine needles of last year and of many other years carpet the ground beneath the tree in a variety of rich browns. Even the guard is captivated by the spell if this place, he lies stretched out under a tree on the soft needles, tells us to take it easy, keep our eyes open for anyone approaching, only then look busy, but meanwhile just relax.

A potato storage depot in town, heaps of potatoes to be moved out of a cellar, a young guard who assumes I am in charge when in fact I am not, but got to sound him out; talk to him, can soon place him in the bracket, this one is in the lowest bracket which makes him a dangerous bastard. He boasts that he has already shot and killed four French prisoners but he has not shot an Englander yet. Take no liberties with him, just get rid of the day and him as quickly as possible but still manage to return to the camp with several potatoes secreted about our bodies in the most unusual places.

Bales of straw to be moved, load up on to lorries, head for town, through the heart of town, its busiest street, pavements full of hurrying civilians, not a smiling face among the lot of them.

A big fat policeman walks along in the gutter, six paces in front of him walks another slight figure, it too walks in the gutter, Jesus, it's a girl! Her hair has been shaved off her head, we are level with her now, a large board hangs on her chest, black lettering written on it in German in large bold handwriting, but only one word stands out clearly to me, the largest word of all, no mistaking it, the word is Juden.

A young Jewish girl, her head hangs forward, chin down on her chest as she stares into the gutter, they walk at a snails pace, must drag the show out, a smile plays around the lips of the bastard that walks behind her as he proudly displays his captive. The towns people stare showing no emotion at the display or they don't bother to look at all, have heard of this sort of thing going on but to actually see it happening there in the road in front of us makes me feel sick. A flood of anger and sheer bloody hatred of everything German floods my mind, they are past, she is behind us, beyond all human help in the hands of these pigs.

A large barn filled with thousands of bales of straw; they reach high up into the very roof of the place, platforms of the bales climb upwards to the top. Each man has a metal hook, arrange ourselves up the series of platforms, toss down the bales from the top for loading on to lorries, can handle them with the hooks quite easily. A simple matter of pulling the bale from its resting place, letting it drop down to the lower platform first ensuring that none of the lads are underneath; unfortunately, the guards keep well clear of the hurtling bales. Take a swipe at the next bale, the hook is aimed too close to the edge of it, cuts straight through the straw like butter, the point of the hook enters my shin bone instead. Stare down at the thing sticking in my leg for several seconds before I realise what has happened, pull the thing out, examine the leg, a small round hole in the shin which is bleeding a bit, but there's nothing to be done, just hope it goes away that's all. Shouting for bales down below, carry on tossing them down.

Hobbling by the time we return to the camp, not much to be done though, see how it is in the morning. Leg badly swollen next morning, can hardly stand on it; report to the sick bay, a British medical orderly sticks me in bed. Daily it gets worse, swelling into a massive size, a large lump appears in my groin. The leg is poisoned they say, ointments, white tablets and paper bandages the only treatment available, those and prayers. Not being a praying man the latter is sadly neglected, don't believe in asking for favours only when you are in trouble.

Edgar and Joe visit every day after their days work is done, we are all worried to death at the very real danger of being separated, working parties are being formed and sent out on permanent jobs, they are having difficulty in dodging them as they try to hang about for me. A couple of weeks of worry, Joe has got caught on a party, can't get off it, comes to say cheerio, Edgar is having a miserable time, won't be able to hold out much longer.

A miracle has happened, the wound has burst; masses of poisonous puss is running out in a river of relief. The sick bay staff are delighted, they could see the loss of the leg or death they say, cheerful bastards. Swelling going down rapidly now, just as well, Edgar has been caught on to a working party at last, can't get off it, leaves in the morning. Ask the medical staff to discharge me so that I can join him, no chance they say, got to rest the leg for a week, I cuss them to hell.

Late afternoon same day, a man is brought in with serious gunshot wounds received on a working party, only one bed they can place him in, mine! Tell me with regret in their voices that they will have to kick me out of the hospital, I scream with delight! Hobble over to the administrative block with Edgar, get my name attached to his working party, we are still together, but a close thing!

A dozen men on the party, we head out of town to become farm workers.

The Unknown Farm, East Prussia, 1941-1942

Being senior man I am nominated to be in charge of the party, my job is to negotiate on behalf of the men when dealing with the guard, not always the happiest of jobs, negotiations being controlled by the prevailing moods of the guard you draw.

A cattle truck, plenty of room to move, relax for the trip which proves to be of short duration, soon a halt, the guard informs us that we have arrived at our destination. Pull back the door, miles of flat open farmland greets our gaze, the only sign of life is a horse-drawn wagon with a seedy looking old man sitting at the drivers seat that waits at the side of the rail track. The train has stopped miles from anywhere as far as we can see, just to dump us. Climb out of the truck, the guard leads us to the horse-drawn wagon, as we do so the train pulls away, the engine ejecting loud puffs of steam in farewell.

The wagon is our transport, thirteen of us including the guard climb aboard, packing gear where we can we sit on the top edge of the side walls. The driver rudely shatters the old horses peace with a snap of his whip, with a resigned manner the horse obliges by moving forward at a funeral pace. A long, tooth-shaking and tiring trip over a rough cobbled roads offering no relief to the eyes from the miles of flat farmland, no houses, no people, our eyes search the open field for signs of other British lads, we wonder if we are the first in this area, but none is seen, we are in a world empty of people.

The driver talks to the horse in endless soft Polish, presumably urging it to better efforts but the appeal is ignored. The wagon too is protesting in its own way, seems to be constructed of many loose bits and pieces, every bump or hole in the roadway causes vies of daylight in the most unexpected places; but the timbers settle back into position with a crash, a portable affair, it sings out in a chorus of loud squeals. We look to each bend ahead hoping that when we turn it something of interest may unfold but it never does. The guard is just as browned off as we are, he keeps adjusting his rifle that drapes his shoulder with the air that suggests he would love to sling the thing far away into one of the passing fields. The bayonet on the end of the rifle stabs upwards to the sky, it's easily the highest point around here for miles.

Life at last, it sits at the side of the road watching our approach. As we draw level, the tiny scruffy object clambers to its feet and walks along the side of the road keeping pace with the wagon. A blonde haired boy of about ten years old, his face is upturned to us directing a pair of large round eyes that search our faces, the probing eyes dismiss the guard as something of no interest. We stare back at the runt in silence for many moments. Suddenly it speaks. "Englanders?" The word is a question. We silently confirm his observations by nodding our heads and continue to gaze back at him in renewed silence. A tiny hand thumps his puny chest as he suddenly volunteers the information proudly that he is Deutch. We nod our heads solemnly in sympathy at this piece of information and continue to gaze at him in silence.

He thoughtfully contemplates the cobbles beneath his feet as he walks and works out his next statement; we wait his pleasure. Soon the tiny head turns to us again, the solemn little face is transformed - radiant with pleasure at what he is about to say. Those of us near him lean over the side of the wagon to catch his words over the noise of the rattling wagon, but there is no need, his words ring out loudly with the clarity of a peal of English bells: "Fucking Bastards!" We gaze at this living proof that other English lads have been in this area sowing their seeds of culture before us with some surprise. He falls back from the wagon, content now that he has displayed his full range of English, the beaming face answering our waves of farewell. Slowly he fades back into a tiny speck in this limitless space of farmland, the world is empty again.

The tired old horse has his way, nobody dashes anywhere, but, at long last some houses; a cluster of them, looks like a farm, the driver is speaking to the guard, pointing to the farm, we guess it's our destination. A large farm. As we get nearer to it the horse looks positively perkier, thinking of his guts I expect. Enter a large yard surrounded by huge barns and stables, bits of rusty old farm machinery scattered about, the guard dismounts with signs of stiffness in his bones, tells us to stay in the wagon till his return, goes into the farmhouse. Soon he returns with another well-fed individual who promptly walk round the wagon examining his brand new stock of workers with a critical eye, we stare down at him with an equally critical gaze, examination over, he speaks to the Polish driver, we head away from the farmhouse to one of the two bungalow type dwellings that stand about four hundred yards away and are about two hundred yards apart.

Single storied and built into two dwellings under one roof, one half has the front window and the front door boarded up with thick timbers; a tangle of barbed wire over the top, the rear window too is boarded and barbed wire. The door has a heavy padlock in place, obviously our future abode. A single room, wooden floor, a tiled fire heating apparatus which reaches from floor to ceiling. Pick our spots on the floor, move in by the simple process of flinging down our gear, will start work next morning, locking us in the guard washed his hands of us for the rest of the day.

Well shut in, but daylight seeps in through the cracks between the boards, not much to investigate, but there is a trap door into the ceiling that needs looking into, see what's up there. It opens easily into a loft that runs over both dwellings, couple of lads investigate, another trap door leads down to the next house. Open it, below is a Polish family in residence, husband, wife, and a brood of children, they are delighted to see us, can walk out of this place whenever we wish to do so; trouble is, would have to go through the Polish family, do that and they will be for the high jump, bloody hell, can't use it!

A little fellow the Pole, can't stop pumping our hands, acts as though we have saved him and his family. Living in the utmost poverty, their food supply is worse than ours; they get no Red Cross parcels. Works for the farmer who he says is not bad by German standards, at least he is allowed to keep his family together, which is all he can hope to get out of life these days. Give them chocolate and soap, which is all we can spare at present, they almost weep at the gifts.

Bright and early next morning the guard arrives with coffee. Snack from our parcels to start the day, our first days work is to pick apples, pick them with pleasure, truly a labour of love. A couple of dozen wind blasted trees, fairly loaded with third rate apples but good enough to fill the belly. Climb the ladders, start to gorge ourselves first, fill all available pockets and the side of the Battle-dress blouse, the guard shouts about a bit professing to be tough, we decide to Christen him with a nice English name, we call him Piss-Tank.

A profitable first days work, stomach and pockets full, we return to the billet. Climb across the loft as soon as the guard locks us in. Our friends the Poles receive the gift of apples with delight, an unobtainable luxury for them as well as us, we are taking them under our wing as much as we can while we are here.

In the other dwelling two hundred yards away are a group of young Polish workers of both sexes, they are fed and housed but receive nothing else in return for the work they do; a dreary colourless life of near slave labour. The house has a dirt floor with no amenities, a wide ring of excrement completely surrounds the premises, a thick cloud of flies fills the air in a haze in the immediate vicinity. The young people are delighted to see us, greeting us as heroes, wish they would not do that, we have no relief to offer them. Some of the girls are beautiful beneath the grime of their conditions, dressed in the town clothes they wore when snatched from their homes they work in all weathers doing more than twice the work that we in our leisurely fashion do.

Miles of open fields; wherever you look bloody great fields filled with rows of young seedlings which disappear into the far distance. Each man is given a hoe, stand astride a couple of rows, must cut down the tiny offending weeds which endangers the seedlings. Start to work under the guards eye, he can see that you make a very good job of it, see how strong and straight the little seedling stands now that I have murdered all the weeds. Soon he loses interest, can get rather boring watching a load of tramps hoeing, he wanders off, sits under a tree for a rest. Strange, the hoe has gone berserk; millions of tiny seedlings are dying, a nice row of weeds take their place, this is going to be a surprise crop for somebody. Stand back, look along the rows, do they not look the same? Nice thin green lines, what more do they want?

Get the guard to go back to the Stalag to see if there is any post for us or maybe Red Cross Parcels. He has to borrow a horse and cart to do this, the trip will take him all day, leaves us in the farmers charge in his absence. The farmer stands watching us working to start with then tells us to work faster, we remind him that we are not his Polish workers and that he can get stuffed. Soon he leaves us alone, for the rest of the day he contents himself with popping out to make sure that we have not left him, a nice relaxed day. Sometimes the guard brings stuff back with him, sometimes he doesn't, it's the luck of the draw.

The seedy old Pole who drove us here on our arrival is a pretty important man around here, he is the cowman and lords it over the other Poles that work on the farm. Not a very nice man, we think he is pro-German, tries to hustle us around when we have to clean out the dung from the cow-sheds; get so fed up with him we decide to give him a nice English name as well, only one name fitting for a face like his, we call him Cunt-face. Scream it out all over the place whenever we want him, he grins at the sound, likes it, asks what it means, we tell him it's an expression of endearment in English, he is delighted, really touched.

Evening soup dished up by the Frau is not bad, quite often bits of solid are found, dare not ask what it is though. Bread is a little more in measure than that received at the Stalag, a lighter coloured bread which has been baked by the Fraus' own fair hands. Now and then one of her favourite top Nazi party members will have a birthday, on these occasions she will send down a thin slice of cake for each man so that we can celebrate too!

The guards tells me in one of his confidential moods that Germany has the perfect answer to the British problem. When the war is over and we are defeated, we prisoners will be allowed to work on in Germany for ten years, at the end of that time we will be permitted to send for our families so that they can work with us. The man really means it and thinks it is quite reasonable.

The fighting on the Russian front fills us with pleasure, it helps keep them off Britains back for a while.

Food and cigarettes arrive spasmodically, usually on a one-between-two men basis, give the young Poles odd tit-bits from time to time but mostly we concentrate on the family next door to us; each time, they look at us in speechless amazement, not believing that such treasures still exist in the world.

Usually finish the day off with a sing-song after the guard has locked us in for the night, getting quite good at harmonising our voices, keep at it until we are satisfied that we sound beautiful by our standards. Old favourites like Nellie Dean bring lumps to our throats big enough to choke a horse. The sad love story of Frankie and Johnny is told time and time again. Now and then we tell of the eagles that shit right in your eye, or relive the amorous adventures of the German Officers who crossed the line. But, whether our choice of song is cultured or not we raise the roof as our melodies float out over the Prussian countryside, the Poles love it, they listen to whatever we have to offer with rapture, these bloody fields around here are soaked too much with sadness. Singing for the Poles went out of their lives more than a year ago, they have nothing to sing about, it's easy for us to sing, shout, and cuss about the place, we are not defeated as they are. Our hope is a practical thing, something to grasp with both hands, theirs is not, they can see nothing but defiance that we alone can offer.

The farmer has been out on a stag hunt today, brings back a huge beast on a wagon with great pomp and ceremony. We have to unload it, notice the great jagged wounds in the body which could not have been made by ordinary bullets. He is describing how he stalked the animal and shot it, boating of his good shooting, he is dressed up in a fancy hunting rig-out. Grey suit, green at the cuffs and collar, pretty little hat with a nice hairy brush stuck in it, he looks a real huntsman. We ask him if he has used explosive bullets to do the job, he says he did; we look at him with the horror of men who shoot stags almost every day at home, tell him that's bad, not at all sporty, pull disapproving faces at him, shake our heads wisely from side to side as fellow sportsmen. He wears a puzzled frown, can't quite make out what he has done wrong, we leave him to work it out.

The Frau has informed us that to celebrate the great hunt we are going to have a piece of the stag as well. Jesus, never tasted venison, supposed to be a luxury. Here we are prisoners going to have venison. A big bucket comes down for the evening meal, venison day, take the lid off to have a look at the piece of meat. A bucket of blood meets the eager gaze, a revolting mess of stewed entrails; we feel sick at the sight of it. Offer it to the Poles who somehow eat the stuff.

A miracle, rain has actually stopped work today. Work only stops normally in this country for an illness near death or an actual death, no other reason on earth counts. But, today the rain did the trick. Out in the middle of nowhere the sky empties, never seen a fall like this, a solid sheet of water. A couple of trees handy, stand under them, but the trees might just as well not be there for all the difference they make, instantly drenched to the skin, the water cascades off the land in a miniature waterfall before the eyes, miserably we stand there waiting for the rain to stop expecting to resume work. The landscape before my eyes has turned to a darkish brown colour. Yes, the water cascading before my eyes is definitely brown, must be the dirt in my hair. The guard stands facing me, he is looking in the general direction of my left shoulder and laughing, can't see what the hell there is to laugh about myself. Ignore the bastard, but, I can't; he still stares at me laughing like a fool. I am getting mad at him, look over my shoulder to see what he finds so amusing, Edgar is lowering an empty bottle from above my head, the coffee it contained has just been tipped over my head, apart from the queer brown colour that flowed before my eyes I had not felt a thing. The guard decides it is too wet to stay outside, takes us back to the billet, farmer decides the rain won't stop, we can take the rest of the day off. Instantly we demand wood to light a fire to dry out our clothes, reluctantly he gives us some, light our first fire, soon the room is full of steaming clothes.

Guard returns from one of his weekly trips to the Stalag for post and parcels, and he is in a hell of a temper. Tells me he has had a chat with one of the lads while at the Stalag, he asked them what Piss-Tank meant, in all innocence they told him. Seems to have hurt his feelings, we wears a very injured expression on his face, says he cannot understand why we should insult a German soldier in this way. Holds me responsible for letting the men do it, deliberately has not brought any parcels back with him just to be cussed but hands over a few letters, informs me that he will be leaving us soon, another guard will be taking over in a couple of days.

Piss-Tank has left us. Having escorted us out to the chosen field for the day he says he will walk back to the farm house where the relief guard should be waiting. Telling us to be good boys and carry on working, which we faithfully promise we will do, he walks out of our lives. Up the gentle slope he goes, over the crest, down the far side. The last thing to disappear is the tip of his bayonet. Immediately down tools, stretch out, relax, plenty of warning of the new guards approach, all we have to do it watch the skyline at the top of the rise for the tip of his bayonet, by the time the man's eyes come into view we shall look exhausted from work.

There it is at last, the tell-tale bayonet tip, something different about it though. Not German, too thin and needle like, French - twice as long as the German ones. He will take longer to come into view, now the muzzle of the rifle, we are half way down the rifle barrel and still no head has appeared. Now the top of his hat, suddenly he is there. Standing on the crest looking down at us, can't believe my eyes, a tiny little man, a dwarf; a clown. A cut-down tunic fits the tiny barrel chest, trousers a different shade to the tunic, baggy at the knees, tucked into top boots that more or less cover his knee caps, the French rifle and bayonet slung over his shoulder towers above his head like a lance. A well developed, well cared for bushy moustache adorns his upper lip, standing there, he nervously gazes down at his new charges. We can only stare back at this comic opera specimen of a soldier in disbelief. A joke in any army, let alone a German one.

Several very silent minutes tick by as we stare at him, he fidgets under our gaze, we await his reaction, at last he has made up his mind on his method of approach. A nervous hitch of the rifle on to his shoulder, he takes the plunge, walks down the slope directly to me, holds out his hand to shake mine. Dazed, I grip it and shake, he tells me his name is Paul, very nice to meet us, walks round all the other lads, shakes their hands too; just over half the height of any of us, he smiles nervously, he is scared to bloody death of us. The man is lost from the word go; he doesn't stand a chance against us, if anybody gives us an inch we naturally take a yard. He is bullied unmercifully, caught between two fires, us and the farmer, he would ask us to do something on behalf of the farmer, but if we don't feel like it his life becomes hell. Have him scurrying back and forth to the Stalag endlessly chasing post and parcels, each time he returns with nothing he is a very worried little man; if he brings something back we pat his head. He would have more peace of mind fighting at the front rather than have a bunch of British P.O.W.'s. A farm worker from the far eastern side of Prussia, he lives only to get back to his big fat wife Anna and his brood of children whose photograph he keeps showing us.

November rolls round again, today we honour our dead, most of us are messing about in the cowsheds, Cunt-Face is in his usual miserable mood; he shouts at us as we fling sown our tools as the time gets near, we all shout back and threaten to rub his nose in a pancake if he doesn't shut up. This subdues him somewhat, we troop outside, form up outside the shed, we shut the stinking world out of our minds for two minutes, Cunt-Face watches us puzzled, we don't bother to explain to trash like him.

A trip on the horse-drawn wagon to fetch some grain, travel four miles each way, pass a row of eight workers cottages, the Polish driver tells me that each house has lost a man, dead on the Russian front, but, they are Polish houses? They have no choice in the matter. Rations cut back to below starvation level, a man cannot see to stand his family starve, but if you join the German Army then your family can have full rations that equal any German, your family will have food and clothing again. We have the greatest sympathy for these men, they seek us out behind the guards back, apologising to us because they must join the German Army. Some shed tears of shame, the helplessness of these men is frightening, most of them will die, we know it, they know it, we can only wish them well. Most of the cottages we pass have dirt floors, chickens, ducks, and goats wander in and out of the houses freely, they bed with the family at night.

Winter is approaching rapidly, the billet is getting cold, tell Paul to get some fuel for us or we shall pinch it. All he gets from the farmer in reply to his request is a lecture on the problems of Deutchland. Ok, so we got to pinch it. Start quite gently at first, little bits of wagon disappear, a pick shaft, then a bloody great plank; break it up, several men fill the inside of their tunics, put some down their trouser legs, under their greatcoats, can't do the cussed things up, never mind, hold the coat across, wend our way awkwardly back towards the billet. Down the lane stands the farmer, watching our approach with interest, not surprising really, our normal physical shapes have completely disappeared, each man is shaped like a shoe box. The farmer looks a bit stunned, it's obvious we have timber under our jackets, walk past him with faces full of innocence; nobody speaks as we pass, he turns with us, studies the view from the rear, but he doesn't say a word. Reach base, soon smoke rises lazily from our chimney.

Day after day we build up our stock as well as supplying the Polish family next door, the mans barns and stables are shrinking beneath his very eyes. Paul the guard is torn between the farmers indignant protests and our insatiable thirst for timber.

A cold job digging sugar beet, the tops are very lush, very green, and always very wet; not just a field of them, more like a plain. As far as the eye can see, countless millions of bloody beet - we shudder at the sight. A short handled tool to get them up with, two long spikes which you can dig deep into the soil at the side of the beet, lever the vegetable up and out of the ground, toss it aside into a heap for cutting and loading, cover a hundred yards, your back will snap in half like a rotten stick. Each man to take three rows at once, in ten yards you are soaked and swearing like a trooper, already in your mind you know which piece of barn is going to get burned tonight, he will have to pay for getting us wet!

The farmer is hovering round us as we work, he can't contain himself any longer. No, no, don't break the long tail off the beet , that's where the highest concentration of sugar is, they must dig up the tail. Bloody fool telling us that; now we know what to do with them, leave them in the ground. The Polish workers have left us far behind, standing in a long line they advance in a wide avenue which sweeps all before it, they work with the smooth efficiency of a well-oiled machine leaving behind neat lines of beet. Our line of beet is a disgrace to Britain, hardly a decent tail can be seen among the lot.

For three days the farmer weeps over the loss of his beet tails, each day he has hoped that our work will improve but we are beyond him, he gets us loading the things onto wagons instead, the Poles are left to dig up the rest. The Poles tell us that the beet are good to eat, cut off the tops, scrub them, boil them till soft, peel and eat. Tastes like sugar beet I suppose, won't become my favourite dish though, but it fills you up and it's hot, we get rid of quite a few this way.

Christmas 1941 arrives and celebrated with the non-arrival of food parcels, sing our blues away instead, also get news that we are to return to the Stalag; the farmer is fed up with us, to save his barns we must go. Little Paul is a bundle of nerves at the very thought of the task of getting us back to Stalag. Never thought it was possible for me to be sorry for a German but for this pathetic little male I am; getting him into trouble with the farmer was part of the game but I have no wish to get him into trouble with his military bosses, they have no sense of humour at all. He has tried his best for us so we don't give him any trouble, we allow him the pleasure of marching us back to the Stalag with the air of a lion in charge of a dozen sheep.

Mariendurg, The Cheese Factory, 1942

The Stalag does not improve at all, Jerry has no intention of letting it do so, he wants us out to work, permanent inmates don't look too good, they get no chance of any extras. Some men are trying to work their 'tickets' as they term it by acting as mental cases, some of the antics they get up to drives us potty just to watch them. One lad skips all day round the compound, arms swinging upwards and downwards to his front, swears blind he is as sane as the rest of us, been at it for months, but who the hell is walking around with tickets I just don't know.

For some strange reason there is a solitary soldier here from Yugoslavia, a very lonely man in the solitude of his own language.

Depressing tales of suicides and shootings, some men in a brainstorm rush the wire trying to climb the impossible tangle, others in terrible stages of depression use the privacy of darkness to slash their wrists, they bleed their life away silently. If someone hears the drip of blood as it hits the floor they might be saved, brought back to the very world they want to leave by other well-meaning men, but mostly they are successful in their bid for freedom. Other men find the rafters of the wash house convenient, again the softness of the night is chosen.

Soup is still pigswill, the 'Glass-House' has a long list of naughty boys by German standards, they wait to do their spell on bread and water, it's like a badge of honour.

Edgar is part of a detail to move potatoes for the day, riding on a lorry load of the things through town, they see a woman walking in the gutter flanked by several policemen dressed in civilian clothes, her hair has been shaved off her head, a board hangs round her neck,. The board tells the German world that she, a German woman, has dared to give herself to a Polish male. As the lorry passes the group, the lads pelt the policeman with a rain of potatoes.

Sooner or later Jerry will call out on morning parade that he requires men for working parties, may require painters, fence builders, cowmen, bricklayers or what have you. If a man feels like a change, fancies tying his hand at bricklaying, he will step forward and swear blind he is the best bricklayer that Britain has ever produced, the fact that he has never seen a brick doesn't matter. By the time Jerry finds out the man will have had a trip out somewhere, had a bit of better grub in anticipation of his skill, wasted a load of bricks and cement and had a trip back to camp. Collapsing walls and fences is the treasured trademark of all British P.O.W.'s in this Stalag, we are proud of the fact, we have no shame.

Two cheese makers wanted, like the sound of that one, in a flash Edgar and I step forward in our best cheese makers fashion. Visions of our teeth sinking into cheeses the size and shape of cartwheels or round ones the size of cannon balls passes through my mind as we do so, a factory in the town they say, not too far to go before we are sinking a couple of pints of milk, might even grow fat on this job. Collect our gear with the confidence of skilled tradesman in this business, we march out of camp into the town, no idea what to expect, take it step by step, at least they won't shoot us when they find out, at least I don't think so.

Medium sized factory, a large yard full of lorries, each one loaded with milk churns, a loading deck just out from the main building, on the deck a set of rollers which leads into the factory, unload the churns on to the rollers, push them across the deck inside the building, empty them into a large weighing tank, pull a lever, the milk empties down into the cellars below.

A comfortable billet by Stalag standards, two tiered wooden bunks, cooking facilities, wash room, a toilet with a real seat. Heating comes from the factory, they have got it made here. Half a dozen British lads and one Frenchmen make up the P.O.W. working staff, a dozen German civilian drivers, Polish and German staff inside the factory. Our job is to unload the churns of milk, empty them, reload the empty churns back onto the lorries. Occasionally we go down to the cellars, move the huge round cheeses from the soaking tank to another, sometimes we stir the content of the large vats of cheese in its preliminary stages.

First thing we are told is that P.O.W. and slave labour is not allowed cheese or milk, it is forbidden! Only the people of the town and the German army are entitled to these luxuries. Once we start work and learn the ropes we are very pleased that we are not able to eat the stuff. Empty a churn of milk into the tank, symbols of hatred will flow out with the white flood, animal dung, a dead mouse here, a rat there, a blood-soaked piece of cotton used by some woman, the slave labour on the farms are doing their work well, they foul the forbidden fruits in the only way they can.

The soup is quite reasonable, can barter bits of chocolate and soap for more substantial items of food, meals can be vastly improved by the use of the cooking facilities and our Red Cross parcels. But we are not happy, we work too hard for Germany, can't slow the tempo down, it's controlled by the arrival of lorries. Guard does not bother us much, likes to talk to us, likes the Englanders he says; I believe he does, keeps our post and parcels coming as best he can, but, we have got to get away from this place as soon as possible, we work as hard as the Poles have to.

Told one day to go out with the lorry driver, collect churns from a few farms, the driver is a scruffy looking German civilian, he immediately starts telling me how devoted he is to his wife and children for some reason, reach the outskirts of town, he picks up a girl who is waiting at the side of the road, climbing into the cab she settles herself comfortably in a corner. Milk churns scattered along the roads on lorry level ramps, I load up the full churns replacing them with the empty ones, sometimes the driver gets out of his cab to stoke up his wood burning lorry, sacks of small off-cuts of wood, a surprisingly small number of wood pieces will keep the lorry moving for many miles, the girl sits in her corner, very quiet, haven't heard her say a word yet. Soon the lorry is full of loaded churns, we head back to town.

A large open field of grass, the driver has turned into it and parked the lorry in the very centre, switches off the engine and asks me to go and have a smoke at the rear of the lorry, he has something to do. His left hand is already up the girls skirt tugging at her pants as he speaks, the silent female is getting to her feet eagerly helping him to get the bloody things off, as I swing down from the cab the pants hit the floor. Stand round the back of the lorry while the randy bastards get cracking, a big lorry but it's rocking on it's springs with enthusiasm and approval. A toot of the horn, the signal that the job has been well and truly done; back to the cab, she sits in her corner looking so innocent. Pull away from the field, he dumps her back at the side of the road, she still hasn't said a word. We head back to the factory, the driver having successfully bridged the gap until he can see his loving wife again.

Things are getting rough round here, can't slow up the tempo of work however much we try, lorries stand waiting to be unloaded nose to tail, the cows out on the farms have gone mad with their endless flow of milk. Can't get a break, we are full of resentment with the amount of work we do. At last a break in the line of lorries, dash into the billet for a rest and a drink. No sooner sat down when the door opens, the guard stands there, a lorry has just pulled in, would I go out immediately and unload it? I blow my top, tell him to go to hell; he says I must go out and do it at once, the people of the town are waiting for the milk and cheese, but I am so mad I tell him that the people in the town and indeed the whole of Germany can get stuffed. I am going to finish my drink. He stands there in shocked surprise at my comments, he keeps his temper in control, is deadly cool. Very quietly he informs me that he is going to leave me, he will go to his billet to pick up his rifle and will return to the room, if I am still here on his return he will have to shoot me, he turns and leaves the room.

Think the thing out quickly. If our positions were reversed I most certainly would not take it from him. Men are getting shot for less than what my undiplomatic tempers had said about his people. I have placed us both in a pretty impossible position, got to ease us both out of it if I can, especially me, can't get shot over a few stinking cans of milk. Return to the deck and resume work, don't think he will shoot me now that I am actually back on the job, but you never can tell with these bastards, know of one guard that walked two miles to get his rifle, the Sergeant in that case died, but I don't think this bloke has that killer instinct.

One eye on the job, one eye open for the guard, many very apprehensive minutes pass as I scrutinise the yard which the guard will have to cross to go into the billet. There he goes, rifle held across his body with both hands, ready for action, he cannot see me where I stand. Watch him enter the billet, a few minutes, out he comes heading for the deck where I should be, there is nowhere to run, I must face him. He has spotted me, walking over slowly towards me, rifle still held across his body, stands below me looking up; stop working, turn and face him squarely, our eyes meet, study each other for many, many tense moments. I look back into his eyes as an equal not as a beaten man, deliberately forcing myself to show no fear to this German, fear of what might happen.

A sudden movement of his rifle as he expertly grasps the sling with one hand, swings it up onto his shoulder, a shrug of the shoulder gets it settled comfortably in place, his face is dead-pan, a slow lift of his hand indicates he is satisfied, he turns and goes back to his billet. A deep sigh of relief rushes out of my lungs, with many other Germans I would be dead by now, the futile weapon in my hand, the milk churn lid, I replace. Things are never the same with the guard afterwards, he seems hurt because I don't like him and his people.

Working in the cellar on odd occasions offers a chance to foul up the goods, stirring the thick milk in the large vats becomes interesting after half an hour collecting spiders, flies, and any other crawly things that choose to come along, scatter them into the mixture, helps to give it body. Large flat round cheeses float in the tanks of liquid, next stage will be to place them on to shelves to mature. Gazing at the things I think how good and appetising they look despite the added ingredients contributed by the slave labour on the farms, but I think they need one more refinement, just to finish them off, I piss on them!

The horse is old, tired, and worn out; standing between the shafts of the tiny cart, I swear the shafts hold the beast up. The dirty, ancient, and smelly object sitting up on the seat is its master, they both wait patiently for me to join them, we go into town to collect swill for the factory pigs. A flat cart, no side walls, it carries four large round metal tubs and two buckets, climbing up on to the bench seat I settle beside the smelly old man. A cluck of the old man's tongue, the horse leans forward against the strap across its chest, it takes the weight and manages to move us forward at a snails pace. Through the quiet streets, silence broken only by the rattling clatter of the steel rimmed wheels over the cobbles, the old man is dumb, doesn't speak apart from an occasional cluck to the horse who totally ignores him, we move with the leisure of Old Man Time, each of us content with our own thoughts.

Wide gates ahead, the entrance to an infantry depot, armed sentries stand one each side of the gate. Unguided, the horse turns into the gateway between the sentries, they ignore us as we enter their domain. A network of narrow roads thread their way between wooden huts, hurrying groups of soldiers dressed in white cotton uniforms, some groups carry sets of boxing gloves, a large brick built structure ahead, pass it, we enter a large square parade ground, the road runs round the outside of the square.

My eyes pop open at the frenzied activities that abound on the square, hundreds of men in full fighting order gallop about like mad things. There, a line of men nestle behind heavy Vickers type machine guns, the gunners look through the sights, number two man lies on his side resting on one elbow as he holds the belt of ammunition in position. A shouted command, the gunner has picked up the gun in his cradled arms and is running forward; number two frantically picks up the ammunition box in one hand whilst the other hand tries to hold the belt in place in the gun, he has to match the gunners speed. A mad scramble as they run a few yards, another command, they are down in position on the ground with a crash of bodies.

Men drag anti-tank guns at speed, leapfrogging round the square as the repeat their gun laying drill, sections with light machine guns, others with rifles, over there an offender, Jesus, he is going through it! He stands in one spot, directly in front, and almost chest to chest stands an N.C.O. who screams into his face, he repeatedly crashes to the ground and is immediately up on his feet again; the speed he has to move his body up and down is impossible, but fear is making him do it.

Never seen machines in action like these before, I cannot take my eyes off the German Army at training. A beautifully turned out figure stands in the centre of the parade ground, lots of silver braid, boots shine like glass. White gloves on his hands, paces around now and then, his eyes dart in every direction watching the mass of frenzied activity. A man to be feared, the top man on parade, his regal splendour dares even a fly to land on him. Like darting blue dragon flies N.C.O.'s report to him, he listens, barks out an order, they dart away again.

I have no notion that the cart has stopped at the entrance to a cellar. Steps lead downwards, the old man is tugging at my trouser leg fussily, has a bucket in his hand, he disappears down the steps, grabbing a bucket I follow him. A small cellar, floor space covered with wooden barrels filled with swill, fill the bucket, up the steps, tip it into the metal containers on the cart. Slow worker my mate, the weight of the bucket bloody nearly pulls him into the barrel as he goes to fill it. Struggles up the steps, I fear he might drop dead on me at any moment.

Each trip to the cart halts me in my tracks as some incident out on the parade ground catches my eye, empty the bucket. I stand gazing, eyes fall on the central regal figure, he is looking at me, making signs, his right arm is stretched out pointing at me; the arm moves down, backwards to remain at a forty degree angle at his side, open palm of the hand indicating the patch of ground next to him. Jesus, the gesture is pure international, the English version hits me fair and square – if I don't get on with my work, he will have me out there! Stay down in the cellar a good five minutes, wondering how sincere the man's invitation is, watch the steps for a possible pair of gleaming boots descending.

Fill a bucket, up the steps, check that the menace is out of view behind the container on the cart, empty the bucket, if he is looking this way all he will see is a bucket and a pair of hands over the top of the container. I slink up and down the cellar steps like a cur, never giving the menace another chance to invite me out there, he will grind me into the dust. Job done, hustle the old man, I am all for a quick getaway but the stubborn old horse has different ideas, he is doing the pulling, we go at his pace or not at all. At snails pace we creep around the parade ground, the menace pivots with us, I spend a lot of time breathing on my finger nails and polishing them on my chest.

Edgar and I are at last sent back to Stalag as undesirable cheese makers but we have disposed of about five months of time! Fellows still dance around the compound trying to convince Jerry that they are nuts, don't seem to be convincing Jerry but they are convincing me.

Soon get fed up with the terrible food, stupid parades and depressing air of the place, time hangs on the hands too much, doesn't move fast enough. Edgar gets caught on a working party for the day, got to go to town an unload a wagon load of bread for the army, he returns to camp in the evening looking for all the world like a pregnant woman; he has managed to pinch two army loaves of bread, how he ever got in through the gate I don't know, the guards must have been blind.

Two men wanted for farm work, a cowman and a ploughman. As one man Edgar and I have stepped forward with the confidence of fully fledged farm workers, obviously as case of our city upbringing fighting to get out, we swear blind we are experts in both ploughing and milking.

Collected by a guard, march through the town to the station, things are looking up. We ride in a passenger coach, tucked away in a corner, nice soft seats, stare back at civilians who stare at us. Ask the guards permission to smoke, we get it, pull out nice fat English cigarettes that we happen to have, blow the smoke all over the compartment. Through the smokescreen the civvy eyes stare at the tubes in our mouths, make great play at breaking off a cube of chocolate, into the mouth nice and slow; push it in through the teeth with one delicate finger, let them see the tit-bit disappear, suck loudly, rudely, and with relish. Silent sullen faces all round, ignore them as we proceed with bright useless chatter. Do we look worried, do we hell? Talk over the forthcoming job as we travel, got to decide who is going to be what, Edgar says he doesn't fancy cows too much, they stink, would prefer the horses; I don't care what I have, so we make him the ploughman on the spot. I will be the cowman. Both happy we have settled that little point, we relax to meet our immediate future.

Fisherbalki, East Prussia, 1942

A country station, a horse-drawn wagon awaits us, the driver has a stiff left leg, he climbs awkwardly up on to the vehicle, looks around for us and the guard but we are already on board and ready to move. Drive a couple of miles, the cobbled road turns to run parallel with a wide river, facing the river and on the opposite side of the road a farmhouse, stable and barn, pull in and stop outside the stable, the driver says that we have arrived and that he is the farmer. Not a very happy looking individual, wait till he finds out our qualifications. The guard is billeted down the road, will leave us now to the farmer but will return later to lock us in for the night.

Into the stable, stalls for sixteen cows, six horses, three pig stys, a small cubicle six feet by five feet, in it two wooden bunks, one on top of the other leaving a two foot strip to move in – our quarters. On the door a padlock. On the bunks, palliasses filled with old straw, the fleas can plainly be seen hopping about on the surface of them, the farmer tells us that we are replacing two Frenchmen.

Free of lice at last, we do entertain the odd flea now and then, but these little mites we consider to be British and can live with them but we are going to have no truck with French fleas! Tell the farmer that the first thing we want is soap, hot water, and disinfectant to clean the place out, next we want fresh straw for the palliasses, he looks at us thunderstruck as though we have asked for the moon, he says he has no straw to spare and that soap is not available, disinfectant is impossible. He has a very definite whine to his voice, very un-German, ok he is going to be a troublesome one, got to start with him exactly as we intend to carry on. In a loud voice which easily drowns his, Edgar tells him that if he doesn't give us the things we want to clean the place out we will immediately start walking back to Stalag. Load of crap of course, absolutely no idea where the Stalag is, couldn't walk anywhere anyway, but he is shattered and believes it.

He is hopping about in his agitation as we stand waiting for him to make up is mind, we help him, thump our chests with our firsts, shouting 'Englanders', indicating that we are God Almighty. Not expecting trouble from the word go, he looks sick. A sudden scream of 'Elizabeth' a woman promptly enters the stable from a door in the shadows, almost as though she has been listening at the door; a plain red faced and most unattractive female. He tells her in injured tones what we require, obviously this is the love of his life, she too is horrified, they talk the crisis over at some length. We stand there with superior attitude awaiting the fate of the French fleas. Reluctantly she nods her head, yes, we can have what we want, off she goes to attend to the items.

He tells us to follow him, out of the stable, across a yard, into a barn, the fresh golden straw reaches from the floor to the roof, he miserably tells us to take what we want. The man has lost the first round, he is going to have a pretty rough time I think.

Get to work, clean the place out, throw out the old straw, wash the palliassess, hang them out to dry. We sleep hard tonight, get the fresh straw in the morning.

Toilet is interesting, a square box on four legs, inside the box roughly at bum level is a board with a hole in it. Stand the contraption anywhere on the dung heap in the yard that you fancy, can move it daily if you don't like the view through the door-less front. You can watch the chickens beneath you that come running to await your offering as soon as you start to undo your pants, the music of their clucking and squabbling becomes part of the ritual, we consider ourselves fortunate that chickens have reasonably short necks.

Have slept well, broken only by grunts and squeals from the pigs, thuds of hooves as the horses restlessly changed position, the den is warm from the heat of the animals, the smells come natural and are acceptable having smelled a lot worse ourselves in recent months. Bright and early at five thirty next morning the guard unlocks the door, the farmer stands at his heels waiting to start the days work. Now for the test, he is asking who the cowman is. I say I am in a tone which implies it was a silly bloody question to ask anyway. Can I milk? I have to answer truthfully that I can't. A resigned expression crosses his face.

Elizabeth, the Frau, has arrived. In her hands she carries two buckets and two milking stools, he tells her that I am the cowman and I can't milk, she gives me a dirty look. She wears a heavy coat and a handkerchief tied over her head, thrusting a stool and a bucket at me she wags her finger indicating that I am to follow her. Out of the stable, round to the rear of the barn, a fenced off enclosure comes into view; a bunch of cows wait our arrival, thirteen of them, black and white in colour, their jaws move endlessly as they chew whatever cows chew, heads turn and take a good look at us as we enter. The frau dumps her bucket under a cow, sits down on her stool, grabs a teat and starts pulling, instantly a white jet hits the bottom of the bucket with the speed of a bullet, to be joined quickly by a second as the other hand gets going. She chatters to me as she works, telling me how to do it I guess, but I don't understand a word she says, a few minutes of demonstration, she gets up, takes my stool and bucket and moves off to another cow, gazing at the empty stool I guess I've got to take over. Sit down to the task, grab a pair of teats and pull like mad for several seconds, nothing happens, try another pair of substantial teats, work them vigorously still nothing happens. The cow looks round at me probably wondering who is taking liberties with her today, I stare back at her with the beginnings of hatred in my eyes at her stubbornness. My hands dance from one stupid teat to another, a dribble that time, a stinging blow round the ear, her tail, filthy with droppings. I swear at her but she takes no notice just increases the blows of her tail round my head. Lost all sense of time in my battle with the teats, had a few dribbles, maybe half a pint, suddenly the nearest hind leg has been lifted in a forward and downward movement, it's in the bucket, smack in the middle of my milk. I stare at it in amazement and utter defeat.

The Frau stands beside me telling me to get out of the way, she will finish it, getting down she proceeds to punch the offending leg with her ham fist as she shouts. Tips the bucket gently, the leg comes out of the bucket instantly without spilling a drop, in seconds the milk is flowing in a stream soon to be finished. She has milked twelve and three-quarter cows to my quarter. Grabbing my hand she examines my finger nails, shakes her head vigorously, nails too long, must cut them to milk cows, apart from that, it will come she says.

Having dispensed with our services the cows wander off back to the open fields, several milk churns stand in the enclosure which the Frau has been filling. Later, she informs me, I will have to take them down the road to the next village to a milk depot. Carrying our buckets and stools we return to the stables. Edgar and the farmer turn up shortly afterwards on a horse-drawn wagon, his lesson this morning had been to drape the harness round the horse, after several tangles he had got it right. Reversing the animal between the shafts of the wagon had given him a few anxious moments, mainly for the horses sake. Losing patience and telling the farmer to shut his mouth, he had coaxed the horse in his way without tearing at the bit as instructed to do.

An outhouse adjacent to the house for eating, two small tables within, one on each side of the room, two chairs at each, Edgar and I sit at one, the other is occupied by another member of the working staff. A kid, about sixteen, grinning at us like a Cheshire cat. Red coloured hair, rough and untidy, blue eyes, freckled face, says that his name is Edward and that he is German. Can't resist the silly cheeky grin on his face, tell him our names and that we are Englanders. The grin lengthens into a beam of sheer delight as though he has been waiting for us to come along all his short life, tells us that he sleeps in a cubicle within the confines of the house, and that apart from us he is the only other man working for the farmer. We ignore the self-imposed status of manhood claimed by the little twerp but we obviously have a useful ally here.

Two girls enter from the holy sanctuary of the house, one places before us plates containing two slices of dark brown bread, the air holes of the bread have been filled with butter. She is a sad looking girl, we smile and thank her but her face does not respond with a smile. The second girl carries two cups of coffee, dumping them before us she greets us brightly, about eighteen, very pretty face, nice figure, she has an abundance of everything physical it takes to make a man happy. They leave the room.

Edward immediately fills us in, the sad one is Polish, might have guessed, her name is Sophia, the happy one is German, her name, like the Frau, is Elizabeth, but we immediately decide to call her FiFi. Sophia is classified as a slave worker, cleans the house, cooks, waits on the Frau hand and foot, does general labouring about the farm as required, the Cinderella of the establishment. Fifi looks after the two kids and drifts around looking sexy. Sophia eats alone within the confines of the house while Fifi eats with the farmers family, she is considered of equal status and breeding. Edward, of a lower social order, eats with us, thus we all fit neatly into our places in this smug world of the farm. The job of Edgar and I is to shake it up wherever we can, that's just plain automatic after all!

Breakfast over, tasks are allocated to us, must deliver the milk to the depot, Edward will come this first morning to show me where it is, load up on to a wagon. Move off, Edward driving, listen to all the German noises that Edward makes to get the horse moving and to make it stop. A small depot, a loading ramp located at the side of the road, unload the churns, pick up the empty ones, get ready to return, but wait. Other British and French arriving with milk from other farms, have a chat, exchange Stalag and war news, Edward waits patiently until I have finished. Tell Edward I will drive on the return trip, his young critical eyes watch me pick up the reins with a confidence I do not feel; my mouth surprisingly produces the correct noise, the horse is moving forward, again the correct noise erupts from my mouth, we stop just where I want to, Edward smiles his approval.

Edgar and I are taken out to the fields by the farmer, a field of young seedlings, they disappear in uniform rows, want us to weed them, have no tools, sit on the ground and pluck with our fingers. He leaves us to it, a beautiful day, what could possibly be more peaceful and relaxed than this. We sit and chat enjoying the peace and solitude. An ear-splitting yell accompanied by galloping hooves and rattling wagon. Edward stands on the floor of the wagon as he gallops at breakneck speed across the next field. The wagon, made up of several pieces loosely held in place by a couple of bolts dances crazily as each piece struggles to take off in its own direction,. We frown at him with the severity of older and wiser men whose peace is being disturbed.

We are part of a working group of men scattered around on farms, they vary in strength depending on the size of the farm, some have three or four men, some two, some only one. Some men work mere plots, some do other odd jobs mostly for women whose men are dead or are serving on some front, one man just upriver works a cross river ferry boat, a flat punt, he pulls on a rope to get his passengers across, his moods control the flow of traffic. The guard is located in a fairly central position on the working area, he cycles round each day checking that he has still got us and to lock us in at night. Each Sunday is a day of rest, all work except milking stops. We walk the half mile to the guards quarter each Sunday for roll call, post and parcel collection if any; on these occasions we spit and polish to the best of our ability in order to present a military front to the German world.

Everyone on the farms calls us by our first names, or as near as they can, having trouble with the pronunciation. Whenever we want the farmer we always shout "Hoy!" to him, usually he comes running, find out that his name is Walter, from then on we scream "Walter" wherever we are, he comes hopping fast.

Rapidly come to the conclusion that Walter and his lady love are a pair of bastards, they treat everyone who works for them and who they consider socially beneath them as dirt, try it on us but we refuse to take it, other people round here have to.

Quickly note that all the farmers round here are little tin gods, working people from the village who wish to speak to Walter have to stand just within earshot of him until he decides to notice them, the superior attitude of the man gets our backs up, got to show these people that he is nothing special; just a dirt farmer. Walter is speaking to the village policeman outside the stable, they are having a laugh and a giggle as they pursue their policy of keeping well in with each other. A very old man and his wife from the village stands within four feet of Walters elbow, the man wishes to speak with Walter, he holds his hat in his hand as they wait, have been there a good fifteen minutes, Walter is well aware that they wait, there is no one else in sight in the whole village.

A tiny crack in the piece of harness that Edgar holds, that will do as an excuse, shout "Walter" at the top of my voice, he stops mid-sentence, looks across, "Come here" first time we have used his first name in public, the policeman's eyes are round with surprise. He looks at Walter to see what he will do about it, but Walter is hopping over quickly to see what is wrong. Show him the leather, he reckons it will be alright, he returns to the policeman, the incident of

P.O.W.'s interrupting the farmer has been seen to be done, a terrible thing, we feel that we have made the old couples day!

Across the road flows the wide river Vistula, it goes direct to the sea and the port of Danzig. How many miles we don't know, all we know is that big ships are there, ships that sail away, maybe even get home! Weigh up the possibilities, talk among the lads on Sundays, try to work out where other men went wrong who have already tried the same thing and failed. No friends round this area to help, even the tiny toddlers report a new face when they see one, it stays at the back of the mind, continuously there, got to be right though, dead right, meanwhile be patient, keep fit.

Edgar has had chicken thrust in his hand by Walter together with a chopper, he has got to kill it, a look of panic on Edgars face, he looks to me for help. I have none to offer, don't want the job any more than he does. Strange, can kill men in the heat of battle and don't lose a moments sleep, but kill and animal or a bird we both panic immediately, but then, we have nothing against animals or birds have we? Can't get out of this one, he painfully prepares to proceed with the execution, lie the birds head and neck on a block of wood in the stable, lift the blade high, a swift stroke but only the beak and half the birds head lies on the ground. Edgar opens his eyes, looks at his handiwork with horror, another swift stroke with his eyes open, the head is severed neatly at the neck leaving a wildly thrashing body. Blood splashes everywhere, quickly, hold it behind a wall of the stall, between it and your own body, soon it's struggles cease, Edgar has killed his first chicken.

Don't think much of the German language at all, does not seem to be a decent swear-word in it as far as I can make out. Saw Walter bash his finger with a hammer today, he danced around on his one good let like a maniac with pain, all he could dig up to scream was the equivalent to 'thunder weather'. This surely is why they are all so miserable.

Have forgiven Edward the boy the liberty of introducing himself as a man, when it comes to work he is quite right, an expert in every aspect of farming he does the work of two men with unconscious ease.

One hundred yards down the road is a small homestead with a few chickens, couple of cows, ducks, a horse, and vegetable gardens, a couple of tiny fields. A woman runs it with the help of a man from London Town, Fred, the lone man of the pace visits us when he has finished work. Tells us one day that his Frau gives him fried potatoes, fried potatoes - heaven above, fried potatoes. For two years we have lived on soup, nothing but soup, every day. Fried potatoes, god it sounds fantastic. Forgotten such things existed, from the second he opened his big mouth we have got to have some, dream about the, talk about nothing else but fried potatoes. They fill our world with their tantalising absence, if we don't have some soon we will die!

Ask the Frau if we can have some fried potatoes, she shakes her head at our request, can't be done, got no fat. Load of crap, we know she has the fat, these farmers have it all! Ok, got to force her hand, we get together to work it out. Half a dozen lousy apple trees in the Frau's garden loaded with apples, if we pinch some of those she will do her nut, any civilian caught taking one would get about three years labour camp; but we are not civilians, don't care a bugger anyway, got to have fried potatoes. Get a nice long ladder after dark, stroll into the garden, climb up a tree, light a cigarette, choke and splutter a bit to make a noise; Edgar holds the ladder below, he lights up a cigarette. Someone comes out of the house to see what all the noise is, a dreadful wail fills the night air, it's the Frau, someone up her apple tree! She calls for Walter who comes rushing out into the dark like a lion, I stand at the bottom of the tree with an apple in my hand. They stare at us in horror, ask why we pinch their apples, we say it's because we want fried potatoes, only fried potatoes can fill our bellies, otherwise it's got to be apples. Hands raised to heaven in horror, more wailing from the Frau, yes, we can have some fried potatoes, very next day, Edward the boy can have some too. Such crimes are cheerfully pursued in answer to the tantalising dreams of food.

Love at first sight between Edgar and the horses, coos over them all day in a sickening fashion, spend hours giving them extra grooming; tells them all about his girl back home, their ears wiggle in appreciation of his descriptions. Gets mad as hell when Walter or Edward uses the whip on them, he gets the same results with his soft persuasion. Now and then the horses tolerate me, will allow me to feed them, will even take the tit-bits that I have scrounged with my own fair hands, will let me groom them from time to time. Working the brush over their beautiful silken coats pleases me, but the pleasure is usually cut short when a large and heavy hoof is dumped squarely on my foot. I scream blue murder at the beast as I wriggle like a worm trying to get free, pleading for a response to my puny hand trying to lift the thick leg, but they merely look round at me with their big soft brown eyes and will remove the leg only when ready. Limping away till next time I swear to God that I shall cut back on their feed if I can.

As I thought, apart from the one who I call Queenie, there is no love lost between the cows and me. Just plain stubborn, they know exactly what they are doing, accidentally stick your finger into a teat, see what happens, they will immediately try to flog you to death with their dirty tails; or wait deliberately until you have a bucket nearly full, then comes the quick double shuffle and a dirty great leg is stuck in the middle of it. Move away - that's another dirty trick they keep up their sleeves, keep edging slowly away, you can wear the legs off a milking stool following the buggers around the field if you let them. Have to do something about their insolence, at least once a week I blow my top at them. Try and punch them and you're likely to break your hand, kick them in the belly and your boot just bounces off as from a tight drum, kick them anywhere else and there's bones in the way, probably break your foot. Took me six months to find out about the big tender nose, walk round to the front of the big pink slobbering nose, punch it. All that will happen though is that great big eyelashes will lower slowly over big brown eyes in mild surprise, but the eyes will accuse you of every atrocity under the sun, they do this deliberately to make you feel bad, but their feminine charms don't win me that easily. Now, Queenie is different; she is a lady, easy to handle, gives her milk freely, if she wants to move her foot she will do it slowly so as to give you warning, gives a man time to move the bucket. Smacks me round the ear now and then with her tail but I swear it is an accident, she wouldn't dream of moving an inch once milking has begun, altogether the nicest cow I have ever met.

So many uniforms walking about this country, the people just don't seem to be keeping up with them fully, they give the party salute to any uniform they meet to play safe. Quite a few strangers pass through the village, we sometimes meet them as we go about our work or on our way to Sunday parade, as you draw close to some of them you can see their brains working trying to figure out which branch of the party you belong to, desperately they try to place you, they can't, ok, play safe, up comes the arm to stab the sky stiffly, "Heil Hitler". We flop our arms in response, loud and clear we reply "Fuck Hitler". They pass, quite happy that they have met other loyal party members!

Edward, like all youth in this country, is a member of the Hitler Youth organisation; he hates it, but has no choice in the matter. He sings the praises of our army more than he does his own, brings along a dummy stick grenade that he has to keep at home to practise with every day; we discuss the merits of theirs and ours, he practices by throwing it at a telegraph pole outside the stable for hours but he never hits it. Challenges me to have a throw, I resist doing so for many days fearing that I too will miss, we have already told the lad that everything we British do is better than the way they do things. I fear to fail in his young German eyes. The little devil is persistent, wears me down in the end, got to live up to our big talk if we can, at last I agree to have a go.

The grenade is nicely balanced in the hand, Edward and his kind seem to throw the thing in the way one would throw a stone, don't seem to line up on target, I will try it the same way we throw ours, see what happens, might come near. Grip the wooden handle firmly, quickly line up on target with the left arm forward to the face, right arm directly behind and low down, a full over arm swing of the right arm over the body as I let the thing go. The missile flies upwards then downwards in a wide arch to hit the pole dead centre - blimey, how did that happen? Edward is absolutely speechless at this display of British military skill, but not as surprised as we are! Couldn't do it again in a million years. Edward is clambering for tuition, wants me to do it again, I refuse to repeat the performance or give him lessons with the superior air of a man who knows he can do it every time. Edward will be going into the army in less than six months time, we teach him nothing! If he survives the war the memory of the Englander and his dummy hand grenade will be implanted in his mind for the rest of his life. On such small things are great and obviously sometimes very false illusions based.

Going to have our pictures taken to send home. The whole commando travels in one very large horse-drawn wagon to a village several miles away, the guard is wedged in the middle of us, pull up in front of a battered old cottage, troop round the back to a garden. Tastefully arranged are tiers of long trestles, sit in front stand at the back pattern, just like wedding groups. Stick the little blokes in front but first a bit of swapping round of tunic jackets, wear the battered ones at the back, come on change pants, let's borrow a hat, soon, all the blemishes are hidden from the eye of the huge old-fashioned camera as an old man dives under his piece of black cloth, every man strains to formulate the word 'CHEESE', got to look like a bunch of lads on a bloody camping holiday or something! After a few days we all get a copy to send home, got to admit the old boy on the camera has made a good job of it. My word, we do look happy! That will keep them quiet at home anyway, will stop their fears a little we hope.

P.O.W. working party 1942, back row from left Arthur, Edgar

Guard caught pilfering our Red Cross parcel stock, immediately sentenced for service on the Russian front even though physically unfit, just as well have made it a death sentence.

Sophia the Polish girl never smiles, she has forgotten how to I think, the ability has been drained out of her, washed away by tears. We try our best to brighten her days but it is difficult, can get very little of her story out of her, only that she does not know where her husband or her baby is, all three are separated from each other, her misery is deep rooted and cannot be shared. We feel that she does not entirely trust us or anybody else, even God. Slip her a few odd items from our parcels when we have them, she softly whispers her thanks, asks no questions, shows no surprise at the appearance of the unobtainable little luxury in her hand, just takes them and goes silently about her work.

We stare at the meal of the day which Sophia has just dumped in front of us is disbelief. On each of our plates lies what looks like a couple of perch. Swear to God that they have just been lifted straight out of the river and slid on the plates, the silver scales gleam, bright red fins. Baleful eyes stare at us, they look sick as all fish do that lie unmarked on somebody's plate, certain that if we put them back in the river this minute they would swim away. Bang on the table shouting "Frau", she comes running, ask her what the hell the things are. Take them away, clean them and cook them; a painful look on her face, we have hurt her feelings, good German food she says, pickled fish. Remind her that we are not bloody Germans, we want some spuds, she takes the fish away and brings us fried spuds instead. Poor Edward looks at his fish with distaste too but he is German, he is supposed to eat it, he can't, he walks out hungry.

A dozen men huddle together in the cow stall, each of them is down on one knee, some dressed in rough suits others in quilted jackets and odd trousers. I come across them unexpectedly not knowing that they are there. Automatically greet them in German, their eyes stare back at me full of fright, no reply, they don't understand me, I walk past them out of the stable. Walter stands outside talking to an S.S. man who shortly herds the men to their feet and marches them away along the village street to disappear from view. Ukrainians, no wonder they were frightened men, anything they see round here in uniform can only be hostile in their minds.

Never a dull moment around here, now the cows need servicing, got to travel a few miles to pick up a bull. Walter uses a light cart for the trip, I travel with him in the cart but I will have to walk back with the bull. Walter reckons he can't handle the bull with his stiff leg, what makes him think that can handle it even with two good legs I don't know! Probably considers me expendable anyway. There the brute stands, just like a bloody Bovril advert, not very tall really, but Jesus, he is wide, built like a locomotive, power in every muscle. His cow pusher, a diabolical looking object, hangs boastfully between his legs; his head swings slowly from side to side looking for a target I think, I keep Walter between it and me as long as I can.

Walter is doing the talking bit quite well to the owner of the beast, in conclusion he points to me with the immortal words that I will escort the beast back to his farm, sounds a bit like a death knell to me though! A steel ring is fixed in the bulls nose into which is attached a piece of timber about four feet long, with this pole one is supposed to be able to lead it anywhere. Looks as though they are about ready to go, the owner unties a rope which fastens the beast to a ring in the wall, grips hold of the pole and leads the lumbering object towards me.

Reminding myself that I represent a certain island across the sea and that any bloody thing a German can do, we of the island can do better, my trembling hand nervously grips the pole. Study the bulls one watery eye that I can see, looks docile enough, got to walk four miles with it, who is going to take who I wonder? Like a little kitten so far, a dead slow lumbering roll. I try a little exploration, a little push of the pole o the right, his head turns to the right, a little pull of the pole towards me, his head turns to the left. Does just what I want him to do, I feel tough, masterful, and strong leading a great thing like him about so easily. A nonchalant spring of confidence in my step as we stride along together man and beast. An itch in the far side of his neck or something, a sudden unexpected turn of his head to the right which rips the pole out of my hands. A frantic dive to retrieve it which places my body close up against his neck, his head is coming back, too late to stop my forward lunge. The pole and his head hits me dead centre in my stomach but somehow the pole is back in my hand, I hang on, it saves me hitting the deck as the wind leaves my body. The power in that neck which could sweep me away like straw has shaken me but he is still dead calm and peaceful, don't think he even felt it! Making good progress, he has stopped on several occasions for no apparent reason, just stops dead in his tracks, looks slowly round as thought saying "Where the hell are the cows then?" Legs well set apart like rocks, usually in the middle of the road, pull as much as you like he won't move until he is ready.

Tie him to a ring on the wall of Walters barn, we leave him bellowing his head off, announcing his arrival to any cows that may be hanging about I guess. Six cows to be serviced, the first one is brought forward; untie the bull, lead him away out of sight of the cow, tie the cow to the ring in the wall in his place, bring back the bull and release him. An investigation to make sure he has got a cow and then he gets to work. Tries to get to work is nearer the truth, a tragic thing, he can't reach, he is too short, but by God, he did try. Stands there now his whole body shuddering with frustration, think he feel the indignity too!

The owner of the beast has turned up to see that his client gets his due I expect, takes the exhausted bull out of sight of the cow again; Walter runs off soon to return with a couple of shovels, makes out a half circle on the soil which matches the cows hind legs in distance from the barn wall, the two farmers start digging a trench. Soon the cows hind quarters stand in the trench no matter which way she turns. Release the bull a second time, the cow doesn't stand a cat in hells chance of getting out of it this time. A very surprised bull, this time he made it, proudly he allows us to lead him away while we change his material for him.

One of the lads on a farm has landed himself in trouble, lost his temper with a farmer he works for, he grabs a picture which is hanging near him off the wall, a well directed blow wraps the frame around the farmers neck. The picture happens to be one of Adolf Hitler, they have him on two counts now, one of attacking a civilian and another of insulting Hitler.

Summer months, after work is finished, Fred from the two-bit farm down the road comes to visit us every day, sit outside the barn, chew straw, watch the world go by and chat. Sometimes we cross the road and take a swim in the river, a bit risky though due to the thick weed which floats in it. Edgar gets caught one day, a few panic moments as we watch him fight to get out of it, nasty stuff. Fred speaks German like a native having the desire and will to learn to do so since his capture, a randy type, he talks a lot about sex which I think he misses more than food!

The small gauge railway track which crosses the farm carries different cargo these days, the open topped trucks are packed to capacity with women of all ages, they stand together so tight that they sway with the movement of the truck in a solid mass. See no sign of packages or bundles, they have only what they stand up in, nationality is difficult to judge, guess that they come from all over except Russia; something about Russians that is different to the eye, partly their dress but mostly it's the expression on their faces. They just stare at you, resist all offers of help, reject friendliness as something suspicious.

Have heard of a large slave labour camp not far from the farm, some nasty tales seep out of the place regarding the treatment of prisoners, guess this train load is heading there. Here and there some of the girls call out and wave to us in greeting, assume they have recognised our Battle-dress, never hear what is shouted but we wave back to them just the same. Ask the farmer what sort of place the camp is, he tells us that it was built as a military depot but is now being used as a temporary political prison. He does not look too happy with our questions about the place and closes the subject, but we have our own ideas.

Sunday muster: post and an issue of Red Cross woolly comforts have come through. Socks, balaclavas, scarves; knitted by the patient practical ladies at home. A tiny piece of paper is rammed into the toe of a sock, on it is written the name and address of the person who has made them, it invites the finder to drop her a line. With pleasure I write and tell her that the gift has reached out onto the remote farm in East Prussia and that it will warm ten grubby British toes this coming winter. A letter arrives from home, it informs us that our father is dead, the German shell of 1914 has at last done its work. We have no strength left to combat the blow, for the first time in this world of total misery we weep.

Fred comes along to visit us, hand him the letter to read, he leaves us alone to our grief. We weep for the love of the man, we weep for the pity of the man; he had to fight the peace years even harder than he fought his war years for the right to live and stand upright like a man, but he was doomed from the start, he could not win, he and his kind had to toe the line in a world full of fit men chasing work that did not exist. We weep for a father forced to ask his sons for the price of a cigarette when we as lads started working. We remember the shame written in his face as he did so. We weep for the memory of his last appearance in front of the 'means test' tribunal. He stood before the table, held up by a pair of crutches, the memory of yet another major operation on his leg wound still fresh in his mind, he answered the probing questions regarding his possible hidden wealth.

"What? Do we understand that you own your furniture and that you have two sons working?"

"Yes" my father truthfully replied, "Two young lads working and we own our bits of furniture".

"So, you have assets! Sell your furniture! With two sons working you can afford a cut in pension"

In a sea of blind humiliated rage my father managed to grasp the edge of the table and tip it into the laps of the tribunal members before he and his crutches crashed to the floor in a helpless heap. They throw him and his crutches out of the place. I remember asking Mother in shocked surprise why Dad was crying when he came home, I had never seen a grown man crying before.

We remember these things and ask ourselves why we are here? Why we bother to fight? Perhaps it's to get rid of the system that ground so many men like Father into the dust between the wars, but we remain the sons of our Father despite ourselves, falling below his measure of courage and endurance is unthinkable. Now he is dead, he could not stand the final operation which removed his leg from the hip socket, his spirit gave way under the ceaseless struggle against pain, the will to fight drained away, now the humiliation is ended. Our lives are suddenly filled with a great emptiness knowing that we shall never again hear his voice, award us the highest praise in the land as he says "Well done son".

A deep sullen depression fills our minds which lasts for several days, the hatred of everything German is intensified until we can hardly bear to look at their world. Wild plans of making a break fills our minds, a dangerous and reckless phase halted only by the stark reality of the impossible odds; without patience and reason Mother could have three dead men on her mind. Gradually we simmer down leaving just hatred.

A report from the village folk tells us that the guard who was sentenced to serve on the Russian front for pilfering our Red Cross parcels is dead, he met death less than two months after arrival.

Harvest time. Crops of wheat to be gathered but first work needs to be done around the edges of the fields with a scythe, make room for the mower to start its long cut. Scythes are thrust at us together with sharpening sticks, up close the things look exceedingly dangerous. Two very old men from the village have arrived to help with the harvest, each have their own private scythes in their hands, they cuddle them with pride, the blades are narrow with many years of sharpening behind them, they gleam like swords. Go into the fields with the old men says Walter, watch how they do it, you will soon pick it up, he talks as though we want to. The old men lead off, a well practised swing of the scythes over their shoulders, they look like a couple of 'old man times'. Move off to follow the old chaps, a nonchalant swing of the scythe over my shoulder, too late. I anticipate the possibilities as the point of the blade heads for my rump, it's tingling as it waits, but no, it's ok!

At the scene of operations the two old men have their scythes reversed, the blades face away from them at face level, sharpening stones in their hands. Arms up, the hands move with the speed of light from the wrists, a flick of the stones each alternate side of the blades, a delicate feel of the blades edge with their thumbs; yes, they are satisfied. Stand back to back to each other, they move off in different directions, each man taking one side of the field. Legs braced well apart, a gentle turn of the bodies to their right starts the motion; a beautiful smooth sweep of the arms across their bodies, an effortless follow up of the body to their left. The long thin blades follow, cutting through the upright wall of stiff stalks. They leave behind two neat rows lying on the ground, not one stalk has dared to cross over another, a second whisper of a swish as the blades leave two more rows neatly on the ground well separated from the first, a low stubble remains, perfectly even, an evenness to shame any lawnmower.

Tell the old men that we will go to the opposite end of the field, work down to meet them, they grunt their approval. We too stand back to back to start off with, ok get set, mentally run through the drill, it's there in the mind. Feet set well apart, hold the blade flat and level just above the ground surface, body a slight turn to the right, a nice smooth relaxed swing of arms and blade across the body to the left, turn the body to follow, this should execute the perfect cutting stroke. How the bloody hell is it then that the point of the blade is buried in the soil by about six inches? Start again, keeping the point up, ok, from the right, before my frustrated eyes the wheat folds over neatly, the ears lie on the ground but the stalks are still attached to the ground; a battered wall of stalks lie flat but uncut, try again, and again, and again. Sick to death of pulling the point out of the ground, a definite bend in the blade, about ten square feet of battered wheat surrounds me, here and there little bits of stubble together with large clods of soil resulting from my excavations. Take a break, see how Edgar is getting on, he has got the idea, doing quite well in fact, but he sweats too much; an efficient man at this game can keep going all day without raining any sweat they reckon. To hell with it, toss the scythes into the nearest ditch, start making up bundles instead. The old men are coming down the sides of the field like a couple of greyhounds, they are happy enough.

Everybody is turning out for this job, even Fifi, the kids and the family Dachshund together with people from the village. Walter turns up in grand style, sitting on his antiquated cutting machine drawn by a single horse. He starts his first cut, soon piles of loose wheat lies in neat rows waiting to be tied in bundles; gather a stick of straight stalks, twist them together to give them strength, gather a heap of gold, bind them round securely, twist, tuck under and stand the bundle upright. Build them into heaps of a dozen or more, let the soft breeze play through them, they are ready to haul back to the farm for threshing.

A large wagon is required to haul the wheat back to the barn, can't see anything big enough round here, but the everyday versatile wagon is the answer. Strip off the sidewalls, ends and floor planks and you are left with two pairs of wheels, each pair joined by an axle. Attached to each axle are two V shaped uprights of timber, both axles are joined by a roughly trimmed pole - remove the pole by taking away two bolts, insert a longer pole, secure with the two bolts, the wagon is now more than twice the length if was before. Drop open sided sidewalls into place, they rest against the V shaped upright timbers on the axles, drop in a long plank to act as a floorboard, the wagon is ready for the harvest. Truly a remarkable collection of bits and pieces developed from centuries of peasant farming.

Pitch forks for everyone, Edward, Edgar and I are to load up the crop out in the fields, everyone else will unload into the barn.

Fritz, the Dachshund, accompanies us out into the fields. Not because he is our friend, he is the biggest Nazi we know normally, got no time for the Englanders, normally he ignores us, but now he is thinking of his guts. He loves the field mice, gobbles them up as fast as they come, he looks like a rat to my mind. Black as the ace of spades, his stubs of legs are giving him trouble in the long grass as he tried to keep up with us. Leaping from time to time trying to see ahead, trying to locate the wheat field, looks at us hoping and expecting us to pick him up and carry him, but to hell with him, he will only remain friendly as long as the mice last, he can't fool us! Edwards arrives with the wagon, pulls in alongside the first stack, he stays on the wagon, we will throw the wheat up to him, he will stack it neatly into the wagon. The dog is rushing around the stack barking like he is crazy with anticipation of the feast to come, as we lift the first few bundles the mice beneath will run to the shelter of the others remaining, only when the last two bundles are lifted will they have to seek shelter further afield, they will have to run to other stacks as much as ten feet away. Stick the last two bundles ready to lift, the dog has gone quiet, he stands staring at the patch of ground that will soon reveal his meal; his body shakes all over with the tension of controlling the springs he is about to unleash. We lift, a mass of twenty or thirty tiny bodies have erupted into darting streaks, the dog too has disappeared into a blurred streak of movement as he darts from one to the other. The tiny darting streaks disappear off of the ground like magic, one or two reach safety but all the others are inside the cavern of the dogs stomach, already the little beast sits waiting at the next stack.

The wagon load builds up, soon it looks like a house on wheels, a neat square house of bundles that Edward the boy produces with the unthinking skill of his kind, only when we cannot toss any more to the top due to its height does it become a load. We rest while the wagon travels back to the barn, the disgusting pig of a dog lies exhausted, his belly is fat and swollen, it drags on the ground when he walks; God knows how many mice he has inside him, been at it non-stop, his intake is beyond belief, still he waits for more. Hot summer weather, sit with our backs resting against a stack, a world of gold surrounds us, the work fills me with pleasure, it has awakened some instinctive joy that only the physical work of gathering the harvest must awaken in every man.

The barn is full to overflowing, Walter borrows a threshing machine. A chain of village folk wind up to the top of the mountain of wheat each creating his or her working platform. The last man stands high near the roof, his job is to toss the bundles down the chain, into the machine which churns out a stream of grain into sacks; a thick cloud of choking dust fills the barn, everyone wears a thick mantle of the stuff. The sacks are heavy, two men swing one up on to the back, stagger into the house, up the stairs and into the loft, tip the contents out on to the floor. Rats temporarily scurry away from the golden raindrops into the dark corners. A change to sack hauling, climb up to the top of the reduced mountain, fork bales down to the waiting chain below, a nice relaxed job. A woman from the village works close to me, keeps feeling the muscle of my arm, tells me how big it is. We are out of sight from those below, wants me to feel her muscles, would like to very much but I don't play ball.

A shout from below, a break, everybody down. Will have to slide down each stage, the body travels over the surface of the straw with the speed of a body on ice, once launched there is no stopping. The last section, launch myself, instantly I see the pitchfork standing directly in my path, standing on its handle, two long steel prongs point upwards. One hope only of not getting transfixed, get a boot to strike between the points on to the curved base. Impact comes as I think, the heel of my boot just finds the curved base between the prongs with a shock that forces the stiffly held leg to bend at the knee, push the body outwards into space to land in a heap, shattered and breathless. No strength to get up for several minutes, a cold feeling in my guts as I study the two shining steel prongs, think of the closeness of what might have been.

A trip by one of the lads to Danzig, he tells of the Russian women slave labour who pick up horse droppings from the streets, they have to use their bare hands as tools, they count as nothing in the minds of these German bastards.

    Happy to say that Walter and the other local farmers are worried, a group of army veterinary men are in the area checking their stock of horses, any they think are good enough for army service they confiscate; every so often they make these trips, the farmers sweat blood each time. This time Walter is lucky, they reject his stock, next time the quality standard may be lowered and the sweating will start all over again; but I am all for anything that makes these farmers sweat.

    A German picture magazine comes to hand, pinched by one of the lads. It is filled with pictures of the attempted Dieppe raid, pictures of knocked out tanks and dead men on the beach, lines of prisoners marching into captivity. They all march without their trousers which have been taken away as an anti-escape measure, we are sad that the raid failed but pleased that the boys are active.

Stand back a bit and you would think you were looking at a field of snow out of season, walk into it and you are surrounded by huge white poppies, a sea of fragile delicate white petals, each has a large black centre pod which Edward says contains things good to eat. Break off a pod, rub it between the hands, the hand is filled with hundreds of tiny black seeds, shovel them into the mouth and chew. A nutty taste, Edward is right, they taste good, we gorge ourselves on poppy seeds as long as the crop stands.

A letter from a lady from Chester, the lady who knitted the socks, a young girl called Jessie, delighted to hear that someone is actually wearing her gift, promises to write again.

A great nest of twigs perches on the roof of the barn, a permanent fixture, it is the home of two very large black and white storks. They sit or stand up there making a loud clattering noise as they work their beaks open and shut, sometimes as we work in the fields they will walk round us with an upright dignity which dares you to sneeze in their presence; look very graceful as they come in to land from flight, the long legs working like pistons to balance the weight of the big bodies. Taking off can sometimes be a bit painful, a long run along the ground, legs going faster and faster, huge wings unfold outwards from the side of the body; a gentle flap which works up to a frenzy, the legs become a blur, a hop upwards but he comes down again like a heavily loaded bomber. You watch his attempts to get up with bated breath, Jesus, he is still running, still flapping his wings like mad; he needs a hell of a long runway, you feel like cheering when he finally makes it, once he is up he is poetry in motion.

Sunday muster and headcount, a large board has been erected outside the guards billet for our special benefit, pinned to the board are large blown up photographs for us to study and think about; mass graves being excavated, bodies in their hundreds being dug out of the ground, close up shots of bullet holes in the skulls of the victims. Under each picture, comments in English which explain that this is the work of our friends the Russians. Each of the bodies is that of a Polish Officer, many thousands shot down in cold blood, a thing the Germans would not do! They must think we are nuts. They forget that we see every day how they treat the Poles and other slave labour that fills this country, the pictures may speak truth, they may not; the German words mean nothing to us, it could just as well be their handiwork. The exercise fails as far as we are concerned, we must be winning this war, otherwise they wouldn't bother to explain anything. They call the place of horror Katyn, a forest located on Russian territory we understand.

A large wooden barrel stands in the corner of the stable, all sorts of muck gets thrown into it and is left to rot, topped up by black stinking water, it's good for the Frau's vegetable garden. Chickens roam about the place freely, Edward finds one dead in an obscure corner, it has been dead for many days, he pops it into the barrel to rot. It floats at the top of the water for more than a week, I see it there each time I pass, one day it is gone, I assume it has sunk to the bottom. Evening meal same day, a plate of boiled chicken soup, think about it a bit, I have killed no chicken today, Edgar has killed no chicken today, nobody else kills them but us these days. A flash of realisation, the chicken out of the barrel. A scream for the Frau that makes the house tremble, she stands before us, the enquiring look of a lady of quality to her serfs as she listens to our questions. Yes, it is the chicken from the barrel; we rant and rave our disgust until she takes it away, a couple of boiled potatoes are substituted instead but poor Edward has to eat his share of the chicken which he had so thoughtlessly thrown in the path of the Frau's eyes.

Fifi is on the hunt for a male, any sort will do, only the old men and boys hang around the village now, the real men are all fighting on the various fronts, she flirts outrageously with both of us when out of sight of the farmhouse, but Edgar is full of his dream girl at home. I study the trim figure, the swell of the soft breasts, the magical promise of the hollow that appears in her dress between her legs as she moves, can take her any time, but I have to say no. A few minutes pleasure is not worth getting separated from Edgar, it is not worth the possibility of her going to a labour camp which might earn her death, but hell, it's hard to refuse the offer! In desperation she turns to Edward the boy, he fills the breach like a man, only too delighted, soon she is with child, Walter and the Frau condemn her and send her away from the farm in disgrace, Fifi disappears from our lives forever. Edward leaves to join the army shortly afterwards, at seventeen he joins the infantry; we can only wish him luck and a safe return.

Fred from the next farm is late tonight for his usual visit, quite dark outside when he does arrive, he is killing himself with laughing, at last his perfect German has paid off as far as he is concerned. He met a German female in the short distance which separates his farm from ours, he chatted her up, God knows what he told her. No problem, at once they are in the ditch, pleasure dispensed with, she goes on her way entirely unaware that it was a British lad who had just made her day. They couldn't even see each others faces, a fine British tactical manoeuvre in the very best tradition, we are proud of the fella.

The cows are brought in for the winter, from now on I shall have to wait on them hand and foot, feed them, milk them, and clear up their mess. Queenie is still the best of the bunch, still the easiest to milk, still the perfect little lady, she doesn't wait until I am behind her cleaning up her droppings to lash out with a wicked kick of the hind leg that spins the shovel out of my hands like the other rotten cows do. Easily she is the nicest German I know, she gets all the little extras I can manage, got to study your friends around here, they are a bit thin on the ground.

Edgar still croons over his horses, keeps reminding me what nice names they have, there's Liz, Shemmel, Old Fox, Young Fox, and of course, Betty. She is his favourite, I swear he has more to say to them than he has to me, they still stands on my foot, can't understand why it isn't broken. If they tread on Edgars foot they seem to hasten to get off.

Go to take a horse down to the village to have new shoes, a busy place, many horses stand waiting for the Smithy's attention in this land of horses. My turn, he tries to get to work on the horse but the animal doesn't like the look of him, wants to kick him to death. I dangle at the horses head trying to sooth him with gentle talk which only seems to make him worse, need Edgars gentle touch, but he is not here. The head of the horse is shaking me like a rat as I hang on, the Smithy is getting mad. Another farmer comes forward from the waiting horses, he holds a small loop of string in his hand, picks up a short length of stick, he grips hold of the upper lip, pickers it together, slips the loop of the string over the lip and starts to twist it. Soon the string is tight around the horses upper lip, as it cuts into the flesh tighter and tighter, the horses neck is stretched outwards, heads held high, eyes pop from their sockets as the agony of his mouth fill his whole body. The Smithy works fast as the pressure of the string is maintained, soon the job is done, I return to the farm with a very subdued horse wearing a nice shining set of shoes.

Winter jobs: digging ditches, spreading much over the fields, new fence posts to hammer into the ground, strengthen barbed wire fences, trips to a nearby forest to collect freshly cut young trees to be used for a variety of jobs about the farm, strip off the bark, cut into lengths, stack into heaps and let them season.

Now and then a shoot, all the local farmers get together for a days fun, slave labour and prisoners act as beaters. A massive circle of men a couple of miles across, to every half dozen men, a gun, the owner of which is dressed to kill in his field grey hunting suit with dark green edging, cheeky fancy hats are worn, liberally adorned with feathers or brushes. The huge circle begins to close slowly with much shouting from the beaters, guns bang away as targets are seen, a fox springs from clover almost from under my feet to speed away towards the centre of the circle as guns in the immediate vicinity blast away at him, they waste their lead, he disappears to fresh cover. We work all day at it, never see anything actually shot but the kills of the day are collected together for display and sharing out, a couple of dozen rabbits, one fox, a dozen pheasants, a couple of hares. With so many guns the share out of the spoils must have had its problems.

The Frau wants her vegetable garden dug, spades with very narrow blades are handed to us to do the job, we dig at leisure in the English fashion lifting a loaded spade, a turn, a neat break-up of the soil to finish the movement. A protesting female voice at our elbows, the Frau stands watching us, tells us that we are not digging correctly; grabs the spade out of my hands to demonstrate, tiny thin slices are shaved off and turned. She insults us, telling us we can't dig now! We tell her that she will get it dug the English way or not at all, she nearly swoons. She shouts for Walter who comes hopping at the sound of his loved ones voice, she explains her problem, he looks at us, we tell him that we take no orders from the bloody Frau, especially his; he agrees with us and tells her to get back in the house. She slinks off in a sulk, the garden gets dug in the English way, guess Walter's love life is going to be a bit rough for a while.

Walter has his shiny top boots on today, that means he is expecting visitors, I have reason to go near the house later in the day, the Frau is calling daintily to me, wants me to meet someone. Enter the outhouse dining room, a woman stands there, obviously of city breeding; beautifully groomed, a sight for sore eyes, she wants to meet the Englander. The Frau introduces her, the woman greets me in English, she comes from Hamburg, been to England on visits, loves England, all the people from Hamburg love the English. Beginning to wonder why we are fighting listening to her. She also wants me to meet someone, her son, she calls out to him in the next room, he steps into the room, a bloody SS man! He stands looking at me with his hands on his hips a though I am something out of a zoo, we both stare at each other poker faced for several minutes with nothing said, now I know why we fight the people of Hamburg! I turn on my heel and leave the room, back to the stable, I enjoy the pigs company better.

Christmas of 1942 passes as nothing, we praise the Lord only that we are still breathing and that our country still fights on, nothing else matters.

Fisherbalki, East Prussia, The Farm, 1943

A bitter cold morning, the usual breakfast of two slices of bread with the air holes filled with dripping is over, we wait outside the stable, ditches to be dug today. Walter says help is coming, we wait about, dressing in our warmest gear; when the labour arrives we shall all move out into the fields together. Through the morning mist a horse-drawn cart approaches along the village road, people are standing in it; men, packed in tight, they rock and sway about as the vehicle rattles over the cobbles.

The men are dressed in what appear to be pyjamas, nothing else. See how thin they are, cheekbones protrude, sunken eyes, shaven head, body bones stick out through the thin material of their garments. Faces blue with cold, their teeth chatter in an uncontrollable rhythm, their rags are a dirty white colour with a narrow blue stripe. The wagon pulls in by the stable, a guard jumps down from the back, he is a giant of a man, big, thick, well fed body, an SS man. Walter rushes to greet him, they shake hands like old friends, Walter seems pleased with his labour as the guard displays them with a wave of his hand. The labour waits in the wagon, their only movement is the shivering of their bodies.

At a word of command from the guard the labour moves with the speed of men crazed with fear; a wild scramble, they stand in a tight packed group within earshot of the guard. Every man's eyes are riveted on the guards face, watching his every breath, waiting his next commands. They watch him with the intensity of a dog watching its master but their eyes are full of fear, their very attitude tells us that the power of life or death over this group of men is totally at the hands of the guard.

Walter leads the way out into the fields, we dash back into our cubicle, grab a few cigarettes and some chocolate, might be able to get something to them during the day. The guard will not allow us to get any closer to them than forty yards, we bide our time, we know the pattern, sooner or later the guard will get bored with his own company, he will drift over to us and start talking. He will tell us what a pity it is that we fight, that we share the same culture, most of them do this, yes, we know the pattern by now. Watch closely the way that he treats them, it will give us a clue as to whether we can make a breakthrough.

One of the men has stopped working, he stands stiffly to

attention, an impossible stiffness of the body, his back arches backwards with effort, he shouts to the guard to ask permission to go to the toilet. The guard tells him to come before him, the man hastens to obey at the double, again stands rigidly at attention directly in front of the guard who is screaming into his face for daring to waste working time. His finger is wagging under the man's nose as he issues threats, the man is forced to listen to a torrent of abuse before he finally gets permission to relieve himself. About turn, run a few yards away from the guard, rip down his pants frantically to avoid wasting time, a quick short squat, pants wrenched back up, double back to the job. The guard is screaming at them to double their efforts, he is the worst possible kind, truly a sadistic bastard, doesn't look possible for us to get anything to them through him!

Got to sound the pig out if we can, he is on his way over now, he talks with the usual approach of his kind, talks about what trash he has to control. To him there are only two peoples fit to live in this world, the Germans and the British. Now comes the culture bit, we lead him on, smiling in the right places. Ask him casually who they are? All he will say is 'Political', won't give their nationality. Pull out cigarettes, light up, has he any objection to us giving the men a few cigarettes between them? Yes he has, he objects strongly! The smokes are still in our hands, his eyes are fixed on them, expects to be offered one, we deliberately put them away, back into our pockets. We resume working, have nothing further to say to him, he leaves us, returns to the men. Instantly he urges them on to yet a further effort, we work leisurely at the pace we want but the agony of the men forty yards away is terrifying.

Back to the stables at the end of the days work, herd them into a stall, they cling to each other as they move, each afraid to be thought lagging. Walter has got to feed them before they go back to their camp, small bowls of liquid which is hot, one for each man. They start sipping the stuff immediately, almost choking themselves in their haste as the guard shows signs of impatience. In a few seconds the bowls are empty and lie on the floor in a heap, the guard walks out of the stable, they follow him in a tight packed group, eyes fixed on his face.

He stands by the waiting wagon, faces the men, a sudden word of command, one of the men breaks from the group at the double, down on both knees at the feet of the guard, with the sleeve of his ragged jacket he is wiping the mud off the guards highly polished top boot. He works frantically, first one sleeve then the other, the lower parts of his jacket now for the other boot; the guard stands with the attitude of a God. The man at his feet is looking up at his face silently begging for approval and release, he squats in the mud waiting as the guard inspects his boots, a nod of approval, a wave of his hand, the man scurries back to the group. Still all eyes are riveted on his face waiting the command to get on the wagon, they must wait for the word to be spoken. Only one thought fills my mind at this moment, I wish for nothing else in the whole wide world than the pleasure of sending a bullet into the guards big fat guts.

The loaded wagon retreats back along the village road, returning the way it had come this morning. Soon it disappears from sight, Walter seems pleased with the work he has got done today. Now we know where the train loads of people go that crosses the farm each week.

Having trouble with my right wrist, feels like a bad sprain, heavy work gives problems, keep it wrapped up tightly in a piece of wet cloth, seems to offer a little relief.

Spring is in the air. I saw a crocus today, tucked away in a corner of the Frau's garden, hope to Christ the Frau doesn't see it, she's bound sure to treat it as an intruder. It is a lovely pale blue, its lonely beauty stands out in the normally drab landscape which surrounds it. Reach out, touch its fragile beauty but don't let the mind dwell on the magic of England at this time, what's the use, this bloom will suffice for now?

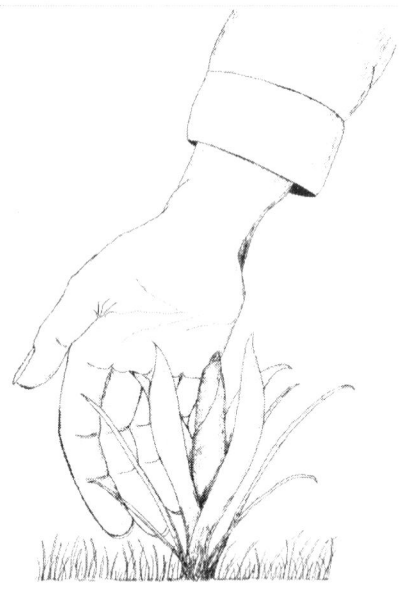

Midwife to the cows, a full time job, both Edgar and I have to attend their labour, coaxing, and sometimes physically pulling the little devils into this miserable world with apologies. A tiny pair of hooves attached to the front legs peep shyly out at us at first, soon the whole legs, a miniature nose followed by the head then the shoulders. Grasp the fragile thing by the shoulders, a pull in rhythm with the cows efforts, there, it is free together with a gush of fluid and the afterbirth. Lower the calf gently to the ground, it lies there like a dead thing, pick up a bucket of cold water which stands by ready, empty the contents over the tiny body, instant reaction as it bursts into movements produced by the cold shock. The body lifts upwards into a sitting position, legs struggle to lift upwards, grasp the body, lift upwards, help her; let go, like a drunk she sways on the thin legs, she sways as though in a strong wind but instantly she is looking for mum. Pick her up, take her to a specially prepared stall, a bed of golden straw awaits her, place her within gently on her legs, she walks with hesitant steps exploring the new world, soon she lies tiredly on the thick cloud of gold. I pat the tiny head, tell her what a nice little girl she is, the liquid eyes close, reluctantly admitting that it's been a hell of a trip.

Queenies son is troublesome, having no desire to enter this world he comes slowly despite the best efforts of his mum, just to be awkward he offers one front leg only, the other is folded backwards within, something must be done quickly to free the other leg before the head appears. Edgars sleeve is rolled up, he inserts his hand into Queenie, hand enters the cavity, searches within; traces the offending limb, guides it, gently bens if forward to the correct position, gently eases his hand out , withdraws his hand holding the tiny hoof securely, there, that's better everything is in place. Queenie is in great pain, something is very wrong, the calf must be pulled out fast, gripping wherever we can pull, get the head and shoulders free, more to grip, pull like mad; reluctantly he comes, there, he is born. Deluge him with water, he struggles immediately to his feet unaided. A big lad, Queenie sinks to the floor exhausted and ignored as we pick up her son and place him carefully into the pen.

Milking as usual, the new mothers milk is discoloured, deep coffee colour, unfit to drink, it's thrown into the slop tub. We use only fresh white milk from the other cows to feed the new calves, but they can't drink it, don't know how. Offer them some in a bucket, submerge my hand into the creamy whiteness, cunningly stick out a finger tip above the surface of the milk, find the searching mouth. The soft muzzle closes over the finger and sucks greedily, lower the hand as the greedy stomach lowers the level of the milk, reluctantly tell him that there is no more for now. This is easily the most gratifying thing I have ever done in my life.

Queenie lies in her stall this morning when she should be up and about, she sits upright in quite a normal looking position at first glance, but study her a bit, see how still she is, not a muscle moves, an unnatural stillness about her, she looks like a study in black and white marble. Head upright, chin resting on the feeding rack quite normal, but she is dead, died during the night. Queenie is dead – I have lost my favourite cow! Queenies son is doing fine, a big lad, he stands head and shoulders above his friends, I make a great fuss of him since the death of Queenie.

The whole farm has gone mad with babies, chicks, ducklings, and goslings get under your feet at every turn, Betty the horse has given birth to a fine young foal, a beautiful light fawn coloured coat, silver mane and tail, a dash of white painted on his soft velvet nose by the delicate brush of nature, he accepts our worshipping hands running over his silken coat as his due. The pigs join in the magic of spring, twenty three young mouths enter the world demanding their food ration immediately they arrive. A string of thirteen endeavour to steal the limelight, emerging into the world as would a string of sausages from a machine, they protest at the confinement of the jackets they arrive in strenuously, gaining their freedom they head for the two rows of abundant nipples. The Frau joins in the parade of births presenting the world with a daughter, but this gift of nature is hidden within the dark confines of the house, we never see it around. I study the two storks so busy chattering up on the farmers barn roof, I eye them with quite a bit of suspicion, all these babies!

Queenies son, is four weeks old when Walter comes into the stall dragging a small table and tells me to get him out of his stall. Walter ties up the animals legs and lays it on the table, I've not idea what he is going to do with it. I hold the animal trying to sooth his fears, his beautiful soft eyes relax as I stroke the length of his head, look at Walter, he has a sledge hammer in his hands, it is raised for a blow. The terrible weight crashes to the animals forehead with a sickening thud. My hands feel the shock of the blow as they lie soothingly on his body, terrible convulsions as I fight to stop him from crashing onto the floor. Walter has a knife, the delicate throat has been slashed almost severing the head, I stare at Walter with horror and revulsion at the unexpected killing of this animal but he ignores me. He works with haste, I suspect that he is doing something illegal, disposing of the calf before the birth is known, soon the son of Queenie is a revolting heap of bits of flesh.

Men of letters have emerged from among our ranks, some reach us via the grapevine from Stalag, some amuse, others boost the spirits, others wax lyrical.

Courage
It is easy to be nice boys when everythings ok,
It is easy to be cheerful when you're having things your way,
But can you hold your head up and take it on the chin,
When your heart is nearly breaking and you feel like giving in.

It was easy back in England among the friends and folks,
But now you miss the friendly hand, the joys, the songs and jokes,

The road ahead is stony and unless you're strong in mind,
You'll find it isn't long before you're lagging far behind.

You have to climb the hill boys, it's no use looking back
There's only one way home and that's off the beaten track,
Remember that you're British and that when you reach the crest,
You'll see a valley cool and green, England at it's best.

By Unknown, P.O.W.

-

All for Love
I read the book one fateful day,
And this to me it did convey,
If eye offend thee, cast it out,
I forthwith started to follow it out.

My eyes ached with beauty tender and fair,
I got rid of the offending pair,
My arms shook with joy longing to hold,
They must go or so I am told.

My legs went to jelly with one sweet look,
Once again I followed the book,
My heart was as light as the blossom on May,
A touch, that's all was needed, it floated away.

My head was awhirl, senseless, insane,
It had to go, worthless, that's a pain,
These offences worry me no more,
Except I'm darned uncomfortably sore.

I've followed the book, you've seen how it ran,
I am now the worlds most imperfect man,
I did it all for love,
But for heavens sake don't follow me, I've just woke up by jove!

(The favourite of Fred, the man of London town who works on the two-bit farm along the road at Fisherbalki)

My Comrades
I think that I shall never see,
A happier bunch than the boys with me,
The work all day come home at night,
And eat their rations by the pale lamp light,
They live on hope, each living for the day,
The gates will open and they will get away.

I know that they feel better,
If they could get a letter,
They march along through rain and sleet,
A smile for everyone they meet,
Some gave their lives, they heard the call,
Good luck to you boys, God bless you all.

By P.O.W.'s Jack Jackson and Guy Gordons

-

God made the world in six days, then he rested.
He then made man then rested again.
He then made woman, since then, neither man, woman, or anything else has rested.

By Unknown P.O.W.

-

Message contained in the P.O.W. German news sheet known as the 'Camp'.
Dearest Daddy's, big brothers and all prisoners. Even though you are far away across the seas, we are with you today more than any other day. We send you our Christmas kiss. We pray that our friend, little Lord Jesus will bring you back before his next birthday. Signed – British children in Argentina, 1942.

The thin column of smoke rises straight up into the air, it drifts slightly as it raises above the tall grass that soon will be cut for the first crop of hay, standing n the dung heap at the rear of the stables you can't miss it as it rises from the flat carpet of surrounding fields. Walter the farmer stands on the dung heap together with his friend the local policeman, he has called in the law to find out what causes the smoke. The policeman is going to do the brave thing, he is moving away from Walter and going in the direction of the smoke, he undoes his revolver holster flap, advances with his gun in his hand, a brave picture of the law doing it's job.

I watch his progress as he walks stealthily into the long grass, nearing the rising smoke, a shot, another figure has appeared near him, a much smaller figure, they are heading back to the farm together, the policeman walks behind. A young lad, perhaps about sixteen, slave labour, dressed in the usual pyjama clothes, shaven head, more than half starved. The policeman has his gun pointed into the middle of the lads back, he is delighted with his captive, he beams at Walter who beams back at him. Somehow the lad has escaped from a working party, was trying to boil a potato to eat, the policeman takes him away I feel to certain death.

Walter says that the pigs have got to be castrated then he leaves the sty door open by accident, immediately the stable is filled with a mass of squealing pink flap eared little object that gallop about in a mad panic, we have got to catch them, find the little boys and operate. A mad chase follows which produces an even noisier ear splitting chorus of squeals.

Capture one, it is a boy thank Christ, Walter stands with the wriggling little beast gripped firmly between his knees, its head with the tiny open mouth is screaming blue murder and is hanging at the back of Walters knees, it's hind quarters which will receive the attention of the razor blade is to Walters front. The hind legs are a blur of movement, the tiny tail is straight with indignation, a quick cut, his potentials as a father are removed, a lump of fat on the cut. Take him back to the sty, a quick dash into the safety of his mountainous mother, his fears are soon lost as he peeps out at me from the many folds of her huge soft belly.

My right wrist is getting worse, gives me a lot of pain. Get the guard to report the symptoms back to the Stalag hospital. Some days later he tells me that he has got to take me back to the Stalag to have the wrist looked at, we will travel by passenger train. Good, a chance to show off an English cigarette, a piece of chocolate, and flash a cake of scented soap at the civilians! The guards is about eight feet behind me as I walk along the side of the road, his stock in trade bayoneted rifle is slung over his shoulder. Normally a silent one he decides to tell me a secret. "America is in the war Tommy". I look suitably surprised at this old bit of news that I am not supposed to know. "They are fighting Deutschland", I turn round and look suitably sad for him, a few minutes silence, I thought he had finished but he hasn't. "Still Tommy, you have the Italians to play with, we have the Americans". Rather surprised at his choice of playthings! He lapses into silence, nothing more to say.

Two German soldiers approach us on the other side of the road going in the opposite direction, the rifle of one of them sticks high into the air, the man who carries it is a tiny little fellow, he looks familiar, as they get closer my suspicions are confirmed. It's Paul, the little guard we had on the farm way back in 1941, as we pass I greet him. At the sound if his name he freezes with shock, quickly he looks away and hurries past, of course he cannot afford to return my greeting, not in front of witnesses. He passes, a tiny insignificant little man fighting his battle for survival his way.

A German military hospital, a collection of wooden huts, a lot of hanging about but eventually I am shown into a room for attention. Quite a lot of fun explaining my symptoms in German to a man dressing Serbian uniform who is also a prisoner and has an equally limited vocabulary in the language. Somehow he gets something down on paper and takes a screen test, studying the illuminated screen he tells me that I have a bone disease, nice fella!

Darkness has overtaken us, the guard won't take a chance on taking me back in darkness, tells me that we shall have to spend the night in town, think I see a sneaking smirk of pleasure round his mouth as he says it. Leave the hospital, wend our way through a couple of streets, enter a building which the guard is obviously familiar with. Through a couple of small workshops, through a door with a padlock on it, enter a room, half a dozen men in Battle-dress lounge about, the guard tells me to settle here for the night, he will return later, leaves me.

Delighted to see fresh British faces, they work in this place, a small factory. They fix me up with food and drinks then tell me all the Stalag news, the situation of Red Cross parcels, deaths, escapes, shootings etc. We gossip over an invisible fence to our hearts content. A gold mine of war news, casually they tell me that they get it almost every day, would I like to hear it? Ignore their invitation at first, think they are joking, but they are not, can hear it within thirty minutes if I like, Jesus, they really mean it! Ok, their guard and my guard have gone out together say the lads which should give us time to hear the news before they return to lock us up.

Follow one of the lads through the workshops, through a door and into the living quarters of the house, a steep flight of carpeted stairs lead up to a second floor. My guide leads the way up them silently, reaches a large landing cut in half by a glass partition with a door in it. Inside the partitioned area is a small table and two chairs, a single electric light bulb hangs directly over the landing illuminating it in a circle of light. A passage leads from the landing to a closed door; my guide knocks at the door, a middle aged male civilian opens it, an exchange of soft Polish, we are ushered quickly into the room.

A room full of bright light and warmth. A woman stands looking at me, she smiles in greeting, they both shake my hand, tell me to sit down and make myself comfortable as we wait for the news time. Jesus, they are so calm and unconcerned about what they are doing, it could earn them death! Fingers to the lips indicating complete silence as they switch on the radio set, ears close to the receiver as I wait breathlessly. Spellbound I listen to the calm voice of London whispering into the room for several minutes. Switch off, must get out quickly. Thank our hosts, turn out the light in the room, open the door a fraction, check if the coast is clear. Bloody hell, two men are sitting in the partitioned section of the landing, backs to the stairs, one of them raises a glass to his lips as we watch, our guards are having a quiet drink.

Got to get past them quick - locking up time soon. Will have to crawl down on the carpet and through the circle of light to get past them, got to do it now or the Poles have had it! We decide that I will go first, I want to get it over with if I can. A last grip of the Polish and British hands as I leave. Drop to the carpeted floor, silently negotiate about fifteen feet of dark passage, reach the edge of the circle of light, edge into it. The guards sit sideways to me at this point, there's danger in a glimpse of movement out of the corner of a mans eye; I move forward so slowly, so flat, a mere fraction of movement, arms dance with tension already. Into the pool of light fully, breathing stops, heart beats wildly; they must be bloody blind thank Christ. I work over to the wall of the partition, get immediately under them, directly behind their backs, can hear their voices distinctly through the thin partition wall, they are calm, unconcerned. About four feet to go to the blessed darkness of the top of the step that leads downwards, inch over towards it slowly, so slowly. Hand grips the edge of the step, can pull my body over the floor easier, arms and shoulders into the darkness, go down the stairs face downwards, the stretching arms control the rate of descent; legs remain in the pool of light, gently curl them up out of the light, ease down the stairs. Fully in darkness now, twist my body, regain my feel, swiftly, silently, reach the bottom of the stairs. My body stinks, a strong smell of sweat or fear! The other lad should be on his way, can just see the top of the guards hats from where I stand, they still face away from the stairs. There, a hand over the top step; how slowly he moves, gently now, almost out of the light. No, he has made it! A silent run down the remaining stairs, run like hell through the workshops back into the billet, collapse like wet sacks, get locked in fifteen minutes later. A near thing, too bloody near, but the news I can take back to the lads makes it all worth it.

The foal is getting a big lad now, has a field all to himself, we visit him every day to give him any tit-bits that we have pinched for him or sometimes just to cuddle him. He plays hard to get at first, galloping round us in circles with a beautiful display of power and muscle, his tail and main stream out in the wind of his speed gleaming like pure silver. Pretend to ignore him, just stand and wait patiently. He will tire of his showing off, will gradually close in his circles, finishing with a gentle trot up to us, his soft muzzle will nudge impatiently, he now wants our gifts quickly, will even allow our arms to go round his neck; he holds his head up high gazing across the fields as we do so accepting our love as his due.

We wend our way along the track, back to the fields as so often before, but today is different. Guns - distant guns ahead. Look up into the sky in the direction of the gunfire, yes, can see tiny distant black specs up there. Can it be? Bursting cotton balls among the specs that grow larger, yes by God, it's our aircraft that fly up there. We have stopped walking, begin to dance on the spot as the aircraft head straight for us, they take shape in formation of fives, scattered over the sky. Bloody great American liberators! Here and there, there are less than five, sometimes only two, an indication of their losses. We are screaming maniacs now, in the middle of the field we hug each other, dance and scream up to the aircraft in frenzied joy at seeing them. They pass over slowly, so very far from home, they pass, we watch them fade back into tiny specs, they are going home, some of them will be home this very day. Heaven be praised, it's impossible to believe. Huge smoke clouds in the sky from whence they came, they have hit something hard, our hearts sing with joy.

News arrives swiftly on the grapevine, the aerodrome at Marienburg bombed at last, more than a thousand dead they say, sadly these are mostly slave labour; I immediately think of the Polish girls that fed me when I worked there in 1941, I pray they missed it somehow. Two British and one German guard killed by falling shrapnel, we grieve for our two dead lades, but our people must bomb, to hell with us. Just bomb and bomb and bomb the bastards.

A woman from the village has been struck by a spent cannon shell which fell from the sky, she is in a bad way. Talk of repatriating sick and wounded men for months, none of us believe it possible but at last men are gathering at Stalag to go home, we follow their progress with bated breaths, praying that nothing goes wrong for them, soon with luck they will be out of it.

The farmer has a visitor for the day, another S.S. man and his brood, Walter seems to be fond of the S.S., probably playing safe. During the day Walter tells me to get a pig out of the sty, take it round to the back of the house. I herd the largest beast round to the spot indicated, six feet from the back door of the house a stake has been driven into the ground, Walter ties a rope around one hind leg and fastens the other end round the stake, the beast is hog-tied.

The S.S. friend waits with a rifle in his hand, a small bore rifle, everybody has turned out for the fun, several children and the two women, we are about to see a German party game. The S.S. man is down on one knee, perhaps eight feet from the animals face, directly in front, a long sighting, his spectators hold their breaths. A shot, a tiny puncture of red in the forehead of the pig, a clapping of hands, shouts of glee from the children. The S.S. man beams at his own cleverness, settles down for another shot, hushed respectful silence as the marksman takes aim at his victim. Cheers of congratulations as another shot strikes home on the forehead, the beast stands facing the torment, body and head swaying from side to side, his leg from time to time pulls at the bonds but mostly he just sways. Six little red holes in the forehead now, a couple of them give small trickles of blood, his swaying is getting more violent but the feet are planted firmly, they don't move, a thin high pitched moan from the animal. At the ninth shot he crashes to the ground, his body heaving, wild squeals of delight from the spectators. Walter has a knife in readiness in his hand, the Frau has a large basin in hers; Walter inserts the knife into the pig's throat, a long cut lengthwise, the Frau quickly holds the basin under the gash as the dark red blood gushes forth.

I stare fascinated at the sheer joy on the faces of these people at the entertainment provided, the children look very pretty in their Sunday best, the adults very smart in theirs. The blood is not flowing fast enough for the Frau, her left hand is buried deep within the gash, half the forearm is in as her hand searches for the pigs heart, the blood comes out faster now in a series of pumping spurts as her hand pumps the heart. The Frau's right hand is in the fast growing bowl of blood as it stirs gently, she looks proudly up into the faces of her guests as she displays her skill, they beam back at her cleverness, I feel bloody sick at the sight of the old cow! There, the blood is all out. The Frau with her ugly blood soaked hands enters the house, her guests follow her in, I return to the stable leaving them to their pleasure.

The S.S. man and his brood have departed with his gift of pork. We go into the house for the evening meal, Sophia brings in two plates, places them on the table and departs. We stare at the things in total disbelief, on each plate reposes a large pigs ear. One for me, one for Edgar, stare at the things for several minutes before we can find enough breath to scream "Frau". A wide eyed frau enters the room, we tell her to take the things away, she does so with the usual injured expression on her face, we have a couple of boiled potatoes instead.

Two letters today, one from Mother with a photograph of my

Father's grave, a mass of lonely flowers, the other is official documentation from an insurance company. Study the thing, I have got to sign it and send it back, that's all, just sign it then my mother can have the paltry thirteen pounds to bury my father. To get my signature this insurance company has forced the complicated and overworked machinery of the Red Cross to seek me out on an isolated farm in East Prussia, the rigid stupidity of this company amazes me almost as much as I admire the achievement of the Red Cross in carrying out the task.

Today is a great day for the village, having been accorded the honour of providing entertainment for one hundred and fifty wounded German soldiers, they are brought up river in fine style to be greeted by approximately three hundred girls with throbbing hearts. The girls have been collected from miles around, I feel sorry for the bloody soldiers really, having to satisfy that lot, but they tackle the task manfully. Soon the ditches and fields are full of wriggling couples, a mass lowering of the knickers is the chief occupation of the day out of respect to the fighting men of the Reich, the breezes of East Prussia eagerly seek the unexpected opportunity to explore normally covered pastures with indecent eagerness.

Fred, the randy one on the two-bit farm next to us is green with envy at the thought of the unmatched talent roaming around the village, but his good looks and first-class German does him no good, this is one act he cannot get in on. A breathless guard finds us working out on the farm, tells me that he has received a phone call to get me back to Stalag for a further examination of my right wrist, we will go next morning. Reach the station, have a long wait, a special train must pass first, Adolf Hitler's armoured train says the guard, it passes through the station very fast, several coaches, at each end anti-aircraft guns complete with crews. We go to a hospital well outside the camp, several wooden huts, German military, we enter one of the huts, hang about all day, nobody takes any notice of us, the guard is getting worried about it. It's getting dark outside, action at last, the guard marches me along several corridors, an open door, the guard shoves me through the doorway, closes the door behind me.

I am in a small office, in the centre of the room there is a desk, behind it sits a German officer, his head is bent over paper work, he does not look up I study his shoulder straps, bags of gold, a big cheese. Stand rigidly to attention to this one, wait for him to look up at me. Bloody knees begin to dance with tension, the bugger still gazes at his papers, playing the waiting game, I'm not used to standing to attention these days. At last, the head lifts, a pair of thoughtful eyes gaze at the specimen that stands before him, in a very surprisingly quiet voice he asks me what is the matter with me.

The question completely floors me. I was expecting to deal with someone who knew my medical history from the previous screen test, rapidly I realise that I am going to get into one hell of a fix trying to explain my symptoms to him in German. With more than common arrogance of most British P.O.W.'s, I have learned only that German which will get me grub and enable me to dodge work; the principle being that if they want to speak to us, speak in bloody English! Can't very well tell this lad to speak in English though. Nothing for it but to sail into my bet Stalag German and see what happens, he has asked for it. Manfully I launch into the mammoth task of explaining to the fella, he sits there for a good seven minutes listening to the noises I make, his face looks as though he is suffering as he listens to the murderous handling of his beloved language. I feel somehow that I am not getting very far with him, that somewhere along the line I have got lost, drifted off into Hebrew or something, but I press on with the stubbornness of our race, cussing him because he can't speak English.

A sudden scream of anguish from the officer, he has rudely cut across my flow of the best German, he is screaming for the guard. The door behind me bursts open, the guard stands there obviously petrified, he stands like a ramrod as the officer shouts at him, a wild wave of the Officers arm into the air which clearly says, "Take this bloody thing out of my sight", I feel my eyebrows rise with indignation at the rudeness of the man. A tap on the shoulder from the guard, a smart about-face, I march out of the room leaving behind a shattered Medical Officer.

Much too dark to take me back to the farm tonight, the guard scratches his head at the problem of what to do with me. He meets some medical staff and asks their advice on his problem, we are to follow them, the guard follows them along several passages, I trail along behind. Enter a large room, an operating table in the centre, a large electric light above it, cabinets round the walls full of instruments, no windows. The guard seems happy for me, he tells me to sleep on the table for the night, lock me in and leaves me. I check the place for anything worth pinching, there are plenty of diabolical carving knives and saws, would be very useful some of them, but I can expect to be searched before we leave in the morning, decide to leave them alone. Lights go out, I settle down on the table, drift off to sleep, no problem.

Guard in a cheerful mood this morning, eager to get off, away from this place, does not search me, hell, could have had a couple of knives! We return to the farm none the wiser as to what we were doing in the place.

The horse drawn wagon brings a load of female slave labour this time, they stand in the wagon shivering in the early morning cold, clad in the inevitable thin pyjamas. They are all young, look thin, their eyes are full of hopeless misery, the usual S.S. guard is in charge but he doesn't seem to hustle them to the same degree as most of his kind does. Out on the land, watch how he treats them, they work quite leisurely but they have to ask to relieve themselves, they walk away from him a few feet, drop their pants and squats while he watches them do it.

Here he comes, they all have to have a chat with us. Out comes the culture bit as expected, but we feel may get somewhere with this guard, ask about a bit of chocolate for the girls, he refuses, we turn our back on him, he walks away. The girls eat their ration of soup in the stall, some of them look beautiful beneath the dirt. The guard sees me studying them, he walks over and asks me which one I fancy, I walk away from the bastard! They load up on to the wagon, disappear into the fading light of day.

An infantry soldier is walking over the fields towards us, not the guard, as he gets closer we recognise Edward the boy of the farm, with a shriek of pleasure he is running to greet us. "Hello, you English bastards!" Looks smart in his uniform, home on first leave, has been in action somewhere in Italy, talks about the big men he has been fighting. Canadians he says, there are many English swear words mixed with his German, practically every second word is a gem, at seventeen he is a good pupil, we feel we have trained him well, he leaves us with our blessing for his safety.

Wrist has given up, can do no more work due to the pain, can't hold a pen to write. Edgar is having to do my work as well as his own, will have to go sick for good, talk it over with Edgar who agrees it's the parting of the ways, I will apply to go into an N.C.O. non working camp but first I must report sick to the guard.

Not gifted with demonstrative displays of emotion, our farewell is outwardly controlled in the way of the English. A lot of love can be expressed in a simple word like "Cheerio" it's the way you say it that counts. On the eighth of December 1943 I part from my brother for the first time in our lives. A last wave to the distant figure as the guard marches me away from the village.

No cigarettes available to tantalise the coach load of civilians today, have some pipe tobacco though, that will have to do. Get out the tin, fold back the curly protective white paper, there before the eyes is a small golden block, pick out the top thin slice, lay it on my knee as I replace the lid. The passengers eyes are fixed on the flat golden slice resting on my knee, looks like a piece of wood, they probably think it is, they gaze at my activities having nothing else to look at. Roll the thin slice vigorously between my hands, their eyes see a magical heap of curly gold resting in my palm. Extract a cigarette paper, needle the tobacco into it slowly, deliberately. Glance around, yes, they are captivated, dead silence as they watch. I light up the cylinder, blow the smoke among them, one of them is asking the guard where a P.O.W. gets tobacco from, I wait for the magic reply, England. German heads wag from side to side.

Marienburg, 1943-1944

Report sick immediately on arrival at the camp, I am placed into a group of non working permanent sick, also apply for transfer to an N.C.O. Non working camp, will have to spend several weeks in this place while Jerry checks with Geneva to see if my rank stands up before they will forward me on to an N.C.O. camp.

Many men in field grey uniforms roam aimlessly within the confines of the camp, they are Italians, thrust behind the wire before they knew what had hit them by their late friends the Germans. They are a well fed lot, uniforms spick and span, some sport beautiful feathers in their hats, Alpine troops. They look as though they have all been plucked directly from their mothers drawing rooms, they walk around with a glazed look in their eyes as well they might, the soup ration appals them and they tread with caution among us.

The lads of the camp tell me of the arrival of the Italians, herded into the camp, a mass of frightened bewildered men, their world turned upside down by the course of events. They stood in the parade ground looking at the screaming senior German guard standing before them, not understanding, completely lost. The German can see that he is not getting through to them, he has got to show him that they (the Germans) mean business, that they are not friends any longer, that they (the Italians) are now prisoners. A fragment of paper lies within the single strand of warning wire which runs round the inside of the perimeter fence, the paper lies on ground that spells certain death. The guard details an Italian to go and pick up the paper, the man does so, not aware of the significance of the wire, and dies under the blast of gunfire. The German made his point - the Italians learned why the lonely single strand of wire was there.

Having had pretty consistent reports of rough treatment given to our lads at Italian hands over the years, we can find little sympathy for their present situation, it's pure poetic justice. Their fear of the unknown bores us, now they tell us they made a mistake, that they are our friends, that they should not have been fighting us.

Great difficulty to move in and out of our huts, Italians fill the doorways to overflowing, their eyes bore into the Battle-dress clad figures within, waiting for one of us to wriggle a finger at them, instantly two or three will rush at you fighting to be the first to reach you. They stand to do our bidding, before us stand men who have tossed their pride to the winds. Some days, if the Red Cross parcels flow smoothly, we make do without the camp swill; rather than waste it, just raise a finger, instantly at the end of it will stand an Italian. Give him your mess-tin, tell him to go and fetch your camp swill; he will return with the tin full to the brim, not having spilled a drop. Tell him he can have it, that you don't want it today, he will look at you as though you are God as he drinks, his eyes will adore you, they make us feel uncomfortable. We tell them to stop crawling about, try acting like bloody men instead. We are experts in the ways of hunger, sorrow and keeping tears at bay, but we have never crawled to any bastard on Gods earth.

Scout around the camp looking for men of the Oxfords; find several of them mostly from my own Company. Talk far into the night about events over the last three and a half years since we last met, walk again with dead friends, stroll through the streets of Oxford, enter each others homes, tell of our hopes and fears, a truly joyous day for all of us.

Too bad I missed the penis competition held a few weeks ago in the camp compound. Someone thought that it might be interesting to establish the longest available, a small table was set up in the middle of the compound and men slapped their offering on to it, then marked the table off with chalk. A Sergeant of the rifle brigade had the honour of winning, the bearer of a dreadful looking object I understand which almost reached his knees. He received a large medal made from cardboard which was presented and pinned on his chest by the German Camp Commandant on parade.

I write lengthy letters to Edgar giving him both the news of the camp and the war news. Waylay the working parties going out on farms, find lads going out in his general direction, they will pass the letters on from man to man, farm to farm until one day they will reach him. Christmas 1943 arrives - I share a piece of stewed chicken which someone has pinched and brought back into camp but my thoughts are back in the cubicle on the farm with lonely Edgar.

Watch the working party being counted out through the gates, two guards on the task, one writes in a book as the other counts off the men in batches of ten. "Eins, zwei, drei, fier, funf, sechs, sieben, acht, neun, zehn, Englander" reports the counter; but one of the ten Englanders has shot out of the file of men, he stands in front of the unfortunate man who has just reported ten Englanders. The man's face is full of indignant fury as the forefinger of his right hand stabs into the Germans chest repeatedly, the guard staggers backwards under the force of the stabbing finger as the man screams into his face: "Nein Englander! Bloody Schottlander!" They stand almost nose to nose, the Scot repeats this vital piece of information over and over again, each time in a higher key. The guards face is a perfect study in blankness as he mentally tries to think what the hell a Schottlander is. Both guards join forces, push the Scot back into line, tell him to get moving or else, he moves on, but the air around him is blue with his muttering. The man's indignant display was beautiful to behold, as a Sassenach I silently and hastily apologise for daring to come from the same island.

New years eve, can only hope that 1944 will hurry up and get us out of this mess, I am rocked to sleep by the antics of a couple of homosexuals on the platform bunk above me. Fed up to the teeth on New Years Day, nothing to do in this place. A Battle-dress clad figure enters the hut asking is anyone required a tattoo done, he will do any picture for the price of a cigarette. Can't understand why blokes have such a thing done myself, it's so stupid, I decide to have one done! Out come the tools, two small sewing needles tied together with thin thread and a bottle of blue ink. My mind searches frantically for a subject to have done. A sinking ship? No, a nude? No. Got no girl friend, can't have a name. Could have a pack of hounds running across my back, the foxes tail up my bum, saw that once, very good, but probably beyond this lad. Settle for the cap badge of the Oxfords on my arm.

A circle of bent heads round my arm, the craftsman and spectators, can't see my bloody arm myself, advice flows freely, warnings flow freely, "Your bloody arm will drop off you know, you will probably get blood poisoning, better lie down." To hell with their advice, good or bad, I feel in a reckless stubborn mood. Hell of a job to draw the shape of a bugle correctly, in the end we compromise with a "that will do". Dip the points of the needles into the ink, prick delicately just under the skin, I sit there with my best man of steel look on my face, the circle of faces round us glance at me from time to time waiting for me to faint or something. A trail if blue is gradually deposited under the skin as the needles follow the pencilled pattern, on top of the skin small globes of blood, soon the shape of a bugle of sorts is imprinted on my arm. Retreat to my bunk to wait for the poison to set in and die within twenty four hours, the artist walks away quite pleased with his fee of one of the English cigarette.

One of the Italians has managed to attach himself to me, comes to see me every day, speaks quite good English, wants to improve it. I like the fellow, he is one of the few Italians in camp who walks with pride of what he is and who he is. I give him a note book and pencil to help his studies, his gratitude shakes me. A farmer from just outside Venice, for the note book his three sisters and his farm are mine! Best deal I have ever had offered.

Confirmation from Geneva at last; tomorrow a party of us will leave for an N.C.O. non working camp. The smuggled letters to Edgar will now have to stop, from now on we can use only the official camp post cards - loaded with our bits and pieces we leave the camp of Marienburg for the last time.

Fort Fifteen, Poland, 1944

A comfortable train trip in a passenger coach. A perky and pretty little blond girl dressed in railway uniform beams and chatters to us for most of the trip, she seems delighted to see so many young men together in one bunch, she ignores the tired old guard completely.

March for a couple of miles, ahead is a large raised mound of earth topped by shrubs and some trees, draw level with it; two massive wooden doors stand open directly into the hillside, a tunnel disappears within. Turn in towards the large doors, armed sentries stand each side, pass between them; enter the tunnel, dim lights burn overhead, walk thirty or forty feet, emerge into a passage that runs both right and left. Turn right, into an office; handing over formalities completed by the guard. British lads escort us to different rooms according to the space available, the passage bends in a continual circle, most doors on the right of the passage. Enter a room which is long and narrow, a large window at the end of the room, I am given a bunk next to the window. Double tiered bunks run each side of the room, filled mostly with reclining figures.

Look out of the window, a wall of red bricks meet the eye directly opposite, they rise upwards as far as the eye can see. To see over the top of the wall you have to get on to the floor and look upwards to find a piece of sky, the wall towers upwards for about forty feet, look down maybe ten feet to the floor of the moat. It is broken into a neat patchwork of tiny and well tended vegetable plots, the width of the moat is approximately forty feet.

The living quarters form a perfectly round island surrounded by the moat, on top of the island the small bushes and trees look like a head of hair in disarray. A path runs round the top of the island threading its way among the bushes, a well worn path beaten out by the tread of countless boot marks on daily exercise. Here and there from its commanding height a glimpse of the outside world can be seen, a strip of road there, another bit there, can see a strip down by the main gate, watch who comes in and who goes out.

Inside the island a well organised community has been set up, the patient work of many years slogging away at Jerry. A theatre, sets of musical instruments, books by the hundred run on professional library lines. Portable gramophones dot the rooms here and there with a collection of well worn records available, darts, cards, and other games. Football matches to equal the vigour of those played at home, lectures by men of recent capture on the modern tactics of warfare, piano recitals, varieties and straight plays performed with the dedication of professionals, the quality is surprisingly good.

A radio in the fort somewhere, each day before lights out the news reader comes round each room, silence falls as the latest B.B.C. news bulletin is read out. Only a couple of men know the whereabouts of the radio, it's hiding place is changed daily. Within a few days I know I have been vetted by innocent questions, a smooth casual screening to ensure I am who I say I am. The guards in the place are a pretty casual lot, there seems to be an understanding between the men and the guards. Men of the Vermach, they require only peace and quiet, they know there is also a radio in the Fort somewhere but they have given up the struggle of trying to locate it.

An additional communal cookhouse where men can go and play with their bits and pieces of Red Cross food, culinary adventures are tried out that would make any housewife swoon with shock.

Two Indians in the Fort, one is a Hindu the other a Sikh, but you would think they came from different planets, they hate each others guts and never communicate. They share a smallish room together, pass the open door and glance in, you can see the Sikh sitting cross legged on his bunk, his bright turban gleams in the gloom; a few feet from him the Hindu reclines on his bunk but although they are so close they are worlds apart. Even their food parcels have to be different to ours and different from each others, I feel that their special food problems must give them many hungry days judging by the erratic delivery of our own more common parcels.

The room owns several records, each day and last thing at night the gramophone is played, easily the favourite tune is the Warsaw Concerto. The machine stands near the window, the beautiful music swells to flood the room, overflows out of the window to fill the moat with its haunting melody. We play it time after time, its sadness flows easily with our mood, it drowns the very soul, no one ever laughs when the music fades away and we turn the machine off, we just lie quiet until aroused emotions stirred by the music settle again. We can do nothing about it, perhaps its setting we find ourselves in, perhaps it's because not too far away from us is all that remains of Warsaw, we lie quiet until sleep claims us.

Must take a trip to a neighbouring fort called Fort Fourteen for an X-ray on my wrist.

An early start the following morning, unhindered by kit of any description I stroll along the side of the road with my own special guard once again, after a couple of miles we reach Fort Fourteen. A large structure built into the side of the hill, doesn't look a bit like a Fort, not like our fortress. A permanent hospital for sick P.O.W.'s this place, go straight in to prompt service. A British Medical Officer examines the offending limb. Must go to the town of Thorn for the X-ray, must go at once. A train trip, march through the streets of Thorn, unimpressed by what I see of the place except for a very long stone bridge, a large part of which is missing, blown up by the Poles years ago. A temporary wooden structure now fills the gap to allow traffic to flow; enter a large brick building, a Germany Military Hospital. Up winding steps to the very top, pass ward after ward of Germans flat on their bloody backs, never seen so many so flat, a wonderful sight.

A landing, two benches to sit on while you wait, the guard and I make ourselves comfortable on one, the other is already occupied by another guard and another fellow in khaki; not British, a brown leather flying jacket, a circular badge high up on the arm, could be American I guess. We study each other casually, dying to speak to each other but not trying it while the guards are present, content ourselves with a nod instead. The guards are getting together, come to some sort of agreement, drift off down the stairs together, we wait until they reach the lower landing, out of earshot, quickly we talk before they return. He is nineteen years old, a crew member of the Liberator shot down over Athens seven weeks ago, hails from Chicago, asks me how long I have been a guest, nearly faints when I tell him three and a half years. Rapidly he fills me up with war news, the guards return, we fall silent. Soon he is taken away, we nod cheerio. X-ray taken we make our way back to Fort Fifteen.

For ten cigarettes the guard will take your photograph, a nice little racket he has worked up, three of us get together and all get into one picture just to beat him down, on a good thing this guard, for ten cigarettes he can buy himself a woman! Stick the picture in for censorship, it gets passed, I send it home. Send letters to Edgar as often as I can, keep him posted on my movements, sometimes I get some from him but he sounds so depressed, his loneliness worries me.

Movement down on the road below, four figures march along the side of the road, as they get closer three Russians and a guard take shape, now quite close. The Russians are in tattered uniforms, ghosts of men, each one carries the insignia of a major on his shoulder, but rank means nothing to the Germans, not if you are born Russian. They pass by slowly, you know somehow that you look at men soon to be touched by the hands of death.

A camp where time hangs on the hands, endless card playing, darts, chess, reading and other dreamed up activities. The gardeners with their tiny plots of vegetable gardens tend the plants with full time devotion, the plants get sick at the sight of them hovering about. Last activity of the day is always the walk around the top, always in one direction the crowd walks, God help anyone who tries to walk against the flow of traffic, complete chaos would arise on the narrow track.

The camp theatre group have a play to offer us tonight, everyone turns out to see the ambitious production of Journeys End. A large cellar deep down in the bowels of the Fort, a high arched ceiling, all whitewashed, a few electric lights here and there give a fairly subdued light. A sloping floor, trestles for seating, at the base of the slope a dingy stage, a grimy curtain looking the worse for wear hangs across the stage hiding the delights within. A hum of subdued chattering voices provide the pre-performance atmosphere of a theatre audience as in any theatre at home, marred only by the field grey figures that sit in the front row, the Commandant and his friends.

We are about to witness the dedicated efforts of a group of men who have sweated blood for many months to entertain us, as the play unfolds the mind boggles at the high quality of the acting, the perfect sound effects, the pinched costumes; if not pinched, scrounged and made up from junk. The scenery and props produced, the only real things are the rifles borrowed from the Commandant for the night, no wonder he sits in the front row, keeping his eye on his bloody guns I expect. I leave the performance deeply impressed. Having seen it performed by professionals in happier days before the war I rate these lads performance at Fort Fifteen as second to none, they did fine, just bloody fine!

Back to Fort Fourteen for a further check on the troublesome wrist, a British Medical Officer again, he has my X-ray which he studies, tells me that I have diseased bones in the wrist, bones that have gone soft, as soft as sponges, got to have the hand and arm in plaster for now, but sooner or later and operation will be necessary.

The trouble is due to malnutrition he reckons, he adds as an afterthought that he has placed my name before the medical commission for possible repatriation, I ignore this last remark as joke.

Return to Fort Fifteen full of news picked up, inform the lads that I am now an invalid and expect understanding and complete consideration in all things. Get mobbed as the brand new plaster is quickly covered with disgusting obscenities, lash out with my new found weapon, a few cracked heads against the hardened plaster earns me immediate respect, nobody argues with me now.

The peace of the room is violently disturbed by the crashing door, the room is suddenly full of S.S. men, machine pistols in their hands, they shout and push us out of the room with haste. The passage is lined with them, they herd us up on to the top of the Fort, seal the entrances to keep us up there, some of the camp guards are here with us, they say the S.S. are searching for our radio set; the guards hate the S.S. men almost as much as we do. We lie on the sandy soil while they search below to their hearts content. S.S. men file up on to the top after several hours, each man has a rake in his hand, they take up position in a long line near where we recline. They move forward slowly raking over ground as they go, obviously they have found nothing below as yet, they think it may be buried in the soil, a slow advance for the line as they rake carefully. Shouts of encouragement from us as we watch, shouts of "You're getting warm!" "No, No, you're bloody cold now!" The S.S. men are getting madder and madder at the taunts, some of them have gone a deep purple with rage but they don't do anything, just keep raking, they make quite a good job of levelling the recreation area for us.

Eventually they leave, their ears ringing with our cheers, we return to our rooms, have been on top of the Fort for most of the day, we are hungry. A scene of complete devastation meets our eyes, a churned up mass of blankets, palliasses, clothes and possessions, many items smashed or broken beyond repair; a couple of days work to sort it all out again but the radio is safe, they could not find it. The S.S. Commandant directed operations form a junction in the passage network, he had stood on a small trapdoor in the floor, the radio was so near to him too - just under his feet in fact, but it won't be there now, already it will have been spirited away to yet another proven hiding place.

Today is a great day in the hopes of many sick and wounded men, in this area the International Medical Board will meet at Fort

Fourteen to decide the applications placed before them, those of us whose names have been submitted must go along to be viewed. Groups of men hang about in the road outside the Fort waiting their turn to be called in for examination; I am in a bit of a daze in the first place to find myself standing in their ranks, not considering myself sick, just disabled. Men disappear from twenty to thirty minutes within the cavern of the Fort, you have to watch their hands as they come out. If the hands are empty the man has failed to pass the board, if however the hands wave a piece of paper in the air it will be a ticket to possible freedom and will be greeted with wild cheering from the assembled men, it means another man may someday soon get out of their hands!

Enter a large room, march into the centre of it, halt, face a long row of tables placed across the room, a long line of doctors entrenched behind the tables, British, German and Swedish. They all gaze at you, it feels and looks like the preliminaries to a Court Marshal. Paper and X-rays pass up and down their line, their eyes bore into you. I need to get out of here quick, wasting their time and mine, don't stand a cat in hells chance with this lot, quite right too. The senior German sits in the middle of the row of tables, he is writing, lifts a rubber stamp, bangs it down, gives it to an orderly who walks over and sticks it in my hand. I look at the British doctors, they are grinning at me, indicating with their heads to get out, it's all over. Turn, march out of the room, along a passage to the beckoning daylight, through the door, out into the road, lift my arm upwards, the piece of paper flutters like a flag, a cheer of approval from the lads. Only then do I look at the paper, this possible ticket with my name on it, tuck it away safely. I leave the Fort with the news that a New Zealand lad has just been found dead in his bunk, the pool of blood from his slashed wrists discovered too late.

Don't feel any different with the paper in my pocket, just a talking point that's all, nothing will come of it. From henceforth I am referred to as the 'Repat' at Fort Fifteen, men gaze at me in awe as though I will be leaving within the hour for England, they have much more faith in the magic powers of the paper than I have.

Not having found the radio in the Fort, they decide to move us from the place, a hurried packing of bits and pieces, we are going to a camp at Thorn. Muster out into the road in ranks five deep, masses of guards mill about; two single columns of guards appear, they march into position one each side of our column of five, the column is now seven ranks deep, two guards for every five of us, very complimentary indeed!

Thorn, Poland, 1944

A text book camp covering a massive sandy area, watch towers at intervals along the length of the fence in addition to the corner sites, large searchlights, men and dogs patrol at night. Full of army personnel from New Zealand, South Africa, Canada, America and Britain, a well organised world within the confines of the wire, each country has its own little area. Here the Americans lush with their abundance of Red Cross parcel supplies and sporting gear, next the Canadians with their abundant supplies, so very many cigarettes, they keep a large wooden box full of the things in their room, just help themselves to a packet as required.

The Yanks play baseball all day, the Canadians play soft ball, both look the same game to me, but say so at your peril! The Canadians say their ball is softer than the Yankee ball, it's a bit larger, but both types fly about like bullets, either one could brain you. Both nations walk about with medal ribbons on their breasts. I ask a Canadian friend what the hell he has got his for? "For volunteering for overseas service" he says, Jesus. "They marched us out into the wilds of Canada, the idea being to march forever, lorries trailed the column, if you agreed to go oversees you got a lift back to the barracks and were given a medal, otherwise you just kept on marching." A good bunch these Canadians, men of Dieppe, a privilege to know them.

The Australians seem to stand round in circles all day tossing coins into the air. New Zealanders drift about, quiet efficient men. South Africans keep very much to themselves, if you wander anywhere near them they will immediately switch from speaking English to Africaan, a sullen lot of men, something on their minds.

Rugby is played with frantic zeal daily for championships, Wales always ready to take on the lot with no holds barred. I watch in amazement as a crowd of men disappear within the heaving wild spray of sad almost digging the ball out.

A wonderful invention called 'the blower', constructed from a collection of empty Red Cross tins and a bed board, the thing operates on the principals of a blacksmiths bellows, get a few wood shavings and the merest scrap of paper, a gentle turn of the fan creates a flow of air, it will boil a tin of water in the wink of an eye, find a scrap of coal dust and you're made!

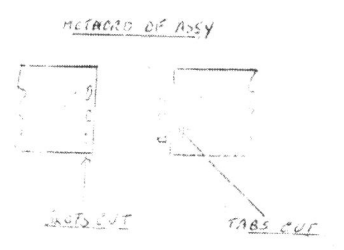

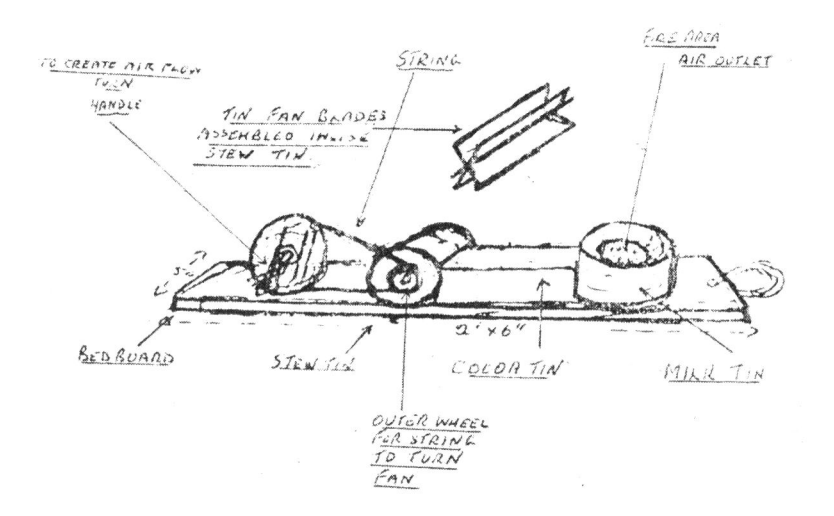

[Diagram: Method of assembly and construction of a "blower" — showing bed board, stew tin with tin fan blades assembled inside, cocoa tin, milk tin, string, outer wheel for string to turn fan, turn handle to create air flow, and air outlet at fire area.]

Bed boards become the obvious source of fuel supply, soon men are balancing as they lie on no more than five narrow boards. The guards start a checking system, daily they count the diminishing bed boards, they rave and shout, replace a large quantity, they too disappear into the hungry furnaces of 'the blowers'. Soon Jerry gets madder, makes us stand out on parade for hours on end, at all odd times of the day, but he still has to count the darn bed boards, daily we stand on punishment parade.

'Blowers' busy all over the place, men squat in absorbed groups as they wrestle with imaginative and definitely adventurous mixes of bits of food, tiny spirals of smoke rise lazily into the air, guards hover about looking miserably at the busy cooks, Christ, they have got to count the bloody boards again, they go off to perform their endless task.

Take a Canadian biscuit, soak it in water, it swells up to more than twice its size, fry it in a bit of margarine or butter, slap a bit of jam on it, you have a P.O.W.'s dream. Get a British hardtack biscuit you can't do much with it but break your bloody teeth, sometimes if we can save enough we soak them in water, needle the mixture with jam, call it a bread pudding!

Natures call must be answered day or night, a present it's night, a thing to be considered seriously in this place, the pit is over the other side of the camp. I have a long walk, a warm night, don't need a jacket, pyjamas serve a dual purpose, vest and underpants by day, pyjamas by night; can be seen clearly, the off white pyjamas ensure that. Fixed searchlights illuminate the whole length of the fences, roving searchlights sweep the compound as I walk across it, a light picks me up as I walk slowly; not worried about the lights, my eyes search for the dogs and handlers. There, out of the dark shadow of a hut steps a man and his dog, they slowly walk towards me and examine me, don't run, but keep the plastered arm ready, if the dog runs at me he is going to get it between his teeth – he will be surprised. They stop half way, the guard speaks to the dog, waves me on, I proceed slowly and deliberately. No sign of them on the return trip, but I know more than one pair of eyes watch my cautious progress.

Running parallel alongside one of the camp fences is the main road to Thorn, an approximate twenty foot strip of grass separates the fence from the road, sit on the soft sand with my back propped against a hut in the sun, I can watch the outside world flow past. German civilians stare at us, we stare back. As I sit there I know that the civilians are in for a surprise sooner or later, the wild savage will come yelling from along the huts with his fearful war cries. He dashes straight at them, they recoil in shocked surprise at the sight of the near naked figure dressed only in a loin cloth which is next door to indecent. In actual fact their lives are saved by the single strand trip wire which he dare not cross. A beautifully proportioned and muscular body completely covered in some brown substance, he brandishes a broomstick spear tipped with a cardboard point, his make-up is spoiled only by the shock of blond hair, day after day he frightens passing civilians who are only looking at us. The column of Russian civilians winds its way slowly along the road past the wire, a column of old men, women, and children of all ages. They look at our silent group inside the wire, but their drawn faces tell the story of their own utter fatigue and hunger, the dull eyes look at us but they don't see, minds are intent only on keeping on their feet as the stagger onwards flanked by armed guards. A long column that takes quite a time to pass. We hear that they have halted along the road, out of sight of the camp, request the camp guards to let them have our days food ration but the request is denied, they say it can't be done.

A course has been marked out, the two contestants kneel at the starting line ready, the two dried prunes are placed on the starting line as well, the men are going to roll the prunes across the sand with their noses, a fight to the finish this race. They're off, two bums stick up into the air as heads go down, they almost immediately have to dig for the prunes, a ring of excited spectators urge them on. I leave them to it, working away like a couple of grubbing pigs, never did find out who won!

Talk among the men of a body and the cess pit, don't bother to ask too many questions, most likely an infiltrator, Jerry has tried it many times over the years but without much success to my knowledge, the men's own internal security arrangements take care of these matters.

The British contingent are getting their concert party on the job tonight, we assemble in the wooden hut in a packed mass, settle on benches that have been tastefully arranged in rows. A single strand of wire runs the length of the rafters from the stage to the back of the hut, all to do with acoustics, a simple technical arrangement which carries the sound to the men at the back. Our eyes pop out at the sight of the prancing long legs of the fantastic chorus girls, Jesus, they look good enough to eat, as good as the real thing. I leave the camp show completely amazed at the wealth of entertainment value in the camp and the dedication of these men who work so hard to entertain us.

News of a major breakout by RAF lads at Stalag Luft III, many are recaptured, some are shot, we are told to expect a batch of men from the camp to join us at Thorn. A busy day today, the boys in blue are expected, we set to work to clean out the huts allocated to them, fill the palliasses with straw, scrounge and collect refreshments of sorts for men who will arrive tired and hungry. Soon they are at the gates, we meet them here, escort them into their huts, they enter among us apprehensively, we British in the camp are mostly men of Dunkirk days and they know it, they think we still don't love the RAF, they don't know that we have forgiven them long ago. I search among them for men of Oxford, find several, fill up with news and gossip of home.

As we recline in the sun at our roadside vantage point, we watch the full scale infantry attack being staged across the road with interest, a wasteland of sand dunes, elderly men in full fighting order, hard at training, with no respect for their age. They crawl up sand heaps and fling themselves down in a wild tangle of arms, legs, and jingling equipment. Some lie stunned at the bottom, the breath knocked completely out of their bodies, but though their bodies may be on the old side their spirit is strong. They try again and again. Cheers of encouragement from the lads, shouted advice to men crawling stealthily between the dunes, shouts of warning to others, "Watch out, the bastards creeping up on you." Some of the looks cast across the road at us should have struck us dead on the spot, some of the Germans look fit to burst with anger, others are so embarrassed under our gaze they can't do a thing right, a fine days entertainment.

Reports of terrible treatment to Russian military prisoners at a camp not far from us, no such thing as going sick for a Russian, they work till they die on the starvation swill. Even after death some of them still go to work, carried out by two other men, an arm held round a neck, dragging feet mean nothing to the guards, take the body to work, claim its ration until the guard realises it is a dead man. The camp tries to get some of our rations diverted to them but again it can't be done. Lost men the Russians, every one of them, we too are lost men, we can do nothing to help them.

All kinds of balls fly through the air as we play at games, sometimes they will roll under the warning trip wire near the fence, need to retrieve the ball but stepping over the wire without permission is a sure way to die. Look up at the nearest watch tower, draw their attention to the ball, make double sure that the guards up the understand clearly what you wish to do, point to the ball, lift up the hand giving the thumbs up sign asking permission, make dead sure he is waving you into the area before you move. Ok, can get it - lift a leg over the single strand of wire, step into the area, one pace, can reach the ball, bend to pick it up, the skin on your back crawls as you do so, you half wait for a shot even though you have permission, your instinct will not, simply cannot, let you trust them. Each time you know you flirt with death just for a bloody ball. Step out of the area, a sigh of relief despite yourself, carry on with the game till the next time.

For many weeks talk of a further exchange of sick and disabled. Men look at me starry eyes at the possibilities for me, but I dismiss the thought from my mind as much as possible.

Someone tries to blow Adolf Hitler up with a bomb. The army guards are changed over for men of the Luftwaffe about this time, elderly men mostly, I gaze at them and wistfully hope they are there because they have no bloody aircraft left to service.

The unbelievable has happened. I have been told to hold myself in readiness to move off on the first leg of a repatriation trip, move out in one week, my mind cannot accept it, don't believe it, my heart has to be kept firmly in place, I just don't believe it. Even if I do move off it won't mean anything, just moving camp that's all. But the men of the camp won't let me forget it, they are overjoyed for me, I get sick of talking about it, every man wishes he were in my boots, they air a lot of dreams through me.

Dash around the camp filling a notebook with addresses and messages to friends and families at home, I will do this, do that, promises of honour to valued friends, may I rot in hell if I don't carry them out. From stern to bows she is a beauty, let my eyes flow along the graceful lines. She is the stuff a man's dreams are made of, close my eyes, I can see the sharp bows cutting through blue seas to lands far away, open my eyes, study the details above deck, see how the tall mast soars up high into the sky, a floating cloud of white sail. A well appointed ship, built with great love over many many months by a man whose first love is the sea, pity she is only about two feet in length. Built from scraps of Red Cross packing cases, the New Zealand builder asks me to get it home for him. OK, a mad scramble to construct a light carrying case, soon a coffin like box is produced, the boat is ready for her voyage to New Zealand. The token of love will travel slung across my back.

The day of farewells, my hand aches with the parting grips, the friendship of such men as these is as breathless to gaze on as the finest jewel, my heart fills to overflowing at severance.

Through the gate, but first, before we leave, a search, hell. Unpack everything, let's have a look through it with a fine tooth comb, I just must have a bomb on me or something. Unpack the boat, the guard looks at it in surprise, the hull could hold many secret things, I hold my breath as I listen to the guards brain asking himself whether he should cut open the hull, I sweat for my New Zealanders handiwork but the guard decides he won't bother. Quickly I replace it back into its hiding place in the box.

We trudge off to Fort Fourteen, a fairly well-laden mule with my bits and pieces, I realise suddenly that if we don't go home now I am saddled with the boat for the rest of the bloody war! Reach Fort Fourteen, collect other ticket holders, we who are able to walk leave Thorn station. Shake the dust of Thorn off our heels with no regrets. None of us believe that we might be going home, not really, but we are moving, that's something, seeing fresh pastures, killing time.

Reach a Red Cross depot called Neu Bentshen, near Posen. A collection of huts, soup is dished up, make a cup of English tea, sleep on the floor. Early start next morning at five fifteen am, a long dreary, stop-start train, halt at a place called Cottbus, brew up another cup of tea, more soup, travel on, reach our destination, the sign at the halt says Annaburg.

Annaburg, Germany, 1944

Unload from the train, a slow march through young pine trees, a building ahead, a beautifully constructed building, a chateau of France dumped out here in Germany. A barbed wire fence surrounds it, a small area by camp standards, a few wooden huts scattered within, guards patrol the fence, lads stand gazing out at us as we approach with bored expressions, counted in, bunks allocated in a wooden hut.

A hospital camp, here we will stay for about three weeks before moving on they say, all of us here are Repats. Judging by the rations there might be something in it after all. Two hot soups a day, two lots of hot water for drinks a day, a fifth of a loaf a day, a Red Cross parcel every week. Got to be trying to make a good impression; God, how the lads at Marienburg would love this place!

My word, they are getting kind - can go outside for a walk now. Got to give your word first that you won't bugger about trying to run off somewhere, who the hell wants to run away from this party? Go out in nice quiet cultured looking groups, walk among the pine trees, the guard strolls with us nice and casual but what makes us stare at him is not because he is a good looking bastard, but because he only carries a tiny decorative pistol in his belt. For the first time a guard without a rifle and fixed bayonet, despite the signs we don't believe it.

Men do try and run away from this camp, have we not two dead to prove it! The Englishman extended his stroll in the woods, went further afield, a policeman shot him. The American couldn't wait any longer either, tried to climb the camp wire, they shot him down. The minds of both men were sick, that's why they were going home. This week they will be buried among the pines they so desperately wanted to leave.

Very correct funerals they accord the two lads, black ornate plywood coffins, the local village horse drawn hearse, a cortege of men from the camp follows the hearse, a squad of German infantry march solemnly to the patch of sandy soil among the pines where other graves are in a neat row, the padre is British. A German officer lays a nice big wreath from the German garrison as a photographer is busy taking many pictures, recording how Germany lays her prisoners to rest. Afterwards they sell us sets of the pictures for a few camp fennings to take home and show our friends.

Each day endless walks around the compound. Two dark skinned little men are heading to cross my path, they have stopped, they wait for me to pass first, nothing will make them cross my path. Ghurka's - wonderful little men, wish they would not do that, they can have my last crust any time.

A great day today. Look up at the heavens, between the mass of great Liberator bombers you can see patches of blue sky, but even that is criss-crossed with vapour trails as hundreds of aircraft muster above our heads from all directions. Oh, happy sight! There is no room up there for German aircraft. Instantly the place is transformed into a camp of raving lunatics, men are screaming up at the aircraft telling them what to do. We leer at the guards panic stricken faces, literally we run around in circles with excitement. The guards are herding us into our quarters, they push and shove us in a panic to get us out of sight of the aircraft. We go in, only to rush to the windows, soon every window is jammed tight with men hanging out and waving the whitest objects they own, every window is a sea of white signal flags to the aircraft above. The guards go mad with shock, they scream at us, bring their rifles to the ready, clear the bolts and take aim. Our bodies withdraw leaving half a shirt or towel or whatever still flapping out of the window defiantly as a target. The bombers leave at different levels, off to their targets, our throats are dry, we are exhausted from the excitement. After a while the guards let us out into the compound, they look at us as though we are mad, which of course we are, who wouldn't want to be mad with a great bunch of lads like these, we sleep with great peace of mind that night.

Men begin to flood into the camp, groups of officers, Canadians, Australians, French De Gaul troops, Indain troops, still the rumour is strong that we shall be moving soon.

At last the day actually arrives, today we move, they have not said where to, but they give us big labels to tie on our tunic button hole, we look like packages. A sight I never expected to see, men who were forced to hand in valuables are actually getting them back, it's got to be seen to be believed. A beautiful day, get my bits and pieces packed again, the boat swings from my back on yet another leg of its New Zealand trip. A slow stroll down to the station, guards accompany us but not a rifle between the lot, just tiny pistols at their belts, they are very friendly, my mind is busy trying to read the signs, trying to guess if it is really going to happen. The signs look good up to now, my mind is afraid to accept the interpretation, guess the sodding guards will still be with us come nightfall, can't imagine life without them

A passenger coach, small compartments, an outer corridor, guards stand about here and there, very relaxed. The train moves off, gathers speed fast, keeps going hour after hour. The German landscape passes by quickly, it recedes away from me as I gaze with little interest from my seat, it streaks past and fades away, away, away, just where I want it to go, a long, long way away. Speed is slowing, travel for many miles gradually reducing speed, groups of small houses appear, they get more numerous, obviously the outskirts of a city, smashed rolling stock at the side of the track, twisted rail tracks, smashed houses. A guard tell us that we are entering Berlin.

The corridor of the now crawling train is packed as we stare out at the scene unfolding before our eyes, an unbelievable sight of stark destruction, we see before us the meaning of saturation bombing, as far as the eye can see is desolation complete. Jagged ugly walls stab the sky here and there but mostly it's just mountains of unbelievable rubble, streets are narrow lanes between heaped rubble, nothing is untouched, nothing is left, Berlin is a rubbish dump, but somehow my heart cannot rejoice. We are silent as we pass through it, the destruction is too great, too vast for our minds to grasp, I feel no pity for the people, only for the city. Endless heaped piles of smashed locomotives, rolling stock and tracks that have been twisted with the ease of thin copper wire now lie on each side of the track. Over there a wooden sidewalk has been built up above street level, it runs parallel with the rail track for several hundred yards, people hurry along it, the timber is bright with unpainted newness, busy looking people, still they carry their briefcases in their hands; they look neither to the left or right as they hurry about their urgent business, they still haven't been hit hard enough.

Reach towards the outskirts, woods appear close up against the rail tracks, you can see the netting stretched between the trees, the busy activity within the shelter. Underground factories I guess, pass many more for several miles, keep the location in my mind, deep within my mind, get the bastards moved if I can have anything to do with it, Edgar and the boys are still back there. Pull away from the place eventually, out into the open country, Berlin is behind us, the symbol of total aerial war is out of sight but the horror picture remains in my mind, imprinted I guess for as long as I live.

Darkness, the train still travels at very low speed, several long silent halts, we are tired and hungry, fed up with the slow progress.

Another halt, wait a bit, told to get ready to get off. Dimly lit sheds, several checks through groups of Germans in shadows, emerge out into the open air, electric lights hanging from the top of the tall posts, naked lights, they shine down on many German troops who stand in an arrow formation in single lines, the point of the arrow is pointed at us, we head directly for it. In the background stands a large ship, lights ablaze on her decks, the spread out ends of the arrow of men extends to each end of the ship, to reach her you must enter through the narrow arrow point.

A long thin line of khaki clad figures winds through the opening between the two men forming the arrow point, the labels tied to our tunics are checked against some records, our discs are taken away, we pass into the patters of unarmed Germans. Across the open space, up a gang plank, on to the ship. Unidentified figures direct us down below to the tiers of bunks, we think we are on a Swedish ship, but don't crow yet, we only think we are.

Hours of silent waiting, nobody tells us anything, my heart doesn't tell me anything, it doesn't feel free, nothing has happened to it as yet. We go to sleep, to hell with it all. Come to, the ship is moving, it's daybreak outside but we can't move, can't leave our bunks for a while, one thing, we are on a Swedish ship. My mind is quite dead, not a bit excited, there are no emotions stirring within, not yet, maybe later.

The ship has docked, we can get off now. File upwards to the deck which is painted overall with the flag of Sweden. Down the gang plank on Swedish soil, we have left Germany behind us. Emotions are still dead, the mind is dull, only the eyes stir.

Gothenburg, Sweden, 1944

On to a train which moves off as soon as it is loaded. Swedish civilian passengers pass to and fro along the corridor, a Swedish soldier enters the compartment, greets us and informs us that we have been landed in the north, we are now travelling south to Gothenburg. My eyes see the passing country but don't register anything. Enter the outskirts of a large city, transfer on to coaches, thousands of people fill the streets. A few very tall men dressed in navy blue uniforms, long overcoats, long swords hang at their sides, they direct traffic and people – policemen.

People everywhere who cheer us like mad. As dusk falls the coach pulls up outside a school, debus, into the school, upstairs into a long dormitory, beds line the wall each side, beautiful nurses stand by each bed. As we peel off to the beds they grab each man eagerly with radiant smiles lighting their faces, for the first time emotions are beginning to stir as I look at them in wonderment, they are so clean.

The nurse is chattering to me in perfect English, trying to put me at my ease, her smile would melt ice but I can only stare and stare at the vision. She stoops, folds back the bed cover, tells me to get in and rest. I only half hear what she has said as my eyes glaze in horror at the snow white sheets that have been revealed. Haven't seen a sheet for more than four years let alone slept in one! She is looking at me a bit surprised because I hesitate, but the sheets make me shudder at the thought of what they will look like in the morning after my dirty body has been in them, the thought of this creature's opinion frightens me. Christ, give me a blanket, that's all I need! She is smiling again, she has guessed what's wrong, says she will leave me for a while, be in bed before she comes back.

Feel the sheets, crisp and so bloody white. Jesus, the springs - never be able to sleep in the darn thing. Slink into it but only because the other lads are getting into theirs, I don't want to hurt my nurse's feelings. She returns, bends over me as she tucks me in like a baby, the fragrance of the scent she wears hits me, my eyes are fixed on the red lips so close, God, if only I could!

Lights out, quietness falls on the room, toss and turn, my mind races backwards, the smell of the sheets, the crisp feel of them interrupts my thoughts, my mind realises that at last I am no longer a prisoner, that I am free. But my heart does not sing as it should, my mind keeps going back to the lads across the water, they are still there, I feel as though I have deserted Edgar, in the darkness I come close to tears. Thought I knew myself. Hardly slept a wink last night, neither did many of the other lads, too many hard beds of late, the habit takes some breaking.

Bright laughing faces fill the ward as the nurses flood back, a hum of English with a nice Swedish accent fills the air, a bright "Good morning" from my blond haired beauty, "You will have a bath now".

"A what?"

"A bath!"

Jesus Christ, is this freedom?

There it is, a coffin without a lid. Gleaming white, just like Mums, steaming water half fills it, more water concentrated there than I have seen in one lump outside a river for many a long time. Crystal clear water, could drink it easily. Suppose it's necessary but five showers over the last few years has done me no harm. A blond head pokes round the door, hurrying me on gently, I use the snow white towel with reluctance, everything around here is blasted white, I don't like it. She waits outside the door for me patiently, I seem to be her personal responsibility, she ain't going to let me out of her sight. Leads me about as though I am blind, this blue eyed vision is holding my hand, I tremble at the touch of the long soft fingers, my heart races at the nearness of the laughing face. God, she knows not what she does to me! Would I write to her, silly question, she has only to ask, I would bloody well die for her at once!

Out into the kids playground, soldiers with rifles stand around the low railing surround, they face outwards, away from us, they face a sea of cheering, laughing, waving people, the soldiers are there to keep them back from us! We answer their greetings, match their waves, strange, feels funny not having anyone or anything in sight to hate, have used up a lot of late, some still smoulders in memory and will never die. The Bavarians of June the fifth 1940, the guard in charge of Walters male slave labour on the farm, no, hate for them will never die, but these people make you smile in their world of peace, they act as though we fight for them.

My angel leads me down stairs, into a large hall, long tables covered in blasted white table cloths again, the tables groan under the weight of food, our breakfast. Many civilians, English residents of Gothenburg, they have come to greet us and have laid on this

English style breakfast, everything strictly in the way of the English. Swedish and British flags decorate the table, everyone loves everyone else, the sudden mass of friendly people hits you below the belt, we are all in a bit of a daze. A dream meal in a dream world, speeches of welcome that hardly register in my mind.

Rest and relax till late afternoon, send letter cards, one to Mother, one to Edgar. Coaches arrive, climb aboard, we head for the boat.

An unbelievable sight in the streets, thousands and thousands of people line the route in wildly cheering masses. See them climbing to the lampposts, spilling out of the windows, perched on the roof tops. Hear how they cheer, we cheer back madly, our hearts filled with gratitude to these wonderful friendly people.

Into the dock, debus, a huge liner towers above our heads, our ship. She waits patiently and in silent dignity for us, she calls herself the Arundel Castle. On her side is painted a huge Union Jack, it's about the length of two buses, it looks grand, big enough for the whole bloody world to see. As I gaze at the painted emblem, deep emotions stir within me, I suppose one could call it love.

Climb upwards on board, downwards to bunks with springs, sheets, and clean smelling blankets. Swedish people mill about on board. Girls and lads in khaki drape about on anything that will take their weight, kisses and cuddles are the order of the last few hours before we sail. Darkness descends, our new found friends must leave, they go with reluctance, but they understand that we are impatient to be on our way to reach the pinnacle of our dreams, England.

Large arch lights hang over the side of the ship to shine directly on to the huge Union Jacks on each side of her, above the decks is a blaze of lights, she moves away from the hospitable land called Sweden, the bows point out into the blackness of the sea, we are on our way.

Smart looking males and females dash about the ship, military, nurses, and welfare workers. Have a lecture, told we have no weapons on board, not even a revolver, jerry would stop us if he thought we had, so we have still got to tread softly, we are not out of the woods yet. We will travel along the coast of Norway, Jerry is still there and watching us closely, the trip will take three days, we are headed for Liverpool.

Bread so white, like biting into a lump of snow, the food is rich and abundant beyond our wildest dreams.

Interview with intelligence, they ask questions, tell them things buried deep within the mind, the Berlin factories in the woods, tell them about them for the lads still back there.

The jagged and ugly coastline stays with us for a long time as we keep close inshore, it looks lifeless, you can't see the eyes that watch the passing ship. Unexpectedly the ship heaves too on her course, soon to be wallowing in the swell, signal lights flash from the shore answered by signals from the ship, rumour flies about that there is a gun on board and that Jerry has found out about it. A fast motor torpedo boat approaches from the shore, as they get closer you can see the German figures on board. Hell, thought we had seen the last of them! They pull into the side of the ship with practiced ease, figures climb aboard, several minutes, they return escorting someone, they take whoever it is away. Escapees had mixed themselves with us it is said, what rotten luck for them, so near to getting away with it.

The ships engines restart, we proceed, next day Norway has disappeared, we are on the open sea, as far as the eye can see there is nothing but water. Walking around the decks, eating and sleeping, nothing else to do. A short attack of sickness on the second day, a combination of food too rich for my stomach and the slow deadly swell of the North Sea.

Somebody shouts that a whale has been sighted, pop up on deck to have a look at it, many miles away can be seen a thin vapour shooting up into the air now and then, but I still can't say that I have seen a whale. Somebody else shouts out that we are passing though the Faro Isles, gallop up to have a look at it, Jesus. Dirty big black rocks pass slowly past the side of the ship, no more than eight feet away. Wet and glistening, the air is full of mist, dash to the other side of the boat, again the massive black rocks slide past by only a few feet, the ship fits between them like a glove, the seamanship is breathtaking, still can't boast that I saw the Faro Isles, I only saw the horrible rocks.

Tugboats dart about on their urgent business, we gaze at the land that has filled our dreams for so long. Very little sign of life can be seen on shore, ahead there is a clock tower, it marks the City of Liverpool, we are steaming up the Mersey. A general air of excitement sweeps the ship, everyone is laughing and giggling like schoolboys, hundreds of eager eyes watch the distance closing to the dock side, with gentle bumps on the padded landing area the ship at last kisses England for us, it is late afternoon.

A few men in working clothes secure the great ship, a few other men in posh civvy suits stand in groups chattering, otherwise the place is empty. Several hours confined to the ship, nobody has got off it yet, impatient nerves and empty hours of waiting has turned our excited joy into frustration and cussing the delay.

England, 1944

Darkness brings movement, we can get off now, wind off in a long single file, though many dimly lit shed, follow the men in front. Civilian faces loom up and pass, unsmiling faces that just stare without seeing you, you want to say hello to them all but somehow the words die in your throat, they are obviously not interested, nothing wonderful is happening in their lives.

On to a train, the windows are blacked out, blue lights burn within. A bag of Red Cross rations. We travel through the night for some hours, halt, file out of the train, on to waiting motor coaches; out of the coaches, into a building, along dimly lit corridors, enter a hospital ward full of empty beds, a nurse indicated a bed per man, climb into them, instant sleep.

Awake early next morning, up for breakfast, plaster removed from my arm, medical particulars checked. I can go home today. At present is seems I am at Shrewsbury.

Motor coach to town station, a waiting train for those of us who travel south, soon the train is full and pulls slowly away, on the platform stands the figure of a man, he stands stiffly at attention, his hand to his cap in a salute as we pass him, he holds the salute till the complete train passes him. Jesus, that was a bloody General or something. Find another lad who is travelling to the same village as me, he has lost an eye.

The station is so quiet and empty, a porter flits briefly into view, otherwise it is dead. We stand and gaze at out station in silence, each with his own thoughts, we have arrived back to the City we left so long ago, our City, Oxford. Share a taxi out to the village of Kennington, knock at my Mothers door, she opens it. We shelter in the comfort of each others arms for many minutes. I submit to her overjoyed fussing with pleasure, her loneliness has ended. I pick up the reins of my father had to drop, I am her man, the one she can see. The one she can touch.

Visit Fathers grave, report my safe return to him in the privacy of the cemetery solitude, tell him that the many many days he stood at the railway track endlessly scanning the windows of passing trains of Dunkirk men in 1940 was not in vain, that one of his sons has returned.

Repatriation leave. Reunions with relations and friends, speed the New Zealanders model boat on the last leg of its trip home. Visit many relations of the boys back in the camp as promised, deliver messages for them, tell their relations that I have just left their sons, husbands, brothers, or fathers. The pleasure on their faces at my words is as a blessing bestowed upon me. Write to many others in far more distant fields, a busy period. Soon leave is over, must report to a college located in the High Street, Oxford, for further instructions. Half a dozen high ranking officers sit on chairs behind tiny coffee tables in a row right in front of me, intelligent looks sweep across their faces, snap decision is made a rubber stamp crashed on paper, I am dismissed.

Examine the papers handed me by a lesser but equally legal rank, I must report to the Kinston Convalescent Depot. Bit surprised really, always thought convalescence came after hospital treatment. A large camp set in what was once parkland, a collection of wooden huts, a huge parade ground surrounded by a tall wire fence, large holes in the wire here and there where the inmates had obviously made breakouts. I automatically look for bloody watch towers, but happily none are visible.

A couple of hundred men gallop about at P.T., others climb up ropes, swing across puddles of water on the ropes, walk aerial wire among the tree tops, or climb large chunks of rope netting, the place is lousy with rosy cheeked and disgustingly fit looking P.T. instructors. Their legs look as though they are made of solid springs, I enter this Tarzan factory with the distant feeling that I have been well and truly misdirected, but no, this is Kingston Con Depot and that's what is written on my bits of paper.

Allocated a bed, meet the other inmates of the hut, they ask me if I arrived on crutches, reckon they never can tell just by looking at a bloke, the bastards on the gate always take away the crutches as soon as you enter the place they reckon. Report sick with my wrist next morning seeking some medical attention, the Medical Officer looks surprised as I unfold my problem, got no idea what the hell I am talking about, I can see I have a problem here. Signs me on with the Sun-Ray treatment for a couple of weeks, I have landed with a right bunch here.

Men flow through the camp quickly as they recover from wounds, illness, periodical casual examinations of case history documents, usually followed by rapid postings to active units. Meet two men of the Oxfords recovering from wounds received in the Normandy Landings, they are going back soon, they confess they will return with fear in their hearts. The Sun-Ray treatment stretches to a month of daily visits, a sheer waste of time for everyone concerned, still I seek proper medical attention, still I need to meet a doctor who knows something about done diseases.

Hang about the place for about two months, another interview, the young dashing Officer who faces me is another stupid bastard who doesn't know what the hell I am talking about, he says that I have been here longer than most, I look alright. He can't see a leg hanging off or anything like that, he reckons I am trying to pull a fast one, trying to work my ticket. Anger erupts at the insult, I tell him to get stuffed and walk out leaving him in mid-sentence. I am getting mad. Caught in a system interested only in shovelling men back to units, got to lie low somewhere till I can meet an Officer interested in medical matters.

Find a solitary toilet in a secluded part of the camp, stay there daily for a further month coming out only for sleep, food, and an evening on the town. Now and then a rocket lands below in the town which rattles me as I sit on the toilet seat, a new disability is developing, getting bloody saddle sore now.

Get introduced to the lurking dangers of the London home-front, look up at a sound see if I can locate the two-stroke motor cycle that passes overhead, the sky is empty to the naked eye, stand still, follow its course with the ears, wait for the motor to stop chugging, suddenly it cuts out as though the hand of death has cut off the ignition, the V.I. rocket is now hurtling to earth, there is no point in running, just hope that it falls far away. A loud explosion follows the prolonged hushed silence, the rocket falls some miles away, London moves again, others will clear up the mess. Later there is the V.2 rocket, a silent, sneaky version, no warning given at all, it gives a fella no time to get his pants up again.

The blackout, hells bells, the blackout - the dangers that lurk under the innocent cloak of darkness. My tobacco pipe is in vogue at present, I feel it gives me a nonchalant air as it sticks out from under my nose. Leave the bright light, step out through the securely blacked out doorway into the darkness of the street, stand still for a minute, let my eyes get used to it. Vehicles creep past aided by the slit of light from the cowelled headlamps, pedestrians tread their way gingerly on the sidewalk aided by small hand torches, I see two widely spaced beams probing the pavement as they approach me, stride out with confidence between the two beams of light into the blackness knowing that it is empty of man. The bowl of the pipe hits the unseen fella first driving the pipe stem directly into the back of my throat, frantically it seeks a way out through the back of my neck, the violent choking and spluttering narrowly averts such a disaster, for a week I can't even swallow a beer.

Yet another medical check in the camp, a completely different Officer, he studies my papers with a puzzled frown.

"Hell man, have you been here this long?"

"Yes sir"

"Must be something wrong with you." I let loose a deep sigh at the news. He signs a chit which will send me to a hospital, at last I have got some action.

A hospital at Woking, check the place to make sure it is not for expectant mothers or something, it isn't, I am reasonably safe. I have local wrist trouble, but I am trussed up in be as though I have not long to live, a doctor stands in front of me looking at the X-ray I had taken in Germany, I eye his intelligent looking face with some suspicion, praying that indeed he is intelligent and knows what he is looking at. Yes, he is intelligent, he mutters "Kienbock Disease" instantly as though he has recognised and old friend, I have found me a real doctor in this country at last.

They get me messing about making soft toys and teddy bears for a week, a the end of which the doctor comes to have a chat with me, tells me that I can take one of two choices regarding my wrist. First, he can remove the connecting joint boned between hand and forearm, which will leave me with a stiff wrist. Second, he can leave the bones in, which will leave some restricted movement, the disease won't spread if the bones are left in he reckons. Knowing how doctors seem to love carving you up, I cheat him, tell him to leave the darn bones alone being as the disease won't spread.

Spend another week creating teddy bears that despite my best efforts finish up looking like Greyhounds, and getting measured for fancy leather supports for the ailing wrist, then the doctor kicks me out of the hospital and H.M. Service as unfit for further duty. Strangely, I don't argue with him one little bit over the point.

But the joys of the de-mob allude me as I study the shifting battle fronts daily, see how the Russian front sweeps in to the area of East Prussia and beyond, my mind erases all else in its concern for Edgar and the other lads, the helplessness of waiting for news, not knowing, fearing the worst, is infinitely harder than sharing the dangers with them.

I watch the postman walk along the path, he hands me a tiny piece of paper, torn off an envelope, on one side is my mothers address and the mark of an American rubber stamp, on the other is written a message:

YOUR SON IS ALIVE AND WELL. SIGNED, A PASSING YANK

My heart leaps with joy at the scrap of information send by the passing good Samaritan, Alive, soon further news should follow. Approximately ten days later a further scrap of paper is delivered by the postman, the message is brief and to the point:
I AM IN HOSPITAL AT NEWTON ABBOT. SIGNED, EDGAR

I catch the first available train heading in the general direction of Devon, many changes en route, enter the first pub I see on arrival at Newton Abbot as darkness falls, I seek refreshment and information. The man and woman have been looking at me for some time, I stand out as a stranger, they approach me, ask if they can help, I tell them my story, yes, they have heard of ex-prisoners arriving in the area, think they can find out just where, but first I need food and sleep, they insist that I spend the night in their house. My new found friends take me to their home, treat me royally, feed and tuck me in bed.

Directions next morning, I have several miles to walk, I leave them with a blessing on my lips. I have been walking for some time, feel I have lost my way, ask directions of the first person I meet. Yes, I am on the wrong road, should be on the other road that runs parallel across the other side of the field, decide to cut across the field to save time and weary legs. Half way across the field a bog develops, flounder directly across it, my nice new de-mob shoes and trousers are in a disgusting state with clinging mud, to hell with them. Reach the road, there before me are large imposing entrance gates that have seen far better days, a long drive leads to a large house.

Reach the house, yes, it is a hospital, yes, ex-prisoners are here, yes Edgar is somewhere within its walls, but I will have to go away and come back on visiting day, can come back in two days, "That's when visiting time is you see!" I explain the circumstances, but to them rules are rules, they must not be broken, I blow my top, but I still cannot get in.

Leave the place, my mind is seething with diabolical plans to break in to the place somehow, my thoughts are interrupted by an approaching ambulance travelling slowly towards the hospital, obviously it's out of work. I stop it, tell my story to the two men on board, they listen intently, "Ok, lad hop on". I go back to the hospital in style, one of the men locates the ward that holds Edgar, he silently leads me through the building, points to a door and disappears without a word.

Push open the door, the place is empty of nursing staff, several dozen occupied beds, most of the lads look awful, my eyes search frantically for signs of Edgars face. There, that grinning skull looking at me, that skeleton covered with skin, that's Edgar, Jesus Christ! I walk over to him, we grip hands hard, nothing is said, nothing need be said, for many minutes we look deep in to each other's eyes as the emotions take control.

The silence is broken by Edgar: "It was a bastard. Glad you weren't there kiddo!"

Cecil Arthur Meads, 1945

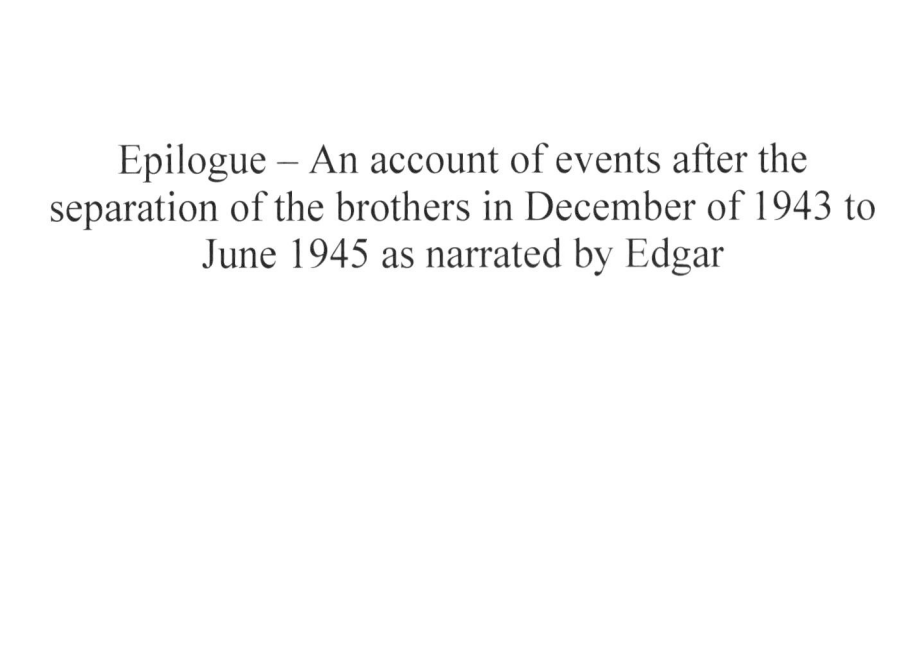

Epilogue – An account of events after the separation of the brothers in December of 1943 to June 1945 as narrated by Edgar

Fisherbalki, East Prussia, 1943-44, The Farm

Strange, never really been separated before, always been together or hanging around close somewhere, but there goes my brother, out of my life, could be forever. He is strolling along the road in front of his guard away from me, his bits and pieces of comfort swing from his body as he rolls along, Red Cross parcel box clutched under his arm. Looks more like a bloody travelling tinker than a soldier. Gradually they fade away down the road, a final wave, he is gone. No good moping about it, there are things to be done, must look to myself, nobody else will.

Work is to be shared by several elderly men from the village, Fred the lad down the road on the two-bit farm, come along to do a bit of milking. Walter also takes on a lone Russian male, a tall thin individual who always wears an old greasy leather cap with large earflaps attached to that hang down at each side of his face. His jacket is of the typical Russian quilted type, battered and well worn top boots wrinkle round the lower part of his thin legs. One of his ears is missing which give his drawn face a lop-sided effect, a man in his late fifties. As he has no bed he sleeps in the barn each night as would an animal. We have difficulty communicating, he has no German, and I have no Russian, but we manage somehow by elaborate sign language. A strange disturbed man, he is subject to brain storms at which times he becomes most violent.

Mostly he spends his time working with a scythe, a master craftsman in the use of the tool, his work instantly registers the skill of a lifetime. Most men can only produce a half circular sweep of a cut with the blade, but this man can arrange his legs into a crossed pattern which, as he unwinds them pivots his body in a complete circle in a corkscrew movement, leaving a perfect circle of cut grass of breathtaking evenness, truly an artist of the first order. One day as I stand grooming the horses in the barn I am startled by a wild scream in Russian coming from behind me. Looking over my shoulder I see the Russian glaring at me with a mad look in his eyes, as I watch he grabs pitchfork which is standing near him, levels it at me and rushes forward. Pure instinctive reflexes cause me to sidestep the prongs just in time while I automatically strike out at him. My fist smashes into his face with great force sending him staggering backward to fall into a large wooden grain bin which stands open behind him, protruding out of the bin I see his legs and the fork which he still clutches. Rapidly taking away the fork I help him out of the bin, he walks away grumbling in Russian but he is much calmer now, and has fortunately lost interest in me.

Deeply puzzled by his attack, I can only put it down to yet another of his brainstorms, but his screaming Russian sentence is imprinted in my mind, I must find out what it meant. I locate a Pole who speaks Russian and ask him what the Russian had been screaming at me, the Pole grins as he tells me that I had been told to go and fuck my mother. Walter the farmer gets rid of the man shortly afterwards, nobody round here felt safe with him about the place.

Winter passes, the monotony is broken only occasionally by the receipt of letters smuggled out to me from the main Stalag from my brother, they give me bits and pieces of interesting information of the world outside the farm. These stop after a while when he is transferred to an N.C.O. non working camp, henceforth the only means of communication between us will be the official letter card.

Completely browned off, must get away from the confines of the farm for a day or I will go mad. I make the excuse to the guard that I have a bad toothache, immediate action; back to the Stalag the very next day. New faces are seen, a day of no work, well worth the perfectly good tooth which I have sacrificed to the dentist. A week later a genuine raging toothache, tell the guard I must have it out urgently, but it kills me for two months before it is finally removed.

One of the lads on a farm has made a fantastic breakthrough, a double-barrelled breakthrough in fact. By servicing the woman of the house in the absence of her man he has access to the radio set, we now have daily news bulletins direct from London every day. Life has become brighter immediately. A great day today, a heavy banging on the stable door at six fifteen am. I open it, there stands John our newscaster, he is blue in the face with excitement, he can hardly speak as he dances from leg to leg. At last he make it and lets me share his great excitement: "They have landed! Us and the bloody Yanks have landed! Landed on the beaches at Normandy!" Holy mother of God. We are screaming to the heavens in sheer delight, a frenzy of hugging and dancing round the stable. The animals think we are mad - we are! At long last our beautiful boys are heading in our direction. We bless this days the 6th of June 1944.

Walter the farmer enters the stall, wants to know what all the fuss is about, we dare not tell him what we know but he knows that something big has happened by our faces. We fight to regain our normal composure in front of him but it's hard, by bloody Christ it's hard not to scream it into his face. Word flies round the farms from man to man, the world is suddenly much brighter, our thoughts are filled with the men who fight in Normandy, we pray that they hurry.

Return to the billet from the fields two days later to find the place torn to pieces, my bits and pieces together with the straw from the palliasses are strewn over the floor, in my absence a search has been carried out with a fine tooth comb. I storm into the farmhouse mad with temper demanding to know what is going on. Walter informs me that two S.S. men have been searching for the radio set. One of the lads has opened his mouth to a German civilian who has immediately reported it to the police, hence the search. One week after the landings the German people are informed on their radios.

All war news is now good, especially on the Russian fronts. I notice a slight change in the way the Germans treat the Polish and Russian slave labour these days, a degree better than usual, they must be getting worried.

Sophia, the Polish girl on the farm has at last found a ray of sunshine in her life having heard from her husband who tells her that they can live together with their child providing he signs certain papers. She asks my advice on the matter, I can only advise her to grasp the opportunity to regain her child with both hands. The husband will have to join the German army but a mother and her child will be reunited, she walks out of my life.

As summer nears its close there is a distinct change in our restricted world, huge barges pass down the river almost daily, they are filled with German wounded, motor torpedo boats tow a string of barges at a gentle pace towards Danzig.

Naval personnel come round the farms to help get the harvest in. A complete 'U Boat' crew gather in the harvest on Walters farm, they also relieve the loneliness of the local women who haven't seen such virile males for years. Every ditch and fold in the ground becomes an organised knocking shop, they are at it everywhere, Jesus, it's hard being a prisoner spectator!

Several times a day now the small gauge railway trucks that pass over the farm fields carry fresh loads of Jewish women of all ages, they stand so tightly packed, between the trucks stand heavily armed guards. I used to stand and wave at them as they pass but I don't now, they just stare at me as they go by, they don't know who or what I am, I can offer them no help, no comfort. I dread to see the empty trucks return, they look so final, I cannot dwell on their fate, there's nothing I can do about it. The old German civilian from the village who works with me is a fine stately old man who I am proud to know, he wears a white Kaiser-type beard with great dignity, he looks at me sadly as the loaded trains pass. "Oh Edard, oh Edard" is all that he can say, tears of shame run down his face.

Quite often I have to tell him off for working too hard, but he is only trying to lighten my load, a man of seventy six, stands a magnificent six feet six in his socks, he keeps offering me his snuff, dreadful stuff, but I take a pinch now and then just to please him, it usually blows the top of my head off, bloody dynamite.

Walter wakes me today, tells me that he must lock me in until further notice but he gives no reason. A guard arrives later, takes away my boots and trousers, locks up and leaves me, again there is no explanation. Locked up for three days, I patrol my three feed by six feet strip for exercise endlessly, then work on the farm is resumed, only then does the reason become clear. There has been a mass breakout by RAF lads at Stalag Luft Three, we hear that three have been caught and shot in the area of Danzig, from then on our boots and trousers are taken away every night.

A concrete shed affair is quickly built in the village, all the men in the area have to file into the place after each day's work; they lock us in together, concrete walls, ceiling and roof, no heating, we are in an ice box as we shiver under our blankets.

The roads are now choked with German troops moving back before the Russian advance, it is mostly horse drawn traffic, they don't look as happy as I feel, but now is not the time to grin at them, not just yet. All civilians use of the railway system is forbidden, it is reserved for military use only, Red Cross parcels and smokes have stopped, life is miserable without them.

Had no news from my brother for a long time now, I wonder how he is making out from time to time.

Have a visitor today, the guard brings an extra man to share our concrete bunker for the night, a Belgian, we gaze at him wondering how we are going to communicate. Fears groundless, as soon as the guard locks us up and departs the Belgian says "How are you fellas? I'm half Yank!" He proves a mine of information, startling us with details of the closeness of the Russians. Being a naval man, Jerry has stuck him on a tug to work which operates out of Danzig, he drifts up and down the Vistula River. Have to help him fill his tug with coal the next morning, no problem carrying the coal, but the fifteen foot long plank suspended between the boat and the river bank gives some anxious moments with its wild springing. We part at the end of the day as he sets off to chug his way back to Danzig, been calling him Yank all day which seemed to please him.

Feeling quite low tonight, the guard has gone to Tiegonhoff to see if any food parcels and cigarettes are available, not a bloody cigarette between the lot of us, the farmer has locked us in due to the guards absence. Getting quite late, a knock on the door as somebody starts to unlock it again, the guard stands at the door, he has no parcels or smokes but he has got one bit of post, a small brown card, he grins as he hands it to me, locks up and leaves us. A Swedish postmark, the card has been signed by my brother, has come from Gothenburg, a Red Cross card that tells me he has arrived in Sweden. Repatriated – safe! I stare at the brown card that tells me he is free, a great feeling of relief sweeps through me, one of us has made it, has got away, I can relax now, six months of wondering and hoping for him is over, he is free, out of their bloody hands. Read the card out to the other lads most of whom know him, at first my words are greeted with dead silence, then it hits them, straight in the guts it hits them, just think, a bloke who was working in this stinking village not long ago has actually made the dream come true, a dream that can happen after all! They go mad, stark staring bloody mad, whoops of joy, thumping me on the cack, shaking my hand, Ginger is crying, he is crying at the miracle of it.

Just up the road lives a very old German couple who are in their seventies, I help them on occasions being a decent old couple; they have one horse and one cow, both animals look as old as themselves. The horse has to be seen to be believed, so old that he falls over nearly every time he goes to sleep standing up, easily the most loveable old creature I have ever had the pleasure to meet. Often asked to help him back on his feet after he has fallen; a bag of bones covered with skin, large flat hooves at the end of long stick like legs, two large ears that always droop like tired stalks. One day the old farmer tells me that the old horse is lost which surprises me, didn't think the poor old thing could move apart from falling over, we are to look round to see if we can find him.

Search high and low for him, can't solve the mystery, assume he must have fallen in the river, probably floating down to Danzig by now. Returning along the river bank to the farm, I hear a deep sigh come from tall grass down close to the water, go down and investigate, there in the grass is the old bag of bones. He lies like a dead thing, no sign of life, poor old sod, he has had it. Place my hand over his nostrils, can faintly feel his breath, lift a floppy ear, shout into it "Hoy, wake up!" Buggered if he doesn't too, he opens a tired old eye and lets forth another deep sigh, he lives.

Back to the farm, get two horses, a tow bar, and chains. Carefully pull him up the bank on to the road, a terrible struggle for three of us to get him on his feet, carefully we lead him back to his stall on tottering legs, there we fix a support strap under his middle to stop him falling down when he goes to sleep, a real old timer that fella.

The cobbles on the road to the village are large and uneven, forbidden to race wagons due to the noise of the steel rimmed wheels and rattling timbers which makes enough noise to wake the dead. Feeling fed up one day I decide to hell with it, will wake the bastards up. An empty hay wagon, two harnessed horses, set them at full gallop through the place, the wagon almost falls to pieces with vibrations as I sweep through yelling at the top of my voice in exhilaration! I pass the village policeman, speedily he mounts his cycle, pedals his guts out trying to catch me up, I ease up at the other end of the village, the policeman dismounts, wags his finger at me as though I am a naughty boy, copies down the farmers name from off the wagon; the farmer will have to pay a hefty fine for my hair-raising, but God it was good!

The old man down the road has given me a puppy for looking after his horse, a tiny black bundle of fur, don't know how I am going to feed him, I sleep on my back at night so that he can lie across my chest inside my shirt. We both like the warmth but I can never get to sleep until he has finished nibbling my chin with his sharp needle like teeth. During the day I work on the land in the saddle, he sits in my coat pocket quite comfortably and without a murmur. Had a bit of luck today, stepped out of the saddle, at my feet lies a large hare frozen with fear, I pick it up, still it does not struggle; hit it a sharp blow at the back of the neck, instantly it is dead, a feast for me and my dog tonight. Boil it up in a bucket behind the barn, it tastes like leather. The puppy eats until he falls over, to look at him I fear I have killed him, I prod his fat little belly from time to time with my finger, it brings no sign of life, the little devil is just too full of food, the glutton. Ask the Frau if I can have a saucer of milk daily for my dog but the old cow refuses, so each morning before the milk churns go down to the factory I steal out and pinch a cup for him, he gets two saucers now instead.

Wonders will never cease in this mad world. We have got to collect napkins now; word has been sent round to all the lads in the area to search our gear for the nearest thing to bits of white towelling, they are wanted for the lad Dawson and his Polish girlfriend on the farm along the road. Fate sent them both to work on the same farm, a case of love at first sight, not the snatched romp in the hay kind of love, but the real thing. The sort of love that weaves the magic of poetry, their love had to find a way. Mere Germans haven't been able to stop it yet, but Dawson is now worried to death, the girl carries his child, their love lives deep within the black shadow of the world of hate, he worries for what might happen to the girl and his child; we worry for all three of them, we can see no happy ending. She is more than eight months gone, her time is near, still she works in the fields, and will probably as many slave labour girls have to do, have it in a ditch. We sort out our near white bits of towelling and send them to the 'Dawson' farm. The girl will cast a magic spell over them with the love of a mother-to-be, she will turn the bits of cloth into nappies for the coming child, it's the least we can do to help lighten her terrible burden of love.

Two of us are on our way to the guards quarters for Sunday roll-call, as we stroll along the bank of the river we see six young Polish girls paddling in the shallows across on the other side. They call out to us in excited greeting "Tommeee", and invite us across to join them. We gaze at the exquisite creatures thinking hard about the invitation, to hell with bloody roll call; we take off our hats, tunics, shirts and vests, take off boots and socks as the girls watch in complete fascination, they don't think we intend to really, but we do. Undoing our belts, our pants drop in heaps about our feet; as we step out of them, then and only then do they realise that we are actually going to call their bluff, that we do intend to swim across to them. With the sudden startled shock of a scurry of pheasants, squeals of simulated panic fills the air, a hasty gathering of clothes as they beat a retreat across the fields away from the randy Tommies. The air rings with female giggles as they run.

Jewish slave-labour girls from the nearby labour camp have come to work on the farm for a couple of days. The guard is a Czech and for an S.S. man he is quite a reasonable fella, he has no objections to me working with the girls. The girls come from all sorts of countries, some from Hungary, I am struck by the finely chiselled features and dark skins of these girls, I guess they are of Romany blood. Others come from France, Germany and Norway. A girl of Norway tells me that her father and two brothers were shot before her eyes outside their house in Norway, both she and her mother were brought to the camp in East Prussia, she has since suffered the sorrow of her mothers death in the camp, now she is alone. She tells me of her dreams, says that she and the rest of the girls, if they live, hope to go to Israel when the war is over. As an afterthought she adds "Of course, that is if you British will allow us to enter". She asks me if I have any socks that need darning because the guard has told her that they will be returning to the farm the next day. I confirm that I have, she asks if I will let her mend them for me, I protest strongly and tell her that she must not wait on me, she insists, says it will give her something to do and will give her great pleasure. I give her my socks, mending wool, and a needle. This little girl from Norway returned them to me next morning, beautifully darned. I can only express my humble thanks but I feel bad about it, I have simply nothing I can give her in return.

The girls are beautiful to gaze upon beneath their grime, I feel so sad for them, two of them are twins, the delicacy of their construction is something to be wondered at. One girl stands out in sheer beauty from all the rest, the eyes can only rest upon her in reverence and wonder at the handiwork of God. She is so beautiful that I can only stare at her as something most holy, too beautiful to be defiled by touching. An elderly woman amongst the group keeps close to the beautiful one in a protective manner, they are related. You can read the fear of what could happen to the girl in the older womans face as she hovers protectively over her young charge.

This is the second day that they have worked with us, the beautiful one is separated together with another girl to work on another farm just along the road for the day. The fear in the eyes of the elderly woman as her charge is lead away by the guard is sickening to see. We have been shamed - our uniform and our values have been spat on in this place; we have been degraded by one of our own men, he has dared to lay his filthy hands on the beautiful one whilst she was working on the farm where he worked, only the angry shouting of the Czech guard had protected the girl. These girls have no-one in the world they can look upon with eyes of trust but us. We have been deeply humiliated by one among us; shamed in their eyes - all the other men in the area are filled with a deep anger and hatred for the man, he must be taught a lesson. Several of the men head for the farm by devious methods, they beat the living daylights out of the bastard who had dared to degrade the girl in our name. Justice is seen to be done.

Meet a lad in the village who works at a flour mill, he asks me if I could use some flour, he will pinch it, we arrange that he will leave it in a certain ditch and I will collect it. I get a big box of the stuff every now and then but can't use it, I've got no facilities to cook so I trade it to other lads on other farms when I take the milk down to the milk depot, it earns me one or two smokes which are a Godsend.

Notice a German soldier cycling over the fields towards me one day, recognise the reddish hair as it gets closer, it is Edward the boy soldier from the farm home on leave. I walk over to meet him, he is grinning broadly as he says: "Hello you English bastard" I reply "Hello you Deutch bastard". We shake hands with genuine pleasure. I thank him for the packets of tobacco that he sends me from time to time, he sends them to his mother in the next village, she, at great risk to herself, slyly throws them into my wagon as I stop outside her house on some pretence or other. He tells me that he had been captured by Americans in Italy but managed to get away, I tell him that he is a stupid young bastard, that he should have stayed, the war will be over by the spring. He agrees now, but he didn't think of it at the time and he did not know things were so bad on the Russian front. He takes my photo and gives me a parcel of food and tobacco, and a small pen knife. He returns to his unit tomorrow. Here is one German soldier who worries about my welfare even when he is away fighting my people. I never see Edward again.

I seem to be getting plagued with children lately. Walter has a visit from a niece of his from Dusseldorf, she seeks relief in the country from the bombing, a very pleasant girl, she seeks me out to talk to me whenever she gets the chance, tries very good French on me but I can't match her skill, we converse better in German much to her disappointment. She has a small son aged three or four, a nice little lad who pesters me as I work in the stables. He tugs gently at my trouser leg one day to draw my attention, tells me that he wants a pee but can't get his penis out, can't undo the buttons of his overall type suit. He wants me to get it out for him. Undoing the button I manfully plunge my hand into the secret depths of his pants to help the fella but my searching fingers can't find the thing, got the location right, got to be here somewhere, but God help me, it's so small, I can't find it by touch. I start giggling as I desperately fumble about, I become hysterical, my guts ache with laughing, the kids laughing too, we are both bloody helpless with laughing because we can't find it, he's forgotten for the moment that he wants a pee. I spot his mum standing by the door, she too has collapsed laughing, she has been watching us all the time.

Walters eldest daughter visits me a lot since I gave her a couple of bits of chocolate, she is another near four year old. She meets me along the lane as I return from the land with the horses, I look down at the stub standing by the horse from my height in the saddle; she wants me to lift her up in front of the saddle for a ride home. She always asks me if I have got a 'package' meaning a Red Cross parcel, she is after more chocolate. If I say "No, no package", she sometimes gets cross about it and will sing a pleasant little nursery rhyme about Englanders being criminals and murderers. On these occasions I stamp my boots at her and say "Boo!" she gallops back to the safety of the house till the next time she feels the urge for chocolate.

A gang of Polish labour have cleared the sugar beet crop out of the ground, I drive the loads to the next village, there I transfer the beet into standard gauge rail wagons, across the other side of the road is the small gauge rail track which crosses the farm, a long line of trucks stand there with their usual load of Jewish females. Two young girls have asked permission to get off one truck, they walk a few paces away from the truck under the watchful eyes of the guards, they lift their clothes and squat to relieve themselves. Suddenly the train is moving before they are finished; in a mad panic they rush to the wagons, try to climb on but beyond them, the truck has pulled away. Blind panic seizes their minds, they scatter away from the train in different directions, their frail bodes fall to the ground shot to pieces by the machine pistols of the guards, my heart screams to heaven with hatred of Germany.

The old man of the village, Herr Frazier, has told me that all civilians of the village have been warned to evacuate at a months notice, only the very old people like him with no transport and no relatives to look after them can stay at their own risk, they would not last long on the road now that the ugly face of winter has arrived. I have warned all the lads on the farm of a possible move soon, we have decided to keep together if we can for safety, trigger happy German troops are roaming about everywhere.

The guards still have not received any orders about us, they are getting a bit panicky as they watch the endless stream of fighting troops retreat.

Christmas Eve arrives with the countryside under three feet of snow, the river is covered with a one foot thick sheet of ice, only the road is made reasonably passable by the amount of troop movement which fills it, forever they are going in the direction of Danzig. In the river almost opposite the farm two large barges lie trapped in the ice, they are loaded with potatoes that were intended for Marienburg and Elbing, today all we prisoners in the area have got to start to unload them. A fifty yard carry across the ice to waiting lorries which will take them on to the towns. Still no smokes or food parcels but I had a letter from my brother which told me that he had arrived home safe and well, thank God.

The barges take three days to unload, Christmas Eve, Christmas Day and Boxing Day. The farmer comes into the stalls only to see if the animals have been fed, he never speaks to me, he is always very white faced since we have had to prepare a wagon to take him on the road of evacuation. He is shocked because his arrogant world is falling apart around his bloody ears, shocked that he must leave his kingdom and his slaves. Reality is here - when he joins the wagons on the road he is nothing, just a refugee; he knows it, I know it, and he knows just what I am thinking, there is no need for words between him and me.

Early evening of the twenty-eighth of December 1944, I can hear the Frau crying in the house, she utters a high pitched wail of anguish from time to time. The farmer comes into the stall, he looks ghastly, can't speak, he beckons me to help him harness the two horses 'Old Fox' and 'Young Fox'. We take them to the barn where the racked wagon is ready and waiting, hitch the horses to the wagon, drive it round to the house where last minute packing is finished.

The Frau comes over to me and says: "Oh Edard, Edard, why isn't it the Englanders or the Americans coming?" I tell her that is isn't, it is the Russians and they will only treat them in the same way that they have been treated.

I watch them go with no pity in my heart after seeing the treatment handed out by them and their kind to those they had authority over, now they too will find out what pain is, what a broken heart is, they can go to bloody hell! Now that the German villagers who can travel have left, all Polish and Russian girl workers in the area are herded into one large barn at the other side of the village, we fear for their safety.

I am alone now on the farm now in charge of fourteen cows, three horses, five pigs and my own dog, the guard should be down later to give marching orders I expect, there will be no fancy transport for us. Blizzards rage daily, in between the blizzards the temperature falls rapidly to freeze everything solid, frostbite will be a real and stark danger under these conditions.

Examine the now empty farmhouse for signs of food and to see how the other half lived. I find no food, the bastards have left me nothing, not even bread for today. Collect four thick empty sacks, cut a hole in the bottom of one to slip over my head, two holes in the sides to slip my arms through, cut a second sack to match, I will wear these under my greatcoat as rough jackets for additional warmth. Cut out rough shaped mittens for my hands with a pen knife, sew them up with cotton thread. A sausage shaped kit bag from the fourth sack to carry across my back, a piece of rope tied at both ends to loop across my chest, this will be essential to cling to when the going gets hard on the road, memories of the 1940 march are still fresh in my mind but I expect this one to be worse. A strip of blanket to tie over my head and ears. I find a child's sledge in the house, will take it to carry two blankets and pack, tie a length of rope to the thing for pulling. I can take no further precautions, I will have to trust in God for the rest. Check my food stock, two tins of marmalade, left overs from far distant Red Cross food parcels, seven raw potatoes.

No sign of the guard today, seems I will have to spend the night on the farm, German troop columns still choke the road outside the farm, moving back towards Danzig, they move with the speed of half frozen and exhausted men. I bolt up the stable and the house for the night, feed my friends the animals, it occupies my mind and keeps them happy. Decide I will sleep in the farmers bed tonight instead of the stable, settle on the thing with a couple of blankets and several sacks to cover me, first bed I have graced for about five years, bloody hell.

Morning of the 29th of December brings the usual sight of troops passing on the road, decide to feed the animals to pass the time away as I wait for something to happen. Worried about my dog, much too small to walk in the snow, I can't carry him or feed him, can't just leave him though. Visit my old German friend across the road, ask him if he will look after the dog for me, he says it will give him the greatest of pleasure to do so. That's a load off my mind. I ask Herr Frazier why he has refused to be evacuated, he replies that he has lived his life, that he will embrace death when it comes without fear. He insists on giving me two slices of bread, I know he can't afford it. I leave him, my heart heavy with sadness, I have been privileged to know for a while a man who I can only describe as a good man in every sense of the word, may God walk with him.

An abundance of animal feed available, fork down as much hay as I possibly can from the loft, all the animals stand more than knee deep in the stuff, it surrounds them completely, swells up on each side of their bodies. I trust it will last them for a few days, can't give them too much grain, it will kill them. Fill their water troughs to overflowing, I can do no more for them. I have fed them for the last time, wonder whose hand will feed them the next time, German or Russian? Perhaps neither, perhaps death will claim them first.

The March 1944-45, East Prussia, Poland, Germany

Three other lads from up river call in to see if I am ready to leave, one of them, the lad who works the ferry boat across the river, has no gloves; I offer him sacks to use as mittens but he refuses, he thinks he will get by without. A final pat on the necks of my friends the horses as I wish them farewell, we head through the village to the guards quarters for muster. As we walk the snow begins to fall in blinding sheets, another blizzard has arrived.

We wait at the muster point for four hours as men drift in, stragglers from distant farms, the tally is completed at approximately forty five men with six guards. The lad Dawson is sick with worry at having to leave his Polish girl and baby, he looks as though he could die of a broken heart. The guards tell us that we have a three day march on the first leg, must reach a river and cross it before the ice breakers do their work, everyone must try and keep up with the column, anyone falling out will be left behind, no help can be offered to us by the guards.

Darkness is lit only by the gleam of the snow underfoot. For many years we have been waiting for this day, for this very moment to see the break-up of Germany, it is happening now, all we have to do is keep on our feet, keep them moving, don't lie down in the open, this cold will bring death. Move off, at first quite briskly, travelling a track that has been partly cleared of snow; turn off the track, head directly across open country, immediately the depth of snow rises over the top of my knees, a deliberate but hurried high lifting of each leg as I reach forward with the foot. Flounder and struggle to keep the pace, soon a nightmare of crashing into the snow face first, up quick, struggle up on to my feet, stagger forward till the next time I go down; body saturated with sweat, dare not stop moving for a minute, the sweat will freeze my body solid.

Blinding snow sweeping into my face is at first annoying but the never ending beating on my face seems to strike nerves under the skin until I want to scream; a pattern of near blindness as my eyelids sink under the pain, breath comes in sobs with an agony in my lungs which scream out for rest but the nightmare continues. Stagger forward, fall, stagger forward, fall, up man, stagger forward. Night follows day, day follows night, night follows day, stagger forward, fall, up man, up, just keep moving. The second day of marching, I have to abandon the sledge and its contents, I have no strength to pull it or carry the blankets.

An endless struggle that lasts two and a half days without stopping, without resting. The third day sees those of us who thought we were reasonably fit completely exhausted, two of the guards look near to death.

At last the river, two ice breaking ships are busy breaking the one foot thick ice, but they work upriver, away from us, about a quarter of a mile. The guards say we must hurry this last stage to cross in front of them then we can all rest on the far bank. Snow has stopped falling, we can see where we go now, given new heart at the thought of a rest, the column flounders in quick step along the bank of the river towards the working ships. Launching themselves at full speed at the ice the vessels rise above the surface to rest half their length on the ice, soon the ships weight plunges them back into the water, reverse, again they charge. Crossing a few hundred yards in front of them, we reach the further bank in safety finding enough strength to salute the crews of the ships with two upright fingers stabbing the air before we collapse on to the snow.

Time is getting lost on my mind, we keep walking through the days, halting only at night by the side of the road; must resist the crazy desire to lie down and rest my body in sleep, especially when it's not snowing, the falling temperature will lull you to sleep forever. Keep on your feet, just stand, arms across the chest, hands under the armpits, must protect my fingers at all costs; shorten my neck, bury my head down into the folds of my collar and doze. Shut the weary eyes as I stand, shut the weary mind from the nightmare please God, but remember to keep the boots planted firmly, keep the legs stiff and straight, must do this to survive.

My food has gone days ago. The marmalade was solid blocks, I had great difficulty in cutting the tin with my pen knife, lived in terror that the blade would break, but by chipping carefully away at the marmalade the magic manna was saved, my stomach is empty now and all but dead.

On a road, can travel better but we have to keep getting off it to let military columns pass. Can't find any barns big enough to get us all in, we pass them with longing in our eyes, have been out in the open for more than a week now, have had no food given to us yet. Moving with a large German army transport column tonight, they don't take any notice of our presence, everyone is so intent on surviving and staying awake.

The guards have at last found a barn for the night, a heavy blizzard is raging. There are no doors on the barn, large holes in the walls and the roof, the force of the blizzard drives the snow straight through the barn; conditions are so bad that the guards have left us to find better shelter for themselves. Can see the outskirts of some houses through the swirling snow just down the road, looks like the outskirts of a town; several lads are drifting off to see what they can find, I too move into the shuffling column of German troops that pass by, they take no notice of us, intent only on staring dumbly to their front with the terrible effort of moving. The high street, houses along each side, a chink of light in one of them it is a bakers shop. Go round to the back door and knock, will try and get shelter for the night. The door opens, a bright and breezy middle aged woman confronts me, she looks at me hard but her face suddenly breaks into a radiant smile. Speaking in Polish she tells me to enter the house, I step into a wonderland of warmth and bright lights, two other British lads stand in the room grinning at me. The flood of friendly warmth makes me feel giddy, I feel light headed, look down at the two freshly baked loaves of bread which the woman has thrust into my hands in total disbelief. We will have to get out of here quick if we want to avoid getting our benefactor into trouble. Hiding the loaves under our coats we step back out into the white world.

Arriving back at the barn we find that most of the lads have drifted off to find better shelter. The shelter offered by the barn against the blizzard is practically nil, to stay here would be to invite trouble, I retrace my steps back to the town and knock on the door of the first house I see. A young Polish male opens the door, I ask if I can sleep on the floor of his house, he grins broadly, says I can and ushers me in. He leads me into a bedroom where nine other British lads are already in residence, a large double bed fills most of the floor space, in the bed the lady of the house reclines surveying the nine bodies stretched out for all the world like a bloody carpet around her. Find a space, squeeze down on the floor, fit myself into the dreamed of luxury and settle down; my body begins to melt in the fantastic warmth of the room, I begin to feel alive again. A knock on the outside door, one of our guards stands there, he begs to be allowed in to share our warm floor; we tell him to piss off, find his own shelter but he won't go, just stands there pleading to be allowed to come in. He begs us to take pity on him, the man is actually crying, ok, let the poor bastard in! He squeezes in among us on the floor, the young Pole locks up the house and climbs into his bed, this man and wife share their humble home with its life giving warmth with eleven men at their feet.

Days follow each other in a wilderness of white freezing cold, my mind is dulled with misery. The guards have to follow directions, first there, then there; occasionally they will manage to obtain a few raw potatoes, enough for a couple per man perhaps, we wolf them down immediately, but mostly they can't get us anything. Nothing else available so we break off pieces of ice, suck and chew them, swallow the tiny crushed pieces, for a few seconds something solid hits the stomach an illusion which cannot fool the stomach and soon passes. Eyes continually search the landscape for the tell-tale signs of mangle heaps but they are almost impossible to locate in this white mantle. If God is good and one is found we kick and claw at the impossible solid frozen mass frantically trying to dislodge some fragment.

Mixed up with a German army column of horse transport this night, we all shuffle along together, ghosts of men hardly moving, another river ahead, thousands of German troops waiting to cross. Wait to cross on the large transported ferry boat that is operating, we wait in despair wondering if they will let us cross. After a few hours an Infantry Officer with one of the columns asks the guard who we are, he tells him that we are Englanders; to our amazement the Officer orders the guard to take us across on the next trip. Half way over the crossing a blizzard descends in all its fury. We disembark and march into the driving snow, travel a few miles, figures dressed in white rise silently up from the snow; German fighting patrols, they order us to halt, spend the night at the side of the road, movement at night is forbidden.

Everyone is standing with their backs to the blizzard, not far away I can see the outline of a barn through the snow, I walk to it to see if I can find something to eat. Can see no sentries posted outside, it must be empty. A small door at the side, open it and enter; my heart almost stops with shock, in the dim light of two electric bulbs I can see lines of cavalry horses munching at feed bags, beside each horse a trooper lies on a thick bed of straw, it is a cavalry unit. The men are looking at me, some are stirring to get up, I raise my hat to the nearest man and say "Pardon monsieur". It is the most un-Russian comment that I can think of, I shoot out of the door back into the cover of the night and the falling snow. Retrace my shuffle back to the group of men standing by the road; three white figures have risen up from the snow in front of me, I stop dead in my tracks, it's a patrol. They ask me who I am and where I am going, I tell them, and await my fate as they think it over, a wave of a hand tells me to move on, I get to hell away from them as fast as I can.

The blizzard rages for three days while we flounder about in it with nowhere to go, when it does eventually stop we find ourselves in a small grove of trees; snow is banked up against the men who have squatted down on their heels, they are almost covered. The temperature has fallen dramatically since the snow has stopped, my body is a frozen lump of pain. Several men have got frostbite, the lad who operated the ferry boat at Fisherbalki and who wouldn't bother to make himself gloves from the sacks I offered him stands there with his hands held up in front of him, they are black and useless, nothing, simply nothing can be done for him. I am worried about my feet, haven't felt them for a long time now, feel so weak I could die.

A misery of daylight or darkness, an endless horror of white, green pine trees by day, black pine trees by night, but always the white snow and freezing, freezing cold.

Fall over a milk churn in the moonlit night, I kick and claw at the lid with a desperate frenzy, get the lid off, the churn's full of frozen milk. Chip at it will my pen knife blade, tiny chips break off, some to be lost in the snow at my feet in my frenzied haste, I can make little impression on the hardness, I have to leave it, catch up with the column.

I am in a barn, can't move, frozen solid, the straw is frozen to my clothes. I feel close to death, can't remember how I get here, can't remember the last three days at all, the lads tell me we are somewhere north of Danzig. Have got to get up and march but I can't move, can't get up, my lungs feel as though they are frozen solid, terrible pains. Several of the lads pull and push me up on to my feet, my hands grip the rope slung across my chest, hang on to that, come on man, get the bloody feet moving. My legs shuffle forward, got to keep them moving to live. Legs are doing their job just fine, the day passes; emerge into a park-like area, a wooden building, two hundred British and two hundred French prisoners here together with many fresh guards. They give us a third of a loaf of bread each, tell us it is to last a week, after a few days rest we start the march down the road through Eastern Germany.

Legs move forward somehow in an automatic rhythm of pain, command my feet to slide over the surface of the snow in a dragging movement. My body is rigid, stiff as it bows with weariness, I don't look left or right, my eyes fight to stay open and look just ahead of my feet. My mind is filled only with the thought that I must not give in to the ever beckoning paradise of sleep on that soft mantle of snow, my head hangs forward, chin on chest. Germans and P.O.W.' all move the same way, bodies are at breaking point. If I can keep on my feet I can move but once down other men have to lift me if they will, I must wait till I get my balance before I can move, down on the ground I am helpless so I must stay on my feet, must not lie down, must stay on my feet forever if I can.

The new set of guards are terrified of the things that are going on around them, they fear the S.S. units that swarm over the area clearing the country in readiness for the retreating front line troops. Guards are desperately looking for a barn big enough to provide shelter for the night. As we emerge from the darkness of a pine forest we see before us a small farm, it gleams in the moonlight, we rush the place in a mad panic before the guards can stop us taking over the barn and the stables. Lucky enough to get into the beautiful warmth of the stables, into a stall, the cows in residence already; look at us in surprise as we lie down beside them, get our bodies up as close as we can to the cows, the nearer we can get to them the warmer we will be, truly paradise. Settling in nicely, the cows don't mind; my body is just beginning to warm up, begin to come alive again, but the guards are among us screaming in fear that the S.S. are here, that we must get out. I have never seen men so crazed with fear like this before, some of them are so terrified that they weep.

With agonised moans and groans we form up outside the stable ready to march; across the road in the moonlight is a long line of men on horses, they are dressed in fur coats and fur hats, they sit silently looking at us. Something about them is different to the ordinary cavalry, something that freezes my heart, the way they look at us with terrible cold eyes; they are Russians, a Cossack S.S. unit with German Officers. Dead silence falls on our ranks as we gaze at them, they spell death, we can smell it, sense it, we are all holding our breaths, you could hear a pin drop. A mounted Officer is speaking to one of the guards, he asks who we are, in a voice shaking with fear the guard tells him that we are English and French prisoners, several minutes silence while the officer thinks over our fate. Suddenly he spits out an order to the guards that he will give us just two minutes to get out of his sight. Never did the column move as fast as it did that night, driven on the wings of the shadow of violent death; only when we had covered several miles do we halt at the side of the road for the night. Some of the guards are so petrified with fear of the S.S. troops they ask us if we have spare Battle-dress to give them, they reckon they will be safer among our ranks. Got to be bloody joking.

I must be going mad, my ears must be playing tricks, but no they are not, in the clear crystal cold air the sound of singing can be heard, men singing. Many men who sing a German army marching song, soon the sound fills the night. A column of men comes into view, they are trying desperately to march. As they draw close the figures take the shape of ghastly looking men dressed only in the thin cotton pyjama type jacket and trouser of slave labour, on their feet, they wear the impossible clogs. S.S. men swing their rifles at any man who doesn't sing lustily enough, urging them to better efforts. As they draw opposite the moonlight paints each man's face with a vivid green colour, the men sing with the fear of men who know they will die on the spot if they stop; our eyes behold a column of men doomed beyond all human help. Three figures lag a little behind the others, two quite small men who struggle to hold up a third, the third man is tall, very tall, even though his head lolls sideways on his shoulders as would that of a rag doll and his feet drag furrows in the snow, he is easily far taller than the two other men who each have one of his arms round their necks, despairingly they drag him along under the rain of blows from the guards behind them.

   The guards look at us and laugh as their busily swinging rifles strike home on the backs of the men, may God forgive our presence here; but the dogs of guards are actually showing off in front of us, they are showing us Englanders how tough they can be with men whom they classify as vermin. I stare at the nightmare and ask myself "Dear God, why do I try to stay alive in this terrible world, there must be something better?" As the column of singing dead men fades away into the cold moonlight I know that something deep within me has died; my heart is sickened and weeps at the depths of man's inhumanity to man, my faith in mankind is dead, a part of me has died forever, and will never be re-born, I am in utter despair. I see nothing to live for.

Move off at dawn, get my frozen limbs to move, fall into the feet dragging shuffle, the endless pattern of misery of cold, utter tiredness and starving hunger. Pass the first few bodies of the slave labour men of the night before, they have found peace at last. Three bodies lie in the snow filled ditch, two of them are very short men, the third is very tall, they have been shot. Soon many others litter the ditches to swell their ranks, some have been shot, others have been clubbed to death, they too have found a peace to last. I thank God from the bottom of my heart at this moment that my brother is not here in this nightmare, that at least one of us is out of it. I do not want to die, but I see little hope, I know I am ill, that my chest is not right, that my legs are giving out, that my strength is fading.

My mind insists on wandering, becomes a blank for long periods of time, sometimes for many days, an incident registers here and there. Men running out of wooden huts, cheerful men full of high spirits - German Air Force pilots, they are scrambling in a mad rush towards fighter aircraft that stand a couple of hundred yards away. They wave and shout greetings as they pass as though they are our best friends, we stare at them with dead eyes and minds.

Night memories, endless walking in vivid moonlight, an endless long road that ribbons onwards night after night. Black pine trees that never leave us, try to shelter among the trees some nights; I feel that the sight of them is driving me mad, I scream at them in hate, my mind and body is frozen in a dreamlike nightmare of numbness, I pray for the sight of a barn, shelter of some sort.

Two figures stand at the side of the road, dressed a bit strangely, they listlessly clear snow off the road; in the wilderness of snow and pine trees they clear the bloody snow. Two young men dressed in khaki, they look at us in amazement, ask who we are, where we have come from and how long have we been prisoners. We tell them, one of them started weeping for us. We pass on, these Yanks are recent prisoners, our years of captivity have shaken them badly.

The land we tread is Pomerania we understand, sick to death of the bloody place, they can stick it, it's nothing but sodding trees.

But one day something wonderful happens, clearings begin to appear among the trees, large clearings with houses that nestle within, some have smoke curling lazily upwards from chimneys, but they are too far away from the road for us to seek their shelter. At least it's a sign of life, hope is rekindled, soon perhaps one will be closer.

At last a farm located near the road, we halt, the guards say they will try and purchase some potatoes. We see a man in khaki busy milking a cow, go over and have a word with him; he keeps his head down as we crowd round him, and in a voice of sheer panic he tells us to go away, that we will get him into trouble with the farmer. We gaze at the specimen in amazement, he is petrified with fear, he is an American. The farmer appears, he has a large stick in his hand which he threatens us with, screams at us to go away, that he will give us nothing. One of our lads steps forward and clips him neatly on the jaw, the farmer now lies flattened in a heap in the snow. Only then do we leave the Yank to continue his milking in peace; we get no potatoes.

Have lost my hat somewhere, don't remember how, wrap my head in a piece of sacking.

A town ahead, a sign tell us that it is called Stolp. Our spirits rise somewhat at the faint possibility of shelter and maybe some food, but we pass straight through it, out the other side. As we reach the open country, we hear terrific explosions as bombs descend on the town behind us. Somebody reckons we have been on the road six weeks now, found five barns for shelter so far, the fifth of a loaf issued to us to last a week happened more than two weeks ago, we have had nothing since. If nothing else we are proving that you can live without food anyway. Seems you can do almost any bloody thing if you try hard enough.

Two of the lads have fallen out, they say they can't go any farther, we leave them at the side of the road, they look in a bad way.

Halt at the roadside for the night, a horse drawn cart slowly approaches us from the direction we have come. As it gets nearer two men can be seen walking behind it, their hands are tied together in front of them, two ropes lead from their bonds to the rear of the cart. The two men who had fallen out this morning have rejoined us it seems, the driver guard cuts them loose on arrival, he has done his job, kept them moving. The dog of a guard couldn't give them a lift, he grins as the men sink to the ground, they look close to death.

Eyes search the road we travel in the wake of military columns for cigarette butts, they are the next soul saving things to food, but there are too many other men doing the same thing, it is hopeless, there is nothing to ease the agony of the stomach.

New faces appear on the march, British and some German civilians, very fit people by our standards, they have filtered into the column from God knows where. A few women here and there, a couple of them dressed in Battle-dress, slave labour girls who refuse to break their special attachments to their British men.

Fresh guards, some of them real bastards. At the back of the column trails a light horse drawn coach affair, it contains a civilian German doctor, his wife, his daughter and an Englishman. The daughter and the Englishman are in love, the doctor and his wife travel the march to keep their daughter and her lover together. The doctor is a good man, he tries to help the sick and lame where he can but his hands are tied, he has nothing much with him.

Houses getting more plentiful, we dig in the gardens with our hands looking for roots to eat. Find a long thin stem, a frenzied bite, my mouth is an agony of hotness, Jesus Christ, a bloody horse raddish! The doctors horse has dropped dead on the road, he becomes food instantly, some men get a piece of meat, others have the liquids which pass for soup. I manage to get a tin of soup, drink it down, it hits the stomach and immediately ejects from my mouth in a stream, I look at it in angry sadness as it soaks into the snow at my feet. Find an unclaimed shin bone of the animal, continue the march sucking and chewing the bone for several days, manage to get some marrow out.

The doctor ceaselessly tries to purchase potatoes from farms that we pass, sometimes he is lucky, we part boil them when we can, a couple per man perhaps. The days pass, we are nearing the city of Stettin having crossed northern Poland and most of Pomerania. The weather has improved, snow has ceased falling, very strong freezing winds blow. We fear the threat of rain, freezing wet bodies will surely kill us off.

All civilian and slave labour marchers are separated from we military and re-routed, several close relationships that have blossomed are ruthlessly severed adding its pain to the agony of living. Leave the road suddenly and plunge in to the depths of a forest to follow narrow tracks, the snow laden trees hide the life giving sun from our bodies, we shiver as we walk.

Second day in the forest, enter a vast clearing among the trees, in the middle of the clearing is a large prison camp, a heavily guarded place. Masses of men press up against the wire to stare at us as we pass; Russians - starved filthy men reduced to a status lower than wild animals, they stare with mad looking desperate eyes. A revolting indescribable stench fills the air which almost makes one vomit, something more than unwashed bodies, excrement -bodies rot somewhere close by unseen. Well clear of the wire German guards are on patrol, each man has a dog, a machine pistol and plenty of grenades in clusters at belts and in their top boots. We pass by that hell, glad to do so.

Find a cluster of deserted wooden huts and a small barn for the night, in the barn I find a spot where one a horse had been kept and cared for. Pressed into the dirt floor here and there ears of grain stare up at me, I pick them out and chew them but the husk cannot pass my throat, I nearly choke in the effort to eject them.

Leave the forest on the third day, back on to a road, my mate Ginger asks me what I think my brother will be having to eat this day in England. We often ask each other this question, it's a game of make believe, takes our minds away to a beautiful world for a few minutes, out of the nightmare, we both share the joy that my brother is not here with us.

We rest on a clear patch of ground on a bed of leaves, near my hand leaves stir, something is pushing the leaves aside; a tiny nose emerges followed by eyes, a head, long ears - a rabbit. There before our eyes is the tiniest bloody excuse for a rabbit you could ever wish to see, he is so weak and new born that he keeps falling over as he takes his tottering steps. First thought is food - but his food value would be as the lick of a stamp, no more! Someone says "Poor little sod, leave the bastard alone". We lie beside him helping him up each time he falls over, send him back on his way to his mum, but we can't find it, we have to go back on the march, we leave the poor little devil floundering about on his own, we can only hope he makes it back home.

Many more houses and farms appear at the side of the road now, shelter might become more available we hope. The winds keep blowing me over, can't do anything about it, no strength to stand against the sudden gusts that hit us, Ginger somehow manages to get me back on my feet again each time, my legs move forward somehow.

Find a large barn in which to spend the night. There are a lot of Russian prisoners already installed, a wild desperate bunch of men, I don't like the look of them. Find myself a hole deep in the straw in the corner of the barn well away from them, lots of movement, shouting in Russian, French and English during the night; men are prowling in the darkness, an uneasy night. In the morning one Englishman and two Frenchmen lie dead from knife wounds. The desperate Russian animals have been searching for scraps of food from men as desperate as themselves, we march away from the place with relief.

I am feeling a bit better now, the sun shines more with a stronger life giving warmth, the countryside is looking a lot more civilised, the wilderness of the east is dropping behind us. See a tiny spot of red colour on the ground at my feet, pick it up, clean off the dirt, a circle of red with a dash of green in the centre, it is the cut off top of a small carrot; it is like sucking sugar, never knew they tasted so sweet before. Eyes open in the shelter of the stable, don't remember exactly how I got here; the wonderful brightness of a strong sun floods the stable, the sight of it enhances the beauty of still being alive. But the glorious feeling is shattered by the shout of anguish from the Frenchman by my side, his mate won't get up for the march, shaking won't wake him, he has died quietly during the night.

The guards tell us that we have got to make faster time over the next three days, must reach Stettin before the Russian tanks cut us off. The thought of trying to march faster fills my heart with horror, but we have no choice. The guards are terrified of being cut off, we pray that the Russians hurry and quickly end it all one way or the other.

After two more days and nights I am ready to drop out, I can go no farther at this speed, the guards tell us that we have just about reached what to them is a safe area, that we can slow up, but unfortunately we have escaped the Russian net.

Dozens of huge fires burning in an open field just off the road, for seconds we stare at them in disbelief. Looks like a load of Yanks round the fires. The guards try to keep us away from the warmth but we sweep them aside like feather sin our mad frantic rush for the life giving heat. The Americans don't want to know us, don't even talk, if they have any cigarettes they keep them to themselves; a miserable lot of bastards. We swarm around their fires, our bodies drinking in the fantastic warmth. Daybreak sees the Yanks marched away, we are on the outskirts of Stettin we understand. Later we move on, greatly revived by the heat of those wonderful fires. We cross the river Oder by ferry boat, march across what appears to be an island, cross a bridge, a sign tells us that we are entering into the state of Hanover, in Germany.

A complete change of countryside, red bricked houses, the start of the Autobahn, which is decorated with a large sign stating: THIS IS AN AREA SUBJECT TO BOMBING. The sign cheers us up, we actually increase our marching speed, a secret pride begins to take shape in our hearts and blooms at what we have accomplished so far in the gentle art of survival, we know that we are a dirty stinking rabble to look at, but bloody Christ we can march.

Reach a barn where we can rest for four days with a ration of two or three potatoes a day. I have my first wash since leaving Fisherbalki in East Prussia in December, it is now mid March. The feel of the sun on my bare body is magic, the cleanliness of the soap and water is heaven.

Back on the march, the ceaseless hunt by the eyes on the ground for anything edible or maybe a cigarette butt, our eyes also travel towards the sky watching the many American bombers that pass, they leave a checkered pattern of vapour trails. Fighter planes streak past here and there, a few German but mostly they are American. The screaming sound of the aircraft engine and the chattering of guns suddenly splits the eardrums and senses apart. As the reflexes project the body away from the road, my eyes register other men falling, a few split seconds, the awful sound and the aircraft has gone followed by a stunned silence broken only by screams and moans of wounded men.

Somehow I have managed to get on my feet unaided, nearby lies one of the guards, the best bloody guard we have got, a real decent fella who has done his best to lighten our burden of living. His legs are shattered to hell by cannon shells, they hang by shreds of flesh. One other guard and thirty of our lads have been hit, many among them have found death from American gunfire this day. Several times every day the fighters attack, they shoot at anything that moves on the roads. Our ears try to get attuned to the sudden scream of their approach but the bastards come and go with the speed of a lightening flash. Death looms everywhere, even our so called bloody friends are trying to kill us now, we are getting a bit browned off with their enthusiasm.

My eyes have been watching the pink piece of paper for some seconds, it looks familiar somehow. The wind lifts it, tosses it playfully along the ground. It comes closer, I bend to pick it up; the guard near me doesn't like me bending to pick things up, his swinging rifle butt misses my head by a fraction of an inch. Examining the pink paper clutched in my hand, looks like a Wrigleys Spearmint wrapper, smell it, God, it smells strongly of Wrigleys Spearmint. I tell the lads that there must be a column of Yanks ahead of us, we increase our pace instantly to try and overtake them; if they have gum they might have other things too, like a cigarette. Soon a small column of marching men comes into view, they are definitely Yanks. As we get closer their uniforms take shape, they are beautifully clean and unblemished. Air Force men, they move very, very slowly, they have great trouble walking. Several guards kick the slower ones up the backside to make them move faster. A horse drawn wagon trails behind the column, it is full of American Red Cross parcels.

Draw abreast of them as we begin to pass, a fantastic heart warming sight meets our eyes, four RAF Officers are strolling along in a nice neat row, they look like bloody school boys in their beautiful blue uniforms. They look at us scruffy lot as we pass with no recognitions in their eyes as British, no reaction on their faces but when one of our lads shouts, "How are the Brylcream boys today then?" they curl up with laughter. They ask us who we are, we reply that we are men of Dunkirk from Poland out for a walk. A London lad among us asks how London is, one of the airmen replies that it is well, that he was there three weeks ago. We gaze at him in holy reverence as a man blessed by the hand of God and marvel at the impossible fact. They have just disembarked at Stettin and it seems are marching to a camp in this area, we soon leave them far behind with no tit-bits gained.

Ginger is losing a lot of blood from his behind, he suffers agony from very bad piles, has to stop from time to time, drops his trousers to get rid of the blood and seek relief. I wait for him on these occasions but the guard sails into Ginger with a mad ferocity of swinging rifle, he beats Ginger without mercy, I can only stand with my arms hanging at my sides, body swaying with the effort of keeping upright. I watch the mad dog beating at Ginger, my heart weeping at my inability to help him, I weep because I want to kill the guard for Ginger and I can't.

Pass through a town, untouched by war, it reminds me a bit of Oxford; wonderful old buildings that look like universities. We estimate that we have marched something over seven hundred miles so far, my mind is dulled by the thought and asks how much longer can we go on? Judging by the direction we march we wonder if our destination is going to be Denmark; suddenly the direction is changed, we now seem to be travelling in the direction of Berlin. Swedish Red Cross ambulances keep passing us on the road travelling to and from Stettin, they fuss along on their mysterious business, we feel strongly that they could bloody well save us for a start.

Early April we enter the city of Brunswick, my breath catches in my throat at the scale of destruction brought about by bombing, everything is a burnt out shell or just flat; they put us in the remains of a brewery, a small section of the roof still hangs precariously in place, we shelter under it.

During the daytime they put us to work on a rail junction, it is a target area for American bombers and fighters, they come over every few hours to blast the place. Our job is supposed to be to replace sections of rail as fast as they get blown up, but we are too weak to even think about it, we struggle only to go through the motions of moving.

Happen to be standing close to a concrete air-raid shelter built above ground as the first air-raid comes over, I am one of the first into the place; it fills up rapidly mostly with women and children. I am well into the back of the place playing with a tiny toddler as the first stick of bombs land all around the shelter, the lights go out as the bombs erupt, ears are deafened with the terrible shocked screaming of the women and children in the confined space. My heart turns to ice at the dreadful sound, it frightens me to bloody death. When the doors are opened to let daylight flood in I can see a huge crack across the roof of the massive concrete which was not there when we entered, the blast has split it in half. I vow never to enter one again preferring to take my chance where I stand out in the open. The continuous sight of so many women snatching babies from their prams to run wildly to the shelters sickens me.

Every day and every night is the same, a hail of bullets and bombs. We are promised a ration of bread one day but in our absence at the rail junction American bombs blow our bloody bread ration sky high, we call them all the bastards under the sun and really mean it from the bottom of our hearts. Every night now we go into the cellars of the brewery for shelter, they are deep and safe, huge barrels line the wall, it is very cold but the bombs can't reach us.

Working at the rail junction, a guard gives Ginger a half of a cigarette which I am to share with him, I will have the last bit of it. My eyes watch Ginger as he inhales, watches the ecstasy that crosses his face, my whole being is screaming for Ginger to hurry, hurry. Fighters come over, the air is filled with flying streams of bullets, men who can run do so, others who can't fade into the ground like magic. The guards have melted from view, they are the only good runners round here, in spite of the activity around me my eyes never leave that stub between Gingers lips, it fills my whole life, I live for nothing else! We limp into a small wooden tool shed which is close by at the side of the rail track, we do it absentmindedly, our whole world is centred only on the cigarette, the exploding bombs around us; the rocking wooden hut, the trembling earth is as nothing. I drift off into the merciful relief of the stub as I inhale the magic - a couple of drags, the magic is finished. We move out of the hut, the devastation that greets our eyes is unbelievable, the shed is the only thing standing anywhere near the junction. We look at each other in complete surprise, we should by rights be well and truly dead.

No sign of life about anywhere, least of all the guards, we start to scrounge around for food, find a cellar, go down into its pitch blackness, feel a barrel standing upright, bash in the top, my hands plunge into a mass of soggy shreds of some substance. Raise a handful to my nose, it smells like Sauerkraut – cabbage; fill my pockets with it, creep back up to the daylight, take great care not to bump into a guard, they can call my full pockets looting and would shoot me.

Some Dutch civilian workers tell me that British tanks are just outside the city, one of them gives me the butt of a cigar, in a frenzy I light it as I stand and inhale deeply, immediately I black out and hit the deck; when I recover consciousness my cigar butt is missing, it has been stolen by some other lucky sod. We pray daily for the tanks to come quickly, German S.S. units pass through the town on their way to the river Oder, a few German fighter planes pass overhead flying low to the ground.

One of the lads that marched with us from Fisherbalki has died in the place, he could struggle no more. I too have reached the end of the road; all my joints have gone numb, they won't function, can't stand upright, can't lift my arms, the fingers won't work, can't manipulate my coat buttons. I can only lie like a wet sack, the impossible hunger and cold has caught up with me, feel drained of everything, physically, mentally and emotionally. I feel nothing, I have had it, the thought of death worried me but little now. A bad night with heavy bombing, the lads are rounded up by the guards to move out to open country. I am carried to a small cellar by the lads before they leave, it contains eight other men who are too sick to march.

The column moves off with my friend Ginger in it, we nine sick are left to our own resources, there is no fear or hope left, we live from minute to minute. We lie there for many hours, the only sounds that enter the background of the mind is the sound of aircraft, exploding bombs and shells, but mostly the mind is dull and empty. A British Officer suddenly bursts into the cellar, a Medical Officer from God knows where, he talks rapidly and excitedly: "Quick, I have persuaded them to take you in to the German hospital. The Americans will soon be entering Brunswick. I am an Officer from the P.O.W. camp, I have a lorry outside." My mind can hardly take in what he says, somehow we stumble and drag ourselves outside, hands push and shove me up into the lorry like a sack of potatoes; we move off, too late I remember I have left behind my sack kit-bag, it contains the only worthwhile thing I possess in the bloody word, a carving executed on wood by my brother with a six in nail in 1940 at Znin. I have literally sweated blood to carry the picture of flowers, now it is gone, I feel sad about it, bloody sad!

A short trip, enter a hospital full of German wounded, I find myself in a room with four Americans and six British, I have never seen any of them before, all of them have been prisoners for a year or less they tell me. German medical staff give us some soup and apologise for not having any bread to give us, it feels so strange to be clean and in a bed again.

A German Sergeant enters the room, he has lost an eye, standing in the doorway he surveys us, he comes over to me and says "Hello. Where have you come from?" he speaks perfect English. I tell him that I have been on the road from the Danzig area since December. He tells me that he lost his eye in the fighting around the Danzig area, gives me some cigarettes. I ask him if he is aware that the Yanks will be coming into the place very soon, he replies that better the Americans than the Russians and returns to his ward.

Behind my bed is a tall window which reaches almost from floor to ceiling, can see quite a lot of hospital grounds including part of an old fort. Bouts of coughing that tears my chest apart keeps me awake at night. Eyes closed, I pray for sleep to chase away fears deep within that I don't want to know about. Suddenly and with the gentle touch of a lovers lightest kiss a cool soft hand rests on my forehead; I open my eyes, by the light of a torch I see two beautiful young German nurses standing there looking at me, their faces full of concern, one asks: "can you not sleep Tommy?" They give me two black pills, mess about with my bed making me comfortable and depart. I sleep immediately but all that coughing was worth having the feel of that beautiful cool hand on my brow for those precious, wonderful few seconds.

I lie between two Americans, both of them hail from the southern states, they moan about their lot endlessly. Both are suffering from a mild attack of dysentery, there's nothing really wrong with them. Young college types, these two men are spineless. There is a third American also from the south, he appears to be of a much lower social class, I think of him as a hill-billy; he waits on one of the college types hand and foot, we British are sick to death of their complaints. The fourth Yank is a northerner, a different breed, he does not complain.

Check my view out of the window next morning, immediately below the window stands an anti-aircraft gun. Jesus Christ, what a place to put it. The gun has been very busy all morning firing at the streams of bombers passing above, an invalid just can't get any bloody peace round here, each round fired shakes me like a pea in a kids rattle. Late afternoon, a roving American fighter plane spots the gun and dives in on it with guns blazing, the window behind me disappears into a shower of glass as it caves inwards over me, bullets knock hell out of the wall that faces me on the other side of the room, I roll out of bed onto the floor and crawl out of the room, none of us has been hit, the gun outside is silent, it never fires again.

A nursing sister tells us that she thinks we will be safer if we take shelter in the old fort in the hospital grounds for the night, she and medical orderlies help us get over to the place. A tiny area inside, the walls are made if huge blocks of solid rock. A few civilians, some wounded German soldiers and we P.O.W.'s is all it can hold, we all sit on the dirt floor. Half way through the night American artillery shells start falling in the hospital grounds, some hit the walls of the fort but the thick stones brush them off with contempt, very little damage is done. A young S.S. soldier with us is screaming hysterically because he can't die for the Fuhrer, he is already shot to pieces and can hardly move, he is ignored by everybody in the shelter, nobody even bothers to tell him to shut his mouth.

The Release, Germany

Near dawn, we listen to the sound of heavy tanks moving, they have got to be American, wait till they get closer to town. One of the lads called Harry stands near the door watching for the first sign of tank movement, he sees one lumbering along quite close, says he is going to flag it down. We watch him run towards it waving his hands in what he hopes is a friendly gesture, the turret of the tank is swinging round in Harry's direction, so is the bloody great gun fixed to it; like greased lightening Harry has turned and is streaking back to the shelter of the fort, he makes it as the gun goes off, we let the bloody tank pass on its way, to hell with it!

Daybreak, we know we are now behind the American tanks but there are none in sight, we leave the safety of the strong walls of the fort, I find that I can just about stand, reach our room in the hospital, collapse on the bed. Watch from the window for the first sign of the American advance patrols, soon they are there, the leading patrol of the 30th American Infantry Division is coming along the road, it is the 13th April 1945. My eyes watch their cautious advance but I don't feel a thing, no relief, no sense of happiness, just nothing, my emotions are dead. Lie in bed, waiting as I have for so many years for events to flow past. The two southern gentlemen each side of me won't even talk to any of us British, we in turn ignore them for what they are.

Suddenly the door is kicked open, into the room comes an American fighting patrol - the biggest, toughest looking crowd of men I have ever seen in my life. Bristling with grenades and automatic weapons, six-guns hanging from the hips for good measure, all of them in their late twenties or early thirties, real bloody men, they look good. The Officer is about thirty five, his Top Sergeant stands immediately behind him, he is a huge gorilla of a man. As soon as they enter the room the two southern gents each side of me start wailing of their hardships and how badly they have been treated. As they wail I study the American guns and equipment, I have never seen a fully dressed Yank ready for war before. The Sergeant turns his head and looks at me, I wink at him, he grins and winks back.

The Officer has got bored of the wailing from his compatriots, he turns to me and says, "How are you fella?" I tell him I could be better but at least I am still here. "Oh", he says, "you're British, where are you from?"

"Oxford"

"Very nice, I've been there, where did they pick you up?"

"Near the Belgian border not far from Dunkirk"

He looks puzzled at this, so does the rest of the patrol who have been listening to the conversation. I continue "Yes, we held a place called Casel once but we were shot to pieces trying to get to Dunkirk".

The American faces are all complete blanks as they struggle to place just what bloody war I am talking about, a pause, the Officer speaks

"When did all this happen?"

I can't help grinning at their faces as I tell them 1940. The Sergeants face is a picture of mental agony as his mind starts working out the years, almost has to use his fingers, suddenly he explodes, "Jesus Christ, that's five years!"

The whole patrol has galvanised into action, they swarm around my bed knocking the breath out of my body with their heavy thumps on my back, every man is shaking my arm off, can't see the cover of my bed for cartons of cigarettes that have appeared like magic, never felt so embarrassed in my life. They say they have got to press on, that they are hunting men of the S.S. Unit who have left sixty-eight dead American prisoners behind somewhere close by. Before they leave they promise to get some food sent along to us from their field kitchen. A fine bunch of men to have as friends, they are men of the north, their brief contact has stirred the nearest thing to an emotion within me.

News comes over the radio that President Roosevelt has died on this day the 12th April 1945. Decide to share out the cartons of cigarette around the Yanks and the lads, ask Harry to do the honours of sharing and distribution. Afterwards I find that I have one solitary packet left, not sure if it's worth while trying to share it. One of the southern gents is off wailing again, something about a Limey having more American cigarettes than him, I fling the packet at him in temper and disgust, the packet hits him in the chest and falls into his lap. Instantly his protective hill-billy is on his feet rushing towards me, I know he intends to hit me, I have no strength to hit back. Harry has moved just as fast, he stand in front of the warlike hill-billy stopping him in his tracks, the Yank takes a swing at Harry but Harry has delivered one much faster, the Yank lies in a heap on the floor not interested in a bloody thing now.

The crew of American field kitchen arrive with an amazing variety of food including canned peaches, the southern gents each side of me immediately get stuck into everything in sight with the starved eagerness of thoughtless pigs. They top everything they eat with amazingly thick layers of peanut butter. I eye the rich food with caution knowing that in my state I could easily land myself with a ripe dose of dysentery if I don't take it easy. I choose a drop if cornflour pudding and two round pieces of beef, my will power screams in protest at my mean and cautious decision, the food is undoubtedly good but my sense of taste is nil, I can taste nothing. When the cooks leave the southern gents are gorged with food, I guess they have the agony to come yet.

A section of American signallers drift into the room, they all look as though they have stepped straight out of school. Young men, full of vitality and well being, they make a great fuss of me; each man swears to bring me back some souvenirs, one of them take my home address and promises to let my mother know that I am alive. They leave me to carry on with their fighting war, a well intentioned group of high spirited northern youngsters.

A two star General and his Padre visit us next, the General delivers a few words to cheer us up, the Padre says a prayer of thanks for our deliverance and gives us each a copy of the New Testament, he reminds me of a missionary at work, getting lost souls back into the fold. I listen to his prayer for us with an open mind, I feel somehow I have few to thank for my survival from the living death of the march, there were a few people and they were decidedly of flesh and blood, not spirits. I felt nothing else walking in my shadow, nothing spiritual, only death.

A young German lad of thirteen wanders into the room dressed in civvy clothes, he is all on his own, comes directly to my bed, sits on it and starts talking to me in good English. He stays for many hours and is full of idle chatter, he doesn't move from my bed all the time he is here, I think he feels safer among us for some reason but he nags me to death.

Taken to a nearby American field hospital which has female staff as well, X-ray taken and a thorough overall check-up, the medical reports are fastened to the stretchers we lie on. Next day we travel to an American airfield, we are unloaded and laid among long rows of wounded in a large marquee, there we wait transportation by Dakota aircraft. As we wait a three star General enters followed by a long retinue of press men and photographers, they all chatter loudly in a southern drawl, you could cut it with a knife. The General swoops on the first American casualty his eyes fall upon, he grabs the man's hand in both of his, stares into the poor fellas face and switches on his sunniest smile as he asks him "How are you ma boy?" A barrage of flashlights as the General holds his sickening pose, he holds it until the newsmen are satisfied. We dive deep within the depths of our blankets at the sight until the fat General leaves.

At last we are airbourne, as we fly I remember the few lurking low flying German fighter planes I have seen two days before and trust that we don't run into one of them in our unarmed Dakota. Study the patchwork of fields below as we glide slowly over them, see the Rhine pass under our wings, as we cross it I think I feel a bit safer now from those German fighter planes. A smooth landing at Orly airport just outside Paris. Ambulances take us to an American base hospital. The two southern gents overeating has caught up with them, you would think they were dying by the wails and groans, their guts hurt they say.

The hospital is run by a southern unit, the stretcher bearers and orderlies and all negroes, nobody in a white skin ever seems to talk to them except to give them orders. No white southern gent wants to talk to we few Limeys either, so we deliberately chat to the coloured lads just for the hell of it. The white girl dressed in American Red Cross uniform keeps passing our short row of beds, first going one way then going back again. She pushes a little wheeled trolley filled with apples and oranges, chocolate and cigarettes, she glances at us Limeys disdainfully as she passes which makes us mad. My eyes stare at the vivid colours of the oranges nestling on her trolley as she wanders past with the bored expression of a budding Nell Gwynne waiting for some poor American soldier to ask for one. As she passes I shout to her "Hey, how much are your oranges?" her southern drawl icily informs me that they are not for sale, they are free. "Oh, I just wondered, I haven't seen one for more than five years but we don't want any, we don't like them." She flounces off with her oranges, almost upsetting her trolley in her haste, her face is bright red, the colour almost makes the vivid colour of the oranges look positively dull.

A young British lad arrives from the British Embassy, he is seeking our particulars, as he sits there in his Officers uniform taking down our stories he becomes terribly embarrassed and ill at ease, a man enjoying a soft war we suspect, he can't get away from us fast enough.

Loaded on to a Dakota aircraft next morning for the flight to England. As we cross the channel I realise that the white cliffs I have been staring at for some seconds is England. Realisation brings nothing, still I feel nothing inside of me, no joy or relief, just a deep sickening sadness in my heart. The ghastly depths of misery and sights seen leave my mind paralysed, the agonising endless pulling towards England over many years has left my heart drained of all emotion. There below me is my paradise, I want to weep but I can't.

We land somewhere near Romsey, ambulances take us to a waiting train, twelve of us British in a world of Americans. Four of our twelve hang on to life only by a thread. The train pulls into a quiet siding, coaches are being unloaded one at a time, we must wait our turn. Pull myself up to a window for a glimpse of England, a man stands in a field close to the track, an elderly man, he has a dog at his heels and a gun under his arm. I call him over to the train, ask him if he will drop a line to my mother, inform her that I am back in England and going to a hospital in Newton Abbot, Devon. He finds a stub of pencil in his pocket, tells me it will be a pleasure to do it for me, produces a scrap of paper, takes down my home address, I silently bless the man.

Stop at an American hospital somewhere on the edge of Dartmoor for one day, the medical treatment accorded to the four men near death is fantastic, someone sits at their bedside all that day and all that night caring and bathing their terrible bed sores, the staff are real angels of mercy, we all of us bless them for what they do. Next day we travel on to a British hospital set up in an hotel near Newton Abbott, Devon. We lie in a row on our stretchers on the floor upon arrival.

A British Medical Officer stands over me, looking down, he speaks: "What's the matter with you? Why aren't you standing up?" I look at him hard, reply that I have walked too far, forgot to eat whilst I was doing it! Indicating the package of American medical reports attached to my stretcher I tell him that it's all in there. He bends down, removes the reports and tears them to shreds before my eyes without even looking at them. He is the second Englishman I have spoken to on my return home, hasn't taken me long to find a real bastard. Yes, I am back in dear old Blighty!

Next day as I lie in bed talking to my Canadian neighbour who is in the next bed, the ward door opens suddenly. Like a bull entering a china shop by brother stands on the threshold, he is made up like a bloody ham bone in a civvy suit, he stands there looking around the place for me, spots me, walks towards me, we are shaking hands hard and gazing at each other for a long, long time, words are not necessary as we gaze our fill, he grins like a silly Cheshire cat, as I remember, I break the silence:

"It was a bastard, glad you were not there kiddo!"

The Last Lap and News of Revenge

I stay in the hospital ward for five weeks, a ward of ex-prisoners, on-one comes near us much except to feed us and dress our wounds. Inspection day for the Colonel of the hospital, the Ward Sister is horrified because we are not standing at the ends of our beds in respect for the Colonel. The Colonel enters, he too is shocked that we recline in our beds, he tells us that we should be standing to him. We remind him that we can't even get out of bed for a piss let alone stand up for him, remind him too that even Jerry couldn't make us do such things, we give him the same reply we gave Jerry – Get stuffed! He takes it without complaint and doubles our food ration to help us on the road to getting out of bed.

The four men who are close to death have been isolated in a room at the end of the ward. There are two closed doors between them and us but we can still smell the stench of gangrene, it fills the whole ward. At night we can hear them calling out for attention but no-one ever comes to them. We take it in turns to stagger in to them to soothe their fears, talk to them, but we have to have a cigarette in our mouths, it helps to deaden the stench.

The Canadian lad in the bed next to me is in a shocking state, the shin bone of one if his legs has been shattered by machine gun bullets, other bullets have ripped his back apart. He lies in agony and frets for his own kind. I feel so sad for these lads with wounds, the unfeeling treatment accorded to them fills me with shame for this British place. I ask the Canadian if he would like to get out of this dump, he is overjoyed even at the thought. I write a letter to Canada house telling them that one of their lads is stuck in with us and to come and get him out. In three days a Canadian medical team arrive with an ambulance and take my friend away back among his own kind.

A loud cheering resounds through the hospital one day, we are told that the noise has been sparked off at the news that Germany has been defeated this day, but our ward remains unexcited and quiet. Eventually a lone Nursing Sister enters the ward, she is full of smiles, she stops in her tracks as she stares at us. "What? Have they not brought you boys a drink to celebrate?" We silently shake our heads, suddenly she bursts into tears, standing in the middle of the ward she sobs her heart out. We gaze at the familiar sight of tears in silence, on this day the 9th of May 1945, we have nothing to say.

At the end of five weeks I can stand on my own feet and walk reasonably well. The image I see in the mirror is vastly different to the one I saw five weeks ago. The skin-covered skeleton frame has gone, in its place stands an over-fleshed individual with bright pink skin, a fresh rosy pink, almost it equals the bloom of that of a baby. A strange effect, but it's not really me, nothing firm about the figure I look at, there's no muscle, it's mostly pure bloody beer, stout and Guinness; for five weeks they have been pouring large quantities of the stuff in to me, building up the figure, blowing it out like a balloon, making it look good so that they can send it on its way. I don't care what they do or don't do as long as they let me go, I want to get out of this place, I just want to get home.

At last, I can go! The outward physical build up is complete, the public can gaze upon me without revulsion. I will not tell anyone at home that I am on my way, I want it to be a surprise, a silent entry, no prepared fuss, just slide into my Mothers peaceful world as though I had never left. They give me a large kit-bag full of military kit to take home with me. I have great difficulty lifting it, my left arm won't work properly, the sinews don't function. They tell me I am officially fit and they have marked me off as A.1. for home service. I'm too tired to argue with them about it.

I leave Devon and travel leisurely drinking in this place called England to the full. If a train is going my way I take it, if not, I sit down and wait contentedly as I study the faces of the passing people who mostly carry bored looking expressions. I bless the fact that they can afford to look so bored, I wonder if they know how lucky they are under the mantle of this island. I leave the train at a village called Radley, it's next to my home village of Kennington. I drag the kit bag along the ground, to lift it is beyond me. See a bus that will take me to within half a mile of my home, the female conductor loads the kit-bag onto the bus for me.

I have several dizzy spells walking the last half mile, times when I have to sit down on the ground to recover. Enter the road which embraces my mothers home, I can actually see the house, never take my eyes off it, I can feel it pulling as would a magnet, the road is silent and empty of people. The dwelling is directly in front of me now, I stand in the middle of the road my eyes feasting on the miracle before me, check the details against my dreams for several minutes, yes, I had it right, my dreams had not failed me. I see movement through one of the window, someone within has spotted me, looks like my brother, it is, he is galloping out of the front door to greet me shouting his head off. We enter the house together, I step into my Mothers arms of welcome and lose myself. I have made it, I am home!

Later a visit to my Fathers grave, I too report my return as had my brother before me. Several weeks leave of complete peace marred only by the problems of thinking and acting in the ways of civilised people again and fighting the terrors or the recent past which persist in my mind. Soon a posting to London where I am somewhat at a loose end, my active military days are over, I wait only for demob now.

Enter a N.A.F.F.I. Canteen for refreshment one day, look around with idle curiosity at the khaki clad figures sitting at tables, note one man who sits alone, he looks familiar, yes it is, it's Dawson - the lad with the Polish girl and baby at Fisherbalki in East Prussia! I walk across and sit down at his table directly in front of him without saying a word. He eyes rest directly on my face but they gaze without seeing, they stare blankly into space, his mind is miles away. My eyes search his face for several seconds waiting for recognition to light his eyes but I wait in vain. I kick his shin, he comes to with a start, his eyes focus, we go mad with the joy of seeing each other alive. We talk for many many hours, we talk of his dreadful problem, his girl and the child. I feel so sick for him, his chances of making contact with them, of establishing their fate is so remote, they are deep within Russian hands now, I feel they are lost to our world. The lad is pining to death before my eyes.

He gives me news of the release of the column that had marched away from Brunswick after they had dumped me in the cellar. I am relieved to hear that my friend Ginger survived the march but we have no idea where he is now. The column didn't get far outside Brunswick before a couple of American tanks came rolling along the road and released them. The decent German guards of the column with nothing to fear from our lads remained where they were and became prisoners in their turn. Other guards ran off across the fields, guards with guilt in their hearts, guards who knew what to expect from men they had so badly treated. Men with the strength to chase the running guards were given guns by the Yanks, guns to do the job, they took off after the fleeing guards soon to return bringing no prisoners. The mad dog of a guard that I had wanted to kill se desperately on the march, the worst guard of them all, the dog who had beaten Ginger and beaten many other men into oblivion is dead, my heart sings at the news of his death. Before he could run he had been knocked to the ground by one of the lads, he died under the rain of blows from a boot. I bless his executioner.

The lads with the collection of German rifles and American guns could not be stopped, they climbed on to the American tanks sitting where they could, and again went into battle seeking Germans who wished to continue the fight. I am proud to know that these men were men of Dunkirk, I feel a great surge of bursting pride for the privilege of having marched with such men as these, I feel humble and proud for having met so many men and women born of a silent courage that soared to great heights when needed over the years of captivity. Think of them as heroes if you dare. A great peal of laughter will echo through the silent stillness of time denying such nonsense, it will remind you that you have it wrong, that they were just people, ordinary everyday people.

We have to say our farewells, Dawson and I must go our separate ways to pursue the art of living, we step out of each others lives for the last time.

Edgar James Meads, 1945

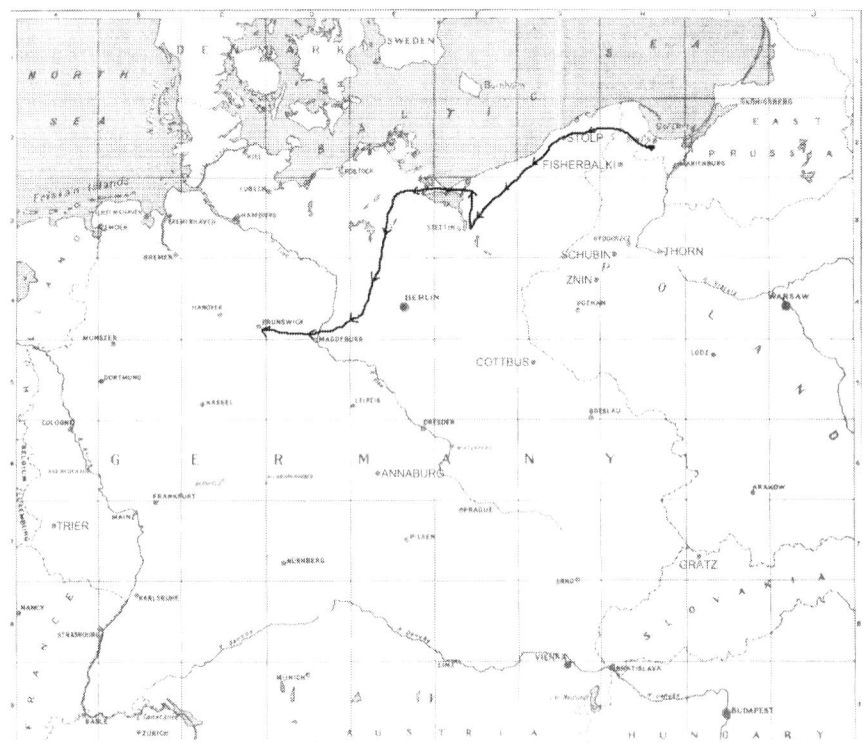

Known locations of Prison Camps and working party sites and approximate route of 1944-45 march from East Prussia to West Germany (adapted from Red Cross and St John war organisation first world war map)